This book explores the ideological origins of the Puritan migration to and experience in America, and shows how Puritans believed that their removal to New England fulfilled prophetic apocalyptic and eschatological visions.

An apocalyptic ideology of history, as a mode of historical thought, enabled Puritans to reconstruct their removal to America within the confines of sacred, ecclesiastical history. By tracing the ideological origins of the Puritan migration within the context of the English apocalyptic tradition, Dr. Zakai shows how Puritans transformed the premises of that apocalyptic tradition by rejecting the notion of England as God's elect nation and by conferring that title upon the American wilderness. The Puritan migration is analyzed further within the wider context of Western colonization of America. Dr. Zakai shows that the unique characteristics of the Puritan settlement in New England derived from the identification of their "Errand into the Wilderness" with the apocalyptic and eschatological "Errand of the Church of the Wilderness" as described in the Book of Revelation. By constructing a unique culture of sacred time and sacred space in the wilderness, and by attempting to reconstruct all dimensions of human life upon the sacred word of God, the Puritans were able as a consequence to interpret their migration to America as the ultimate culminative event in the all-time mystery of human salvation and redemption. In their de-sacralization of the Old World and their sacralization of the New, the Puritans produced thereby the first original American ideology of history.

Cambridge Studies in Early Modern British History

EXILE AND KINGDOM

Cambridge Studies in Early Modern British History

Series editors

ANTHONY FLETCHER
Professor of Modern History, University of Durham

JOHN GUY
*Richard L. Turner Professor in the Humanities and Professor of
History, University of Rochester, NY*

and JOHN MORRILL
*Lecturer in History, University of Cambridge, and
Fellow and Tutor of Selwyn College*

This is a series of monographs and studies covering many aspects of the history of
the British Isles between the late fifteenth century and the early eighteenth century. It
includes the work of established scholars and pioneering work by a new generation
of scholars. It includes both reviews and revisions of major topics and books which
open up new historical terrain or which reveal startling new perspectives on familiar
subjects. All the volumes set detailed research into broader perspectives and the
books are intended for the use of students as well as of their teachers.

For a list of titles in the series, see end of book.

EXILE AND KINGDOM

History and apocalypse in the Puritan migration to America

AVIHU ZAKAI

Senior Lecturer in the Departments of History and American Studies,
The Hebrew University of Jerusalem

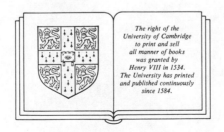

The right of the
University of Cambridge
to print and sell
all manner of books
was granted by
Henry VIII in 1534.
The University has printed
and published continuously
since 1584.

CAMBRIDGE UNIVERSITY PRESS

Cambridge
New York   Port Chester
Melbourne   Sydney

Published by the Press Syndicate of the University of Cambridge
The Pitt Building, Trumpington Street, Cambridge CB2 1RP
40 West 20th Street, New York, NY 10011–4211, USA
10 Stamford Road, Oakleigh, Victoria 3166, Australia

© Cambridge University Press 1992

First published 1992

Printed in Great Britain at the University Press, Cambridge

A catalogue record for this book is available from the British Library

Library of Congress cataloguing in publication data

Zakai, Avihu.
  Exile and kingdom: history and apocalypse in the Puritan
migration to America/Avihu Zakai.
    p.   cm.–(Cambridge studies in early modern British history)
  Includes index.
  ISBN 0 521 40381 2
  1. Puritans–New England.   2. History (Theology)–History of doctrines
3. United States–Church history–Colonial period, ca.
1600–1775.   I. Title.   II. Series.
BX9355.N35Z35   1992
285′.9′0973–dc20   90-29094   CIP

ISBN 0 521 40381 2 hardback

To
Amotz and Alon

The world [is] all before them, where to choose
Their place of rest, and Providence their guide.

JOHN MILTON

CONTENTS

ACKNOWLEDGMENTS

In the course of writing the book I have incurred debts and obligations from many friends and colleagues. In particular, however, I am deeply grateful to Yehoshua Arieli, Jack P. Greene, J. G. A. Pocock, Sir Geoffrey Elton, and Michael Zuckerman, for their constant encouragement and interest; to Richard Polenberg, David Weinstein, Walter Nugent, Stephen Whitfield, Michael Heyd, Uzi Amit-Kohn, John Pankratz, and Anya Mary Mali, who read earlier drafts, and in various ways helped make the book better than it might have been.

I have been assisted by research grants from The American Council of Learned Societies, American Philosophical Society, United States Information Agency, and United States–Israel Educational Foundation. I want also to acknowledge the generous help and hospitality of the John Carter Brown Library, the Huntington Library, and Wolfson College, Cambridge. Though the book was completed at the Hebrew University of Jerusalem, the writing was begun during a sabbatical year at the Philadelphia Center for Early American Studies. Bat-Sheva Gefen has typed this book more than once. In getting the work ready for publication, I have been fortunate to have the assistance of the superb staff of Cambridge University Press, particularly the editorial work of Bill Davies and Jean Field. An earlier version of chapter 1 has been published in *History and Theory*, portions of chapter 6 in the *Journal of Ecclesiastical History*, and parts of chapter 7 in the *Journal of Religious History*. I am grateful to the editors for permission to use these materials here.

INTRODUCTION

The initial premise of this book is that a serious study of the Puritan sense of time and view of history is warranted and in some respects long overdue. Throughout history religious movements have constructed new modes of historical thought and presented their own vision of history in order to explain and justify their rise and appearance upon the stage of history. In this context, the Puritan migration to America was, by its very nature as an ideological movement, no exception. The Puritans sought to construe a meaningful sacred, historical context within which to explain their removal to, and presence in, the wilderness of America within the course and progress of salvation history (*Heilsgeschichte*) – the unfolding story of God's plan of salvation and redemption – or within the annals of ecclesiastical history. Almost inevitably, then, as this study will attempt to show, serious analysis of the Puritan philosophy of history is indispensable in order to understand the meaning and significance which Puritans conferred on their action within the confines of the history of salvation, or within the unfolding drama of salvation and redemption, and how they understood their role in the context of the sacred history of the church upon earth.

The Puritan migration to New England was based essentially upon a well-defined Christian philosophy, or ideology, of history according to which Puritans explained their migration to and experience in the wilderness of America. I am referring here to *church history*, or *ecclesiastical history* – a unique mode of historical thought, or Christian philosophy of history, according to which the church is considered to be the main agent in history, and the process of history is perceived as evolving during time mainly in light of the sacred course and progress of the church, or God's chosen people, in the world. Ecclesiastical history is sacred history, for it concerns the divine dispensation of God and his revelatory redemptive acts in history, or more precisely, the whole of Christ's divine economy of salvation upon earth.[1]

[1] Today indeed the most common, ordinary and regular usage of the term "ecclesiastical history," or "church history," refers to the history of churches as institutions. The reader will

1

Puritans of course did not invent ecclesiastical history as a unique mode of historical thought. The formation of this Christian philosophy of history can be traced back to the time of the Church Fathers. More specifically, the fourth century did see the development of a major new form of historiography, that of ecclesiastical history, and this new Christian conception of history prevailed as the tacit framework for Christian thought in the following centuries. It is important to recognize, then, that the Puritans were using this inherited mode of historical thought to define their own sense of time and view of history. Ultimately, it was through the prism of sacred, ecclesiastical history that the Puritans viewed with frightened eyes the gloomy course of the Reformation in England. They drew on the ideology of salvation history to explain the ultimate necessity of God's saints to depart from sinful England, to justify the meaning and significance of their migration to America, to construe the sacred, redemptive and revelatory meaning of the American wilderness, and last but not least, to interpret their life and experience in New England.

When Cotton Mather, the famous seventeenth-century historian of Puritan New England, argued, "But whether [Puritan] *New England* may *Live* any where else or no, it must *Live* in our *History*," he was referring to ecclesiastical history as a coherent and well-defined philosophy of history. And it was indeed within this mode of historical thought that he examined Puritan New England's singular role in sacred, providential history. "But of

immediately recognize, however, that in my usage of the term "ecclesiastical history" throughout this study I am referring more particularly to a coherent, well-defined Christian philosophy of salvation history (*Heilsgeschichte*). The reason is that throughout the history of Christianity, this usage of ecclesiastical history as a unique mode of historical thought, or as a unique Christian ideology of salvation history, was common in the writings of Church historians. Therefore, in using the term "ecclesiastical history," or "church history," to denote a unique Christian philosophy and ideology of history, I follow, for example, such famous ecclesiastical historians as Eusebius Pamphili, "the father of Church History," John Foxe and Cotton Mather. For their use of the term "ecclesiastical history" as signifying a unique Christian mode of historical thought, see Eusebius Pamphili, *Ecclesiastical History* (323), translated by R. J. Deferrari, 2 vols. (Washington, 1981), vol. I, pp. 35–7; John Foxe, *Acts and Monuments* (1570), the preface "To the Right Virtuous, Most Excellent and Noble Princess, Queen Elizabeth;" and Cotton Mather, *Magnalia Christi Americana, or, the Ecclesiastical History of New England* (London, 1702), "A General Introduction."

Among the studies concerned with Christian views of history, see C. A. Patrides, *The Phoenix and the Ladder: The Rise and Decline of the Christian View of History* (Berkeley, 1964), and *The Grand Design of God: The Literary Form of the Christian View of History* (London, 1972); K. Lowith, *Meaning in History* (Chicago, 1957); H. Butterfield, *Christianity and History* (London, 1960), and *The Origins of History* (London, 1981); C. T. McIntire, *God, History, and the Historians* (New York, 1977), and C. T. McIntire and Ronald A. Wells (eds.), *History and Historical Understanding* (Grand Rapids, 1984); Robert Nisbet, *History of the Idea of Progress* (New York, 1980); M. I. Finley, *The Use and Abuse of History* (New York, 1975); A. Richardson, *History Sacred and Profane* (London, 1964), S. Pollard, *The Idea of Progress* (Middlesex, 1968); E. L. Tuveson, *Millennium and Utopia* (Gloucester, 1972), and *Redeemer Nation* (Chicago, 1968); F. C. Haber, *The Age of the World* (Baltimore, 1959).

all *History* it must be confessed," declares Mather in his monumental *Ecclesiastical History of New England*, "that the *Palm* is to be given unto *Church History*," because "the *Church* wherein the Service of God is performed, is much more Precious than the *World*, which was indeed created for the Sake and Use of the *Church*." Praising ecclesiastical history above all other modes of historical thought, Mather adds:

> 'Tis very certain, that the greatest Entertainments must needs occur in the History of the *People*, whom the *Son* of God hath *Redeemed* and *Purified* unto himself, as a *Peculiar People*, and whom the *Spirit* of God, by *Supernatural Operations* upon their Minds, does cause to live like *Strangers* in *this World*, conforming themselves unto the *Truths* and *Rules* of his Holy Word, in Expectation of a *Kingdom*, whereto they shall be in another and a better *World* advanced.[2]

Undoubtedly, in order to appreciate more fully the mind-set and motivations of the Puritans, and to illuminate more clearly the ideological context for their migration to, and experience in, America, it is necessary to analyze the idea of ecclesiastical history as a unique mode of historical thought.

"Any history written on Christian principles," wrote R. G. Collingwood, "will be of necessity universal, providential, apocalyptic, and periodized."[3] Ecclesiastical history, by its very nature as the history of the Christian Church, is obviously the supreme example of this mode of historical thought. It is universal history inasmuch as the church claims universal validity for its teaching, appealing to the whole world and not merely to one nation, dealing with the origins of man and the universal promise of God, with Creation and the end of history. And although ecclesiastical history considers the church to be the central agency in the providential drama of human salvation and redemption, it has no particularistic center such as race, nation, or people. Ecclesiastical history is providential history because it espouses the belief that the whole universe is a theocratic universe ruled directly and immediately by God's divine providence; hence, history is God's domain, a space of time regulated and controlled by God's divine

---

[2] Cotton Mather, *Magnalia Christi Americana*, "A General Introduction," in Perry Miller and Thomas H. Johnson (eds.), *The Puritans: A Source Book of Their Writings*, 2 vols. (New York, 1963), vol. I, pp. 167–8.

[3] R. G. Collingwood, *The Idea of History* (Oxford, 1961), p. 49. Christian historiography, of course, is only one important example of man's attitude toward time and history. On the general issue of man's sense of time and vision of history, see Joseph Campbell (ed.), *Man and Time*, Papers from the Eranos Yearbooks (Princeton, 1983); J. T. Fraser (ed.), *The Voices of Time* (Amherst, 1981); Donald J. Wilcox, *The Measure of Times Past* (Chicago, 1987); G. J. Whitrow, *Time in History: Views of Time from Prehistory to the Present Day* (Oxford, 1989); Anthony F. Aveni, *Empire of Time: Calendars, Clocks, and Cultures* (New York, 1989); Reginald L. Poole, *Studies in Chronology and History* (Oxford, 1934); Frank Kermode, *The Sense of an Ending: Studies in the Theory of Fiction* (Oxford, 1967); John G. Gunnell, *Political Philosophy and Time* (Chicago, 1987); Stephen Toulmin and June Goodfield, *The Discovery of Time* (Chicago, 1982); Ricardo J. Quinones, *The Renaissance Discovery of Time* (Cambridge, Mass., 1972).

providence, as a play preordained and directed by God's hand. It is a periodized history because it divides history into past, present, and future according to divine prophetic revelations. These epochs in God's all-embracing divine providence include the period before Christ, that after his First Coming, and the glorious period which is to unfold after the anticipated Second Coming. Finally, ecclesiastical history is apocalyptic history, dealing with prophetic, redemptive revelations based on the apocalyptic visions in the New Testament, especially the Book of Revelation, and founded upon the belief in providence and the anticipation of the fulfillment of divine prophecies and revelations. Because it progresses in a continuum from historical revelation to the future unveiling glory, from the promise made in Christ's First Coming to its realization in his Second Coming, each age came to perceive this apocalyptic and eschatological dimension of history differently.

Ecclesiastical history constituted an important mode of historical thought from the rise of Christianity to predominance in the western world during the fourth century until "the secularization of theological teleology of history" announced by the Enlightenment of the eighteenth century.[4] Founded upon a definite and coherent Christian conception of history, or more precisely, upon a historical economy of salvation, ecclesiastical history is a system of thought in which history is defined exclusively as the story of salvation and redemption, comprising a special dimension of space and time in which progress is made from promise to fulfillment, from prophecy to realization. In contrast to secular history which deals with peoples, societies, and institutions, during time, sacred history deals with the unfolding of God's divine plan of salvation, or with God's saving work and his mighty redemptive acts in history. Indeed, all history, secular and sacred, displays

[4] Rudolf Bultmann, *History and Eschatology* (Edinburgh, 1957), p. 65. On the rise and development of ecclesiastical history, see: O. Cullmann, *Salvation in History* (London, 1967); M. A. Fitzsimmons *et al.* (eds.), *The Development of Historiography* (New York, 1967); H. E. Barnes, *A History of Historical Writing* (New York, 1962); J. W. Thompson, *The History of Historical Writing*, 2 vols. (New York, 1942); James T. Shotwell, *The History of History* (New York, 1939); D. Hay, *Annalists and Historians* (London, 1977); Ferdinand Christian Baur, *On the Writing of Church History*, translated and edited by Peter C. Hodgson (New York, 1968); Herbert Butterfield, "The Establishment of Christian Historiography," in *The Origins of History*, pp. 158–84; A. Momigliano, "Pagan and Christian Historiography in the Fourth Century A.D.," in *Essays in Ancient and Modern Historiography* (Oxford, 1977); John J. Dawson, *The Dynamics of World History* (New York, 1956); Reginald L. Poole, *Chronicles and Annals* (Oxford, 1926); Langdon Gilkey, *Maker of Heaven and Earth: A Study of the Christian Doctrine of Creation* (New York, 1959); Peter Guilday (ed.), *Church Historians* (New York, 1926); Jaroslav Pelikan, *The Mystery of Continuity: Time and History, Memory and Eternity in the Thought of Saints Augustine* (Charlottesville, 1986), *The Vindication of Tradition* (New Haven, 1984), and *The Excellent Empire: The Fall of Rome and the Triumph of the Church* (San Francisco, 1987); R. A. Markus, *Saeculum: History and Society in the Theology of St. Augustine* (Cambridge, 1970).

the working of God's divine providence. Yet, it is only sacred, ecclesiastical history which tells what meaning and significance historical events have in the overall divine economy of salvation. The foundation of sacred, redemptive history is therefore the biblical narratives of God's saving work among his chosen people, the promise made in the Old Testament and the fulfilment in the New, as well as the prophetic revelations concerning Christ's Second Coming and the transformation of the world into the Kingdom of God.

At the center of ecclesiastical or salvation history stands Christ. He is the focus of church history for some obvious reasons. First of all, it is through faith in Christ and by belonging to the church – which is his symbolic body on earth – that the believer can secure participation in salvation. Moreover, since Christ's First Coming is perceived as a historical revelation, all of history prior to His arrival becomes infused with meaning, and all subsequent history is seen to bear His mark until the anticipated Second Coming – an event signifying the end of time and history. With the First Coming, Christ entered time and history as the Son of God; his Second Coming is inseparable from occurrences within time or developments in the history of the church.

The church, as the spiritual body of Christ, inevitably assumes a central place in the sacred history of salvation, since until the Second Coming history is determined by the revelation of Christ as embodied in the church and its faith. Furthermore, because the process of history has a real significance and meaning in ecclesiastical history, history in fact became a divine epic stretching back in time to Creation and pointing forward to that magnificent event of the transformation of the world into the Kingdom of God and of his son Christ. For throughout all the vicissitudes of time and history since the Fall, God's divine providence selected, elected, and predestined certain people to restore humanity and reconcile it with its Creator. Accordingly, in this divine epic of salvation and redemption, as, for example, St. Augustine argued, the expulsion from Eden marked the beginning of sacred, providential history whose essential feature consists in the apocalyptic struggle between the "city of God", or the church, and the "city of Satan."

Within the context of ecclesiastical history the church thus becomes the necessary, perhaps even the main, instrument of salvation without which there is no grace and without which Christ's Second Coming is unimaginable; and which is, consequently, essential to the transformation of the world into the Kingdom of God. In this divine economy of salvation, that is, the historical process of human salvation and redemption in which man sins against God and God is willing to redeem him, the history of the church (hence the term 'ecclesiastical history," or "church history") has a most prominent place. By denying any possibility of salvation outside itself (*extra ecclesiam nulla salus*), the church thus transformed itself into the primary means through which man, alienated from God, could become reconciled with him. Ecclesiastical history, then, is based on the notions of man's sin and God's saving grace; for without sin and redemption, history, as the space of time from the Fall to Christ's Second Coming, has no meaning.

Ecclesiastical history, then, is essentially the story of the attempts to bring the fallen world to reconciliation with God – with the church as the central agency in the drama of human salvation and redemption. It is a history that deals with the vicissitudes of the church during time, its struggles, persecutions, and triumphs. And indeed in Christian historiography this focus became the very theme of history itself. To be more precise, within ecclesiastical history, earthly events are significant only insofar as they relate to the sacred history of the church. However, in this Christian scenario of time and history, past and present events obtain their full meaning not only in relation to the history of the church, but mainly and more fundamentally in relation to the eschatological future and the decisive apocalyptic event of salvation and redemption which is to transpire at the end of time and history. The apocalyptic and eschatological revelation of God at the close of history, the culminating event in which God's glory is proclaimed along with the salvation of the elect, is the stated goal of ecclesiastical history. Thus, it is only in relation to this eschatological scenario that historical events acquire their significance.[5]

The relationship between sacred, prophetic revelation and the goal of history is the main concern of ecclesiastical history. For according to this mode of historical thought, there has been unfolding from the beginning of time the grand design of God's miraculous providence, a divine scheme, directing, conditioning, and controlling each and every event in history. History, therefore, is linear and teleological. The task of ecclesiastical history is to record and illuminate the sacred, providential, and redemptive course of events in the history of salvation. Thus, within this Christian ideology and philosophy of history, the past is perceived as replete with symbols and prophecies pointing to the glorious future, the millennium, the Kingdom of God, or the heavenly city of God – the New Jerusalem.

The Puritan conception of church history was based upon the premises of Protestant historiography, and more specifically upon the formation of a Protestant apocalyptic tradition in England during the sixteenth century.

---

[5] On the relationship between history and apocalypse, see Bernard McGinn, *Visions of the End: Apocalyptic Traditions in the Middle Ages* (New York, 1979); Klaus Koch, *The Rediscovery of Apocalyptic* (London, 1972); C. A. Patrides and Joseph Wittreich (eds.), *The Apocalypse in English Renaissance Thought and Literature* (Ithaca, 1984); Thomas J. J. Altizer, *History as Apocalypse* (New York, 1985); Austin Farrer, *A Rebirth of Images: The Making of St. John's Apocalypse* (New York, 1986).

Chapter 1 explores how Protestant historians and theologians in Europe, beginning with Luther and Melanchthon, justified the break between the Protestant and Catholic churches and fashioned a unique ideological context of sacred time and history in order to explain the special role of the Protestant Reformation within the larger framework of salvation history. In the ecclesiastical and theological controversies surrounding the forces of Reformation and Counter-Reformation, Protestants turned increasingly to history in order to find meaning for the Reformation in the course and progress of the church in the world. Protestant historiography based itself upon a historical interpretation of divine prophecies and regarded the Apocalypse as the guide to the entire course of the history of salvation and redemption. Consequently, the Reformation gave rise to a new mode of historical consciousness, or a distinctly Protestant historiography based upon apocalyptic interpretation of history. Within the apocalyptic scheme of history, then, the Protestant Reformation was situated at the end of time and history, as an eschatological event preceding that moment when the whole mystery of providential history was to be resolved.

The Protestant apocalyptic tradition exercised an enormous influence in England. Claiming that the English Reformation would reveal the full significance of England's singular role in sacred, providential history, it established an illustrious vision for England in the drama of salvation and redemption. Protestant historians, such as John Bale and John Foxe, gave prominence to English history within the confines of ecclesiastical history by presenting it as an ongoing apocalyptic struggle between Christ and Antichrist. In this apocalyptic scenario, England played a unique part, almost to the point where English history and ecclesiastical history became inseparable. Thus, in the hands of the Protestant apocalyptic historians in England, English history had truly become a mirror of sacred, providential history. The English Reformation was in this sense the pinnacle of English history.

The Protestant vision of England's unique role in sacred, providential history, however, underwent a radical and revolutionary transformation in the early seventeenth century with the failure of the Puritan movement under Elizabeth and the early Stuart kings. By declaring that the Church of England had a unique and prominent role in providential history, Protestant apocalyptic tradition envisioned the ultimate sacralization of England as God's chosen nation in ecclesiastical history. However, the Puritan failure in England led instead to the gradual abandonment of this vision, and Puritans increasingly began to think of England rather as an obstacle, or locus of apostasy, impeding the struggle for the true reformation. Consequently, Puritan apocalyptic thought in fact brought about the ultimate de-sacralization of England's role in providential history, and thus turned the eyes of the godly to seek outside the boundaries of England the realization of their

eschatological vision and millennial expectations. This major transformation owed much to the writing of Thomas Brightman and William Perkins,
to name only two of those who provided the justifications for a Puritan
initiative to construe a new apocalyptic ideology of ecclesiastical history in
which the Church of England, having failed to execute the true reformation,
forfeited its glorious role in the all time drama of the history of salvation
and redemption. Hence, the de-sacralization of England in providential
history resulted in the Puritans' move to establish a new center of sacred
time and sacred space in the wilderness of America.

Any discussion of the Puritan migration to New England should
obviously take into account the meaning and significance assigned in providential history to religious migration. Within the confines of sacred,
ecclesiastical history, religious migration holds a unique and prominent
place. Controlled and directed by God's divine providence and conceived as
an economy of salvation, the sacred history of the church manifests a long
and continuous series of migrations of God's saints which mark the spread
and advance of the church, and concomitantly the progress of the Gospel,
upon earth. For if the ultimate mark of human existence on earth is based
upon the drama of alienation from, and reconciliation with, God, then
salvation history itself reveals a dialectical turn: a pilgrimage between Egypt
and the Promised Land, or between Babylon and New Jerusalem. Between
these two poles of the drama of human salvation, migration symbolizes the
prophetic journey marking the end of alienation from and the total
reconciliation with God.

Salvation history, therefore, consists in imminent flights of liberation
from sin into grace, from the profane to the sacred. In this redemptive
context, migration indeed constitutes the heart of ecclesiastical history. It
acquires its prominence in sacred history precisely because it symbolizes the
whole course of the history of salvation as alienation from and reconciliation with God. In this sense, religious migration is indeed a revelatory,
prophetic, and redemptive event; a sacred journey directed by God's divine
providence which unveils the meaning of a certain time and a certain space
in the progress of the history of salvation. Thus, through the sacred dimension of time, or within the unfolding course of the drama of redemption,
migration reveals new terrestrial places and consecrates them as sacred
places in the drama of salvation. In this prophetic, redemptive context,
indeed, the Puritan de-sacralization of England, led inevitably to the
ultimate sacralization of New England in providential history.

The Puritan apocalyptic interpretation of history, then, ultimately constructed a new mode of sacred time and sacred space, or a new vision of the
course and progress of church history, which in turn enabled them to assign
sacred, revelatory and redemptive meaning rather to the wilderness in

America instead of to England. Yet, historically speaking, the Puritan eschatology and apocalypse of America was not the first instance of the European spiritual conquest of the New World in terms of the premises of ecclesiastical history. Nor was it the first example of the European justification of the colonization of America in terms of the carryover of the Gospel to the New World. Chapter 2, therefore, deals with the apocalypse and eschatology of America, or with the incorporation of the New World as a sacred space into the framework of church history during the Age of Reconnaissance and Discovery.

In ecclesiastical history there has always been a close and inseparable connection between sacred time and sacred space. Throughout history, now conceived as salvation history, God's divine providence led to the incorporation of certain places as sacred spaces within the providential course of the church in the world. Furthermore, the issue of the reconstruction and consecration of sacred time and sacred space in salvation history is inseparable from the singular, redemptive and revelatory role assigned in the history of the church to religious migration. Religious migration is a crucial feature of ecclesiastical history because it constantly connects, through God's providence, sacred time and sacred space. Over time, then, the progress of the Gospel in the world inevitably leads to the de-sacralization of previously revered places, nations and peoples, and to the sacralization of new ones. Hence the singular role which ecclesiastical history assigns to religious migration as a prophetic, revelatory and redemptive event, one which invests certain places with sacred meaning in the framework of the church's continued wandering upon earth. Ultimately, religious migration constituted an important part of the dissemination of the Gospel throughout the world; since the Fall, God's divine providence has invested sacred meaning not only upon certain times and certain people, but also upon certain places during the progress of the church in the world.

Two important types of religious migration emerged in sacred, providential history which Europeans had greatly used in order to consecrate sacred meaning on the New World in providential history, and obviously, no less in order to justify the conquest and settlement of America. On the one hand, there is the *Genesis* type, which is a peaceful religious migration based both upon God's promise to his chosen nation that he will appoint a place for them to dwell in upon earth, and on the idea of spreading the Gospel in the world. And, on the other hand, there is the *Exodus* type, which is a judgmental crisis and apocalyptic migration, marking the ultimate necessity of God's chosen people to depart from a sinful past and corrupt human traditions. With the discovery of the New World and the beginnings of European colonial activities there, the powerful sacred image of the *Genesis* type of religious migration had played a unique role in the justification and rationalization of

Catholic Spain and Portugal's conquest of America, and thus contributed greatly to the incorporation of America as a sacred space in providential history.

With the beginning of the English colonization of Virginia, the religious wars between the forces of Reformation and Counter-Reformation were transferred to the New World. Chapter 3 deals with the eschatology of the Protestant settlement of Virginia, and how English Protestants construed America as holding sacred meaning in providential history. Evidently, the apocalypse and eschatology of the Protestants' settlement of Virginia was based upon the premises of Protestant apocalyptic tradition in England, the transfer of the apocalyptic struggle between Catholicism and Protestantism into America and, above all, upon England's glorious role in providential history. Despite the obvious differences between Spanish, Portuguese, and English Protestants concerning religion, however, their justification for the settlement of America was commonly based upon the *Genesis* type of religious emigration taken from the annals of ecclesiastical history, namely, God's Promise to his chosen nation to go and spread the Gospel throughout the world.

The Puritan eschatology and apocalypse of the New World constituted a radical and revolutionary departure from previous European attempts to incorporate America as a sacred space within the confines of ecclesiastical history. Having failed to execute the true reformation in England, Puritans turned their gaze on the New World. Their experience in England, the experience of failure, was radically different from that of Catholics in Spain and Protestants in England who sought to transport to America the glorious religious cultures of their own countries. Puritans on the contrary sought to create in America that which had been denied them back home. Inevitably, as I demonstrate in chapter 4, the Puritan eschatology and apocalypse of America were not based upon the *Genesis* type of religious emigration, as was the case with Spain, Portugal, and Protestant England, but rather upon the *Exodus* type of religious migration, a judgmental, apocalyptic migration based upon the ultimate rejection of, and total separation from, what was seen as corrupted history and degenerating human traditions. With the Puritan migration, then, there appeared for the first time a unique reconstruction of America as a sacred space in providential history in which the total desacralization of the Old World led inevitably to the ultimate sacralization of the New World in the history of salvation. In the Puritan apocalyptic scenario, America became a sacred space in ecclesiastical history, a shelter, as it were, and a refuge for God's saints who felt obliged to flee into the wilderness of New England because of God's impending judgment on the old, sinful world.

Puritan eschatology and apocalypse of America determined not only the creation of New England as a sacred center, both in terms of sacred time and sacred space, in the history of salvation, but ultimately served also as the basis for the creation of a sacred Puritan errand into the wilderness of America. Chapter 5 illuminates how the Puritans fully utilized the sacred, prophetic, redemptive and revelatory vision of the Errand of the Church of the Wilderness, or the Woman in the Wilderness of the Apocalypse. It also examines the eschatological and apocalyptic dimension of this errand, and describes how Puritans used this sacred prophetic vision in order to define the meaning of their holy experiment in the wilderness of America within the boundaries of sacred, ecclesiastical history.

The Puritans' eschatology and apocalypse of America, and the reconstruction of New England as the ultimate sacred center in providential history, had obviously tremendous social and political implications for Puritan life in New England. The last two chapters deal therefore with the crucial relationship between Puritan modes of conviction and modes of conduct, or between reflection and realization. Chapter 6 shows how the Puritans' failure in England to establish holy Christian fellowships according to their own vision of social and religious reformation, had led to the migration to New England, a place in which Puritans could realize their holy calling to lead a godly Christian life in both church and society in keeping with their special relationship with God. Likewise, chapter 7 explores how the Puritan theocratic impulse to establish every dimension of human life upon the sacred word of God, eventually led to the formation of a holy Christian commonwealth, or theocracy in New England, a unique political and social system in which both church and state were based upon a covenantal relationship with God.

The creation of sacred time

Religious reformation, history, and eschatology: Protestant historiography in England during the sixteenth century

Then came, at a predetermined moment, a moment in time and of time,
A moment not out of time, but in time, in what we call history: transecting,
  bisecting the world of time, a moment in time but not like a moment of
  time,
A moment in time but time was made through that moment: for without the
  meaning there is no time, and that moment of time gave the meaning.

T. S. Eliot, The Rock, VII

And when he had opened the seventh seal, there was silence in heaven . . .
But in the days of the voice of the seventh angel, when he shall begin to sound,
the mystery of God should be finished . . .
And the seventh angel sounded; and there were great voices in heaven, saying, the
kingdoms of this world are become *the kingdoms* of our Lord, and of his Christ;
and he shall reign for ever and ever.

The Apocalypse

Sanguine fundate est ecclesia, sanguine crevit, sanguine succrevit, sanguine finis
erit. (The church was established in bloodshed; it grew and thrived on blood; it
was renewed by blood; and its end will be in blood.)

Nathaniel Holmes, "Preface" to John Cotton,
The Way of Congregational Churches Cleared, 1648

REFORMATION AND HISTORY

When describing the impressive growth and revival of learning during the
sixteenth century, Francis Bacon suggested that the source for this important cultural and intellectual transformation, later known as the "Renaissance" and "humanism," should be seen in the context of the Protestant
Reformation. More specifically, he argued that it all began with Martin
Luther, who out of his struggles

against the bishop of Rome and the degenerate traditions of the church . . . was

12

enforced to awake all antiquity, and to call former times to his succours to make party against the present time: so that the ancient authors, both in divinity and humanity, which had long time slept in libraries, began generally to be read and revolved.[1]

Greatly impressed by the coincidence in time between the pursuit of religious reformation and the advance of learning, Bacon had no other way of explaining this singular phenomenon than to see it as clear evidence of God's providence:

when it pleased God to call the Church of Rome to account for their degenerate manners and ceremonies . . . at one and the same time it was ordained by the Divine Providence, that there should attend withal a renovation and new spring of all other knowledges.[2]

While a historical explanation based upon God's providence is no longer acceptable today, Bacon's argument concerning the relationship between religion and the revival of learning in the sixteenth century nevertheless reveals an essential truth about the Protestant Reformation: in the ecclesiastical and theological controversies surrounding the forces of Reformation and Counter-Reformation, Protestants turned increasingly to history, to the study of past events and the interpretation of their significance, in order to find meaning for the Reformation in sacred, providential history. The pursuit of religious reformation led to the creation of a unique mode of historical thought – Protestant historiography based upon an apocalyptic interpretation of history, or upon an apocalyptic mode of historical thought.

From the very outset of the Reformation, Protestants were vulnerable to consistent charges made against them by Catholics concerning the validity of their theological assumption and the historical warrant for their ecclesiastic reformatory efforts. The entire historical justification of the Protestant Reformation within the context of sacred ecclesiastic history hinged upon the answer to the question: "where was this church of yours" before the time of Luther?[3] Indeed, it was their attempt to provide a historical basis for the break with the Church of Rome, and to demolish the historical foundation upon which the Papacy built its claim to exclusive power, that led the Protestants to launch their appeal to the study of history that became a major dimension of the Reformation itself. Beginning with the publication of the first major work of Protestant history, *Carion's Chronicle*, in 1532, a unique, coherent and well-defined pattern of Protestant historiography began to emerge from the religious wars of the sixteenth

[1] Francis Bacon, *The Advancement of Learning*, ed. A. Johnston (Oxford, 1974), p. 25.
[2] *Ibid.*, p. 42.
[3] John Foxe, *Acts and Monuments*, ed. G. Townsend and G. R. Cattley, 8 vols. (London, 1837–41), vol. I, p. 9.

century. Ultimately, Protestant historiography signified a new mode of historical thought. Based upon a close correlation between history and prophecy, it was primarily characterized by an apocalyptic view of history, which in turn gave rise to a new form of historical consciousness. Not only did the study of history become now a crucial dimension of the religious war which the Protestants waged against Rome, but the whole attitude toward profane, secular history was changed in Protestant historiography from what had traditionally been accepted in Christianity. Protestant historiography based itself upon a historical interpretation of prophecies and stressed the apocalyptic scheme of events, that is, that the Apocalypse is to be regarded as the guide to history. Within this framework the Reformation is situated at the end of time and history, as an eschatological event preceding that moment when the whole mystery of providential history would be resolved. Thus, "Protestant history becomes the handmaiden of Protestant theology and Protestant politics."[4]

This new historiographic approach is especially prominent in regard to England, where the development of Protestant historiography signified the creation of a singular interpretation of English national history in which the Church of England, due to its apostolic origins, was to play a central role in the final stage of providential history which began with the Reformation. From the beginning of the English Reformation, the search for religious reform "stimulated a patriotic interest in the past as well as a desire to justify the break from Rome."[5]

This close association between religious persuasion and the rise of a new mode of historical thought, such as occurred in Protestant Europe, is clearly reminiscent of the correlation Bacon had made between the pursuit of religious reform and the revival of learning. In England there was a special relationship between Humanism and the pursuit of religious Reformation. As Ernst Cassirer wrote: "The great Italian humanists looked upon traditional objects of religious faith with cool and deliberated scepticism," yet "in England humanism takes the opposite course from the first. Its criticism is directed against scholastic systems and against antiquated and 'barbaric' forms of theological learning, but never against religion. On the contrary, the forces of humanism work for the sake of religion."[6] In this context it comes as no surprise that from the very outset of the English Reformation "the new learning of humanists was put to the test of political and theological debate. Increasingly, after the 1530s," or when the official break with the Church of Rome took place, "scholars and statesmen turned to history

---

[4] James W. Thompson, *A History of Historical Writing*, 2 vols. (New York, 1942), vol. I, p. 527.
[5] J. R. Hale (ed.), *The Evolution of British Historiography* (London, 1967), p. 11.
[6] Ernest Cassirer, *The Platonic Renaissance in England* (Austin, 1953), p. 12.

to justify the ways of church and state to Englishmen."[7] Furthermore, due to the special conditions of the Reformation in England as a national movement aiming to free both state and church from papal usurpation, ecclesiastical controversies in England "became more consciously historical," as the Protestants "had made purposeful use of history for specific polemical ends."[8] What eventually emerged in Tudor England was in general terms the creation of "a unified Protestant literary tradition,"[9] and in particular the creation of a distinct mode of historical thought – English Protestant "apocalyptic tradition,"[10] which was based upon an apocalyptical view of English history and which increasingly came to define the Reformation in England in eschatological, apocalyptic terms.

English historical apocalyptic tradition exercised enormous influence on the Reformation in England, especially from the time of Queen Elizabeth's accession to the throne and up to and during the Puritan Revolution of the seventeenth century. Many historical studies have already demonstrated its importance to an understanding of the religious and political developments in England during that period.[11] My aims, however, are somewhat narrower: to describe the formation of the apocalyptic tradition in England as a

---

[7] F. Smith Fussner, *The Historical Revolution: English Historical Writing and Thought* (London, 1962), p. 17.

[8] Arthur B. Ferguson, *Clio Unbound: Perceptions of Social and Cultural Past in Renaissance England* (Durham, 1979), p. 171.

[9] John N. King, *English Reformation Literature: The Tudor Origins of Protestant Tradition* (Princeton, 1982), p. 407.

[10] On the development of Protestant apocalyptic tradition in England, see the excellent studies of Katharine R. Firth, *The Apocalyptic Tradition in Reformation Britain: 1530–1645* (Oxford, 1979), and Richard Bauckham, *Tudor Apocalypse: Sixteenth Century Apocalypticism, Millenarianism and the English Reformation, from John Bale to John Foxe and Thomas Brightman* (Oxford, 1978).

[11] Among the studies concerned with English apocalyptic vision from the English Reformation to the Puritan Revolution, see Bryan W. Ball, *A Great Expectation: Eschatological Thought in English Protestantism to 1660* (Leiden, 1975); Bernard S. Capp, *The Fifth Monarchy Men: A Study of Seventeenth-Century English Millenarianism* (London, 1972); Paul Christianson, *Reformers and Babylon: English Apocalyptic Vision from the Reformation to the Eve of the Civil War* (Toronto, 1978); Christopher Hill, *Antichrist in Seventeenth Century England* (Oxford, 1971); William Lamont, *Godly Rule: Politics and Religion, 1603–1660* (London, 1969) and *Richard Baxter and the Millennium* (London, 1979); Tai Liu, *Discord in Zion: The Puritan Divines and the Puritan Revolution* (The Hague, 1973); J. G. A. Pocock, "Modes of Action and Their Pasts in Tudor and Stuart England," in *National Consciousness, History and Political Culture in Early Modern Europe*, ed. O. Ranum (Baltimore, 1975), pp. 98–117, "Time, History and Eschatology in the Thought of Thomas Hobbes," in J. G. A. Pocock, *Politics, Language, and Time: Essays on Political Thought and History* (London, 1972), pp. 148–201, and *The Machiavellian Moment: Florentine Republican Thought and the Atlantic Republican Tradition* (Princeton, 1975); Peter Toon (ed.), *Puritans, the Millennium and the Future of Israel: Puritan Eschatology* (Cambridge, 1970); Ernest L. Tuveson, *Millennium and Utopia: A Study in the Background of the Idea of Progress* (New York, 1964), and G. J. R. Parry, *A Protestant Vision: William Harrison and the Reformation of Elizabethan England* (Cambridge, 1987).

unique mode of historical thought during the sixteenth century, and to speculate upon its meaning. More specifically, I wish to explore the significance of English historical apocalyptic tradition in relation to the Christian sense of time, or view of history.

However, before dealing with the Protestant apocalyptic tradition in England, it is necessary first to explore the premises and substance of Protestant historiography in Europe during the sixteenth century.[12] The foundations of English apocalyptic tradition were inextricably connected to the rise of Protestant historiography in Europe. Many of the major English Protestant historians had taken refuge in Protestant centers in Europe during the periods of the Henrican and Marian Exiles, and worked there in close association with other Protestant scholars and historians. There they formed an integral part of an intellectual community within which was laid the foundation of Protestant historiography.

PROTESTANT HISTORIOGRAPHY

The Protestant Reformation was indeed a revolution, but as G. R. Elton reminds us, "it is easy to mistake the nature of that revolution." The essence of the Reformation was a "religious revolution," a fundamental quest after the "restoration of God at the heart of religion and theology."[13] While attacking vehemently the Church of Rome's usurpation of the means of salvation by arrogating to itself the Power of the Keys, the Protestants endeavored to restore God to the center of religious life and experience. With this important restoration of the deity to the very core of religious faith, long-cherished religious and ecclesiastical traditions of the Church of Rome were denounced as the fundamental prerequisite for salvation was changed from *ex opere operato* ("by the work done") to *Sola Fide* ("through faith alone"). Not content with the restitution of the power of God in religion and theology, the Protestant reformers strove also to restore God's glory in a theocratic universe and to return to him his direct role within history. By viewing history as the proper domain of "the theatre of God's judgement,"[14] as the dimension of time which is the subject of divine revelation, the Reformation gave rise to a new historical consciousness based upon a close reading of Scripture and its correlation to historical

---

[12] The most useful survey of Protestant historiography for our present purpose is Thompson, *A History of Historical Writing*, vol. I, pp. 520–645, and A. G. Dickens, *The Reformation in Historical Thought* (Cambridge, Mass., 1985).

[13] G. R. Elton, *Reformation Europe, 1517–1559* (London, 1963), pp. 274–6.

[14] According to Philip Melanchthon, "all the world is God's theatre in which he displays examples of all our duties." This quotation is from A. G. Dickens, *The German Reformation and Martin Luther* (London, 1974), p. 205. See also Thomas Beard, *The Theatre of Gods Judgments* (London, 1612). Beard was Oliver Cromwell's schoolmaster.

events. Directed by the literal rather than the allegorical interpretation of divine prophecy, the Protestants turned to history in order to explain the historical process in the light of God's word, endeavoring to prove that it was the force of God's hand which directed the course of events. In terms of philosophy of history, Protestant historiography may be characterized as an apocalyptic mode of historical thought which viewed history as a dimension of time subject to prophecies.

Protestant reformers, it is true, turned first to Scripture in their quest to refute the ecclesiastical and theological positions of the Church of Rome, and they vehemently denounced the church on the grounds that it opposed apostolic tradition and introduced innovative religious beliefs and practices. Luther, for example, constantly referred to the teaching of the See of Rome as "pure invention," and strongly attacked the papacy's claim of exclusive power over "the interpretation of scripture or the confirmation of its interpretation" as "a wickedly invented fable."[15] Calvin, when accused by Catholics of invention in his teaching, criticized his accusers with the retort that "by calling it 'new', they do great wrong to God, whose sacred Word does not deserve to be accused of novelty."[16] In their attacks against Rome, Protestant reformers were initially far more interested in proving their position through Scripture than they were in appealing to any historical arguments, a preference which reveals something about the Protestants' early view of history. "The pagan called history the mistress of life," wrote Calvin, but he was firmly assured that indeed "scripture alone deserves that high position."[17] However, as the struggle between the forces of Reformation and Counter-Reformation intensified during the course of the sixteenth century, the Protestants gradually changed their attitude and came to appreciate the study of history and its possible uses in refuting the historical foundations of Rome and the papacy. As Luther admitted in 1535, "though I was not at first historically well informed, I attacked the papacy on the basis of Holy Scripture. Now I rejoice heartily to see that others have attacked it from another source, that is, from history," and he happily acknowledged "how clearly," through the work of Protestant historians, "history agrees with Scripture," so that what he had "learned and taught from Paul and Daniel, namely, that the Pope is Antichrist, that history proclaims, pointing and indicating the very man himself."[18] Luther had come now to regard history as "the mother of the truth," and "refused

---

[15] Martin Luther, "An Open Letter to the Christian Nobility of the German Nation" (1520), *Works of Martin Luther* (Philadelphia, 1943), vol. II, pp. 66, 74–5.

[16] John Calvin, *Institutes of the Christian Religion*, Library of Christian Classics, 2 vols. (Philadelphia, 1960), vol. I, pp. 15–16.

[17] Calvin cited by Donald R. Kelley, *The Beginning of Ideology* (Cambridge, 1981), pp. 157–8.

[18] Luther cited by Firth, *The Apocalyptic Tradition*, p. 13.

to recognize any conflict between the Bible and history properly understood."[19]

Luther's statement signified an important moment in the development of Protestant historiography, for those words, recorded in the preface to Robert Barnes' *Vitae Romanorum Pontificum (The Lives of the Popes of Rome)* (1535), indicated full acknowledgment of the achievements of Protestant historiography in the battle over "the truth." Above all, Luther's contention that history concurred with the word of God revealed an essential premise of Protestant historiography: divine prophecies as recorded in Scripture were subject to historical interpretation. And as a direct consequence of the association, secular, profane history – as the domain within which God's providence revealed itself through the fulfillment of prophecies – became integrally linked to sacred, ecclesiastical history. Regarded now as the ground on which the apocalyptic struggle between Christ and Antichrist takes place, secular history was projected by Protestant historiography to the dimension of sacred, prophecy-fulfilling history.

Carion's Chronicle (1532), the first major historical work of Protestant historiography, derives its great significance from this very transformation that was performed on secular history. With the Reformation providing an impetus in the 1520s to historical investigation Protestant historiography began to take shape. Luther duly "regretted in 1520 his failure to read history and poetry and the time he had wasted on the inanities of the philosophers and the sophists;"[20] and indeed the actual task of formulating Protestant history was left to others, most notably Philip Melanchthon. It was Melanchthon and other scholars who undertook to revise *Chronicle* by John (Johannes) Carion, a book about the history of the world from Adam to the early sixteenth century. This greatly revised version, which was published under the name of *Carion's Chronicles*, and in which the original book had been "literally rewrote" and "made a new book," constituted the first Protestant writing "to show the influence of the apocalyptic thought."[21] For the first time using prophecies – the Prophecy of Elias and the Book of Daniel – as the basis of the course of history, "Melanchthon's revised book became a work of Lutheran propaganda. It set a precedent for sixteenth-century historical writing with a theological content and purpose."[22] Fur-

---

[19] Donald R. Kelley, *Foundations of Modern Historical Scholarship: Language, Law, and History in the French Renaissance* (New York, 1970), pp. 155–6.

[20] Matthew A. Fitzsimons, Alfred G. Pundit, and Charles E. Nowell (eds.), *The Development of Historiography* (New York, 1967 [1954]), p. 120.

[21] Thompson, *A History of Historical Writing*, vol. I, p. 527; Firth, *The Apocalyptic Tradition*, p. 6.

[22] Thompson, *A History of Historical Writing*, vol. I, pp. 529–31; Firth, *The Apocalyptic Tradition*, p. 15.

thermore, this universal history became "an historical textbook in Germany for some two hundred years."[23]

Not the least of its merits, in terms of Protestant historiography, was the intimate relationship it set forth between history and prophecy. "God hath given us al maner of prophecyes" so "that the accomplishment of their chaunce, we myght have wytnesse," and this in order "that we shuld be warned when Christ must come, and when the ende of the worlde is to be loked for." The historical dimension of prophecy was further stressed in the argument "that all thynges spoken on in the prophets are come to passe, that we may believe, that those shall happen also, the which holye scripture sayeth shall befal."[24] Thus history and prophecy were inextricably bound to one another, with prophecy placed within the historical dimension, and history – as the realization of prophecy – situated within the prophetic dimension. With history and prophecy so closely joined, a knowledge of history becomes necessary for the understanding of prophecy, and familiarity with prophetic writing becomes indispensable to the interpretation of history: "to understande prophecyes arighte it is greatlye necessary to knowe the order of kingdomes, the nombre of the years, and many other thynges," for this historical knowledge "is chiefelye necessarye for Chrysten men, that they may the better understande the prophecies, and have better judgment of them."[25] Indeed, it was Melanchthon's deep conviction that "history forms a succession of divinely predestined events and patterns."[26]

Carion's Chronicles marked the creation of a Protestant ideology of history. The apocalyptic element of Protestant historiography, first introduced there, was to become more pronounced over time. Moreover, two major achievements emerged from this book which determined to a large extent the future course of Protestant historiography. First, by being divided into the periods of the four great monarchies, Babylonian, Assyrian, Persian, and Roman, history was set in a predestined apocalyptic direction; this in turn placed the Reformation within a well-defined historical context whereby it could be regarded as the final stage before the end of time. Second, Melanchthon succeeded in erasing the boundaries between sacred and secular history and uniting both into one history evolving along a special dimension of time in which promise leads to fulfillment, and prophecy to its realization.[27]

[23] Fitzsimons, *The Development of Historiography*, p. 121; Thompson, *A History of Historical Writing*, vol. I, p. 528.
[24] Firth, *The Apocalyptic Tradition*, p. 16.
[25] *Ibid.*, p. 16.
[26] Dickens, *The German Reformation and Martin Luther*, p. 205.
[27] Firth, *The Apocalyptic Tradition*, pp. 15–22; Thompson, *A History of Historical Writing*, vol. I, pp. 527–8.

The extent to which Protestant historiography influenced the conception of the relationship between history and prophecy is nowhere more clearly seen than in Luther's change of opinion, through the works of Protestant history, such as *Carion's Chronicle* and Barne's *Vitae Romanorum Pontificum,* concerning the prophetic visions described in the Revelation of St. John and their historical significance. Although Luther's exegesis of Revelation ought not be treated as a historical work, it marked a departure from an allegorical interpretation of prophecies to a literal interpretation and a tendency to view them in historical terms, so that the whole course of history came to be revealed through a historical interpretation of prophecy.

Luther wrote two prefaces to "The Revelation of St. John." In 1522, in the first, he frankly admitted that he actually "missed more than one thing in this book," and therefore "hold it to be neither apostolic nor prophetic." "First and foremost," Luther declared, "the apostles do not deal with visions, but prophesy in clear, plain words." Not knowing how to interpret the "visions and figures" which were the main content of the Apocalypse, Luther argued that "no one knows what is [the Book of Revelation], to say nothing of keeping it." He gave serious thought to letting "everyone think of it as his own spirit gives him to think," yet he expressed his deep hesitation to deal with the book himself: "my spirit cannot fit itself into this book" because "Christ is not taught or known in it."[28]

A remarkable shift in view is evident in the second "Preface," which appeared in 1545. Luther was constantly revising his translation of the Bible into German, and was assisted in this task by his "Wittenberg Colleagues,"[29] Melanchthon among them, at their weekly meetings. The edition of 1545 was the last to be supervised by the great reformer himself, and in it he revised not only his translation, but also the prefaces he provided for each book of Scriptures. In this edition, one particularly remarkable passage may be said to contain the essence of what had newly emerged as the Protestant historical interpretation of the Apocalypse:

Since it is intended as a revelation of things that are to happen in the future, and especially of tribulations and disasters for the Church, we consider that the first and surest step toward finding its interpretation is to take from history the events and disasters that have come upon the Church before now and hold them up alongside these pictures and so compare them with the words. If, then, the two were to fit and agree with each other, we could build on that, as a sure, or at least an unobjectionable interpretation.[30]

---

[28] Luther, "Preface to the Revelation of Saint John" (1522), *Works of Martin Luther,* vol. VI, pp. 488–9.

[29] C. M. Jacobs, "Introduction" to Luther's "Prefaces to the Books of the Bible," *Works,* vol. VI, p. 365.

[30] Luther, "Preface to the Revelation of Saint John" (1545), *Works,* vol. VI, p. 481.

Certainly the most amazing aspect of this passage is the explicitness with which history is pronounced necessary for the understanding of prophecy. Here, Luther appears to have accepted the method of correlation between "text" and "chronicle," or prophecy and history, which had been developed by Protestant historians, according to which historical "events" were compared with "pictures" or visions of the Revelation, and placed in a coherent mesh based on the "words or interpretations."[31]

It was with this approach that Luther endeavored to provide now an interpretation of the Apocalypse. "Many have tried their hand at" the Apocalypse, wrote Luther, "but until this very day they have reached no certainty." Now that he was "certain of its meaning, or interpretation,"[32] Luther undertook to interpret its visions and symbols in such a way as to situate the Reformation in an apocalyptic historical context. By identifying the Sack of Rome by the armies of Charles V in 1527 with the destruction of "Babylon the Great" (Rev. 18), the Turk's invasion of Europe with "Gog and Magog" (Rev. 20), and the Papacy with Antichrist,[33] Luther unmistakably was able "to place the Reformation in the final years of history."[34] Furthermore, by interpreting history in terms of the prophetic revelations of the Apocalypse, Luther was able to find significance in the Reformation through providential history; "here," in Revelation, "we see clearly what cruel offenses and short-comings there have been before our times, and one might think that the Church was now at its best, and that our time is a golden age compared with those that have gone before."[35] Indeed, the Apocalypse "shows enough of terrible and monstrous beasts, horrible and vindictive angels, wild and awful plagues," yet Luther was sure that "through and above all plagues and beasts and bad angels, Christ is with His saints, and wins the victory at last."[36]

Within the works of Protestant historiography, none can be compared to the monumental historical study known as the *Magdeburg Centuries* (1559–74). Initiated by Matthias Flacius Illyricus, and composed with the collaboration of colleagues, the *Centuries* was a major Protestant historical enterprise. At considerable financial cost, the authors engaged in the searching out and collecting of books and manuscripts from all over Europe. Essentially an ecclesiastical history, the *Centuries* traced the history of the church from the birth of Christ to the thirteenth century with the goal of demolishing the historical foundation of the Church of Rome, mainly by refuting the authenticity of documents upon which the Catholic Church

[31] *Ibid.*, p. 480.   [32] *Ibid.*, p. 480.   [33] *Ibid.*, pp. 486, 484.
[34] Firth, *The Apocalyptic Tradition*, p. 12.
[35] Luther, "Preface to the Revelation of Saint John" (1545), p. 487.
[36] *Ibid.*, pp. 487–8.

based its claims to exclusive power. Filled with accusations that the pope is Antichrist and the Catholic Church the empire of Antichrist, the work's importance in the context of Protestant historiography rests in its attempt to demonstrate the endurance through the centuries of the true church with its pure Christian faith and doctrine. The *Centuries* in essence came to present

the Ecclesiastical History of the perfectly conceived church of Christ, as to situation, propagation, persecutions, periods of peace, and as to doctrine, heresies, ceremonies, government, schisms, councils, important individuals, miracles, martyrdoms,

and so forth, all of these "comprehended in a clear manner according to centuries" (hence the name of the work) and "compiled with great diligence and honesty from the best historical, patristic and other writers."[37] As an ecclesiastical history, the *Centuries* aimed to reveal the decline of the church under the papacy, and it described "anyone who resisted" the Church of Rome as "a morning star of the Reformation."[38] Thus, again, within a theocratic universe history was regarded as the dimension of time along which an apocalyptic struggle was waged between the true and false church, or between Christ and Antichrist. The mark of history, stressed the *Centuries*, "is the warfare between good and evil, between evangelical truth and the intrigues of Anti-Christ."[39]

With the appearance of *Carion's Chronicle*, Luther's exposition of the Apocalypse, and the *Magdeburg Centuries*, Protestant historiography emerged as a unique mode of historical thought, which, being based upon the strictest correlation between prophecy and history, might be defined as an apocalyptic ideology of history. The revolutionary character of this ideology is clear in light of the previous orthodox Christian attitudes toward time and history. Before the Reformation, the Christian philosophy of history was largely grounded upon the legacy of the Fathers of the church, most notably St. Augustine of Hippo, whereby eschatology and apocalypse were removed from history, and the entire culmination of the redemptive process was placed beyond time. The fulfillment of prophecy and revelation, once considered a dimension of history itself, as is reflected in the chiliastic and millennial expectations in early Christianity, was now sought outside history. During the patristic period, this "de-eschatologization process"[40] gradually displaced Christ's Second Coming from this world to the "world

---

[37] Denys Hay, *Annalists and Historians: Western Historiography from the Eighth to the Eighteenth Centuries* (London, 1977), p. 123; Thompson, *A History of Historical Writing*, vol. I, pp. 530–1; Fitzsimons, *The Development of Historiography*, pp. 121–3; Harry E. Barnes, *A History of Historical Writing* (New York, 1962 [1937]), pp. 124–5.

[38] Hay, *Annalists and Historians*, p. 125.

[39] Thompson, *A History of Historical Writing*, vol. I, p. 530. Fitzsimons, *The Development of Historiography*, p. 122.

[40] Alfred Braunthal, *Salvation and the Perfect Society: The Eternal Quest* (Amherst, 1979), p. 146.

to come" and irrevocably separated prophecy from history. No longer considered an intrinsic part of the historical process, eschatological revelation receded into some undefined realm outside the boundaries of history. "The two cities, the earthly and the Heavenly," according to Augustine, "which are mingled together from the beginning to the end of their history," would be "separated by the final judgment, each receives her own end."[41] Thus, the eschatological day of judgment inaugurating Christ's Second Coming, and the millennium itself, was removed from the dimension of history and no longer considered a historical event.

With Protestant historiography, eschatology and apocalypse – and hence the millennium – were once again included within the boundaries of time and history. This new approach brought about a radical change in the Christian attitude toward history, which had been exemplified by Augustine who exerted great influence on the Christian view of history before the Reformation. Divine providence, Augustine believed, is concerned with salvation, not with history as such, and therefore the intrinsic dualism characterizing the historical process, the struggle between the heavenly and profane cities, would be resolved only beyond time and history. Firmly intertwined with one another in history, these two cities signified by their contest the essence of history and the immanent feature of the historical process. History is the arena in which the crucial struggle between the two cities takes place, and only on the eschatological day of judgment is that struggle resolved. An integral part of this dualistic view of history is Augustine's conception of the *saeculum*, or secular history, and of man's existence in the world. There are "no verbs of historical movement in the *City of God*, no sense of progress to aims that may be achieved in history," and it appears from Augustine's writings that

the most obvious feature of man's life in this *saeculum* is that it is doomed to remain incomplete. No human potentiality can ever reach its fulfillment in it; no human tension can ever be resolved. The fulfillment of human personality lies beyond it; it is infinitely postponed to the end of time, to the Last Day and the glorious resurrection.[42]

History, devoid of all human progress, was therefore regarded by Augustine as without meaning, and his attitude toward history, and hence the world, was thus based upon alienation from it, and not upon reconciliation. "Citizens of Jerusalem," Augustine preached to his fellow Christians in Carthage, "O God's own people, O Body of Christ, O high-born race of foreigners on earth . . . you do not belong here, you belong somewhere else." A permanent pilgrimage upon earth – this essentially is the state of

[41] St. Augustine, *City of God*, trans. J. O'Meara (Middlesex, 1984), p. 842.
[42] P. Brown, "Saint Augustine," *Trends in Medieval Political Thought*, ed. B. Smalley (Oxford, 1965), p. 11.

Christian life in the world as "resident strangers," or "resident aliens,"[43] and this existential state determined, *ipso facto*, the Christian view of history. In terms of sacred, providential history as well, to Augustine's mind profane history was devoid of any significance:

that since the coming of Christ, until the end of the world, all history is homogeneous, that it cannot be mapped out in terms of a pattern drawn from sacred history, that it can no longer contain decisive turning-points endowed with a significance in sacred history. Every moment may have its unique mysterious significance in the ultimate divine *tableau* of men's doings and sufferings; but it is a significance to which God's revelation does not supply the clue.[44]

Protestant historiography then, must be considered within the context of the pre-Reformation Christian philosophy of history, and in terms of man's existence in the world and the significance of his action in time. With its apocalyptic orientation to history and strict correlation between history and prophecy, Protestant history infused the *saeculum* (history in its secular meaning) with divine significance, thereby transforming the role which the world and secular history assumed in sacred, providential history. This mode of historical thought first of all bears evidence to the rising belief in man's ability to comprehend the course of history. Second, by incorporating the saeculum into sacred, providential history, Protestant historiography utterly abolished the dualistic view of history, as exemplified in Augustine's notion of history as a constant struggle between the two cities. Eschatology and apocalypse, excluded from time and history by pre-Reformation church thought, were thus firmly reestablished within the boundaries of history and made intrinsic to the historical process; divine Providence now worked through and within history. Third, men's existence in the world and especially the saints' role in history was now changed from that of alienation from the world to active participation within it. With history situated along the dimension of prophecy, the saints, as Christ's army, took their stand alongside Him, where they played a singular role in the unfolding drama of salvation.

ENGLISH APOCALYPTIC TRADITION

Protestant historiography, which developed in Protestant centers in Europe during the sixteenth century as a movement aimed at demolishing the historical foundations of the Church of Rome and exposing the papacy's sinful and unwarranted usurpation of ecclesiastical and regal powers, tended more and more to be nationalistic in its character. As the Reforma-

---

[43] P. Brown, *Augustine of Hippo: A Biography* (Berkeley, 1969), pp. 313–14, 323.
[44] R. A. Markus, *Saeculum: History and Society in the Theology of St. Augustine* (Cambridge, 1970), pp. 20–1.

tion movement spread across Europe, it stimulated a strong interest in national history in countries such as Poland, Bohemia, Hungary, France, Denmark, and Sweden. Many of the historiographic works in Protestant countries emphasized the particular nation's role in the historic struggle against the Church of Rome; at the same time, these works denied all historical significance to Rome and the Catholic Church, and sought to fill the vacuum thereby created by introducing national historical content.[45]

Armed with a new critical awareness and historical consciousness, Protestant historians set out to examine past national experiences in light of the struggle with Rome. This was especially true in England, where Protestant historiography laid the foundations for interpreting English national history within the context of providential history. Providing a singular place for the Church of England in providential history, the Protestant apocalyptic tradition in England made it the core of English history as a whole, describing all of English history solely in terms of the history of the Church of England. Consequently, Protestant historiography gave rise to high expectations that the Reformation in England would finally reveal the full significance of the English nation in providential history. Through this development, the revolutionary implications of Protestant historiography were most fully revealed.

English Protestants took a leading role in the establishment of Protestant historiography on the continent. Many English reformers during the Henrican and Marian Exile, such as William Tyndale, John Bale, John Foxe, and others, worked hand in hand with Protestant historians and theologians on the continent in the research, writing, and publishing of historiographic and theological polemical tracts. Protestant intellectual centers flourished in Europe during the Protestant Reformation, and within them the premises of Protestant historiography were forged as a revolutionary ideology of history. Exile became an important avenue for English reformers to diffuse ideas back to England upon returning to their native country. The Henrican and Marian Exiles, in particular, took part in this way in the great cultural and religious revival initiated by the Reformation. This was nowhere more apparent than in the field of Protestant historiography.

Slowly but surely, English reformers in exile and at home developed a unique Protestant historiography singularly fitted to the English historical context, which interpreted the break with Rome in increasingly nationalistic terms. In a sophisticated interpretation of English history, pure apostolic Christianity was claimed to have been transferred intact to England well before the intrusion of the Church of Rome, thus implying that it was the

---

[45] Kelley, *Foundations of Modern Historical Scholarship*, pp. 151–82; Thompson, *A History of Historical Writing*, vol. I, pp. 531–4.

Church of England, and not Rome, that was founded upon apostolic origins, and that the former was in decline because of the usurpation of the latter. From this point of view, English history appeared as an endless struggle of the English Church and monarchy to resist Rome's usurpation of regal and ecclesiastical powers. This argument came to constitute the core of Protestant historiography primarily through the writings of John Bale, John Foxe, and Thomas Brightman, the leading exponents of the Protestant apocalyptic tradition in England during the sixteenth century. It was largely as a result of their writings that Protestants regarded the English Reformation as central to English history. Later, during the seventeenth century, their works became the source of the upsurge in eschatological visions and millennial expectations which characterized the Puritan Revolution.

John Bale and the two churches

The Protestant historiographer John Bale (1495–1563), forced to leave his native country after the fall of his patron Thomas Cromwell, fled to the continent and settled in Germany in 1540. Earlier in his career, after his conversion to Protestantism and as an advocate of reformed doctrine, Bale did no more than write some historical and miracle plays, most notable among them *King John* (c. 1536). Once secure on the continent, however, and part of that "afflicted family" of "believing brethren" whom the Lord "hath exiled" from the "realm of England," Bale took upon himself a mission of such proportions as would transform him from minor dramatist into a major protagonist of English Protestant historiography. "I have considered it no less than my bound duty, under pain of damnation, to admonish Christ's flock" in England by exposing the "present revelation of their perils past, and the danger to come for the contempt of the gospel."[46] The outcome took shape as the *Image of Both Churches* (1541–7), an ecclesiastical history of universal scope yet singularly adapted to England, and modeled after Augustine's *City of God* ("either we are citizens in the new Jerusalem with Jesus Christ, or else in the old superstitious Babylon with Antichrist the vicar of Satan"). It was, essentially, a history based upon "the most wonderful heavenly Revelation of Saint John the Evangelist," or the Apocalypse.[47] "So highly necessary, good Christian reader," thus opened Bale's book, "is the knowledge of St. John's Apocalypse or Revelation (whether you wilt) to him that is a member of Christ's church"; for this prophecy

---

[46] John Bale, *Image of Both Churches* (1550), in *Selected Works of John Bale*, ed. H. Christmas (Cambridge, 1849), pp. 254–5.
[47] *Ibid.*, pp. 252, 251.

containeth the universal troubles, persecutions and crosses, that the church suffered in the primitive spring, what it suffereth now, and what it shall suffer in the latter times by the subtle satellites of antichrist, which are the cruel members of Satan.[48]

Concerning the relationship between history and prophecy, the Apocalypse according to Bale "is full clearance to all the chronicles and most notable histories which hath been wrote since Christ's ascension, opening the true natures of their ages, times, and seasons." Indeed, "in the text," or in the Apocalypse, historical events and occurrences are "only proponed in effect, and promised to follow in their seasons, and so ratified with the other scriptures; but in the chronicles they are evidently seen by all ages fulfilled." "Yet is the text a light to the chronicles," stressed Bale, "and not the chronicles to the text."[49] The key to history, the meaning of historical events, is to be found in the text of divine prophecy. This indeed was the Protestant revolution in the Christian philosophy of history: a historiographic revolution whose rallying cry was for a literal, figural, and historical reading of Scripture, giving rise to a tight correspondence between prophecy and history. Eric Auerbach best described this correspondence as follows:

Figural interpretation establishes a connection between two events or person [or ceremonies], the first of which signifies not only itself but also the second, while the second encompasses or fulfills the first. The two poles of the figure are separate in time, but both, being real events or figures, are within time, within the stream of historical life. Only the understanding of the two persons or events is a spiritual act, but this spiritual act deals with concrete events whether past, present, or future . . . since promise and fulfillment are the real historical events, which have either happened in the incarnation of the world, or will happen in the second coming.[50]

Having established the connection between prophetic text and historical event, between prophecy and history, Bale then turned to the reconstruction of ecclesiastical history based upon an apocalyptic mode of historical thought. A struggle takes place within history and time, he said, between the true and false churches, between Christ and Antichrist. This apocalyptic struggle characterized the essence of history, the latter being exclusively associated with the progress of the church, and England held a special role in this contest. Following the example of Augustine's *City of God*, Bale described history as the space of time within which a struggle is waged between two opposite powers, but instead of Augustine's two cities, Bale defined it in his *Image of Both Churches* as a struggle between two churches, the one belonging to Christ and the other to Antichrist: the first is

[48] *Ibid.*, p. 253.
[49] *Ibid.*, p. 253.
[50] Eric Auerbach, cited by Mason I. Lowance, *The Language of Canaan: Metaphor and Symbol in New England from the Puritans to the Transcendentalists* (Cambridge, Mass., 1980), p. 13.

"the true Christian church, which is the meek spouse of the Lamb without spot," and the second is "the proud church of hypocrites, the rose-coloured whore, the paramour of antichrist, and the sinful synagogue of Satan."[51] The great difference between Bale, and indeed Protestant historiography in general, and Augustine, is that while in Augustine's thought the struggle between the two cities marks the essence of profane, secular history, and will be resolved beyond time and history, according to Bale the apocalyptic struggle between the two churches is inherent in providential history and is played out and resolved within time. It is in history (now redefined as "providential history"), Bale argued, that "the two churches" receive their due fate: "the one turned over into the most fearful and terrible destruction, under the title of the old whorish Babylon, the other obtaining a most glorious raise, under the name of the holy new Jerusalem."[52] Moreover, in sharp contrast to Augustine's pessimistic view of history as devoid of any sacred or human progress, and his resultant concept of alienation from the world, Bale and other Protestant historians developed a sense of history as the arena in which the drama of salvation is unfolding, a realm in which sacred, and hence human, progress is made from divine promise to its fulfillment. In sharp contrast to Augustine, Protestant historiography perceived history as rich in immanent meaning.

It is noteworthy that while Bale abolished Augustine's dualism between heaven and earth as the mark of history, he nonetheless retained a dualistic view concerning the fulfillment of prophecies. He believed that the realization of the millennium and the establishment of the New Jerusalem would take place both as an earthly and a heavenly phenomenon. Thus, concerning the millennium, the saints "reigned with Christ, the pastor and high bishop of their souls, not only here, [upon earth] where as they suffered with him, for a thousand years' space, but also above, where as he sitteth on the right hand of God's majesty-seat a thousand without end."[53] In the New Jerusalem on earth, "all her citizens are of one faith, and there shall be one glorious unity and concord," because "perfect are their consciences, and their conversations godly." In its primary manifestation the New Jerusalem is a historical, earthly event, whereupon it undergoes "regeneration, when she meeteth her spouse in the air."[54] For indeed, Bale argued, it was said in the Apocalypse "that the new Jerusalem shall come down from heaven: but not so that it shall not up again. For Christ's elects shall be where as he is."[55]

Closely related to the issues of the millennium and the New Jerusalem is the question of when the key to the drama of salvation would finally be disclosed. Bale offered no great eschatological visions or millennial expec-

---

[51] Bale, *Image of Both Churches*, p. 251.   [52] *Ibid.*, p. 514.
[53] *Ibid.*, pp. 566–7.   [54] *Ibid.*, pp. 582–4.   [55] *Ibid.*, pp. 587.

tation toward the final conflagration, for he did not expect God's mysteries to be revealed during his lifetime. Rather, he saw his time and the Reformation in general as the period of the sixth seal, or as the sixth and penultimate age in the history of the world. "Since Christ's ascension hath the church continued by six other ages . . . comprehended in the six seals, in the latter end of whom we are now." From the time of "creation," history continues within "the space [of] six ages, till the coming of Christ, which brought with him the sabbath of the Spirit," or the seventh age.[56]

Bale's importance in the Protestant apocalyptic tradition in England lies mainly in his interpretation of the origins of the Church of England. The Church of England was founded, according to Bale, not by St. Augustine of Canterbury (d. 604 or 605), who was sent by Pope St. Gregory the Great to England in 597, but rather by St. Joseph of Arimathea, "the councillor," who after the Crucifixion buried the body of Christ (Luke 23:53, Matt. 27:60, Mark 15:46). This idea was first broached by William of Malmesbury in the twelfth century, who claimed that St. Joseph came to England with the Holy Grail and established the first church there; with this story at hand, Bale had material on which to base his view that the Church of England was virtually apostolic in its origins, appearing well before the rise of Rome to predominance in the world. Having argued that, Bale could proceed to say that "Gregorye" sent "a Romyshe monke called Augustyne, not of the order of Christ as was Peter" to England in 596, "there to sprede ther Romyshe faythe and relygyon," yet "Christes faythe was there longe afore."[57] And just as the newly created Roman papacy introduced evils and superstitions into the primitive, apostolic church, in general, so it corrupted the Church of England. According to Bale, the sending of St. Augustine of Canterbury to England by Pope St. Gregory the Great signified the entrance of "monks and Italyanes" who were "wele armed" with "Aristotles artylerye, as with logyck, Phylosophy, and other crafty scyences, but of the sacred scripturs, they knew lyttle or nothyne."[58] The Church of England thus came to exemplify the fate of the true church in general: with primitive apostolic origins well preceding the rise of Rome, it is eventually corrupted by sinful Roman faith.

Bale gave further prominence to English history by presenting it as a model of ceaseless resistance to the Pope's usurpation of regal and ecclesiastical powers. This tendency is particularly noticeable in the historical play *King John* (King Johan) which Bale wrote during the 1530s as part of Protestant propaganda. "John as a martyr-king, forced against his will to submit to papal tyranny" was meant to serve Henry VIII as a historical

---

[56] *Ibid.*, pp. 449.
[57] F. J. Levy, *Tudor Historical Thought* (San Marino, 1967), p. 91.
[58] *Ibid.*, p. 91.

model in his struggle against Rome. John, the king who resisted the papacy
so strongly and fiercely, was thus rescued from oblivion that he might be an
example to the English monarchy in the sixteenth century. Bale's apocalyptic view of history does have its effect on the play;[59] *King John*, therefore
may impress the reader as an early attempt by Bale to correlate prophecy
and history prior to writing his major ecclesiastical history, the *Image of
Both Churches*, a decade later. The historical setting of the play is the
struggle between John, king of England, and Pope Innocent III in the early
thirteenth century over the pope's appointment of Stephen Langton as archbishop of Canterbury in the face of John's opposition. The king's
sovereignty in his realm was an issue which Bale utilized fully in his play.
John "was of God a magistrate appoynted, to the gouernaunce" of England
in order "to see mayteyned the true faythe and relygyon, but Satan the
Deuyll, which that tyme was at large, had so great a swaye that he coulde it
not discharge." Furthermore, "King Iohan of England, bycause he hath
rebelled" against the Pope's power to install Archbishop Langton at Canterbury, had "to gyve up hys crowne."[60] Yet at the end of the play, in the
epilogue which was written after Elizabeth's accession, Bale expressed his
great hope that the queen and "hir ofsprynge maye lyve also to subdewe the
great Antichriste, with hys whole generacyon."[61] As a historical play, *King
John* demonstrates that the Protestants in England, confronted with the
problems of the English Reformation, had now become history-minded and
increasingly concerned about the past.

The historical approach went hand in hand with Bale's apocalyptic interpretation of history. Through his works a Protestant historiography began
to emerge in England which emphasized the apostolic, primitive origins of
the Church of England, denounced the Church of Rome as having brought
corruption and superstitions to the English Church, and consequently interpreted the entire course of English history from the beginning of Roman
influence in England as a continuous apocalyptic struggle between Christ
and Antichrist, or between the Church of England and the papacy. Bale
anticipated that the present king of England would rise to the task and fight
the papacy as John was said to have done, and thus he extended his "daily
prayer" that "the most worthy minister of god, king Edward the sixth,"
which "hath so sore wounded the beast," after his accession in 1547 to the
throne, would continue to "throw all" the "superstition" in the Church of
England "to the comfort of his people."[62] Indeed, the Reformation in England "by the gospel-preaching" led so far to "the suppression of

---

[59] Barry B. Adams (ed.), *John Bales' King Johan* (San Marino, 1969), "Introduction," p. 59.
[60] Bale, *King Johan*, pp. 101, 98.
[61] *Ibid.*, p. 147.
[62] Bale, *Image of Both Churches*, p. 640.

monasteries, priories, convents, and friars' houses . . . But be of good comfort and pray in the meantime," Bale advised, "for the Holy Ghost promiseth here they [the bishops] shall wither away, with all that the heavenly Father hath not planted." For according to Bale, the time has come for God's judgment, "now is the axe laid to the root of the tree, to hew down the unfruitful branches, the withered reserved to unquenchable fire."[63]

In the hands of Bale, English history had indeed become a mirror of providential history, a nation in which historically two churches were fighting for predominance. The English Reformation was in this context a pinnacle of English history, intrinsically associated with English nationalism and the turning away from Rome.

John Foxe and the elect nation

It was left to Bale's young friend and fellow Marian exile, John Foxe, to articulate the Reformation in England as a national reformation. Foxe made explicit in his writings, most notably in his *Acts and Monuments*, what was merely implied by Bale; that is, he took "the grand scheme evolved by John Bale and developed it into a fully articulated church history."[64] For his great competence as historian and martyrologist "John Foxe toweres above all the Englishmen who contributed to shaping English history into a Protestant mold," and "significantly helped to create a national faith that was shared by the English Reformers at large."[65]

A further difference between Bale and Foxe concerns the accession of Elizabeth I to the throne. Unlike his young friend, Bale was never able fully to utilize this event as an important sign of the triumph of Protestantism in England. Twice compelled to flee his native country, during Henry VIII's and Bloody Mary's times, when he finally returned to England in 1559 he was too old even to resume his position as bishop of Ossory which he had held during the reign of Edward VI. It was Foxe, then, returning to England that very same year, who placed the occasion of Elizabeth's accession within the context of the Protestant apocalyptic mode of historical thought. "By now by revolution of years we are come from that time of 1501," the time in which "the Lord began to show in parts of Germany wonderful tokens, and bloody marks of his passion" – to "the year now present 1570. In which the full seventy years of the Babylonish captivity draweth now well to an end."[66] In this time, "what the Lord will do with this wicked world, or what

---

[63] *Ibid.*, p. 485.
[64] Levy, *Tudor Historical Thought*, p. 194.
[65] V. Norskov Olsen, *John Foxe and the Elizabethan Church* (Berkeley, 1973), pp. 40, 38.
[66] John Foxe, *Acts and Monuments*, vol. I, p. 520.

rest he will give to his church . . . his will be done in earth as seemeth best to his divine Majesty."[67] Becoming more specific, Foxe continued: "At length the Lord sent this mild Constantine to cease blood, to stay persecution, to refresh his people." Thus was Elizabeth compared with Constantine the Great who made Christianity the religion of the empire. "In much like manner what bitter blasts, what smarting storms have been felt in England during the space of certain years, till at last God's pitiful grace sent us your Majesty to quench firebrands, to assuage rage, to relive innocents."[68] With such words, Elizabeth was assigned an important role in the triumph of Protestantism in England, not only stopping Bloody Mary's persecutions against the true church, but also greatly advancing the Reformation in England: "what a provident zeal full of solicitude, you have, minding . . . to furnish all quarters and countries of your realm with the voice of Christ's gospel and faithful preaching of his word."[69] Clearly, Foxe had a keen grasp of the importance of Elizabeth's accession within the framework of English history and he applied it to his ecclesiastical history.

Like Bale before him, Foxe began his historical writings while still in exile, with the intention of writing an ecclesiastical history that would place the Protestant Reformation in the context of providential history. "It have here purposed," he wrote,

to digest and compile, not so much to delight the ears of my country, as to intent to profit the church of Christ, so that we, in these reformed days, seeing the prodigious deformities and calamities of these times now present, and comparing the same with the times that were before, may therefore pour out more abundant thanks to the Lord for this his so sweet and merciful reformation.[70]

Foxe aimed in his work to present that which he considered the true association between prophecy and history, which in turn would draw the people more to God. "Ecclesiastical history," such as he attempted to write in the *Acts and Monuments*, "out not to be separate" from "the office of the ministry,": for "as by the one, the people may learn the rules and precepts of doctrine, so by the other, they may have example of God's mighty working in his church, to the confirmation of their faith, and the edification of christian life." For it is through ecclesiastical history that Christians come to know the acts of divine providence in time, through the manifold examples and experiments of God's great mercies and judgments in preserving His church, in overthrowing tyrants, in confounding pride, in altering states and kingdoms, in conserving religion against errors and dissensions, in relieving the godly, in bridling the wicked, and so forth. It was in the hands of Foxe that Protestant historiography truly became a theology of history:

[67] *Ibid.*, vol. I, p. 520.
[68] Foxe, cited by Christianson, *Reformers and Babylon*, p. 41.
[69] Foxe, *Acts and Monuments*, vol. I, p. 504.
[70] *Ibid.*, vol. I, p. 4.

the observing and noting whereof in histories minister to the reader thereof wholesome admonitions of life, with experience and wisdom both to know God in his works, and to work the thing that is godly; especially to seek unto the Son of God for their salvation, and in his faith only to find that they seek for, and in no other means.[71]

First and foremost, Foxe's ecclesiastical history came as a response to the Catholic charge that the reformed church did not exist before Luther's time.[72] So he set about to prove "that the same form, usage, and institution of this our present reformed church, are not the beginning of any new church of our own, but the renewing of the old ancient church of Christ."[73] In order to do so, he divided "the whole tractation of this history into five sundry diversities of time." The first period extended from the apostles to Constantine the Great; the second period, from "the flourishing time of the church" until the year 600; the third period marked "the declining or backsliding of the church" and continued "until the loosing out of Satan, which was about the thousandth year after the nativity of Christ." The fourth period "followed the time of Antichrist, and the loosing of Satan or desolation of the church, whose full swinge containeth the space of four hundred years"; this period Foxe correlated with the predominance of the papacy in the world. "Fifthly and lastly, after this time of Antichrist reigning in the church of God by violence and tyranny, followeth the reformation," which signalled the final battle, the historical apocalyptic struggle with Antichrist and "his church decreasing." Although, Foxe noted, "the durance of" the Reformation and "the true church increasing . . . hath continued hitherto about the space of two hundred and fourscore years," yet "how long it shall continue more, the Lord the Governor of all times, he only knoweth."[74]

In this apocalyptic scenario, England held a special place, almost to the point where English history and ecclesiastical history were inseparable. It was this singular role assigned to England in sacred, ecclesiastical history that made the book so highly influential in that country. "It became almost the Bible of Protestant England, and was ordered by Convocation to be placed in churches where everyone might have access to it." Originally intended as a general ecclesiastical history, a universal history of the church from its beginning to his time, the *Acts and Monuments* became increasingly Anglicized in its focus, particularly after Foxe's return to England. As the author himself conceded upon completing his work, it was mainly a history of the acts and monuments of the Church of England, intentionally written "in the popular tongue" for the "ignorant flock of Christ" who lived "in this realm of England," and who "have been long led in ignorance, and

[71] *Ibid.*, vol. I, p. 504.   [72] *Ibid.*, vol. I, pp. 9, 513, 3–4.
[73] *Ibid.*, vol. I, p. 9.   [74] *Ibid.*, vol. I, pp. 4–5.

wrapped in blindness, for lack especially of God's work, and partly also for wanting the light of history."[75] While the *Acts and Monuments* commences with a general description of "the first primitive age of Christ gospel," the work as a whole is divided by major events in English history, and concludes with a historical event that is exclusive to the English Reformation, namely, "the end of queen Mary," or Bloody Mary, "and the beginning of this gracious queen Elizabeth."[76] Like Bale, but with more historical ability, Foxe depicted English history as revolving around the history of the Church of England, and he envisaged the Reformation of the English Church as a climactic event that would finally reveal England's special role in providential history. Generations of Protestants, reading his book, were thus conditioned to look upon the fulfillment of the Reformation in England as the crucial task of their time; theirs was a unique nation, and they a chosen people. This deep conviction is well described by Milton in his *Areopagitica* (1643):

the favor and the love of Heaven, we have great argument to think in a peculiar manner propitious and propending toward us. Why else was this nation chosen before any other, that out of her, as out of Sion, should be proclaimed and sounded forth the first tidings and trumpet of reformation to all Europe?

Indeed, the entire thrust of the *Acts and Monuments* was to demonstrate to the English reader that theirs was a chosen nation that had received the pure faith during the time of the apostles, had struggled increasingly to preserve it undefiled against Rome and the papacy, and finally, with Wyclif, had initiated the Protestant Reformation. Consequently, Foxe spared no efforts to prove the pre-Augustinian origins of the Church of England. Among the many arguments he used to prove this point, is the story about Joseph of Arimathea who "after the dispersion of the [early church by] Jew, was sent, by Philip the apostle, from France to Britain, about the year of our Lord 63: and here remained in this land all his time; and so with his fellows, laid the first foundation of Christian faith among the people of Britain." Based upon this and much other evidence, Foxe could absolutely and vehemently deny the Catholic allegation that "the church of England was first derived from Rome."[77] Once having established the apostolic origins of the Church of England, Foxe like Bale before him, could then proceed to describe the history of England as a constant struggle between the true and the false church – the Church of England and of Rome – a struggle in which King John, who "like a valiant prince, had held out the tyranny" of bishops, assumed a leading, though eventually tragic role.[78]

[75] Thompson, *A History of Historical Writing*, vol. I, p. 615; Foxe, *Acts and Monuments*, vol. I, p. 504.

[76] Foxe, *Acts and Monuments*, vol. VIII, pp. 753–4.   [77] *Ibid.*, vol. I, pp. 152, 306.

[78] *Ibid.*, vol. IV, pp. 144–5, 131; vol. II, pp. 324–42.

According to Foxe, since England had given the great fourteenth-century reformer John Wyclif to the world, it was England which had inaugurated the Protestant Reformation. As Foxe wrote in his *Acts and Monuments*, after the triumph of Constantine the Great and the establishment of Christianity as the religion of the empire, "according to the preordinate counsel of God . . . it pleased him to show mercy again, and to bind up Satan, the old serpent, according to the twentieth chapter of the Revelation, for the space of a thousand years: that is, from the time of Licinius," in the year 324, "to the time of John Wickliff and John Huss."[79] Throughout that millennium Satan was bound up, and during the fourth period according to Foxe's division of ecclesiastical history, or the period "from Gregory VII . . . till the time of John Wickliff and John Huss,"[80] occurred the loosing again of Satan and the time of Antichrist. In this very time, in which "all the whole world was filled and overwhelmed with error and darkness," by "God's providence" Wyclif "sprang and rose up, through whom the Lord would first waken and raise up again the world."[81] Thus, the Reformation, or "the last time of the church," is "counting from the time of Wickliff." However, "this religion," or the religion of the Protestants, which "hath sprung up and risen but of late," in fact "hath been spread abroad in England of old and ancient time," and not only created "from the time of Wickliff."[82] Although Wyclif, and hence England, inaugurated the Reformation, Foxe made it clear that the true faith was preserved in England through its history.

The climax in England's unique role in providential history was reached, according to Foxe, with the accession of Elizabeth to the throne and the consequent triumph of Protestantism through the English Reformation.

And first to begin with our thanks, most due, to Almighty God, what cause have we all Englishmen so to do, that is, to render most ample thanksgiving to the mercifulness of God, who hath granted, conserved, and advanced, the seat-regal of this realm, so good, godly, and virtuous a queen.

Elizabeth secured the Reformation in England, and Foxe was convinced that under that godly queen, the Church of England would become God's glorious church:

of this I am sure, that God, yet once again is come on visitation to this church of England, yea, and that more lovingly and beneficially than ever he did before. For in this visitation he hath redressed many abuses, and cleansed his church of much ungodliness and superstition, and made it a glorious church.[83]

The question still remained, however, when and how the Last Act in providential history would take place, and to this, Foxe, like Bale, had no answer:

[79] *Ibid.*, vol. I, pp. 292, 249–50. [80] *Ibid.*, vol. I, p. 5. [81] *Ibid.*, vol. II, pp. 793, 796.
[82] *Ibid.*, vol. III, p. 580. [83] *Ibid.*, vol. VIII, p. 601; vol. I, p. 94.

"but so it is, I cannot tell how, the elder the world waxeth, the longer it continueth, the nearer it hasteneth to its end, the more Satan rageth."[84]

Above all, Foxe's *Acts and Monuments* reflects the supreme achievement of Protestant historiography, the shaping of English history to its own ends, and the creation of a new historical consciousness among Englishmen. Foxe succeeded in imparting to Englishmen a national ecclesiastical history unique to England, a Protestant view of English history centered exclusively on the Church of England, from its early apostolic origins until the time of Elizabeth. In "this account of Church history," wrote William Haller, Foxe showed that a "long succession of the native rulers down to Elizabeth" owed "their authority directly to divine appointment" and "made plain that by all the signs to be found in Scripture and history the will of God was about to be fulfilled in England by a prince perfect in her obedience to her vocation, ruling a people perfect in their obedience to her authority."[85]

The enormous popularity of the *Acts and Monuments* merely underscored the book's great influence in raising a new historical consciousness in England during the second half of the sixteenth and the first half of the seventeenth century concerning the special place to which God's providence had appointed the Church of England, and hence England, in ecclesiastic history. Nowhere was English history more successfully described in terms of Protestant history, or was the course of England through time more deftly delineated in terms of the history of the Church of England. And just as the history of the English Church had been situated within the apocalyptic dimension of time, so the entire course of English history was now imbued with apocalyptic, eschatological significance. Protestantism and English patriotism had now become inextricably joined, with the role of England in sacred history based upon the independency of both the church and the crown.

An examination of the differences between Foxe and Bale may facilitate a greater understanding of Foxe's contribution to Protestant historiography. Foxe's attempt to reveal the apocalyptic dimension of history and the historical dimension of prophecy shows that he had adopted Bale's apocalyptic interpretation of English history. And it was in line with the apocalyptic scheme developed by Bale that Foxe concentrated exclusively on the Church of England as the clue to English history. Yet, there is a crucial difference in the works of these two great exponents of the Protestant apocalyptic tradition in England. Bale's *Image of Both Churches* consists merely of a presentation of a few historical apocalyptic examples pertaining

---

[84] *Ibid.*, vol. VIII, p. 754.
[85] William Haller, *Foxe's Book of Martyrs and the Elect Nation* (London, 1963), pp. 224–5; "John Foxe and the Puritan Revolution," in Richard F. Jones (ed.), *The Seventeenth Century* (Stanford, 1951), pp. 209–24.

to England, whereas Foxe's *Acts and Monuments* provides a fully articulated historical interpretation of England based upon the apocalyptic mode of thought. Bale merely applied a handful of examples from English history to his apocalyptic interpretation of history; Foxe, on the other hand, far more historically minded, described English history as the unique embodiment of the prophecies of Revelation, based on very methodical research. He attempted to demonstrate the historical forces at work within English history, the cause of its changes and transformations, and in sum, the whole course of English history in terms of prophetic revelations. "Foxe was the first British author to write a Protestant apocalyptic history that attempted to explain changes in time in terms of an unfolding pattern of events."[86] Foxe thus led the way for generations of Englishmen to perceive their history within the context of the Apocalypse, and provided them with an understanding of the forces operating within English history.

Bale and Foxe's works should be considered above all in the context of the threatening course and development of the Reformation in England, especially during the Catholic reaction under Mary. Both wrote while living on the continent, and the experience of exile shaped, to a great extent, the thrust and content of their writings. Both returned to England along with other Marian exiles following Elizabeth I's accession to the throne in 1558, which secured the victory of Protestantism. The reign of Elizabeth signified for them, as well as for other Protestants, not only the triumph of the Protestant religion in England, but also and equally important the vindication of Protestantism within sacred, ecclesiastical history. In other words, the victory of Protestantism in England justified the premises of Protestant historiography concerning the course and progress of ecclesiastical history, or the history of the church, which stressed the apocalyptic struggle taking place between the forces of Reformation and Counter-Reformation. In England, this struggle of faith, a constant and violent battle for the soul of the English people, was finally resolved with the coronation of Elizabeth.

The Apocalypse of the Geneva Bible

Another work written in exile during the reign of Bloody Mary also contributed enormously to the development of the Protestant apocalyptic tradition in England: the Geneva Bible of 1560. Its extraordinary popularity in England left an indelible mark on Protestants and Puritans. "The vitality of the Geneva Bible was wonderful. It had commended itself to general acceptance, for it had been made by earnest and scholarly men, driven by persecution out of England," wrote John Eadie. Furthermore, "it did not die

---

[86] Firth, *The Apocalyptic Tradition*, p. 110.

under episcopal frown, nor was its circulation promoted to any extent by episcopal patronage. The people loved it for itself and its history."[87]

The Geneva Bible was the product of zealous Protestant exiles who took refuge in Geneva during the Marian persecution in 1554, and it marked the culmination of efforts by English Protestant scholars to provide a new translation of the Bible compatible with the new trends in Protestant biblical scholarship on the continent as well as with the development of Protestant historiography in Europe. The Geneva Bible obtained enormous popularity in England, though it lacked royal and ecclesiastical authorization. Issued in handy form, instead of in folio, with compendious notes of a Calvinist flavor, it was the most-read Bible in private use in England. No less than 120 editions were issued between 1560 and the appearance of the King James' version in 1611, and this number climbed to nearly two hundred by the outbreak of the Civil War.[88] It was widely used in Scotland as well, and later, with the colonization of America, in the English colonies. It was especially popular in Puritan New England. The extraordinary popularity of the Geneva Bible was based upon the fact that with it "for the first time, the English people had a Bible, scholarly in its translation, but also designed for use by the laity."[89] Furthermore, "its handy comprehensiveness made it the family Bible of the English people and it was the first Bible printed in Scotland" (1579). Most important, "in both countries the majority welcomed its strong Protestantism, even its Calvinism." These merits, among others, account for the fact that the Geneva Bible "superseded the Great Bible" of 1539, and "retained its popularity against the Bishops' Bible" of 1568, "and, for generations, against the Authorized Version" of 1611.[90]

The English Protestant scholars who produced the Geneva Bible, among them William Whittingham, Miles Coverdale, Christopher Goodman, Anthony Gilby, Thomas Sampson, and William Cole, were fully conscious of the role which they hoped it would play in the religious wars of the truth. In an age which bears witness to "so horrible backesliding and falling away from Christ to Antichrist, from light to darkness, from the living God to dumme and dead idols," and in a time of "so cruel murther of Gods Saints" under Queen Mary, the translators explained that God's divine providence

---

[87] *The Geneva Bible: A Facsimile of the 1560 Edition*, ed. Lloyd E. Berry (Madison, 1969). The quotation is from John Eadie, *The English Bible* (London, 1876), vol. II, pp. 51–2, as cited in Berry's "Introduction" to the *Geneva Bible*, p. 22.

[88] Richard L. Greaves, "The Nature and Intellectual Milieu of the Political Principles in the Geneva Bible Marginalia," *Journal of Church and State* 22 (1980), 233.

[89] Lloyd E. Berry, "Introduction," *The Geneva Bible*, p. 13.

[90] S. L. Greenslade, "English Versions of the Bible, 1525–1611," *The Cambridge History of the Bible: The West from the Reformation to the Present Day*, ed. S. L. Greenslade (Cambridge 1963; reprinted 1978), p. 159.

still continues to work in time and history "with most evident signes and tokens of God especial love and favour" towards his saints. Now, the surest way to be mindful of "these great mercies" is "atteyned by the knollage and practising of the worde of God," because the Bible

is the light to our paths, the keye of the kingdom of heaven, our comfort in affliction, our shields and sword against Satan, the schoole of all wisdome, the glasse wherein we beholde Gods face, the testimonie of his savour, and the only foode and nourishment of our soules.[91]

Therefore the small band of English exiles in Geneva thought that they could not do something "more acceptable to God and comfortable to his Churche than in the translating of the holy Scriptures into our native tongue." The new translation was needed not only because former "translations required greatly to be perused and reformed," due to "the infancie of those tymes" in which they had been written and because of the "imperfect knollage of the tongues" in the past, but because, most importantly, "of this ripe age and cleare light which God hath now reveiled." In the context of the apocalyptic wars of the truth in England, then, the Geneva Bible was produced not only in order "to set forthe the puritie of the worde" of God, but also in order to illuminate the "right sense of the holy Gost for the edifying of the brethren in faith and charitie."[92]

Seen in this context, the Geneva Bible was supposed to do more than merely supply Englishmen with the best and most appropriate translation of the Bible. Ultimately, it came to provide an interpretation of the course and progress of the church within time and history based upon the premises of Protestant historiography and the apocalyptic mode of historical thought which would expose English Protestants to the meaning and significance of their own time in the context of sacred, providential history. This contention is evident in the role which the translators of the Geneva Bible reserved for Elizabeth in sacred history and in the role their Bible was expected to play in furthering the Reformation in England.

Because the translation of the Geneva Bible began during the reign of Queen Mary and was finished after Elizabeth's accession to the throne, the translators dedicated the preface of their work, or the "Epistle," to the Protestant queen. They compared Elizabeth to "Zerubbabel" who built "the matrial Temple, according to the commandment of the Lord" in ancient Israel. And they appealed to her by reminding her that, "God hath laid upon you in making you a builder of his spiritual Temple" in England. "God hath made" her, they argued, "as our Zerubbabel for the erecting of his most excellent Temple, and to plant and mayteyn his holy worde to the advancement of his glorie." Thus Elizabeth's divine role in providential

---

[91] "To the Reader," *The Geneva Bible.*   [92] "To the Reader," *The Geneva Bible.*

history not only relates to her "owne honour and salvation" of her "soule," but more importantly, concerns "the singular comfort of that great Flocke" which "Christ Jesus the great shepherd" had "committed" into the queen's charge "to be fed both in body and soule." This holy task was formidable "considering therefore how many enemies are, which by one meanes or other," aim "to stay the building of that Temple" of God in England, especially the "Papistes" who "under the pretence of savoring Gods worde, traiterously seke to erect idolatrie and to destroy" the queen.[93]

The translators of the Geneva Bible also assigned great importance to its role in furthering the progress of the Reformation in England. For in these holy wars of the truth, a new translation of the Bible was an "expedient and necessarie" means of preserving the true faith from the papists and other idolators. Furthermore, according to its translators, because "the worde of God is an evident token of his love and our assurance of his defence," the new Bible was to "be the first foundation and ground worke, according whereunto the good stones of" the Reformation in England "must be framed, and the evil tried out and rejected." The Bible was to be the cornerstone of the Reformation under Elizabeth, because

without this worde we can not discerne between justice, and injurie, protection and oppression, wisdome and foolishnes, knollage and ignorance, good and evil. Therefore the Lord, who is the chefe governour of his Church, willeth that nothing be attempted before we have inquired thereof at his mouth.[94]

In the overall context of history as an economy of salvation, the translators of the Geneva Bible believed, like Bale and Foxe, that England occupied a singular place in the drama of providential history. Furthermore, they were convinced that England's prominent role in sacred history was inextricably associated with the role assigned to Elizabeth in ecclesiastical history. For after the triumph of Protestantism in England, "the eyes of all that feare God in all places beholde" England "as an example to all that beleve." Elizabeth's life symbolized the vicissitudes of the Reformation in England, and, with her accession to the throne after Mary, England's deliverance and special role in sacred history. "The prayers of all the godly at all tymes are directed to God for the preservation of her majestie," wrote the translators of the Geneva Bible in their preface. And they appealed for "Gods wonderful mercies towards you at all seasons, who hath pulled you out of the mouthe of the lyons" during the Catholic reaction under Mary. Elizabeth's accession was clearly a sign of God's providence which showed that she would have a singular role in serving God and His church in England. So, because "from your youth you have bene broght in the holy

---

[93] "Epistle," *The Geneva Bible.*   [94] *Ibid.*

Scriptures, the hope of all men is so increased, that they can not but looke that God should bring to passe some wonderful worke by your grace to the universal comfort of his Churches."[95]

The dedicatory epistle to Elizabeth suggests in general terms the historical role which both the Protestant queen and the Geneva Bible were expected to play in advancing the Reformation in England. The translators also added brief annotations, or marginal commentary, both textual and explanatory, which elaborated particular passages in Scripture in the light of the premises of Protestant historiography. These annotations, gathered "both by diligent reading of the best commentaries and also by conference with the godly and learned brethren,"[96] constituted a formidable weapon for understanding the Bible according to the Protestant interpretation of time and history. No wonder, then, that the extraordinary popularity of the Geneva Bible resided to a great extent on these marginal commentaries. "The single most important features of the Geneva Bible, to both laity and the clergy, consisted in the marginal notes."[97] Written from the extreme Protestant point of view, they provided a popular exposition of the Protestant ideology of history. Furthermore, "there is much evidence that both the unlettered clergy and the laity relied on" these "notes for proper interpretation of Scripture."[98] According to Thomas Fuller, who wrote a seventeenth-century history of the Church of England, as the Geneva Bible became more unavailable, people began to complain that they "could not see into the sense of Scripture for lack of the spectacles of those Genevan annotations."[99]

Written as a popular exposition of difficult passages in the Bible, the brief annotations gathered in the Geneva Bible offer the reader an extreme Protestant point of view concerning the course of ecclesiastical history as an economy of salvation. The radical Protestant thrust of these brief annotations is nowhere more clear than in the Book of Revelation. Based upon the premises of Protestant historiography and its ultimate goal of correlating history and prophecy, the marginal notes on Revelation in the Geneva Bible treat the Apocalypse as historical prophecy, and interpret history as prophetic history. This was the essential character of the apocalyptic tradition in England, as developed by Bale and Foxe. But now, in the Geneva Bible, it became the only available and authoritative exposition. In the Geneva Bible, therefore, the premises of Protestant historiography became an indispensable feature of the Book of Revelation, so that everyone who read about the Apocalypse could not avoid interpreting it along the lines of

[95] *Ibid.*
[96] "To the Reader," *The Geneva Bible.*
[97] Lloyd E. Berry, "Introduction," *The Geneva Bible*, p. 15.
[98] *Ibid.*, p. 19; Greenslade, "English Versions of the Bible," p. 158.
[99] Eadie, *The English Bible*, pp. 51–2, cited in Lloyd E. Berry's "Introduction" to the *Geneva Bible*, p. 23.

the Protestant sense and view of the history of the church. In the hands of the translators of the Geneva Bible, the prophecies of the Apocalypse became a formidable tool with which to expound church history, since Christ's first coming, as an apocalyptic struggle between the true church and the Church of Rome.

According to the "argument," or the synopsis, preceding the translation of Revelation, the Apocalypse is that "moste excellent booke" in which the "holie Gost" gathered "a summe of those prophecies, which were written before, but shulde be fulfilled after the coming of Christ." Accordingly, these prophecies tell of "the Divinitie of Christ, & the testimonies of our redemption." No longer considered obscure and uninterpretable as Luther had claimed in 1522, the Book of Revelation now acquired, due to the great transformation of Protestant historiography, a prominent role in elucidating sacred history. It became, in the hands of Protestants, the ultimate means for understanding the meaning of their time in providential history. Consequently, the translators of the Geneva Bible encouraged everyone to read the Apocalypse: "Read deligently: judge soberly, and call earnestly to God for the true understanding thereof." Understanding the Apocalypse became, therefore, an important ingredient in the Protestant sense of time and history, and in order to facilitate the reading of these prophecies, the brief annotations served to explain the historical application of the prophetic visions in Revelation.

The marginal notes to Revelation in the Geneva Bible thoroughly incorporated the premises of Protestant historiography and thus provided an actual historical context within which to interpret the meaning of the book's prophecies and visions. These notes furnished a full historical explanation of the prophetic revelations contained in the Apocalypse. For example, the "tribulation" of the Church of Ephesus (Rev. 4:9), is interpreted as taking place during "the persecution under the Emperor Domitian" (AD 51–96). A shooting star at the time when "the fifth angel sounded" (Rev. 9:1) is characterized in the marginal notes as signifying "the Bishopes and ministers, which forsake the word of God, & so fall out of heaven & become angels of darkenes" (Rev. 2:1). Most prominent in this historicization of sacred visions and prophecies is the identification of the pope with the Antichrist. Hence it follows that "the Pope" [is the] "king of hypocrites and Satan's ambassadour": (Rev. 9:11), who acquired "his power out of hel and cometh thence" (Rev. 11:7), and his jurisdiction "compared to Sodom" (Rev. 11:8). Furthermore, the prophetic vision during the time of the seventh seal, which according to God's divine providence proclaimed "the kingdomes of this worlde are our Lords, and his Christ, and he shal reigne for evermore," was expounded in the marginal notes as signifying the victory over Satan and his instruments, "the Pope" and "Turke" (Rev. 11:15).

The historicization of prophetical visions in the brief annotations on the Apocalypse becomes more pronounced as the apocalyptic struggle in Revelation between Christ and the Antichrist reaches its culmination. Consequently, the Apocalypse mirrored the Protestant struggle against Rome and the Catholic faith. And so, through the radical attempt of Protestant historiography to correlate prophecy and history, the Book of Revelation was transformed into a revolutionary apocalyptic ideology of history with which Protestants defined their religious war with Rome. Hence, Rome is identified with Babylon, because "the vices which were in Babylon, are founde in Rome in great abundance" (Rev. 14:8), and "Rome" is "the second Babylon" (Rev. 16:12). In the same vein, the great whore in Revelation is identified with the "Antichrist," who, in turn, is compared to "the Pope with the whole body of his filthie creatures" (Rev. 17:4). And the destruction of Babylon, according to the annotations, signified that God's "judgements are true & just," and the saints therefore "ought to praise him evermore for the destruction of the Pope" (Rev. 19:4).

The historicization of prophetic revelations in the Apocalypse enabled Protestants to show that some prophecies had already been realized within time and history, while others had yet to be fulfilled in the future course of sacred, providential history. The enhancement of the prophetic dimension of history reached its climax in the explanatory notes on Revelation in the Geneva Bible. This was because, according to Revelation, "the testimonie of Jesus, is the spirit of prophecie," which meant, as explained in the marginal notes, "that we must beleve no other spirit of prophecie, but that which doeth testifie of Jesus, and lead us to him" (Rev. 19:10). Religious belief, prophecy and history, therefore, are inextricably connected; belief justifies the validity of prophecy, and the latter, in turn, defines the course and meaning of history. Hence, the sacred validity of the Apocalypse is historically final and irrefutable. And hence, understanding history as an economy of salvation is dependent upon the belief in the prophetic testimony of Christ.

The culmination of sacred, ecclesiastic history in Revelation is indeed the millennium. This period signifies the great transformation of the world from alienation to reconciliation with God; or, conversely, it implies a return to a theocratic universe ruled and governed directly by God's divine providence after the destruction of the Antichrist and Babylon. The destruction of Babylon preceded the millennium, but before Christ could exercise his millennial role with his saints, Satan too had to be expunged from the stage of history. He was chained for a thousand years, which according to the annotations in the Geneva Bible, meant the period "from Christs nativitie to the time of Pope Sylvester the seconde" (Rev. 20:2). Given the fact that Sylvester II was pope from 999 to 1003, the historical period corresponding to the chaining of Satan is the first thousand years after Christ's First Coming. Since the historical realization of the prophecy concerning Satan had already taken place, the stage of history was already prepared for the coming of the millennium. Consequently, the glorious period of the millennium was conceived, and here lies the radical thrust of the marginal commentaries in the Geneva Bible, as an earthly, terrestrial phenomenon taking place within time and history.

The millennium, in which the saints "lived, & reigned with Christ a thousand yere," was expounded in the marginal notes of the Geneva Bible as a period to be enjoyed by them "while thei have remained in this life" (Rev. 20:4). Taking place within time and history, the millennium was therefore a terrestrial phenomenon. In the same vein, the first resurrection was interpreted as taking place within this world. It meant "to receive Jesus Christ in true faith, & to rise from sinne in newenes of life" (Rev. 20:5). Only those who had shared in the first resurrection would reign with Christ "a thousand yere," or "for ever" (Rev. 20:6). Later Satan would be set free, which means that "the true preaching of Gods worde is corrupt" (Rev. 20:7). The final apocalyptic battle would then take place between Christ and Gog and Magog, the servants of Satan, who symbolized the "enemies of the Church of God" including "The Turke" (Rev. 20:8).

The historical interpretation of Revelation in the marginal notes of the Geneva Bible can also be clearly seen in the anticipated transformation of the world after Christ's victory over Satan and Antichrist. Thus, "a new heaven, & a new earth" signified that "all things shalbe renued and restored into moste excellent and perfect estate, and therefore the day of resurrection is called, The day of restauration of all things" (Rev. 21:1). In this moment of perfection and holiness, the New Jerusalem would appear, comprised of "the holie company of the elect" (Rev. 21:2). God's rule in a theocratic universe is acknowledged as "Kings & Princes (contrarie to that wicked opinion of the Anabaptists) are partakers of the heavenly glorie, if they rule in the feare of the Lord" (Rev. 21:24).

The notes on Revelation in the Geneva Bible of 1560 fully reflected the premises of Protestant historiography and thus contributed enormously to the rise of the apocalyptic tradition in England. Providing a historical interpretation of the Apocalypse, they transformed the Revelation into a mirror of the struggle between the Reformation and the Counter-Reformation. The historicization of the Apocalypse also exemplified the thoroughly literal, and hence terrestrial, approach of Protestant interpretation. And because the realization of prophetic revelations was taking place within history,

history in turn became a crucial and inevitable dimension of prophecy. Yet, as previously noted concerning Bale and Foxe, the Protestant translators of the Geneva Bible hesitated to pinpoint the moment at which the eschatological transformation of this world into the Kingdom of God would take place. Their hesitation was caused by their fear of allowing men's imagination to determine the eschatological moment of the Lord's Coming. In short, the Apocalypse should not be considered "as the other prophecies which were commanded to be hyd til the time appointed" (the Book of Daniel, for example), but rather the prophecies in Revelation "shulde be quickely accomplished & did now begin" (Rev. 22:10). And yet because "the time is at hand," caution was needed in order not to falsely interpret the signs of time and history. For "seing the Lord is at hand, we oght to be constant and rejoyce, but we must beware we esteme not the length nor shortenes of the Lords coming by our owne imagination" (Rev. 22:20). Although Christ's Second Coming was imminent, the eschatological moment still lay within the unfolding drama of sacred, providential history and no human was capable of precisely determining when it would occur.

Historical circumstances led Bale, Foxe and the authors of the Geneva Bible marginalia to stop short of drawing the full revolutionary conclusions embodied in Protestant historiography. Based upon its strict correlation between prophecy and history, Protestant apocalyptic historiography implies that there will come a point in time, a historical moment, when the two will be irrevocably joined. This will be the eschatological day of judgment, Christ's Second Coming, or the millennium. Divine prophecy foretells this final providential event, as for example in Revelation concerning the time of the "seventh seal" in which the sounding of the "seventh trumpet" signifies the moment when "the mystery of God should be finished" (Rev. 10:7), for when "the seventh angel sounded" then "the kingdoms of this world are become the kingdoms of our Lord, and of his Christ; and he shall reign for ever and ever" (Rev. 11:15). Based upon the literal interpretation of prophecy, Protestant historiography was compelled to give a historical interpretation to this eschatological event in which the whole mystery of providential history would be unveiled. Both Bale and Foxe awaited the opening of the seventh seal, or the sounding of the seventh trumpet, in time and history. Bale thought his time was that of the sixth seal, very close but not yet belonging to the seventh. Foxe also believed that "this seventh trumpet certainly is not far off, when by marvellous inversion of things and times the past shall grow old and all things new, a new heaven and a new earth shall be constituted."[100] Neither Bale, Foxe, nor the marginal notes on Revelation in the Geneva Bible, therefore, furnished any historical interpret-

---

[100] Foxe, cited by Olsen, *John Foxe and the Elizabethan Church*, p. 99.

ation concerning the last and final prophetic revelation in providential history. This task was left to Thomas Brightman, whose great contribution to English apocalyptic tradition lies in the historical interpretation he offered concerning the seventh trumpet, an interpretation which enabled Englishmen to look upon their time as the period of the millennium at hand.

Thomas Brightman and the seventh trumpet

In the English apocalyptic tradition of the sixteenth and seventeenth centuries, Thomas Brightman holds a prominent spot. His exegesis of the Book of Revelation had a tremendous influence on the course of the Puritan movement in England before and during the Puritan Revolution, and the revolutionary solution he offered in terms of the relation between prophecy and history singularly inspired radical Puritans, in England as well as New England, to attempt to realize through their own actions their millennial expectations and eschatological visions. Brightman's historical interpretation of the Apocalypse constituted a unique philosophy of history which supplied the Puritans with coherent perceptions concerning both the meaning of their time in providential history and the crucial role of the saints in the time of the millennium at hand. His basic assumption was that through time and history the Kingdom of God would rise on earth, and that in this world and not the next the mystery of the great providential drama would be revealed. This view created a new sense of religious and political obligations among Puritans regarding their own role in the cosmic battle between Christ and Antichrist. Brightman's radical solution concerning the relationship between prophecy and history conclusively replaced St. Augustine's dualistic view of the world by finding a moment in history when the heavenly city and the earthly city would unite, thereby *immersing* the millennium in time and history. Essentially, Brightman's work raised a new historical consciousness in England during the first half of the seventeenth century. It aroused a sense of the imminent fulfillment of prophecy within time and history, a deep-seated conviction within each individual that his was the time of the millennium at hand and that it was thus the duty of the saints to come to the aid of Christ in transforming the world into the Kingdom of God. For as Brightman declared: "now is the time begun when Christ shal raigne in all the earth, having all his enemies round subdued unto him and broken in peeces."[101]

Brightman's contribution to the English apocalyptic tradition can most fully be appreciated in the light of the premises of Protestant historiography.

---

[101] Thomas Brightman, *Apocalypsis Apocalypseos, or a Revelation of the Revelation* (Leyden, 1616), pp. 491, 502. On Brightman's influence in England during the first half of the seventeenth century, see William Lamont's important study, *Godly Rule*.

As noted earlier, Protestant historiography stressed the literal, historical interpretation of divine prophecy. As a historical outlook its main goal was to transform the meaning of history from a field of human action almost totally divorced from sacred, providential history, to a domain firmly situated within the dimension of prophecy, and to unveil the hidden pattern of providential history unfolding in world events and directed toward the millennium and the end of time. Accordingly, history as realized eschatology is by its very nature predestined to reach that moment in time of eschatological salvation. Both Bale and Foxe, however, in their apocalyptic historical interpretation, stopped short of explaining that crucial moment in providential history in which the mystery of God's providence would be revealed. Brightman, on the other hand, went further, offering his contemporaries a historical interpretation of the time of the seventh trumpet of Revelation, which he correlated with Elizabeth's accession to the throne in England. According to Brightman, it was unto England "which Christ sent our most gracious Elizabeth to be Queene at the first blast of the seaventh Trumpet in the yeare 1558."[102]

The difference between Brightman and Foxe should be seen against the background of the changing historical circumstances in England, especially concerning the state of the English Reformation during the second half of the sixteenth century. To Foxe, as to many other Protestants of that time, the early years of Elizabeth's reign offered renewed evidence of England's destiny as a chosen nation in providential history: the true reformation in England would come to fruition through the imperial instrument, the prince, who was leading the fight against Antichrist in the world. But what if the prince were to fail in this divine mission? "The certainties of one age," noted R. H. Tawney, "are the problems of the next," and toward the end of the sixteenth century many Protestants in England faced nothing but problems.[103] For despite all their efforts, the prince had failed in the long-expected reformation of the Church of England, upon which depended England's unique place in providential history. With the Puritan failure under Elizabeth, this "orthodox" relationship between the Church of England, the prince, and the millennial prospect, which is most fully exemplified in Foxe's writings, underwent a radical reassessment, and the Protestants' millennial expectations of the prince began to wane and disperse. Centrifugal millenarianism replaced centripetal millenarianism.[104]

Brightman's celebrated book on English apocalyptic tradition, *Apocalypsis Apocalypseos*, or *A Revelation of the Revelation* (1609), is important to

---

[102] Brightman, *Apocalypsis Apocalypseos*, p. 490.
[103] R. H. Tawney, *Religion and the Rise of Capitalism* (New York, 1954), p. 231.
[104] On the concept of "centrifugal millenarianism," see William Haller, *The Rise of Puritanism* (Philadelphia, 1938), pp. 16, 179, and Lamont, *Godly Rule*, pp. 25, 51.

this thesis for two reasons. First, it serves as evidence of the Puritan failure to reform the Church of England under Elizabeth. "Brightman argued against expecting too much from a Godly Prince," because for him "the Godly Ruler frustrates, not advances, Godly Rule."[105] Rather than looking upon the prince as the main instrument in the realization of England's singular role in providential history, Brightman exhorted the believers themselves to work toward advancing the reformation in England. Second, and more to the point, it offered a radical interpretation concerning the relationship between prophecy and history. This historical apocalyptic interpretation laid the groundwork for the shift in the early seventeenth century toward centrifugal millenarianism, and profoundly influenced Puritans up to and during the Puritan Revolution.

Brightman's unique role in the English apocalyptic tradition resided in the fact that he had proposed a revolutionary solution concerning the relation between prophecy and history, or between the prophecies of Revelation and the Puritan experience in England at the turn of the sixteenth century. The essence of Brightman's radical solution is his contention that the Book of Revelation not only described events to come but also contained prophecies with actual historical substance. Events depicted in the Apocalypse, he argued, or the Epistles sent to the seven churches or cities, correspond to actual periods of ecclesiastical history, past and present. "These seaven Epistles," wrote Brightman, "respected not onely the present condition of the seaven Cities, but do . . . comprehend the ages following for a long time."[106] Accordingly, the Church of Ephesus in Revelation he associated with the apostolic church until Constantine; and Smyrna, with the period of time "from Constantine . . . until Gratian, about the year of our Lord 382." The Church of Pergamum corresponded to the sinful Roman church, "from the yeare 380 . . . until about the yeare 1300." The fourth church in Revelation, Thyatira, Brightman correlated with "the tyme from the yeare 1300, until the yeare 1520." The last three churches of the Revelation, and hence their historical periods, fall within the era of the Protestant Reformation. Sardis corresponded to the German Reformation, Philadelphia to the most reformed Protestant churches of "Constance, Basill, Strasburgh, Geneua and others." And finally, the church of Laodicea, upon whom the Lord had promised to pour his wrath, Brightman correlated with England.[107] Consequently, if in Revelation the churches, barring Philadelphia, moved from the ancient purity of apostolic times into decline, they also moved *in time* – according to the holistic pattern of this book – toward history's climax and the apocalyptic events surrounding Christ's Second

---

[105] Lamont, *Godly Rule*, 51.
[106] Brightman, *Apocalypsis Apocalypseos*, 155.
[107] *Ibid.*, pp. 74, 84, 97, 118–22, 140, 158–9.

Coming. The gulf between secular and providential history was thus finally bridged, as history and prophecy became one.

Brightman's interpretation allowed for a historical, earthly unification of the visible and the invisible church. Neither Bale nor Foxe, never daring to interpret their age as the last period in the realization of eschatology, attempted to propose such a union in their apocalyptical historical interpretations. It was only Brightman who, advancing one significant step forward, boldly claimed his age as the historical stage upon which the realization of eschatology would take place. "For now is the last Act begun," he averred,

of a most long & doleful Tragedy, which shall wholy overflow with scourages, slaughters, destructions, but after this Theatre is once removed, there shall come in roome of it a most delightful spectacle of perpetuall peace, joined with abundance of all good things.[108]

Brightman was certain that the blast of the seventh trumpet in Revelation had already sounded in time and history. Following the Book of Revelation, which states that "in the days of the voice of the seventh angel, when he shall begin to sound, the mystery of God should be finished," or more specifically, that with the sounding of the seventh trumpet "the kingdoms of this world are become *the kingdoms* of our Lord, and of his Christ; and he shall reign for ever and ever" (Rev. 10:7; 11:15). Brightman believed himself alive "in these last ages" when "Christ shal raign in all the earth,"[109] and specifically, "in these last times from the yeare 1558, wherein the seaventh Trumpet blew."[110] The period of the sounding of the seventh trumpet is portrayed in Revelation as that time in which the entire dualistic structure of the universe is broken: a war, begun in heaven, extends to earth, so that the earth becomes the ultimate scene of the cosmic drama from which emerges the Kingdom of God. This is the period, then, in which the millennium is finally at hand after many apocalyptic events, including the destruction of Babylon. And it was the historical event of Elizabeth's accession to the English throne which Brightman perceived as its commencement. Thus, wrote Brightman,

the time is at hand; the Event of things immediately to be done . . . the things to come are no lesse certaine; But for us, who have seene the consent between the event and Prophecy for the space of a thousand & five hundred yeares, that is, ever since the days of John, we can not possibly doubt, any longer touching those few events which yet remaine to be accomplished.[111]

This sense of the millennium at hand, so characteristic of Brightman's exegesis of Revelation and so different from previous apocalyptic commen

---

[108] *Ibid.*, preface "to the Holy Reformed Churches of Brittany, Germany, and France."
[109] *Ibid.*, p. 497. [110] *Ibid.*, pp. 490–1. [111] *Ibid.*, p. 1,135.

taries, stems from the historical perspective in which he placed the prophecies of the Apocalypse. According to Brightman, during the rule of
Constantine (who made Christianity a church state in the Roman Empire),
"the Divell was bound . . . for thousand years." In 1300, he maintained, the
Devil or Satan escaped from captivity and began to wage war on Christ and
his saints. And the late seventeenth century he regarded as the time of the
end of Antichrist: "the last end of Antichrist shall expire at the year 1686."
It was between these two periods, then, that the battle between Christ and
Antichrist transpired, in which the saints gathered around the Lord in his
wars on Mount Sion as described in the Apocalypse. Throughout this
period, therefore, the church paraded as the Militant Church, gradually
spreading the Kingdom of Christ on earth through religious reform against
Satan and Antichrist. Since according to Revelation Satan and his agents
were to battle Christ for only 390 years, Brightman calculated that at the
end of the seventeenth century, after the final destruction of Antichrist, the
saints together with Christ would rule on earth. Then, "all the nations
shalbe at the Churches command, & that at a becke, requiring & taking
lawes & ordinances from it, whereby they may be governed."[112]

With Brightman, therefore, the millennium was immersed in time and
history. According to his interpretation, from 1300 onward, Christ and the
saints were engaged in the apocalyptic drama foretold by Revelation, and
from that time on world history revealed the spreading of God's Kingdom
on earth, culminating in the sounding of the seventh trumpet and the
approach of the millennium. By calculating that the blast of the seventh
trumpet proclaiming the coming of the Kingdom of God upon earth
occurred in the year 1558, Brightman infused a strong eschatological
impulse into early seventeenth century Puritan millennial discourse. Three
decades after Brightman, Thomas Goodwin could write: "This is the last
time because it is the perfection of the other . . . and therefore seeing these
are the last days, the nigher the day approacheth, the more shall we
endeavour to do God service."[113] And Milton, who in his ecstatic vision saw
England as "a noble and puissant Nation rousing herself like a strong man
after sleep, and shaking her invincible locks," or as "an Eagle muing her
mighty youth, and kindling her undazl'd eyes at the full midday beam;
purging and unscaling her long abused sight at the fountain it self or
heav'nly radiance," was similarly convinced that

thy Kingdom is now at hand, and thou standing at the dore. Come forth out of thy
Royall Chambers, O prince of all the Kings of the earth, put on the visible roabes of
thy imperial Majesty, take up that unlimited Sceptor which thy Almighty Father

---

[112] *Ibid.*, pp. 519, 569, 852, 1119.
[113] Thomas Goodwin, "Three Sermons on Heb. I, 1, 2," in *The Works of Thomas Goodwin*,
ed. J. C. Miller (Edinburgh, 1861–5), vol. V, pp. 533–4.

hath Bequeath'd thee; for now the voice of thy Bride calls thee, and all creatures sign to bee renew'd.[114]

By insisting upon the strictest correlation between prophecy and history, Brightman transformed the millennium into an attainable, historical goal to be realized in an immediate future by the saints and Christ under some terrestrial reign. It was through this historical interpretation of prophecy that Brightman instilled new meaning into the search after reformation in early seventeenth-century England. For when correlating events described in Revelation with time and history, with historical events and periods, Brightman not only presented history as the dimension of realized eschatology, but he also described the final eschatological revelation, the millennium and the Kingdom of God, as coming to pass within the framework of history. Through his construction of the Church's history out of Revelation, from the First until the Second Coming of Christ, Brightman inspired Puritans to look upon their time as that of the seventh trumpet when the mystery of providential history would be revealed in full.

Giving rise to a new historical consciousness in England, concerning the imminent fulfillment of prophetic revelations, Brightman saw it as his task to outline the particular role that England would assume in the period of the approaching millennium and the establishment of the Kingdom of God upon earth. In his delineation of church history, he endeavored to link each church in Revelation to an actual historical counterpart, and each epistle of Christ to his churches in Revelation to a particular historical period of time. Each church in Revelation symbolized for Brightman a specific period in the history of the church from Christ's First Coming until his Second Coming. It was only when he came to identify the sixth church of Revelation, Philadelphia – God's only truly reformed church and that to which Christ promised that he "will write upon [her] the name of my God, and the name of the city of my God, which is New Jerusalem" (Rev. 3:12) – that Brightman made the historical correlation not with the English Church, but rather with "the Church of Helvetia, Suevia, Geneve, France, Scotland."[115] Brightman's refusal to associate the Church of England with Philadelphia is perhaps the clearest indication of his radical departure from the prevailing apocalyptic tradition in England, and especially of his distance from Foxe's vision of England as playing a unique role in providential history.

Writing almost half a century after the accession of Elizabeth to the throne and the establishment of the Elizabethan Settlement, Brightman was fully aware of the Puritan failure to reform the Church of England. There-

---

[114] John Milton, cited in Douglas Bush, *English Literature in the Earlier Seventeenth Century, 1600–1660* (New York, 1952), p. 373; Milton, *Animadversions*, cited in Haller, *The Rise of Puritanism*, p. 357.

[115] Brightman, *Apocalypsis Apocalypseos*, pp. 139, 140, 142–5, 155.

fore, it is not surprising that, disappointed by the Prince's unwillingness to reform the church, the aging historian chose to identify the Church of England not with Philadelphia but rather with Laodicea, the corrupted church of the Apocalypse. In this manner, Brightman drastically altered England's position in providential history from Foxe's elect nation to that of the sinful church in Revelation which rejected God's word and was therefore warned by the Lord that He would "spue thee out of my mouth" (Rev. 3:16). If Laodicea was England, as Brightman believed, then Christ's prophecies about Laodicea in Revelation applied equally to England. In that case, a special punishment awaited England – the historical Laodicea – in addition to the general destruction promised by God in Revelation to all who refused to acknowledge him. For in the end, all churches but Philadelphia would be destroyed in the final judgment, while Laodicea faced a double specter: it would be cast from Christ's mouth to Satan, before being consumed in the general conflagration along with other churches not implementing full reformation. In terms of the Puritan movement, Brightman's correlation between England and Laodicea created a deep sense of crisis concerning England's role in providential history.

With the Puritans' hopes in the reforming zeal of the monarch fading rapidly during the reign of James I and Charles I, and with the Church of England becoming increasingly corrupted, there emerged a crisis of terrifying proportions indeed, as many feared that England would soon be called to account. In the scenario described by Brightman, with England as Laodicea, England could expect nothing but the righteous ire of God. This divine wrath was a very real possibility to generations of Puritans who were accustomed through their reading of Protestant historiography to view their time and place as the historical applications of prophetic revelation. Just how successful Brightman was in transforming the role of England in providential history from Foxe's concept of the elect nation to that of doomed Laodicea, awaiting the Lord's final judgment, is suggested by the frequency with which England is associated with Laodicea in Puritan writings. To a large extent, then, the whole course of the Puritan movement up to and during the Puritan Revolution was determined by Brightman's correlation between England and Laodicea. This correlation led to the migration of thousands of Puritans to New England during the 1630s with the aim of saving themselves from doomed Laodicea, or England.[116] Moreover, the Puritan Revolution in a sense constituted an attempt to bring England back to the center of providential history, from corrupted Laodicea to Philadel-

---

[116] On Brightman's influence on the Puritan migration to New England, see my "Exile and Kingdom: Reformation, Separation and the Millennial Quest in the Formation of Massachusetts and its Relationship with England, 1628–1660," Ph.D. dissertation, Johns Hopkins University, 1982.

phia, and consequently to build in England the New Jerusalem. In short, greatly influenced by Brightman, the Puritan Revolution in England is evidence of efforts made to fulfill the role of the saints in providential history by aiding Christ against Antichrist.

With Brightman's radical interpretation, Protestant historiography in England based upon an apocalyptic mode of historical thought reached its culmination. The whole thrust of the Protestant apocalyptic tradition, the attempt to correlate to the outmost prophecy and history, had been developed by Brightman into a revolutionary apocalyptic interpretation of redemptive history in which eschatological revelations, such as the millennium and the Kingdom of God, were not only considered to be within time and history, but were conceptualized as a feasible historical goal attainable within the life span of the present generation. For the seventh trumpet, according to Brightman, had already blasted in time and history, proclaiming the very near approach of that eschatological end in which the whole mystery of time would be revealed and Christ with his faithful would reign upon earth, a time in which the kingdoms of the earth would become the Kingdom of God. Furthermore, in terms of apocalyptic interpretation of history, Brightman argued, "a full understanding" of the past is impossible "before the last trumpet," or only after the sounding of the seventh trumpet. "But nowe when al things were at last accomplished, it was a fit time to see the whole garment," or the whole course of providential history, "displaid at once."[117] This was the sense of the imminent fulfillment of prophetic revelations within the boundaries of time and history, a sense of the millennium at hand, that Brightman infused into English apocalyptic tradition in the early seventeenth century. His was a revolutionary apocalyptic interpretation of history which boldly proclaimed the moment in time when the mystery of sacred, providential history would come to its final consummation and realization.

In the ideological wars of the sixteenth century, Protestant historiography played a crucial role in the struggle between the forces of Reformation and Counter-Reformation. As a philosohy of history based upon an apocalyptic mode of historical thought, it attempted not only to demolish the historical foundation of the Church of Rome, but also to provide Protestants with a coherent view concerning the significance of the Reformation and their own actions in providential history. From its very beginnings during the 1530s, Protestant historiography used divine prophetic text as the basis of its historical interpretation. Eventually, prophecy was treated as intrinsic to history, and even as directing and controlling the very historical process. As the meaning of prophecy changed from the allegorical to the literal, the

---

[117] Brightman cited by Firth, *The Apocalyptic Tradition*, p. 177.

significance of the *saeculum*, or profane history, also became greatly altered: the Christian attitude of *contemptus mundi* was discarded, and in its place emerged the view of history as the domain of realized eschatology, as that space of time in which prophetic revelations are fulfilled. This radical inclusion of eschatology and apocalypse within the boundaries of time and history gives clear expression to the nature of the Protestant revolution in historiography. Essentially, Protestant historiography abolished the Augustinian dualism between the sacred and profane history by developing a unique relationship between prophecy and history: it placed prophecy within the historical dimension, transforming it into historical prophecy; and it situated history within the prophetic dimension, turning it into prophetic history. Sacred and profane history, therefore, became one and the same, giving rise to a new sense of history. This is the perception of history as an economy of salvation, a course of redemption consisting of a special dimension of space and time in which progress is made from promise to fulfillment, from prophecy to its realization.

Accompanying the Protestant historiographic revolution was the notion of a theocratic universe in which God's providence immanently directs historical events. Within such a universe, ecclesiastical history was the only history to have any meaning. The church, as the body of Christ, inevitably assumes the central place in divine, providential history, since until Christ's Second Coming history is determined by the revelation of Christ as embodied in the church and its faith. Ecclesiastical history, then, with its portrayal of the vicissitudes of the church within time – its struggles, persecutions, and triumphs – became in Protestant historiography the very theme of history itself. In other words, events of this earth are significant only insofar as they relate to the history of the church. Furthermore, as an economy of salvation, ecclesiastical history is by nature inseparable from prophecy. It was the task of Protestant historiography to reveal the glorious future of the church through its unique interpretation of divine prophecy.

The Protestant apocalyptic tradition in England held a special place for its unrelenting efforts to correlate prophetic revelations to English history, and for its success in providing a coherent apocalyptic historical interpretation of the history of England. Due to the special historical conditions prevailing in England, where religious and national struggles against Rome were so closely interwoven, Protestant historiography played an important role in creating a new historical consciousness among Englishmen toward the significance of English history in general and the meaning of the English Reformation in particular, in the course of sacred, divine history. Indeed, the emergence of a Protestant apocalyptic tradition in England during the sixteenth century marked the nationalization of the Book of Revelation. Due to the apostolic origins attributed to the Church of England, a church said to have adhered to the true faith throughout its history, divine revelation was believed to have special implications for England. With its view of the Church of England as the essence of English history as a whole, Protestant historiography beginning with Bale presented the English Reformation as the culmination of a long struggle between the true and false church, or between Christ and Antichrist.

Once circumstances changed in England, and the triumph of the Reformation was secured with Elizabeth's accession to the throne, Foxe turned Bale's contention concerning the uniqueness of the Church of England in sacred history into a full national destiny: England as a chosen nation, God's elect nation, whose history from beginning to end revealed the course of providential history leading to prophetic realization. The nationalization of the Book of Revelation reached its peak with Foxe: a chosen nation with pure apostolic faith struggles against Rome, and finally, through Elizabeth's godly rule, will play its crucial role as providential history nears its climax. The enormous popularity of Foxe's book testifies to the fact that by the second half of the sixteenth and first half of the seventeenth century the majority of the English people strongly and heartily adhered to Protestant historiography.

The full implications of the apocalyptic tradition in England became manifest in Brightman's thought. His radical correlation between prophecy and history stated clearly that with Elizabeth's accession to the throne the seventh trumpet of the Apocalypse had already sounded in time and history, and that in the ensuing time of the millennium at hand, the apocalyptic struggle between Laodicea and Philadelphia as foretold in Revelation was to take place. Given that the long-awaited reformation in England had not yet been accomplished, it was the duty of the saints to engage themselves here and now to return England to the center of providential history by fighting Laodicea and transforming the Church of England into Philadelphia or the New Jerusalem. In the time of the millennium at hand, the ultimate and pressing mission of the saints was to save England from the fate of doomed Laodicea. To a great extent, the story of the Puritan movement in England during the first half of the seventeenth century, and above all, the course of the Puritan Revolution, is the story of the Puritan attempt, following Brightman's apocalyptic interpretation, to bring England back to the center of the providential history of salvation.

2

The creation of sacred space I

The geographies of the mind: the incorporation of
America as a sacred place in ecclesiastical history

THE ENGLISH APOCALYPTIC TRADITION AND THE SETTLEMENT OF AMERICA

The ultimate achievement of the apocalyptic tradition in England was undoubtedly the deep-seated conviction among Protestants and Puritans alike that prophetic revelations constitute the very essence of history. History, therefore, was placed within the sacred dimension of time and prophetic revelations situated within the dimension of history. Consequently, the accepted Augustinian view that an essential gulf divided sacred and profane history, or prophecy and history, was totally abolished in the English apocalyptic tradition. Prophecy became history, and history became prophecy. In other words, historical events were interpreted as the realization of prophetic revelation while divine prophecy was seen as the source for explaining the progress of history. This process was nothing less than the sacralization of historical time, or the creation of sacred time – the view that history not only revealed but also fulfilled the realization of divine prophecies.

The root of this process of sacralization of historical time lies, as we have tried to explain in the previous chapter, in the belief that the ultimate issue regarding apocalyptic interpretation or understanding prophecies, is related to the question of time. Now imbued with sacred meaning, history and time constitute the medium by which prophetic revelations reach their realization. With the rise of the apocalyptic image of history within English Protestant historiography, then, history itself became a revelatory event as a history of salvation. Through God's divine providence, therefore, history and revelation were inextricably interwoven with one another. This great transformation in the English apocalyptic tradition regarding prophecy and history had crucial consequences for the vision of history as an economy of salvation. Interpreting divine prophecies historically became an urgent task in explaining the course and progress of the history of salvation.

By 1617, Richard Bernard, a Puritan divine, summed up the revolutionary character of the apocalyptic tradition in England in these words:

The matter then of this prophecie [the Apocalypse] is historicall, as it cometh to be fulfilled. It is therefore not spiritual or allegoricall, but an historicall sense, which in this booke we must attend unto . . . For to John was reuealed what things should come to passe here upon the earth, before the worlds end, as far as concerned the Church . . . if we then doe loose the historical sense, we loose the proper sense of this booke, what other spirituall vse soeuer we make of it. By this then we see what necessity there is to reade histories, into which wee must looke and search diligently . . . according to the course of this prophetical narratio.[1]

For Joseph Mede, one of the major figures in English apocalyptic tradition, divine prophecies should also be explained historically:

For the true account therefore of *Times* in Scripture wee must have recourse to that SACRED KALENDER and GREAT ALMANACK of PROPHESIE, *The Four Kingdomes of Daniel* which are *A Propheticall Chronology of Times measured by the succession of Foure principall Kingdomes, from the beginning of the Captivity of* Israel *until the Mysterie of God should be finished.*

The mystery of sacred, providential history can be explained only through divine prophecy which is "a Prophetical-Chronology of Times" from the beginning of time and history until their very end, or until "all the *Kingdomes* of this World should become the *Kingdomes of our Lord and his Christ.*"[2] Yet, if prophecy gives meaning and significance to time, it is history which reveals the mystery of prophecies. Thus, according to Stephen Marshall's triumphant sermon before the Long Parliament in 1643, "time (one of the best Interpreters of Prophecies) hath produced the *events* answering the types [of prophecy] so full and clear, that we have the whole Army of Protestant Interpreters agreeing in the generall scope and meaning of it."[3]

This overt confidence regarding the course of sacred, providential history evidently led Puritans to the optimistic conviction that theirs was the epoch in which prophetic revelations would soon be realized. For example, writing in 1648 in New England, Thomas Hooker argued:

For these are the times drawing on, wherein Prophecies are to attain their perform-

[1] Richard Bernard, *A Key of Knowledge for the Opening of the Secret Mysteries of St. Johns Mysticall Reuelation* (1617), p. 123.
[2] Joseph Mede, *The Apostasy of the Latter Times* (1641), in *The Works of . . . Joseph Mede, B.D.*, ed. J. Worthington, 2 vols. (1664), vol. II, p. 807.
[3] Stephen Marshall, *The Song of Moses the Servant of God, and the Song of the Lambe* (1643), p. 1.

ances: and it is a received rule and I suppose must sane, when Prophecies are fulfilled they are best interpreted, the accomplishment of them is the best commentary.[4]

No wonder, then, that some could argue, as did the Puritan William Hicks in 1659, that "the Revelation is no longer a mystery, but a Book of History of memorable Acts and passages."[5] A century later, Jonathan Edwards, the chief architect of the Great Awakening in New England, declared that, through prophecy and history, "mankind" is informed of God's "grand design" in "the government of the world."

In the Bible, we have an account of the whole scheme of providence, from the beginning of the world to the end of it, either in history or prophecy, and are told what will become of things at last; how they will issue in the subduing of God's enemies, and in the salvation and glory of his Church, and setting up the everlasting kingdom of his Son . . . How rational, worthy, and excellent a revelation is this![6]

The apocalyptic tradition in England, therefore, brought about the sacralization of history, and, hence, the idea that England would play a singular role in sacred, providential history. But the creation of history as sacred time in the drama of salvation should be considered as only one essential dimension of the apocalyptic interpretation of history. Another dimension, equally important, was the creation of sacred space, of a holy land selected by God's divine providence for his chosen people who would have a crucial role to play in the unfolding drama of salvation. When John Bale and John Foxe developed the apocalyptic tradition in England, the view that England, due to the Reformation of the Church of England, as a sacred place inhabited by a chosen people was essential to their thought. In the apocalyptic view of history, therefore, the two dimensions were indispensable to each other, because prophetic revelations deal equally with both sacred time and sacred space in the drama of mankind's salvation.

By the end of the Elizabethan age, the English people were convinced that they were a chosen people dwelling in a holy land consecrated by God's divine providence. The notion among English Protestants of the singularity of the reformed Church of England led directly to the vision of England as an elect nation, of a chosen people dwelling in a sacred land. Sacred time and sacred space, the two essential dimensions within which prophetical revelation would be realized, comprise the very essence of apocalyptic interpretation of history. Therefore, the Protestant Reformation of the Church of England during Elizabeth's reign led to the notion of England as an elect nation. William Haller defines it most persuasively:

---

[4] Thomas Hooker, *A Survey of the Summe of Churche Discipline* (1648), preface.
[5] William Hicks, *The Revelation Revealed: Being a Practical Exposition on the Revelation of St. John* (1659), preface.
[6] Jonathan Edwards, *History of the Work of Redemption*, in *The Works of President Edwards* (New York, 1968 [1817]), vol. V, p. 277.

The idea of a predestined salvation reserved for the elect, of the Church as a communion of elect souls beset in all ages by enemies without and within, of the progression of the elect from age to age towards an apocalyptical vindication – these conceptions assumed in many minds a meaning and application which went beyond their merely religious context . . . For the Church as they conceived it appeared now as one with the nation, and for many, besides the champions of a still more perfect reformation, the nation itself assumed something of the nature of a mystical communion of chosen spirits, a peculiar people set apart from the rest of mankind.[7]

Because the apocalyptic tradition in England viewed the church as the central agency in sacred history, it is obvious that the providential role of the English nation was determined exclusively by the progress of the reformation of the Church of England. So far as English Protestants believed their church to be the true church, they assigned England the title of elect nation; a title which accorded England a unique role in the unfolding apocalyptic drama of salvation both in terms of sacred time and sacred space. When the Puritans who emigrated to New England denied England its title as elect nation, their bold repudiation of England's prominent role related both to the dimension of sacred time and the dimension of sacred space. They refused to accord England the prominent role in providential history with which Protestants had previously invested it since the accession of Elizabeth. They also denied England's location as a sacred place in the history of salvation. With the Church of England failing to execute a true reformation according to Puritan premises, they gradually repudiated England's pretensions to being elect. So, for example, when John Winthrop wrote to his wife in 1629 that England's "sinnes giues vs so great cause to looke for some heauvy Scquorge and Judgment to be cominge vpon us," the great leader of the Puritan migration to America was testifying to the desacralization of England, both in terms of sacred time and sacred space. Given England's failure and fate, Winthrop was confident that God "will prouide a shelter and a hidinge place" for his true church in the wilderness of America.[8]

The Puritans' twofold desacralization of England was a clear consequence of developments within the apocalyptic tradition in England as described in the previous chapter. For the transformation within the English apocalyptic tradition from Bale and Foxe's vision of England as the elect nation into Brightman's identification of England with the most sinful church of Revelation – Laodicea – marked a turning point in the course of the Reformation in England. From the end of the sixteenth century to the era of the Puritan Revolution, two conflicting visions concerning England's role in sacred, providential history existed and dominated the stage on which the struggle

---

[7] William Haller, *The Elect Nation: The Meaning and Relevance of Foxe's Book of Martyrs* (New York, 1963), pp. 244–5.

[8] John Winthrop, "John Winthrop to his Wife" (May 15, 1629), *The Winthrop Papers*, ed. Allyn Forbes, 5 vols. (Boston, 1929–47), vol. II, p. 91.

for the soul of the English people was taking place. On the one hand, the Protestant vision of England, based upon Bale and Foxe's writings, emphasized England's singular role in sacred history due to the Reformation of the Church of England and its historical struggle against Rome. Based upon this sense of election, Protestants developed a nationalistic outlook toward the world, stressing England's superior religious, cultural, and political life. "Foxe developed a new structure for apocalyptic time, one in which England – the elect nation – with its history became the principal actor in the struggle against Antichrist." England was seen as "the true vehicle of Christian redemption," or more specifically, a nation whose history was in fact "the embodiment" of the whole course of the history of salvation.[9]

On the other hand, however, a vision of England emerged which was based upon the Puritan failure to reform the Church of England. This competing vision was best articulated by Thomas Brightman and William Perkins and stressed the imminent judgment awaiting England unless it implemented a more thoroughly religious reformation. "We are in danger to be *spued out of Christ mouth*," wrote Perkins in 1595, "for it was written" in the Apocalypse "for our instruction, and for all Churches," that because of England's "luke-warme" approach to religion "we trouble Christ, and therefore are like to be cast out" from the church, as was Laodicea's fate.[10] The Puritan vision, therefore, stood in sharp contrast to the Protestant one. Puritans denounced the insufficiency of the Reformation in England, and their failure to reform the Church of England led them to foresee a bitter and frightening fate for England unless it mended its religious ways. In clear contrast to the Protestant vision, the Puritan vision of England's fate was gloomy and desperate. This transformation within the English apocalyptic tradition is crucial to any understanding of the Puritan movement. To a large extent, the Puritan Revolution was an attempt to return England to the very center of sacred, providential history. The transformation of the English apocalyptic tradition is crucial, as well, to understanding the Puritan migration to New England because the desacralization of England, both in terms of sacred time and sacred place, led some Puritans in the early seventeenth century to sacralize New England. New England became the holy land consecrated by God's divine providence. Therefore, New England was to play a singular role in the course of the history of salvation.

The role of the apocalyptic tradition in England during the sixteenth and seventeenth centuries has received considerable attention from historians in

---

[9] J. G. A. Pocock, "England," in *National Consciousness, History and Political Culture in Early Modern Europe*, ed. O. Ranum (Baltimore, 1975), p. 108.

[10] William Perkins, *Lectures Upon the Three First Chapters of the Revelation* (1604), p. 310. Perkins originally preached these lectures in 1595.

recent years. Less attention, however, has been given to the crucial role that this tradition played in the English settlement of America both in terms of the incorporation of America within the confines of the unfolding drama of providential, ecclesiastical history, and of the reconstruction of America as a sacred place in the history of salvation. Yet, to a large extent, the justifications for and the vindications of the Protestant settlement of Virginia and the Puritan migration to New England were based upon the premises of the apocalyptic tradition or upon the apocalyptic interpretation of history. Indeed, it is hard to conceive of the English colonization of America without the apocalyptic dimension according to which the settlement of America was seen as a divine duty to spread the Gospel in remote corners of the world. In the apocalyptic struggle between Christ and Antichrist, or between the true Protestant Church of England and the false Catholic church of Spain and Portugal, the battlefield spread across the Atlantic Ocean to America. The New World increasingly became the stage upon which the rivalry between the European forces of Reformation and Counter-Reformation took place. With the migration of the apocalyptic struggle between Christ and Antichrist to the New World, America gradually began to occupy a unique role in the course of sacred, providential history. The apocalyptic dimension, therefore, was crucial in defining the significance of the newly discovered New World for the European mind.

Yet despite the common ground shared by the English Protestants and Puritans concerning the fight against the Antichristian missionary efforts of Catholic Spain and Portugal in the New World, great differences existed between the Protestant justification and vindication of the settlement of Virginia and Puritan reasons for emigrating to New England. And it would be a grave mistake to claim, as the Puritans in America in fact argued for many years, that the difference between Protestant Virginia and Puritan New England lay in the fact that the first was established for earthly aims and goals while the second was founded for religious ends or for God's sake. The religious justifications behind the settlement of Virginia cannot be overlooked, as we will see later. The most important difference, however, between Protestants and Puritans lay in their differing attitudes to England's role in sacred, providential history. To a large extent, then, the transformation of English apocalyptic tradition from Bale and Foxe's vision of England as elect to Brightman and Perkins' identification of England with doomed Laodicea directly affected the different justifications Protestants and Puritans gave for the settlement of Virginia and New England.

Different apocalyptic visions concerning England's role in sacred, providential history, therefore, had enormous consequences for the meaning of America in the history of salvation. Believing their nation to be elect, Protestants justified the settlement of Virginia on the ground that, due to its glorious religious, cultural, and political institutions, England had a divine warrant to settle America and to establish "a New Britain in another world," and to teach the "heathen barbarians and brutish people" of America "the speech and language of Canaan."[11] In the same vein, the poet Michael Drayton called upon the English people "brave and heroique mind / worthy of your countries name," to commit themselves to settle "Virginia / Earth's only Paradise."[12] For English Protestants, therefore, the colonization of Virginia became a crucial trial of England's unique role as the elect nation in sacred, providential history. William Symonds, for example, compared James I with "Constantine the pacifier of the world, and the planter of the Gospell in places most remote," and demanded of James I:

Lord finish this good work thou hath begun; and marry this land, a pure Virgine, to thy kingly soone Christ Jesus; so shall thy name be magnified: and we shall have a Virgin or Maiden Britaine, a comfortable addition to our Great Britain.[13]

Viewing the colonization of America in the context of sacred history, Protestants found in the annals of ecclesiastical history a sacred model by which to justify and vindicate the settlement of Virginia. The sacred model which Protestants thought best described the English colonization of the New World was that of Abraham's migration (Gen. 12:1–3). They did so because Abraham's migration, or what I call the *Genesis* type of religious migration, symbolized a peaceful migration based upon God's promise to Abraham to make out of him and his seed a great nation. The *Genesis* type of religious migration, therefore, best fitted the Protestant vision of England as a nation of chosen people who had a singular role to play in providential history. Because Englishmen are "the sonnes of Abraham," there cannot be any doubt that the same "Lord that called *Abraham* into another country, doeth also by the same holy hand, call" now England "to goe and carry the Gospell to a nation that never heard of Christ."[14]

Clearly, the Protestant apocalyptic vision of England's singular role in sacred, providential history determined the prominent role Protestants

[11] Richard Crakanthorpe, *A Sermon Solemnizing the Happie Inauguration of our Most Gracious and Religious Soveraigne King James . . . Preached at Paules Crosse, the 14 of March last, 1608* (1609), in *The Genesis of the United States*, ed. Alexander Brown, 2 vols. (Boston, 1890), vol. I, p. 256; John Parker, "Religion and the Virginia Colony 1609–10," in *The Westward Enterprise: English Activities in Ireland, the Atlantic, and America 1480–1650*, ed. K. R. Andrews, N. P. Canny, and P. E. Hair (Detroit, 1979), pp. 254–5.

[12] Michael Drayton, "Ode to the Virginia Voyage," in *The Genesis of the United States*, vol. I, p. 86; Edward D. Neill, *Early Settlement of Virginia and Virginiola As Notice by Poets and Players* (Minneapolis, 1878), p. 8.

[13] William Symonds, *Virginia, A Sermon preached at the White-Chappel . . . April, 1609. Published for the Benefit and Use of the Colony, Planted, and to bee Planted There, and for the Advancement of their Christian Purpose* (1609), The Epistle Dedicatorie.

[14] *Ibid.*, pp. 16, 19.

assigned to England in the colonization of America. Protestant vindications of the settlement of Virginia were based upon the concept of England as elect, and England's mission in America was, therefore, simply an extension of its glorious and historical role in the drama of salvation. The Protestant apocalyptic view of the New World, therefore, was inextricably associated with the Protestant apocalyptic vision of the Old World. The *Genesis* type of religious migration, then, based upon God's promise to his chosen people, best fitted Protestants in their attempt to define England's role in the colonization of the New World. The reason for this is obvious. For the *Genesis* type of religious migration discloses a center in providential history, Abraham and his seed, through which God fulfills divine prophetic revelations in the progress of the history of salvation. And as God made Abraham into a great nation, so now it was through England, the elect nation and the locus of providential history, that God would fulfill His promises and prophecies, both in the Old and in the New World. In Protestant thought, therefore, America acquired its singular role in sacred history only through association with England. The New World had no other meaning or significance in providential history.

An examination of Puritan reasons for emigrating to New England, on the other hand, reveals a totally different revolutionary picture. Following Brightman and Perkins' identification of England with Laodicea, the Puritan emigrants denied England any important role in sacred, providential history except that of apostasy, and therefore emphasized time and again the apocalyptic gulf separating England and New England in the history of salvation. Having failed to bring about a more perfect religious reformation in the Church of England, Puritans increasingly tended to view their relationship with the established church as an apocalyptic struggle between Christ and Antichrist. Their migration to America was based, to a large extent, upon a deep eschatological consciousness of the true church fleeing into the wilderness in face of the imminent fate soon to befall sinful England and the Old World in general. "And if it should be please God to punish his people in the Christian counteries of Europe," preached Robert Cushman in 1621 in Plymouth, New England, "here is a way opened" in New England "for such as have wings to flie into this Wilderness."[15] Later, in the spring of 1629, leaders of the future great Puritan migration of 1630 argued that "all other Churches of Europe" had been "brought to desolation" during the events of the Thirty Years' War (1618–48), and it seemed to them that God's divine judgment was "cominge upon us" too in England. "Who knows," they

---

[15] Robert Cushman, *A Sermon Preached at Plimmoth in New England, December 9, 1621* (1622), The Epistle Dedicatory. See also by the same author, *Reasons and Considerations Touching the Lawfulness of Removing out of England into the Parts of America*, (1622).

asked, "but that God hath provided this place [Massachusetts], to be a refuge for many, whom he meanes to save out of the general destruction."[16]

Indeed, the conflicting visions of Protestants and Puritans concerning England's fate in sacred providential history can hardly be more opposed. Against the Protestant glorious vision of England in the history of salvation, the Pilgrim Father, William Bradford, claimed that "ever since the breaking out of the light of the Gospel" in England, England had become the stage of an apocalyptic struggle in which "Satan hath raised, maintained and continued" to wage his wars "against the Saints."[17] More specifically, Puritans were fully convinced that if the Church of England continued to "imytate Sodom in her pride and intemperance," "Laodicea in her lukewarmness," or "the Sinagogue of Antichrist in her superstition," it would certainly evoke God's wrath.[18] Fortunately, they knew that because God's divine providence had "carried his people into the wilderness," He would provide them a "comfortable refuge" there. They were wholly confident that "God hath provided this place [New England] to be a refuge for many whom he meanes to save out of the general callamity."[19]

It was in this context of an apocalyptic struggle between Christ and Antichrist that John Cotton declared that "here is then an eye of God that openes a doore there [New England], and sets him loose here [in England]." For "when God makes roome for us, no binding here, and an open way there."[20] And what Cotton expressed implicitly, Thomas Hooker and Francis Higginson boldly declared in most explicit words. In 1631, Hooker affirmed, "God begins to ship away his Noahs," from sinful and doomed England, "and God makes account that New England shall be a refuge for his Noahs . . . a rock and a shelter for his righteous ones to run unto."[21] And Higginson, too, thought that "New England might be designed by heaven, as a *refuge* and *shelter* for the *non-conformists* against the storms that were coming upon" England.[22] Accordingly, with the desacralization of England as a sacred space in providential history, some Puritans thought that the New Jerusalem of the Apocalypse lay across the ocean in New England. "I

---

[16] "General Observations for the Plantation of New England" (1629), *Winthrop Papers*, vol. II, pp. 114, 138–9.

[17] William Bradford, *Of Plymouth Plantation, 1620–1647*, ed. S. E. Morison (New York, 1967), p. 3.

[18] "John Winthrop to his Wife" (1629), *Winthrop Papers*, vol. II, p. 122.

[19] "Reasons to be Considered, and Objections with Answers," (1629), *Winthrop Papers*, vol. II, pp. 138–9.

[20] John Cotton, *Gods Promise to His Plantation* (1634 [1630]), p. 12.

[21] Thomas Hooker, *The Danger of Desertion* (1631), in *Thomas Hooker, Writings in England and Holland, 1626–1633*, ed. George H. Williams, Norman Pettit, Winfried Herget, and Sargent Bush, Jr. (Cambridge, Mass., 1975), p. 246.

[22] Francis Higginson, cited in Cotton Mather, *Magnalia Christi Americana; or, the Ecclesiastical History of New England*, 2 vols. (Hartford, 1820), vol. I, p. 328.

pray god account you and preserue you," wrote a Puritan from England in 1631 to his friend in the new colony of Massachusetts, "as worthy stones in buyldinge his newe Jerusalem" in the American wilderness.[23]

The prevalence of the terms "shelter," "refuge," "hiding place," and "wilderness" in their rhetoric points unmistakably to the fact that Puritans thought of their migration to New England in ways which were radically different from the ways in which Protestants saw their settlement of Virginia. Having failed to reform the Church of England according to their liking, and deeming themselves God's saints persecuted by Satan's rage in England, it was no wonder that the Puritan emigrants to New England utilized radically different sacred models and prophecies in order to justify their removal to America. Thus, if the Protestants' justification for the settlement of Virginia was based upon God's promise to Abraham and his seed, or upon what we have called the *Genesis* type of religious migration, Puritans tended to use the prophetic vision of the Woman's flight into the wilderness (Rev. 12:6–17), or the flight of the true church into the wilderness in face of Satan's fury. Most importantly, in terms of the sacred patterns represented in the annals of ecclesiastical history, Puritans chose the sacred model of Israel's exodus out of Egypt, or what I have called the *Exodus* type of religious migration, as the basis for justifying their migration to New England. So, for example, as God "carried the Israelites into the wilderness and made them forgette the fleshpotts of Egipt," wrote Winthrop in the summer of 1629, "God will by this meanes" of Puritan migration to Massachusetts "bringe vs to repent of our former Intemperance and soe cure vs of that desease which sends many amongs vs vntimely to our graues and others to Hell."[24]

For English Puritans in general, the exodus theme of Israel's flight out of Egyptian bondage indeed became the mirror of the whole history of human salvation and redemption. Illustrating this is the picture on the title page of the Geneva Bible of 1560 which depicts the "Israelites" standing on the shore of the "Red Sea," their backs towards the mighty Egyptian army and their faces towards the vision of the Promised Land looming in the distance. The Geneva Bible, sometimes called the Puritan Bible, was the most popular version in Puritan circles in England and New England. For Puritan emigrants to America, the flight from England to New England symbolized in vivid and concrete terms their exodus from bondage in Egypt, or England, to the promised land of Canaan. Theirs was a migration of a "Nation" driven out of another nation into the wilderness with a "speciall Commis-

---

[23] Edward Howes, "Edward Howes to John Winthrop, Jr." (1631), in *Winthrop Papers*, vol. III, p. 54.

[24] John Winthrop, "Reasons to be Considered, and Objections with Answers" (1629), in *Winthrop Papers*, vol. II, p. 144.

sion from heaven, such as" was the case with "the Israelites" in past times.[25] "Is not the way to Canaan through the wilderness?" asked Richard Mather. "Doubtless," he continues, "through the wilderness you must go, if ever you will come to Canaan."[26]

By its very definition in ecclesiastical history, the wilderness represents an intermediate zone between Egypt and the Land of Promise; it is, therefore, an essential part of the *Exodus* type of religious migration. Consequently, Puritans in America identified their migration with Exodus, claiming "God hath dealt with us as with the people of Israel; we are brought out of a fat land into the wilderness."[27] So powerful was this image of migration to America as an exodus that even during the time of the Puritan Revolution in England, some Puritans in New England warned against going back to England as a return to Egypt. "Will you be gone back again to *Egypt*," Cotton admonished his brethren in Boston, New England. And he warned them that return to England, or Egypt, means that "you must worship the beast or the image of the beast."[28]

Clearly, the *Exodus* type of religious migration used by the Puritans to justify their removal to New England is radically different from the *Genesis* type of religious migration used by the Protestants to vindicate the colonization of Virginia. The *Exodus* type is wholly apocalyptic in its character. It is based upon a crisis in the history of salvation which could be solved only through God's divine providence acting directly and immediately within history. Israel, a chosen nation, oppressed and persecuted by God's enemies, is delivered out of the state of bondage and slavery in Egypt only through the mighty hand of God's providence, which opens the way for the Israelites to return to the center of the history of salvation. Through the punishment of Egypt, God's divine providence delivers them out of Egypt and leads them toward the Land of Promise, guiding them in their wandering in the wilderness and eventually directing them to the Promised Land of Canaan. In contrast to the *Genesis* type of religious migration, which emphasizes the peaceful and gradual spread of the Gospel in the world, the *Exodus* type of religious migration symbolizes the fact that redemption could only be attained through direct divine intervention in the course of world history. Most importantly, the apocalyptic and judgmental character of the *Exodus* type demonstrates that only by severing ties with a sinful nation and corrupt history could God's chosen nation return to the center of providential

---

[25] John Cotton, "God's Promise to His Plantations," p. 5.

[26] Richard Mather, *A Farewell-Exhortation to the Church and People of Dorchester in New England* (Cambridge, Mass., 1657), p. 3.

[27] Peter Bulkeley, *The Gospel Covenant* (1651), cited in *The Puritans in America: A Narrative Anthology*, ed. A. Heimert and A. Delbanco (Cambridge, Mass., 1985), p. 118.

[28] John Cotton, *An Exposition upon the Thirteenth Chapter of the Revelation* (1655), p. 20.

history and play its unique role. Only by turning away from degenerate human traditions could Israel reach redemption. Thus, while the *Genesis* type develops the notion of a sacred center, Abraham and his seed, and its expansion within time and space, the *Exodus* type stresses the apocalyptic separation from sins and ungodliness. It signifies a flight from corrupt history and a fresh beginning in the history of salvation. In sum, because it is based upon crisis and judgment, the *Exodus* type of religious migration points unmistakably to the fact that, in the drama of the history of salvation, an apocalyptic gulf separates Egypt from Canaan and England from New England.[29]

Conflicting apocalyptic visions concerning England's role in sacred, providential history eventually led Protestants and Puritans in England to articulate different apocalyptic visions concerning the meaning of America as a sacred place. Yet, the overt contrast between the Protestant vindication of the settlement of Virginia and the Puritan justification of the migration to New England should not hinder us from seeing that, for both groups, migration to the New World essentially signified a revelatory event in the sacred history of salvation. For in the annals of ecclesiastical history, it was through the migration of God's chosen people, based upon God's divine prophecy, that a certain place acquired its prominent role as a sacred space in providential history. Prophecy and migration, for example, constituted the sacred meaning of Canaan in the history of salvation (Gen. 12:5–7). Just as prophetic revelation supplies meaning and significance to time and history, it determines as well the essence of place as a sacred space in the drama of human redemption and salvation.

Thus, having previously dealt with the issue of the creation of sacred time, or the process by which Englishmen rendered history sacred through prophetic revelation and in that way transformed it into sacred history, our task in the present chapter is to see how Englishmen, through their reading of divine prophecies, incorporated America as a sacred place within the confines of sacred, ecclesiastical history. Just as divine prophecy gave meaning to time and history, so also divine prophecy imparted significance to place in the history of salvation. For the Puritan migration to America, the role of New England as a sacred space was of ultimate importance. While for Protestants, Virginia's role as a sacred place in ecclesiastical history was inseparable from the notion of England as the elect nation, for Puritans the significance of New England as a sacred space was determined by total separation from corrupt England. The precondition of Puritan migration to New England, therefore, depended on reconstructing New England as a sacred place in providential history. Given the unfolding apocalyptic drama

[29] About the idea of Exodus in Western political thought, see M. Walzer, *Exodus and Revolution* (New York, 1985).

in England, Puritans were compelled to forge a sacred place in the wilderness of America to which the saints would fly from doomed England.

Before we deal in detail with the Puritans' vision of New England as a sacred place, we must first show how the discovery of space, exactly like the discovery of time, depended upon prophetic revelation. The attempt to deal with the issue of the incorporation of America as a sacred place in the history of salvation ought to begin, therefore, with the general issue of the "geographies of the mind," or with men's attitudes towards space. Then, because both Protestants of Virginia and Puritans of New England regarded the settlement of America as a religious, revelatory migration, we also have to deal with the concept of religious migration as a revelatory event in sacred, ecclesiastical history. Furthermore, because Spain and Portugal were the first to attempt the incorporation of the New World within the confines of sacred, ecclesiastical history through the interpretation of prophetic revelation, we ought to deal as well with the Apocalypse in the Age of Discovery and Reconnaissance. For, to a large extent, the reconstruction of America as a sacred space by Protestants and Puritans, despite the crucial differences between them, was aimed at refuting Spain and Portugal's apocalyptic vision of the New World as a sacred space according to the premises of the Roman Catholic Church. Only after examining these premises will we be able to understand fully the Protestant ideology of the settlement of Virginia, and most importantly, the revolutionary character of the apocalyptic ideology of the Puritan migration to New England. In contrast to Spain, Portugal, and even English Protestants, the New England Puritans were the first to formulate, through the *Exodus* type of religious migration, an ideology which emphasized the distinctiveness of America in ecclesiastical history. With American Puritans, indeed, we find for the first time the beginnings of a coherent American ideology, an ideology, that is, based on the premises of the ultimate separation of America, the New World, from the corruption and degeneration of the Old World. Seeing their migration as an apocalyptic revelatory event, American Puritans were the first to accord America a singular, independent role as a sacred place in the history of salvation.

THE GEOGRAPHIES OF THE MIND

Historical movements create not only external social and political changes, but also yield new modes of thinking about time and space and hence develop new categories for experiencing time and space. An essential argument of Kant's Copernican Revolution in epistemology was his contention that, as he wrote in *The Critique of Pure Reason*, in 1781, the forms of experiencing time and space are determined by the mental apparatus of the observer. Therefore, because our sense of time and space is indeed subjective, the experience of time and space varies considerably along, for example, religious and nationalistic lines.[30] Previously, we saw how prophetic imagination gave meaning and significance to time and history and how sacred, divine prophecy shaped the experience of time among English Protestants and Puritans. The same can be said about the experience of space, or the reconstruction of space according to prophetic revelations. The philosophic attention given to time and space should not hinder us from seeing that both can be usefully applied in understanding cultural and intellectual history, or from seeing that we may interpret culture as a function of time and space.[31] This is especially true concerning religious culture where the experience of time is inextricably tied to the experience of space.

In religious thought, the concept of sacred space is inseparable from the notion of sacred time. While divine prophecy construes certain places as sacred, the essence of sacred space lies in the realization of prophetic revelation. So, for example, the very notion of the Promised Land, or Canaan, is inextricably tied to the vision of a chosen nation in the history of salvation and vice versa. Consequently, in religious culture, the experience of sacred time determines as well the experience of sacred space. Prophetic imagination affords meaning not only for time and history but for space as well. In other words, within the context of sacred ecclesiastical history, divine prophecy transforms unknown and merely terrestrial places or *Terra Incognita*, into a sacred space as singled out by God's providence to play a unique role in the unfolding drama of salvation. In this context, then, the notion of "geographies of the mind," or the place of imagination in geography, is crucial to understanding the meaning of sacred space in the course of the history of salvation.

"Terrae Incognitae" was the title of John K. Wright's influential presidential address delivered before the Association of American Geographers in December, 1946. Wright, a prominent geographer and intellectual historian whose works admirably demonstrate the intrinsic connection between the history of geographical exploration and the history of ideas, addressed the issue of "The Place of the Imagination in Geography."[32] This seminal essay opens new avenues to the study of geographical knowledge, or, as Wright termed it, "geosophy" ("geo" meaning earth, and "sophia" meaning knowledge). Geosophy, or the study of geographical knowledge, deals with the ways and means by which people transform *Terra Incognita* into *Terra*

---

[30] Stephen Kern, *The Culture of Time and Space, 1880–1918* (Cambridge, Mass., 1983), pp. 1, 206. See also the important discussion of time and space in Stephen W. Hawking, *A Brief History of Time, From the Big Bang to the Black Hole* (New York, 1988).

[31] Kern, *Culture of Time and Space*, pp. 3–5.

[32] John K. Wright, "*Terrae Incognitae*: The Place of the Imagination in Geography," in *Human Nature in Geography* (Cambridge, Mass., 1966), pp. 68–88.

Cognita, or a land unknown into a known land. In geography, said Wright, "the words *terra incognita* signify a land unknown to the map maker." Therefore it indicates unknown space "beyond the ken of the geographers and cartographers of Western civilizations." Evidently, the transformation of a space from *Terra Incognita* into *Terra Cognita* depended, on the one hand, upon geographical exploration and discovery and, on the other hand, upon what Wright called "the geography of the mind," or upon imagination. "The imagination not only projects itself into *terrae incognitae* and suggests routes for us to follow, but also plays upon those things that we discover and out of them makes imaginative conceptions which we seek to share with others." Human imagination, therefore, helps us "to convert the *terrae incognitae* . . . into *terrae cognitae*."[33]

A word of caution is obviously appropriate: *Terra Incognita* is not a land totally and wholly unknown to us for it has some contact with the known world. We have, at least, some knowledge of its existence. Its future transformation into *terra cognita*, however, essentially depends upon imaginative conceptualization. Wright's contention about the crucial role that imagination plays in conquering *Terra Incognita* and transforming it into *Terra Cognita* is therefore of utmost importance because it highlights the crucial process of the spiritual conquest, or the imaginative creative conquest, of space by the human mind. For "unlike the mental images that we can merely invoke from the memory," said Wright, "an imaginative conception" of unknown geographical space, "is essentially a new vision, a new creation" by which we incorporate unknown terrestrial place into our knowledge and thereby give it meaning and significance.[34]

Wright's claims are of the utmost importance for the historical study of men's sense of, and attitudes towards, terrestrial space. In the same way that we imbue time with sacred meaning and thus construct sacred history, we also project sacred meaning into certain places and thereby construct sacred space. In this context, Wright's concept of "geosophy" is fruitful because it relates to "the study of geographical knowledge," or to what also may be termed the study of the history of geographical knowledge. Geosophy is "to geography [what] historiography is to history." It deals with "the nature and expression of geographical knowledge both past and present" regarding men's sense of terrestrial space. Yet, because this geographical knowledge has to do with subjective conceptions, or with imaginative conceptions, it reflects not only men's sense of geographical limitations and boundaries, but also their attitudes towards space. Geosophy, therefore, deals with "human desires, motives, and prejudices" towards space in time.[35] Just as we portray time according to our imagination and wonder, we depict space according

---

[33] Wright, *"Terrae Incognitae,"* pp. 83, 70–3.   [34] *Ibid.*, p. 34.   [35] *Ibid.*, p. 83.

to our motives and inspirations. Both spheres, then, express our desires and goals because we reconstruct both imaginatively. Time and space, to conclude, are essential dimensions in which men express their visions and goals in every age and therefore both are worthy of historical inquiry.

Missing, however, from Wright's seminal essay of 1946 was any detailed discussion of how people in each age reconstruct their "imaginative concepts" of terrestrial space. For if each period has its own repository of ideas concerning space, or its own geographical lore, then clearly every age has different attitudes toward space. Wright himself addressed this important issue in another seminal essay, "Notes on Early American Geopiety," in which he described with greater clarity the variety of men's religious attitudes toward terrestrial space. Claiming that "geography is also a form of awareness," Wright explored some of the dimensions of the religious, emotional bond of man toward space. And because of his fondness for coining terms, he created the term *geopiety* to denote the special dimension of man's religious, emotional attachment to his terrestrial space. As the term suggests, "geopiety could be regarded as a province in a larger kingdom of *georeligious*," which in turn is "part of the still greater unnamed empire where religion and geography meet." In general, then, geopiety deals with "religious awareness," such as religious "perceptions, emotion, cognition, belief," and so on, of terrestrial space.[36]

"Georeligion," or as Wright sometimes called it also "religiogeography," is "*religion* that has to do with geographic actualities," or the role of terrestrial space within the confines of religious thought and experience. This special dimension of awareness "constituting geopiety," or what may be called more broadly "georeligiousness," Wright continues, "could be called geopious awareness." For example, places like Jerusalem and Mecca arouse "geopious emotions on the part of geopious persons." In the context of sacred, ecclesiastical history, which is our major concern, Wright adds two additional concepts. The first is *geotheology*, which deals with the science of the divinity in terrestrial space. In the context of "the geographies of the mind," the term "geotheology" signifies the theological nature and meaning of space. The second term is *geoteleology*. (Since "tele" means end or goal, it concerns the end of geographical space within the design and purpose of the universe.) Yet, as the Greek word 'telos" suggests, it is not about the mere physical termination of the world, but rather about the "end" or "the goal (purpose; 'end sought')" of the world. Geoteleology, then, deals with the destiny of the world within a theocratic universe, controlled and directed according to the divine scheme of God's providence. Or as Wright puts it, geoteleology can be defined "as the concept or doctrine

[36] John K. Wright, "Notes on Early American Geopiety," in *Human Nature in Geography*, pp. 251–2.

of divine providential dispositions of terrestrial circumstances primarily for God's glory and secondarily for the use of man." For example, Creation, the Deluge and the End of the World, are "the major geoteleologic providences" in the annals of sacred, ecclesiastical history.[37]

Among men's religious emotional bonds to terrestrial space, which Wright so brilliantly analyzes, of crucial importance for us is geoteleology which deals with the End of the World, or the fate of the earth in the final conflagration. A crucial aspect of geoteleology is the eschatological and apocalyptic dimension, or the destiny of a given space in the unfolding apocalyptic mystery of the history of salvation, of Christ's Second Coming and his millennial role with the saints upon the earth. Following Wright, the eschatological role of a given space in providential history can be termed "geoeschatology."[38] And we may add here a new term, "geoapocalypse," or the fate of a given space within the course of apocalyptic history. Geoeschatology and geoapocalypse, as branches of both geotheology and geoteleology, deal with men's attitudes towards space according to eschatological and apocalyptic visions, or according to prophetic imagination. Thus, for example, the Puritans' desacralization of England as a sacred place in providential history, reveals their geoeschatologic and geoapocalyptic awareness that England was not elect but rather represented apostasy within the course of the history of salvation. And geoeschatologic and geoapocalyptic consciousness gives evidence as well of the sacralization of an alternative place within the eschatological and apocalyptic drama of salvation and redemption.

As we have seen, this is indeed one of the most important characteristics of the Puritan vision of New England. God, that is, "creates New England to muster up the first of His Forces in." These godly armies the Lord's divine providence chose to locate in New England in order "to proclaime to all Nations" of the old world "the neere approach of the most wonderful workes that ever the Soones of man saw": Christ's Second Coming and his millennial rule with his saints upon earth.[39] The Puritan poet, Michael Wigglesworth, provides a vivid picture of this geoeschatologic and geoapocalyptic awareness of New England.

> The time drew nigh wherein
> The glorious Lord of hosts
> Was pleasd to lead his armies forth
> Into those forrein coastes . . .

---

[37] Wright, "Notes on Early American Geopiety," pp. 252, 251, 255, 257.

[38] *Ibid.*, pp. 266–7.

[39] Edward Johnson, *Wonder-Working Providence of Sion Saviour in New England, 1628–1651*, ed., J. Franklin Jameson (New York, 1910), pp. 23, 60–1.

Here was the hiding place, which thou
Jehova didst provide
For thy redeemed ones, and where
Thou didst thy jewels hide.[40]

The study of "the geographies of the mind," or the role of the imagination in geography, then, is crucially important to any historical understanding of men's attachment to terrestrial space and to the transformation of *Terra Incognita* into *Terra Cognita*. It is also crucially important regarding the incorporation of a given terrestrial space into the confines of sacred history by which such a place acquires a singular, providential role in the history of salvation according to prophetic imagination. "No exploration in any part of the world (or, now, out of it)," wrote John L. Allen, "can be fully assessed without reference to that agency of the human mind," or imagination, which according to John Milton in *Paradise Lost*, "misjoyning shapes, Wilde worke produces oft." The entire process of geographical discovery, exploration, and, consequently, of men's emotional bond to terrestrial space, "is conditioned by the imagination, and thus the study of [geographical] exploration should focus on imagination's influence."[41] Imagination is, after all, what distinguishes men's attachment, or reverence, toward a place from that of animal territorial attachment. "Human territoriality, in the sense of attachment to place," wrote Yi-Fu Tuan, "differs in important ways from the territoriality of animals unburdened by symbolic thought," or imaginative conceptions. In this context, geopiety indeed belongs to the realm of the history of ideas; it is "an exercise in self-awareness" regarding men's sense of, and attachment to, terrestrial space which ultimately "reveals the depth of the emotional bond between man and nature, man and place."[42]

The study of "the geographies of the mind," or the role of the imagination in geographical discovery and exploration, is crucially important to the field of religious history because, in the past, religious faith and experience

---

[40] Michael Wigglesworth, *God's Controversy with New England* (1662), in *Seventeenth-Century American Poetry*, ed. H. T. Meserole (New York, 1968), pp. 43–5.

[41] John L. Allen, "Lands of Myth, Waters of Wonder: The Place of Imagination in the History of Geographical Exploration," in *Geographies of the Mind: Essays in Historical Geosophy*, ed. David Lowenthal and M. J. Bowden (New York, 1976), pp. 57, 41, 58.

[42] Yi-Fu Tuan, "Geopiety: A Theme in Man's Attachment to Nature and to Place," in *Geographies of the Mind*, p. 13. *Geographies of the Mind* is a collection of essays in honor of John K. Wright produced by his students. See especially the following important essays: Philip W. Porter and Fred E. Lukermann, "The Geography of Utopia," pp. 197–223; and David Lowenthal, "The Place of the Past in the American Landscape," pp. 89–117. See also David Lowenthal's important study of man's attitudes toward his past, *The Past is a Foreign Country* (New York, 1985), and Victor Turner and Edith Turner's excellent study of pilgrimage and attachment to sacred places, *Image and Pilgrimage in Christian Culture: Anthropological Perspectives* (New York, 1978).

provided the ultimate sanction regarding the bonds between man and space. This is nowhere more clearly seen than in relation to the religious, spiritual "discovery" and "conquest" of the New World in which prophetic imaginative concepts were ultimately responsible for the transformation of America from *Terra Incognita* into *Terra Cognita* in the European mind during the Age of Discovery and Reconnaissance. To a large extent, as we will see later, this transformation of the New World was made possible through the incorporation of America into the confines of sacred, ecclesiastical history, the most commonly accepted ideology of history in the Christian world at the time. What was available for the Europeans during the Age of Discovery was, after all, the prophetic, imaginative concepts of sacred, ecclesiastical history by which they would explain the meaning of the newly discovered New World. In this important process, imaginative religious concepts facilitated the spiritual conquest of America and thus fostered the gradual incorporation of the notion of the New World within the European mind.

Yet, before dealing with the Apocalypse in the Age of Discovery, or with the incorporation of the New World as a sacred space within the unfolding history of salvation, we ought first to explore the concept of religious migration within sacred, ecclesiastical history as a revelatory, prophetic event. For religious migration was the key concept by which Europeans explained and justified the colonization of America; it stood behind such concepts, or myths, as the spreading of the Word of God to the remote corners of the world, the movement of the Gospel from East to West, and the eschatological significance of the Indians' conversion in America. As a revelatory, prophetic event in sacred ecclesiastical history, the concept of religious migration eventually led to the apocalyptic interpretation of the New World.

MIGRATION AS A REVELATORY, PROPHETIC EVENT

Within the confines of sacred, ecclesiastical history, or that mode of historical thought based upon the church as the central agency in the history of salvation, migration holds a unique and prominent place. Controlled and directed by God's divine providence and conceived as an economy of salvation, sacred history manifests a long and continuous series of migrations which mark the spread, advance and progress of the church, and concomitantly the Gospel, upon the earth. For if the ultimate mark of human existence on earth is based upon the drama of alienation from, and eventual reconciliation with God, a compulsory exile from Eden and final voluntary (predestined) return to the New Jerusalem, then sacred history itself reveals a dialectical turn: a pilgrimage between Babylon and Jerusalem or between Egypt and the Promised Land of Canaan.

Between these two antagonistic poles of the drama of human salvation, migration symbolizes the prophetic journey marking the end of alienation from and the total reconciliation with God. Being essentially the drama of human salvation and redemption, "the Christian Epic," as George Santayana called sacred ecclesiastical history, consists in imminent flights of liberation from sin into grace or from the profane to the sacred.[43] These migrations are expounded not only in terms of sacred time, or prophetic revelations, but also in terms of sacred place. Religious migration, therefore, almost always takes place between two definite and antagonistic spaces in providential history – Babel, Babylon, Sodom, Gomorrah, and Egypt on the one hand, and Jerusalem, New Jerusalem, Canaan, and the Land of Promise on the other. The first signifies total alienation from God and the latter the full reconciliation with Him.

In existential, spiritual terms, an important dimension of the history of salvation, indeed its ultimate dimension, is according to St. Augustine, "the pilgrimage of this life."[44] Or, as Robert Cushman, deacon of the separatist congregation in Leyden and latter a business agent of the Pilgrim Fathers' colony in Plymouth, New England, movingly observes:

We are all, in all places, strangers and pilgrims, travellers and sojourners; most properly, having no dwelling but in this earthen tabernacle. Our dwelling is but a wandering; and our abiding, but as a fleeting [a hastening away]; and, in a word, our home is nowhere but in the heavens; in that house not made with hands, whose maker and builder is God; and to which all ascend, that love the Coming of our Lord Jesus.[45]

Especially "to the Protestant," wrote Richard Niebuhr, "life seems a pilgrim's progress which, whether made solitarily or in company, proceeds through unpredictable contingencies and crisis toward the destination beyond life and death where all the trumpets blow."[46] As an existential mode of Christian life, religious migration is an important form of spiritual pilgrimage. It exhibits the main features of spiritual pilgrimage in general: "separation" from a sinful place and "aggregation" in a holy one, "detachment" from corruption and "attachment" to godly life. In sum, as a

---

[43] George Santayana cited by Harry Elmer Barnes, *A History of Historical Writing* (New York, 1963 [1937]), p. 42.

[44] St. Augustine cited by Jeroslav Pelikan, *The Mystery of Continuity: Time and History, Memory and Eternity in the Thought of Saint Augustine* (Charlottesville, 1986), p. 109.

[45] Robert Cushman, *Reasons and Considerations Touching the Lawfulness of Removing out of England into the Parts of America*, (1622) in Edward Arber (ed.), *The Story of the Pilgrim Fathers* (New York, 1969 [1897]), p. 497.

[46] H. Richard Niebuhr, "The Protestant Movement and Democracy in the United States," in *The Shaping of American Religion*, ed. J. W. Smith and A. L. Jamison (Princeton, 1961), vol. I, p. 23.

spiritual journey, "pilgrimage . . . offers liberation from profane social structures."[47]

Yet religious migration in general, quite apart from a personal spiritual pilgrimage, signifies the heart of ecclesiastical history. It acquires its prominence in sacred history precisely because it symbolizes the whole course of the history of salvation as alienation from and reconciliation with God. In this sense, migration is indeed a revelatory, prophetic event; a sacred journey directed by God's divine providence which unveils the meaning of certain time and certain space in the progress of the history of salvation. Through the dimension of sacred time, or within the unfolding course of divine providence, migration reveals new terrestrial places and consecrates them as sacred places in the drama of salvation. Exactly as the Book of Revelation and other prophetic writings decree the meaning and goal of time, so divine prophecy requires, for example, migrating from Babylon as a condition for reaching the New Jerusalem – only those who leave Babylon eventually become citizens of the city of God. Religious migration, therefore, is a revelatory prophetic event both in regard to time and space. As with time and history, prophetic revelation sheds light upon the role of place within sacred, providential history. Consequently, just as sacred history has its beginning and end, so space too acquires a beginning and end in sacred history through divine prophecy. After all, Creation means both the formation of time and space,[48] and eschatological visions are related to the fate of both time and space in the final conflagration. In the whole scheme of sacred providential history, religious migration revealed the rhythm and geographical course of the progress of the history of salvation upon earth.

The first religious migration in ecclesiastical history, and hence the first experience of exile, also constituted the opening and beginning of history itself, namely the forcible expulsion from the Garden of Eden. So, according to Eusebius(*c.* 260–*c.* 340), bishop of Caesarea and the Father of Church History as a mode of historical thought,

Immediately in the beginning, after the first life in blessedness, the first man, despising God's command fell into this mortal and perishable life and exchanged his former life of luxury with God for this curse-laden earth.[49]

And according to Otto of Freising (*c.* 1114/15–58), the famous ecclesiastical historian, "while the first man dwelt" in Paradise, "he became disobedient to the word of God, and so by the righteous judgment of God he was cast

---

[47] Turner and Turner, *Image and Pilgrimage in Christian Culture*, pp. 2, 4, 9.

[48] According to St. Augustine, "The beginning of the world and the beginning of time are the same;" *City of God*, trans. John O'Meara (New York, 1984), p. 435. See also Pelikan, *The Mystery of Continuity*, pp. 39, 43.

[49] Eusebius Pamphili, *Ecclesiastical History*, trans. Roy J. Defferrari, 2 vols. (Washington, DC, 1981), vol. I, p. 43.

out into his pilgrimage" in the world.[50] No wonder, then, that ecclesiastical historians chose to begin the history of the church with the Fall, or according to Eusebius, "with the story of the most capital and lordly events" which stood at the beginning of history.[51] For Augustine, too, in the *City of God*, the expulsion from Eden marked the beginning of sacred, providential history whose essential feature consisted in the apocalyptic struggle between "two societies of human beings, one of which is predestined to reign with God for all eternity, the other doomed to undergo eternal punishment with the Devil."[52]

Having been excluded from Eden because of their alienation from God, or because of "the excess of their self-chosen wickedness," the Lord established earth as a place of exile and trial for His creatures, a space in which, Eusebius continues,

the Guardian of all, pursued them with floods and conflagrations . . . and with successive famines and plagues and wars in turn and with thunderbolts from on high He cut them down, as if checking some terrible and quite obstinate disease of their souls with more severe punishments.[53]

The earth, therefore, played a singular role in sacred, providential history as the place where humanity would eventually reconcile itself with God. For God "in His exceeding love of man" did not hide himself nor alienate himself from his fallen creatures on the earth, but rather, through his divine providence, continued to take care of them.[54] In the concluding lines of his great epic, *Paradise Lost*, John Milton marvelously depicted this expulsion from Eden and yet continued caring by God:

> The world was all before them, where to choose
> Their place of rest, and Providence their guide.
> They hand in hand with wandering steps and slow,
> Through Eden took their solitary way.[55]

Throughout all the vicissitudes of time and history since the Fall, then, God's divine providence selected, elected, and predestined certain people and certain places in order to restore humanity and reconcile it with its Creator.[56] Hence, the forced expulsion from Eden is only the first in a long series of religious migrations in sacred history. With the Deluge, God

---

[50] Otto, bishop of Freising, *The Two Cities: A Chronicle of Universal History to the Year 1146 A.D.*, trans. Charles C. Mierow (New York, 1966), p. 123.
[51] Eusebius, *Ecclesiastical History*, vol. I, p. 38.
[52] Augustine, *City of God*, p. 595.
[53] Eusebius, *Ecclesiastical History*, vol. I, p. 43.
[54] *Ibid.*, p. 44.
[55] John Milton, *Paradise Lost*, in *The Portable Milton*, ed. Douglas Bush (New York, 1955), p. 548.
[56] Augustine, *City of God*, p. 671.

destroyed all flesh upon earth because of the persistent wickedness of the whole human race. In ecclesiastical history, the story of Noah's ark serves as "a symbol of Christ and the Church," according to Augustine, or as "a symbol of the city of God on pilgrimage in this world."[57] As a migratory event, this story is also a revelatory event; divine prophecy led Noah to escape the Flood where God's wrath destroyed the whole earth. "A mystery of the highest solemnity was being enacted here," wrote Augustine of the story of Noah's ark. It was "a symbolic presentation of a reality of the greatest importance," namely a symbol "designed to give a prophetic picture of the Church."[58] Yet, carried by the mighty wings of divine providence, Noah's migration lacks a final, terrestrial destination. It was only directed toward the preservation of godly people. No wonder, then, that only after the Deluge the notion of sacred space finally emerges. And the age of compulsory migration, the one from Eden and the other from corrupt earth before the Flood, comes to an end. Now, with "the era that begins with Abraham,"[59] religious migration becomes a voluntary, conscious act leading toward a Land of Promise. Sacred, terrestrial space finally becomes an essential dimension of sacred, providential history.

According to Augustine, Abraham's migration inaugurated a "new era" in providential history because "from that time onwards our knowledge of" the city of God, or the church, "becomes clearer and we find more evident promises from God which we now see fulfilled in Christ."[60] Consequently, God's promise to Abraham, and hence Abraham's migration to Canaan, the Land of Promise, is a great prophetic, revelatory event in the history of salvation. Through a divine prophecy, a chosen nation dwelling in a sacred place became the means for spreading the Gospel in the world.[61] Migration, then, is no less than a prophetic revelation about the course and progress of the history of salvation. Furthermore, with Abraham's migration and paralleling the conceptual family of a chosen nation and sacred space, an opposite conceptual family of the profane and sinful, corrupted space emerges. With this divine congruency between the character of people and the nature of the space in which they live, religious migration and terrestrial space acquire radically different importance. A new type of religious migration emerges in ecclesiastical history, namely a divine judgmental migration which involves the destruction of corrupted space.

In clear contrast to Abraham's peaceful migration, Lot's removal from Sodom, for example, is a judgmental migration. Accordingly, after God warned Lot to escape from Sodom, He poured his wrath upon "that ungodly city" and "reduced it to ashes." Furthermore, "the punishment of the men of Sodom was a foretaste of the divine judgment to come" in the

---

[57] *Ibid.*, p. 643.   [58] *Ibid.*, pp. 647–8.   [59] *Ibid.*, p. 670.
[60] *Ibid.*, p. 670.   [61] *Ibid.*, pp. 675–7.

end of time and history.[62] With the creation of a chosen people and of sacred space, then, God's divine providence assumes more and more of an apocalyptic role in the history of salvation. And while it protects and promotes godly people and their place of living as sacred space, it also bitterly condemns the profane and their place of habitation. The two most *exemplary* models of judgmental migration are, of course, Exodus and the apocalyptic destruction of Babylon in Revelation. Concerning the story of Exodus, in order to "release God's people" from "the crual and burdensom yoke of slavery" in Egypt, God's divine providence inflicted "ten memorable plagues" upon "the Egyptians,"[63] and so restored His chosen people to the center of the history of salvation or set them free to reach their eschatological destination in the Promised Land. Another famous example of divine, judgmental migration is the separation of the godly from the Whore of Babylon before God poured his wrath upon that sinful city as described in Revelation (14:8, 18:4–9).

Religious migration, then, as a prophetic revelatory event connecting two opposite and antagonistic poles of providential history, illuminates the whole course of the history of salvation not only through the dimension of sacred time but also through the dimension of sacred space. So if sacred time is always associated with a certain terrestrial space, sacred space is always inextricably bound to the sacred history of salvation. Furthermore, in terms of divine migration as a prophetic revelatory event, sacred time determines sacred space and vice versa. We may therefore apply Stephen Hawking's notion of "time-space", or "space-time," from his *A Brief History of Time*, to the relationship between sacred time and sacred space in religious migration as a prophetic, revelatory event in providential history. Moreover, again following Hawking, we can also define religious migration as "event horizon," or as "the boundary of the region" of sacred "space-time" in providential history.[64] For as a prophetic, revelatory event, religious emigration in ecclesiastical history constitutes a special region of sacred "space-time" along the course of providential history. Each migration is an event which only reveals the present boundary, or the present state, in unfolding providential history. And with each consecutive migration, God raises another curtain on the stage of the mystery of the history of redemption and salvation.

In sacred, ecclesiastical history, then, God's providence reveals itself at certain moments and in certain spaces. But because to move in time means to move between spaces, migration is essential to the fulfillment of prophetic revelation. Hence, migration itself assumes the meaning of a prophetic, revelatory event which exemplifies God's divine providence. Religious

---

[62] *Ibid.*, p. 692.   [63] *Ibid.*, p. 708.
[64] Hawking, *A Brief History of Time*, pp. 25, 94.

migration, therefore, is an essential dimension of the history of salvation from its very beginning with the Fall to its eschatological and apocalyptic end. Christian historiography and geography, time and space, are inextricably interwoven through the concept of religious migration. This is clearly evident in the notion of the *translatio imperii*, or *translatio religionis*, that is, the progress of the Gospel from East to West during the course of providential history.

Few concepts in historiography have endured so persistently as that of the *translatio imperii*. "The idea of transference sought to explain the major crises of world history by which supremacy is taken from one people and given to another." Originating in Roman historiography, it was introduced into Christian historiography by St. Jerome (*c.* 342–420). Later, in the twelfth century, when "the number of world monarchies came to be fixed at four in accordance with Daniel's vision," it found its most "coherent and definitive expression with Otto of Freising." During its development, the idea of *translatio imperii* was applied to various human activities such as the transfer of wisdom, virtue, and political power. It was applied as well to the concept of *translatio religionis* in which "God's rejection of the Jews for the Gentiles" provided the basis for the "idea of the transfer of religion, grace or the Kingdom of God" within the world.[65]

In the twelfth century, however, with Otto, Bishop of Freising's *The Two Cities: A Chronicle of Universal History to the year 1146 A.D.*, "the process of world history became a movement of power from the East to the West." In his book, Otto first refers to the transfer of learning:

The careful student of history will find that learning was transferred from Egypt to the Greeks, then to the Romans, and finally to the Gauls and the Spaniards. And so it is to be observed that all human power or learning had its origin in the East, but is coming to an end in the West, that thereby the transitoriness and decay of all things human may be displayed.[66]

In another place, however, Otto closely associated the transfer of the power of learning and wisdom with that of religion. "One need not wonder at the transfer of power or wisdom from the East to the West, since it is evident that the same transfer has been effected in matters of religion."[67] In apocalyptic and eschatological terms, the migration of the Gospel from East to West is also evident in the fulfillment of prophetic revelation; geographical progress of the church upon the world coincides with the course of sacred time. According to Otto, one scholar writes, "with the completion of this movement in the West, and with the decay of the empire, the end was at hand."[68] Time and space would merge together in the end of time and

---

[65] John M. Headley, *Luther's View of Church History* (New Haven, 1963), pp. 240–1.
[66] *Ibid.*, p. 241; Otto, bishop of Freising, *The Two Cities*, pp. 95, 322–3.
[67] Otto, bishop of Freising, *The Two Cities*, p. 448.
[68] Headley, *Luther's View of Church History*, pp. 241–2.

history and the geographical progress of the Gospel would reach its final eschatological destination.

The idea of *translatio imperii* from East to West, as introduced by Otto of Freising, had a powerful impact on ecclesisastical history as a mode of historical thought. For now a nation's geographical location could easily determine its role in sacred providential history. Ernst Kantorowicz has noticed that, for the Carolingian kings of France in the eighth century, "Jerusalem" wandered to Gaul, and that during the thirteenth century, "the kingdom of France . . . was considered the home of a new chosen people."[69] Later, during the sixteenth century, Spanish Catholics claimed that "Jerusalem" wandered across the Pyrenees because "God had raised Spain above all the kingdomes of the earth, and He had designed the Spaniards as His new chosen people."[70] And Luther accorded Protestant Germany a similar role in sacred history:

Dear Germans, take advantage, because our moment has come. Gather in, while it still shines and is good wheather. Use God's grace and Word while they are present. For you should know that God's Word and grace is a traveling object that rains blessings. It does not return to where it has once been. It was with the Jews, but away it went and they now have nothing. Paul brought it into Greece. But again it went away through neglect, and Greece now has the Turks. Rome and the Latin lands have also had it, but away it goes and they now have the pope. And you Germans are not allowed to think that you will have it forever, because it cannot be retained by those who show ingratitude and contempt. Grasp it and retain it, whoever can.[71]

This sense of providential election and the sacred westward movement of the Gospel strongly prevailed in Protestant and Puritan England during the sixteenth and seventeenth centuries. For example, Thomas Goodwin declared in 1646,

This Isle in which we live . . . is the richest Ship, that hath the most precious jewels of our Lord and Saviour Jesus Christ in it, and the greatest treasure, of any kingdome in the world.[72]

According to the idea of *translatio religionis*, God's divine providence designated certain places and peoples in the great migratory, and hence revelatory, course of the Gospel upon earth. The importance of this powerful image lies in the fact that it locates the sacred meaning of certain spaces and certain peoples or nations along the course of the prophetic, revelatory progress of the church from East to West. Herein lies the ultimate signifi-

---

[69] Ernst Kantorowicz, *Laudes Regiae: A Study of Liturgical Acclamations and Mediaeval Ruler Worship* (Berkeley, 1946), p. 59, and *The King's Two Bodies: A Study in Medieval Political Theology* (Princeton, 1981), p. 237.

[70] John L. Phelan, *The Millennial Kingdom of the Franciscans in the New World* (Berkeley, 1970), p. 11.

[71] Luther, *To the Burgomaster and Counsellors*, 1524, cited by Headley, *Luther's View of Church History*, p. 242.

[72] Thomas Goodwin, *The Great Interest of States & Kingdomes* (1646), p. 51.

cance of *translatio religionis* for the incorporation of the New World within the confines of sacred, ecclesiastical history. For beginning with Columbus' voyages, Europeans began increasingly to interpret the significance of the New World within the providential scheme of history, or according to the great prophetic, revelatory transfer of the Gospel from East to West. "God made me the messenger of the new heaven and the new earth of which he spoke in the Apocalypse of St. John," declared Columbus in 1500, "and he showed me the spot where to find it."[73] Disappointed by the state of religion in early seventeenth-century England, the English poet George Herbert declared,

> Religion stands on tiptoe in our land
> Readie to passe to the American strand.[74]

And for Jonathan Edwards, "the discovery of America, coinciding with the Reformation, opened up the possibility 'for a glorious renovation of the world' of which the 'great awakening' of New England was a conspicuous sign."[75] Even for Thomas Paine, "the Reformation was preceded by the discovery of America – as if the Almighty graciously meant to open a sanctuary to the persecuted in future years, when home should afford neither friendship nor safety."[76]

With the decline of providential interpretations of history, the idea of *translatio religionis* was replaced by the more general idea of *translatio imperii* regarding America's role in world history. Bishop George Berkeley believed that in America,

> There shall be sung another golden age,
> The rise of empire and of arts . . .
> Westward the course of empire take its way;
> The four first last acts already past,
> The fifth shall close the drama with the day;
> Time's noblest offspring is the last.[77]

[73] Christopher Columbus cited by Pauline Moffitt Watts, "Prophecy and Discovery: On the Spiritual Origins of Christopher Columbus's 'Enterprise of the Indies,'" *American Historical Review* 90 (1985), 73.

[74] George Herbert, "The Church Militant," c. 1610s, in *The Poetical Works of George Herbert*, ed. A. B. Grosart (London, 1876), pp. 242, 249.

[75] Jonathan Edwards, *Thoughts on the Revival of Religion in New England*, cited by Yehoshua Arieli, *Individualism and Nationalism in American Ideology* (Baltimore, 1966), p. 41.

[76] Thomas Paine, *Common Sense* (1776), in *Common Sense and Other Political Writings*, ed. Nelson F. Adkins (Indianapolis, 1953), p. 23.

[77] George Berkeley, "America, or the Muse's Refuge" (1726), cited by Arieli, *Individualism and Nationalism*, p. 42, and Lowenthal, *The Past is a Foreign Country*, p. 110.

Americans themselves, of course, adopted these glorious views concerning their country. For example, according to Nathaniel Ames,

The Curious have observ'd, that the Progress of Human Literature (like the sun) is from the East to the West; thus it has travelled thro' Asia and Europe, and now is arrived at the Eastern Shore of *America*.[78]

And, finally, Hector St. John De Crevecoeur firmly believed that it was America's destiny, according to the idea of *translatio imperii*, to fulfill all human hopes and expectations:

Americans are the western pilgrims, who are carrying along with them that great mass of arts, sciences, vigour, and industry which began long since in the east; they will finish the great circle.[79]

Previously we saw how prophetic imagination was used by Protestant historiography to interpret the signs of sacred time and the path of providential history. Now, with the concept of religious migration as a prophetic, revelatory event in ecclesiastical history, and its important articulation in the idea of *translatio religionis* as the grand migratory progress of the Gospel from East to West, we can easily see how prophetic imagination explains the course of sacred history through geographical direction as well, or how geography helps in further understanding the mystery of the history of salvation. For viewing the grand geographical westward transfer of the church within the apocalyptic and eschatological context of religious migration as a prophetic revelatory event, it is evident that geographical discoveries are essential parts of the unfolding providential drama in which God's "Divine Providence hath Irradiated,"[80] to use Cotton Mather's words, certain terrestrial places and singled them out as sacred sites for the fulfillment of prophetic revelation. Hence, Jerusalem, Rome, France, Spain, Germany, and England held, at different times, prominent roles in the great circular movement of the Gospel from East to West. Geography, then, became an essential dimension of providential history. Now in the Age of Discovery, after God lifted the providential curtain over America, it was the New World's turn to play a singular role in the history of salvation. Consequently, as we are about to see, many Europeans, who interpreted the discovery of the New World in apocalyptic and eschatological terms, saw the settlement of America as a prophetic, revelatory and migratory event.

---

[78] Nathaniel Ames, *Astronomical Diary* (1758), cited by Wright, "Notes on Early American Geopiety," p. 275.

[79] Hector St. John De Crevecoeur, *Letters from an American Farmer* (London, 1945 [1782]), pp. 43–4.

[80] Cotton Mather, *Magnalia Christi Americana; or, the Ecclesiastical History of New England* (London, 1702), "A General Introduction," in *The Puritans: A Source Book of Their Writings*, ed. Perry Miller and Thomas H. Johnson, 2 vols. (New York, 1963), vol. I, p. 163.

To the European mind, the discovery of America was inextricably connected with apocalyptic visions and eschatological expectations. It was the last
act of providential history with "the long day of mankinde drawing fast
towards an euening, and the worlds Tragedie and time neare at an end."[81]

THE APOCALYPSE OF THE AGE OF DISCOVERY

The Apocalypse of the Age of Discovery refers to the discovery of
the Apocalypse of the New World. For as prophetic imagination led to the
discovery of sacred time and history, so it led to the discovery of the
apocalyptic significance and meaning of America or, in sum, to the
incorporation of the New World within the confines of sacred, providential
history. Centuries of interpreting history in terms of sacred, ecclesiastical
history conditioned Europeans to view the discovery of the New World in
terms of the prevailing providential scheme and ideology of history, that is,
according to Christian historiography. During the Age of Discovery,
explorers "viewed the events of geographical exploration and colonization
as the fulfillment of the prophecies of the apocalypse." And it is indeed in
this sense that we may rightly speak of "the apocalypse of the Age of
Discovery."[82] In other words, the spiritual imaginative conquest of the New
World was fundamentally defined by the incorporation of America within
the confines of sacred, ecclesiastical history which, through geographical
discoveries and expansion, in turn transformed the assumptions of
ecclesiastical history.

Christopher Columbus, who established the first link between the Old
and the New World, found "a false Asia in the West," and "persisted in that
belief until his death."[83] His misconceptions derived from the geographical
lore then current, namely that nothing stood between Europe and Asia
except the vast ocean. Moreover, his misconceptions clearly reveal how the
process of exploration and discovery were conditioned by imagination.
According to John K. Wright:

Explorers have seldom gone forth merely to probe about for whatever they may
happen to discover. They have gone in quest of definite objectives believed to exist
on the basis of such information as could be gathered from the geographical lore of
their own and earlier times.[84]

[81] Sir Walter Raleigh, *The History of the World* (1614), ed. C. A. Patrides (London, 1971),
p. 154.
[82] John Leddy Phelan, *The Millennial Kingdom of the Franciscans in the New World*
(Berkeley, 1970), p. 17.
[83] J. H. Parry, *The Discovery of the Sea* (Berkeley, 1981), p. 184. See also another important
book by J. H. Parry, *The Age of Reconnaissance: Discovery, Exploration and Settlement
1450 to 1650* (Berkeley, 1981).
[84] John K. Wright, "Where History and Geography Meet: Recent American Studies in the
History of Exploration," in *Human Nature in Geography*, p. 27.

And as John L. Allen wrote, the "use of the term 'discovery' to describe the major event of exploratory venture suggests pre-awareness of something to be discovered."[85] With Columbus, the essential dimension of his geographical lore was indeed the apocalyptic interpretation of history. For as he claimed in reference to the meaning and significance of his "discoveries":

God made me the messenger of the new heaven and the new earth of which he spoke in the Apocalypse of St. John after having spoken of it through the mouth of Isaiah; and he showed me the spot where to find it.[86]

It is crucially important that the first explorer of the New World emphasized the intrinsic link between prophecy and discovery and tended to view the meaning of his geographical discovery in terms of the realization of prophetic revelations. In his mind, Apocalypse and "discovery" were inseparable, and this is because, for him, the word "Revelation" seems to denote "discovery" and vice versa. Consequently, if the Apocalypse unveils the course of time and history through prophetic imagination, the same can be said regarding space in which the Apocalypse reveals the meaning of geographical discoveries in the context of the providential drama of salvation. Columbus, therefore, inaugurated the important process by which the New World was incorporated into the confines of sacred, ecclesiastial history. And because prophecy and "discovery" were but one and the same thing, the Apocalypse shifted to the other side of the Atlantic Ocean with the first act of the discovery of the New World. More than a century later, in the early seventeenth century, Samuel Purchas, the great English compiler of British geographical exploration, compared the English discoveries in the New World to "Solomon's Discoveries," which by God's "Revelation" were aimed "to prepare us for that holy Jerusalem, descending out of Heaven from God, having the Glory of god." Because "Solomon seemes to signifie Christ, his Navy the Church," and because "the Heavenly Solomon" was destined "to the building of that Temple in the new Jerusalem" through the discovery of "Ophir," Purchas argued that in "this History" of English discoveries "will appear also a Mystery and Type of Eternitie." For in the providential context of prophecy and discovery,

Every Christian man is a ship, a weak vessell, in this Navie of Solomon, dwelling in a mortall body, is within less than foure inches, then one inch of death.[87]

The story of the "Admiral of the Ocean Sea," and his long struggle to obtain royal support from the Aragonese court of Queen Isabella for his

---

[85] Allen, "Lands of Myth, Waters of Wonder," in *Geographies of the Mind*, p. 43.

[86] Columbus, cited by Pauline Moffitt Watts, "Prophecy and Discovery: On the Spiritual Origins of Christopher Columbus's 'Enterprise of the Indies,'" *American Historical Review* 90 (1985), 73.

[87] Samuel Purchas, *Hakluytus Posthumus, or Purchas His Pilgrimes* (1625), 20 vols. (Glasgow, 1905), vol. I, pp. 4–14.

"Enterprise of the Indies," which he eventually received after almost seven years in 1492, is well known.[88] Yet, an examination of Columbus' spiritual life illuminates the essential connections between his discoveries and the apocalyptic and prophetic significance he ascribed to them. He believed that "he was predestined to fulfill a number of prophecies in preparation for the coming of Antichrist and the end of the world." Deep in his soul, he felt that he was "Christ-bearer," and this conviction shaped the role he sought to play in sacred, providential history: "Columbus's apocalyptic vision of the world and of the special role that he was destined to play in the unfolding of events that would presage the end of time was a major stimulus for his voyages." His apocalyptic view of history, in other words, was inextricably interwoven within the geographical and cosmological lore of his time, so that "his apocalypticism must be recognized as inseparable from his geography and cosmology."[89] No wonder, therefore, that Columbus' "discoveries" were wholly apocalyptic in their character and that he claimed to have found, in his own words, "the location of the terrestrial paradise, as approved by the Holy Church."[90]

Columbus was also very familiar with contemporary works on geography, astronomy, history, and cosmology, especially Pierre d'Ailly's *Imago Mundi* (1410). Moreover, he had been engaged for a long time in writing a work which remained uncompleted called *Book of Prophecies* (*c.* 1510), in which he "intended to set forth" the course and progress of divine "eschatology and to explain his role in it." In eschatological terms, as revealed in the *Book of Prophecies*, Columbus had "a virtual obsession with the recovery of Mount Zion, the symbol of the Holy Land," and he was much occupied with the issue of "the conquering and conversion of the heathen." Thus, the "Enterprise of the Indies," according to Columbus, symbolized the whole course of providential history:

In this voyage to the Indies Our Lord wished to perform a very evident miracle in order to console me and the others in the matter of this other voyage to the Holy Sepulchre.[91]

In Columbus's apocalyptic framework, therefore, prophecy and discovery went hand in hand; as sacred history is unveiled through the realization of prophetic revelations, so the pilgrimage towards the Holy Land is realized through the revelation, or discovery, of a new terrestrial space. And as geographical discoveries revealed the course of providential history, so the fulfillment of prophetic revelations gave meaning and significance to newly

[88] Samuel Eliot Morison, *Admiral of the Ocean Sea: A Life of Christopher Columbus*, 2 vols. (Boston, 1942).
[89] Watts, "Prophecy and History," p. 74.
[90] Columbus cited by Watts, "Prophecy and Discovery," p. 83.
[91] Watts, "Prophecy and Discovery," pp. 92, 85, 92, 96.

discovered places. In this context, indeed, Columbus' apocalyptic interpretation of his "discoveries" is a fitting example of "geoteleology" or of "geoeschatology."

Columbus's geographical lore was greatly influenced by the apocalyptic mode of historical thought which led him to believe that he was living in the final stage of providential history or in an age in which "the world was rapidly approaching its end." Following d'Ailly's calculation of the duration of the world, which was based upon Augustine's seven-age theory of periodizing history, Columbus estimated that "there are lacking about one hundred and fifty-five years for the completion of the seven thousand at which time the world will come to an end."[92] In eschatological terms, before the end of the world, all divine prophetic revelations would be fulfilled within time and history with the transformation of the world from alienation to reconciliation with God. It was within this apocalyptic eschatological context that Columbus interpreted his explorations and discoveries. "The Admiral of the Ocean Sea was dazzled by the vision that Christianity," which always claimed to be universal, could "become geographically worldwide" through his discoveries. Viewing himself as "the instrument of Divine Providence," Columbus was deeply convinced that the Holy Ghost had sent him to open "the door of the Western sea" in order to fulfill the apocalyptical prophecy of the spread of the Gospel to all corners of the world which was to take place before the end of time and history.[93] In his mind, then, geographical "discovery" was inextricably interwoven with prophetic revelation in regard to the progress of the history of salvation.

So far as he was concerned, Columbus had reached Asia and not America. Therefore, he was deeply convinced that he had found "the terrestrial paradise," the earthly paradise mentioned in Scriptures: "And the Lord God planted a garden *eastward in Eden* and there he set the man he had formed" (Gen. 2:8). Again, the importance of this "discovery" should be seen within the eschatological context. With the approach of the end of time and history, prophetic revelations were being fulfilled including the spread of the Gospel throughout the world whose boundaries Columbus' discovery had definitely established. This was why, in part, Columbus insisted that "the world is but small." "I have treated . . . the location of the terrestrial paradise, as approved by the Holy Church," he wrote, and therefore he boldly concluded that "the world is not so large as vulgar opinion makes it."[94] The finding of "terrestrial paradise" thus brought to an end the whole prophetic and revelatory course of *translatio religionis*, or the church's pilgrimage upon earth. The return of the church to its place of origin

92 *Ibid.*, pp. 96.
93 Phelan, *The Millennial Kingdom*, pp. 20–1.
94 Watts, "Prophecy and Discovery," pp. 83, 77.

signified the fulfillment of the apocalyptic prophecy concerning the spread of the Gospel throughout the world before the end of time and history. Geographical discovery, then, unveiled the signs of time and history and thereby revealed the eschatological moment of sacred, providential history.

Ultimately, Columbus' apocalyptic view of history determined the significance he assigned to his geographical discoveries. "He was looking back through fifteen hundred years of Christianity, [and] it seemed to him that his discoveries represented the grandiose climax of Christian history." Yet, Columbus knew well that his own discovery of "the terrestrial paradise" comprised only one part of the apocalyptic drama of sacred history which was approaching its eschatological end. Columbus considered "the discovery of the Indies, the conversion of all Gentiles, and the deliverance of the Holy Sepulcher," or the liberation of the Holy Land, "to be the three climactic events which foreshadow the end of the world."[95] The fulfillment of these great prophetic and revelatory events, Columbus was convinced, would transform the world into the Kingdom of God:

the universal ends of the earth will remember God and be converted to him and the people of the earth will adore his fatherly aspect since God is king and rules over the people.[96]

Thus, with ideas as well as deeds, through his geographical and spiritual explorations in both time and space, Christopher Columbus began the essential process of incorporating the New World into the confines of sacred, providential history. He inaugurated the process of the spiritual conquest of the New World which is so crucial to understanding the settlement and colonization of America.

Columbus was the first, but by no means the last, "to interpret the discovery of the New World apocalyptically." With the creation of the Spanish and later the Portuguese colonial empires in America, a host of theologians and historians "viewed the events of geographical exploration and colonization as the fulfillment of the prophecies of the apocalypse." Their writings contributed enormously, therefore, to the transformation of the New World from *Terra Incognita* into *Terra Cognita*. Their problem, obviously, was that of justifying the conquest of America, a land never occupied by Christian rulers and inhabited by peoples who had never heard the saving words of the Gospel. The outcome was that "no colonial empire in modern times was built upon so extensive a philosophical and theological foundation as the empire that the Spaniards created for themselves in the New World."[97] The spiritual, imaginative conquest of the New World,

---

[95] Phelan, *The Millennial Kingdom*, pp. 22–3.
[96] Watts, "Prophecy and Discovery," p. 94.
[97] Phelan, *The Millennial Kingdom*, pp. 17, 5; Parry, *The Age of Reconnaissance*, ch. 19, "The Rights of Conquerors and Conquered," pp. 303–19.

therefore, was no less important than the astonishing military conquest of the Conquistadors. And so, as the European geographical horizon expanded during the Age of Discovery, the scope of Christ's Gospel of salvation widened with the incorporation of the peoples of America within the mystery of the history of salvation. In this context, the Apocalypse of the Age of Discovery became the geography of the Apocalypse in the New World.

From the very beginning of the discovery of the New World, spiritual religious considerations played an important role in the conquest of America. The right of the Spanish crown to rule over America was based upon Pope Alexander VI's two *Inter cetera* bulls of May 3 and 4, 1493, which had not only granted Spain the newly discovered lands and islands in the New World, but had also imposed spiritual obligations to convert the Indians to the Christian faith. During the fifteenth century, and within the prevalent belief in a theocratic universe ruled immediately by divine providence, "the pope's universal jurisdiction *in spiritualibus* and his limited, indirect jurisdiction *in temporalibus*," had been widely acknowledged in Christian Europe. As yet, several years before the Protestant Reformation, no one had openly refuted the pope's spiritual jurisdiction upon earth. The Alexandrian bulls of 1493, therefore, supplied the Spanish right to conquer the New World, in both spiritual and military terms. In these bulls, the pope had expressed thus what he desired from Ferdinand and Isabella: "Hence, all things considered and especially the exaltation and expansion of the Catholic faith, you are to subject these lands and islands and their inhabitants, and with the help of God's mercy, bring them to the Catholic faith." Further, declared the pope, by "the authority of the Almighty God granted to us through St. Peter and of Christ's Vicarship which we exercise on earth," he had granted to Ferdinand and Isabella "all lands and islands discovered or still to be discovered" in the New World. It should be noted that, for Ferdinand and Isabella "the Alexandrian bulls had only subsidiary value in claims to dominion over the new lands," because it was widely accepted at the time that the POPE's jurisdiction *in temporalibus* was limited and indirect. But *in spiritualibus* these bulls had "essential value in whatever concerned the evangelization of the Indians." The Alexandrian donation of the New World to Spain, therefore "imposed spiritual obligations regarding the evangelization" of the inhabitants of America.[98]

There cannot be any doubt concerning the genuinely religious intentions

---

[98] Miguel Batllori, S.J., "The Papal Division of the World and Its Consequences," in *The First Images of America: The Impact of the New World on the Old*, ed. Fredi Chiappelli, 2 vols. (Berkeley, 1976), vol. I, pp. 214–18. See also Luis Weckmann-Munoz, "The Alexandrian Bulls of 1493: Pseudo-Asiatic Documents," in *The First Images of America*, vol. I, pp. 201–9.

of Spain in the New World. The Spanish crown "regarded the conversion of the Indians as establishing the 'justness' of Spanish rule" in America. The spiritual conquest became indeed an integral part of the colonial empire that Spain built in America. According to one estimation, "some six million Indians were baptized by 1540." Dominican and Franciscan missionaries worked hand in hand with Conquistadors to discover America and to reveal to the Indians the mystery of the history of salvation. The discovery of the New World thus opened up the confines of sacred, ecclesiastical history with the inclusion of millions of Indians upon the stage of providential history. This was especially true in regard to the gradual awareness among Europeans that America was a distinct continent separated from both Asia and Europe. This new view of America inevitably brought to the fore the issue of the Indians as the descendants of the ten lost tribes of Israel, whose conversion to the Gospel was considered in apocalyptic thought to be a sure eschatological sign in providential history, as could clearly be seen among Franciscan and Dominican missionaries during the sixteenth century and among Puritans in England and New England in the seventeenth century.[99]

Columbus indeed had found a false Asia in the West, and it was only some decades later that "the notion of America's existence came gradually" into the European mind.[100] The notion of America as a distinct continent separated from Asia had its origins with Amerigo Vespucci's voyages to the New World in 1499 and 1501. "The main, the certain result of Vespucci's two voyages was the knowledge that a great continent existed" in the West, the same land Columbus and other explorers believed to be part of Asia. This new geographical knowledge was made available to the public in a popular work, *Mondus Novus* of 1504–5, and thus the idea that "a new continent had been found and that Amerigo Vespucci had discovered it" became "general in the mind of the reading public" in Europe.[101] No wonder, then, that because Amerigo Vespucci "was the 'discoverer' of the new continent *qua* continent: it is just that it should bear his name."[102] This new geographical "discovery" concerning America, which gradually became part of the geographical lore of the sixteenth century, had a considerable influence on the Apocalypse in the New World.

---

[99] Lewis Hanke, "The Theological Significance of the Discovery of America," in *The First Images of America*, vol. I, p. 367; Phelan, *The Millennial Kingdom*, p. 26.

[100] Weckmann-Munoz, "The Alexandrian Bulls," p. 203.

[101] Parry, *The Discovery of the Sea*, pp. 218–19.

[102] Weckmann-Munoz, "The Alexandrian Bulls," p. 207. See also, David Beers Quinn, "New Geographical Horizons: Literature," in *The First Images of America*, vol. II, pp. 635–58; Hildegard Binder Johnson, "New Geographical Horizons: Concepts," in *The First Images of America*, vol. II, pp. 615–33; Luis Weckmann, "The Middle Ages in the Conquest of America," *Speculum* 26 (1951), 130–41; and Lynn White, Jr., "Christian Myth and Christian History," *Journal of the History of Ideas* 3 (1941), 145–58.

Columbus believed in a small world, a tripartite world consisting of Asia, Europe, and Africa, and he therefore thought that he could reach Asia by a relatively short sea voyage from Europe. In geographical terms, this was the ultimate mission of his "enterprise of the Indies." Consequently, the New World for him was merely a geographical extension of the Old World. Accordingly, the Indians described in the Alexandrian bulls of 1493 were in fact another group of Orientals. Now, in contrast to Columbus' tripartite world, Vespucci's revolutionary view of a quadripartite world established America as a new and unique terrestrial space, a distinct New World inhabited by a distinctive human group, the Amerindians. This new geographical – and indeed anthropological – discovery altered in a revolutionary way the Apocalypse of the Age of Discovery. Thus, for example, the Catholic Serafino da Fermo wrote, in the middle of the sixteenth century, that although the Protestant Reformation had brought many tribulations upon the Church, God's divine providence was still working within time and history "in the discovery of new worlds and especially of America." Accordingly, with the picture of a quadripartite earth, "it was necessary for God's Word to go forth into the four corners of the earth and now the fourth has been discovered."[103]

The Apocalypse of the New World was intrinsically connected with the Apocalypse of the Old World. Previously we have seen how Columbus' apocalyptic interpretation of his discoveries was closely associated with his notion of Spain as an elect nation in providential history. This contention is also true in regard to the prophetic and apocalyptic imagination of the New World on the part of the Spanish missionaries and visionaries. For Geronimo de Mendieta, the Franciscan missionary in Mexico, "the kings of Spain" were "the greatest princes of the New Testament," resembling for example Constantine the Great or Charlemagne. Accordingly, Mendieta claimed that Philip II (1527–98), "is the Promised one, the Messiah – World Ruler who is destined to convert all mankind on the eve of the Last Judgment." Assigning a singular role to Spain in providential history, obviously, provided Mendieta with the context within which to interpret the sacred significance of the Spanish colonial empire in America:

Who knows whether we are not so close to the end of the world that the conversion of the Indians is fulfilling the prophecies for which we pray that the Jews may be converted in our time. Because if the Indians descend from the Jews, then the prophecy is already fulfilled.

Hence it follows that Hernan Cortes was called by divine providence to lead the enslaved Indians out of Egyptian bondage of the Aztec into the Promised

---

[103] Serafino da Fermo, cited by Marjorie Reeves, *Joachim of Fiore and the Prophetic Future* (New York, 1977), p. 126, and by the same author, *The Influence of Prophecy in the Later Middle Ages: A Study in Joachimism* (Oxford, 1969), pp. 469–70.

Land of the Gospel. "Cortes was the new Moses whose conquest [of Mexico] liberated the natives from the slavery of Egypt and led them to the Promised Land of the Church."[104]

Franciscans and Dominicans interpreted the inner meaning of the New World history in apocalyptic terms, and thus incorporated America into the providential scheme of sacred, ecclesiastical history. Indeed, in an eschatological context, divine providence "shall not cease until the number of the predestined is reached, which according to the vision of St. John" in the Revelation, "must include all nations, all languages and all peoples."[105] The apocalyptic interpretation of the New World was also most prominent among the Jesuits in Portugal and Brazil, where we can see once again how the Apocalypse of the Old World ultimately determined the Apocalypse of the New World. "The remarkable global expansion of Portugal lent itself to messianic and apocalyptic interpretations" which emphasized that "the small Portuguese nation" is "the Chosen Race of the New Testament whom divine Providence has chosen as the instrument to spread the True Faith across the whole globe," or that "Portugal would be the Fifth Monarchy prophesied by Daniel." Consequently, because of their divine election in providential history, the Portuguese would wash their swords

in the blood of heretics in Europe and the blood of the Muslims in Africa, the blood of the heathen in Asia and America, conquering and subjugating all the regions of the earth under the aegis of one crown and gloriously be placed beneath the feet of St. Peter.[106]

The colonization of the New World was based to a large extent upon the apocalyptic interpretation of history. Both Spain and Portugal justified their conquest and settlement of America on the premises of sacred, ecclesiastical history in which the church was considered to be the central agency in history. Discovery and conquest of the New World, therefore were defined in the larger apocalyptic context of the great prophetic migratory course of the church upon the earth, or of the advance and spread of the Gospel in the world, in which the preaching of the Gospel in all the corners of the world, along with the conversion of the Indians, were considered certain signs of the imminent end of the world. With the Age of Discovery, then, the New World was increasingly incorporated into the confines of sacred, ecclesiastical history, acquiring a prominent role in providential history as a new stage upon which prophetic revelations would be realized. Furthermore, because Spain and Portugal each claimed to be God's chosen nation, each viewed its colonial activities in providential context, and looked upon the New World

---

[104] Phelan, *The Millennial Kingdom*, pp. 12, 26, 103, 122–5.
[105] *Ibid.*, p. 12.
[106] *Ibid.*, pp. 119–21; Reeves, *Joachim of Fiore and the Prophetic Future*, pp. 132–5.

as the place within which to fulfill its divine election in sacred history. In terms of the sacred patterns exhibited in ecclesiastical history, this type of religious migration, and hence of colonization, is what we tend to define as the *Genesis* type; namely, God's chosen nation which was elected to accomplish a singular, divine mission in the unfolding drama of salvation. Yet, as we are about to see, English Protestants also defined and justified the settlement of Virginia in the early seventeenth century as a *Genesis* type of religious migration, founded upon the vision of England as God's elect nation with a singular role to play in providential history by the colonization of the New World and the preaching of the Gospel of salvation to the Indians.

3

The creation of sacred space II

The eschatology of the Protestant settlement of Virginia

ESCHATOLOGY AND APOCALYPSE IN THE ENGLISH SETTLEMENT OF THE NEW WORLD

Spain and Portugal had laid the foundation for the incorporation of America as a sacred place within the confines of providential, ecclesiastical history. Theirs, however, was the Catholic apocalyptic interpretation of history which saw Luther "as the real Antichrist," and the Protestant Reformation as the eschatological "great time of troubles" before the end of the world. Accordingly, in view of the apocalyptic and eschatological events taking place in Europe with the great schism which the Protestant Reformation brought in the Christian Old World, the New World increasingly acquired a prominent role in the providential history of salvation. For some Catholics "the Church's losses in the old were being compensated by her gains on the other side of the Atlantic," and with the great harvest of the Indian souls' conversion to the Catholic faith it seemed that "the New World was restoring the religious balance of power which the Old World had been unable to maintain."[1] The great prophetic migratory transfer of the Gospel to America was seen, therefore, not only in the eschatological context of the Indians' conversion to Christianity and the spread of the Gospel to all the corners of the world, but also in the context of the apocalyptic struggle in the Old World between Christ and Antichrist, or the Church of Rome's struggle against the great tribulations Satan brought to the church with the Protestant Reformation. The religious upheavals of the sixteenth century had an immediate impact upon the apocalyptic interpretation of the New World.

When Englishmen, however, began to ponder the idea of settling

---

[1] John Leddy Phelan, *The Millennial Kingdom of the Franciscans in the New World* (Berkeley, 1970), pp. 24, 32.

94

America, they developed a radically different apocalyptic and eschatological interpretation of the New World, one based ultimately upon the premises of Protestant historiography, or upon the premises of the apocalyptic tradition in England, as described in the first chapter. According to this tradition, the mark of time and history is the essential struggle between Christ and the true apostolic church against the pope as Antichrist and the false Christ. During the sixteenth century, the symbol of this apocalyptic struggle was the battle between the forces of Reformation and Counter-Reformation. When England began to settle America, however, it was almost a century after Columbus had discovered the New World and many decades after Spain and Portugal had imposed the Catholic faith on the Indians. It was only natural, then, that with the beginning of the English settlement of America, the religious wars of the truth would be transferred into the New World, and that Englishmen would see their colonization efforts as part of the rivalry between the Protestant and the Catholic faith. Yet, because this rivalry involved an essential ideological conflict between them concerning the apocalyptic interpretation of history, the English settlement of America necessarily gave new meaning and significance to the New World as a sacred space within the confines of sacred, ecclesiastical history. Now, according to the Protestant vision, America too became the stage upon which the whole apocalyptic struggle between Christ and Antichrist, or between the forces of reformation and counter-reformation, took place. Consequently, with the English colonization of America, exactly as was the case with Catholic Spain and Portugal, the Apocalypse of the New World was inseparable from the Apocalypse of the Old World.

RICHARD HAKLUYT AND THE QUEST FOR ENGLISH COLONIZATION OF AMERICA

Despite the overwhelming differences among them, however, English Protestants and Spanish and Portuguese Catholics all shared an important conviction regarding the European settlement of America; namely, all of them defined the colonization of the New World as following the sacred pattern of the *Genesis* type of religious migration. The glorious mission of God's chosen nation was to fulfill its divine election by advancing the cause of the true church and by spreading the true faith in both the Old and the New World. The *Genesis* type of religious migration, based upon God's promise to Abraham, thus entailed a sense of uniqueness bestowed upon a sacred center, or elect nation, whose role is to fulfill prophetic revelations, and, eventually, transform the world into the Kingdom of God. No wonder, then, that Spain, Portugal, and England, each claiming to be God's chosen nation, tended to justify its colonization of America by the *Genesis* type of religious migration. This can be clearly seen in Richard Hakluyt's *Discourse on Western Planting* (1584), one of the earliest attempts in a long series of Protestant writings to arouse the spirit of Englishmen to settle America, in which the colonization of the New World was depicted as a consequence of England's unique role as God's chosen nation.

Hakluyt had no doubt concerning the meaning of the discovery of America in sacred, providential history, and the role England ought to play in the New World: "this westerne discoverie" of America "will be greately for thinlargemente of the gospell of Christe, whereunto the princes of the refourmed relligion are chefely bounde, amongest whom her Majestie" Queen Elizabeth "ys principall." The arguments that Spain had already been given jurisdiction over the New World by the Alexandrian bulls were totally rejected by Hakluyt, who claimed that "the Bull of the Donation of all the West Indies graunted to the Kinges of Spaine by Pope Alexander the VIth" was in fact "falsly geven oute by the popishe clergye and others his fautors, to terrifie the princes of" the Protestant "relligion and to abuse and blynde them."[2] So, by refuting the Spanish and Catholics' claim over America, Hakluyt invoked the notion of England's right and duty, deriving from its singular place in providential history as God's elect nation, to settle America and to preach the Gospel of salvation to the Indians.

In the context of the history of salvation, the discovery of the New World shows unmistakably that "the people of America" from Florida to the north "are idolaters" and "worshipped the sonne, the moone, and the starres." Yet, they are "very desirous to become Christians." Therefore, Hakluyt argued, it should be seriously considered "by what meanes and by whom this most godly and Christian work may be perfourmed of inlarginge the glorious gospell of Christe, and reducinge of infinite multitudes of these simple people that are in errour into the righte and perfecte way of their salvation." The very fact that the northern part of America, according to Hakluyt, "is yet in no Christian princes actuall possession" now obligates England to engage herself in this so glorious and divine duty. For this sacred task should be undertaken by those who "have taken upon them the protection and defence of the Christian faithe. Nowe the Kinges and Queenes of England have the name of Defendours of the Faithe," the title which was given to Henry VIII by Pope Leo X in 1521 after the former had written a tract against Martin Luther. It is this title, continues Hakluyt, which now obligates the kings and queens of England not only "to mayneteyne and patronize the faithe of Christe, but also to inlarge and advaunce the same"

---

[2] Richard Hakluyt, *Discourse on Western Planting* (1584), in *Documentary History of the State of Maine*, 2 vols., Maine Historical Society Collections (Cambridge, Mass., 1877), vol. II, pp. 3–7.

in the world. "Neither oughte this" divine mission in providential history "to be their laste work, but rather the principall and chefe of all others." Accordingly, England ought to plant "one or two colonies of our nation" in America, and thus "with discretion and myldenes distill into" the Indians' "purged myndes the swete and lively liquor of the gospel."[3]

As to the question "what may wee hope . . . in our true and syncere relligion" to gain out of the preaching of the Gospel to the Indians, Hakluyt argued that the main goal of this divine mission is

the gayninge of the soules of millions of those wretched people, the reducinge of them from darkenes to lighte, from falsehoodde to truthe, from dombe idolls to the lyvinge God, from the depe pitt of hell to the highest heavens.

Furthermore, this divine task is most pressing now because "the people of america crye unto us . . . to come and help them, and bringe unto them the gladd tidinges of the Gospell." And it is all the more urgent "because the papists confirme themselves and drawe" the Indians to their faith, "shewinge that they are the true Catholicke because they have bene the onely converters of many millions of infidells to Christianitie." Seeing now that the New World, as well, had become the stage upon which the struggle between the forces of Reformation and Counter-Reformation was taking place, Hakluyt had argued that "the princes" of the Protestant "relligion (amonge whome her Majestie ys principall) ought the rather to take in hand" this "godly action" of the spreading of the Gospel into the New World. Hakluyt was very confident indeed that "the time ys at hand when her Majestie" would assume on herself this divine mission in regard of "Godds harvest among the infidells" of America.[4]

Due to its prominent role in providential history, it is "from England" that "sincere relligion" would be planted in America, in contrast to the false Catholic conversion of the Indians in the New World. Yet, in the wider context of the religious wars in Europe, the English settlement of America, according to Hakluyt, would "provide a safe and a sure place to receave people from all partes of the worlde that are forced to flee for the truthe of Gods worde." The notion of America as a place of refuge and as a shelter from religious persecutions in Europe is established here for the first time in the English-speaking world. It closely associated in Hakluyt's mind with the notion of English colonization of America as a means to free the Indians from all the "pride and tyranie" with which "the Spaniardes governe" them. "Tied as slaves" under the Spanish rule, the Indians "all yell and crye with one voice, *Liberta, Liberta*, as desirous of libertie and freedome" which only "the Queene of England" can provide them. Consequently, once Elizabeth

---

[3] *Ibid.*, pp. 7–9.   [4] *Ibid.*, pp. 10–12.

will establish her domain in the New World and rule "the natural people there with all humanitie, curtesie, and freedom, they will yelde themselves to her government, and revolte cleane from the Spaniarde."[5]

Richard Hakluyt's *Discourse on Western Planting* is one of the earliest attempts in which Englishmen began the essential process of incorporating the New World as a sacred space within the confines of ecclesiastical history. Seen in the larger context of the unfolding providential history of salvation, the colonization of America signifies the transfer of the true Protestant faith to America and the introduction of the Indians to the saving grace of God's word. Yet, given the fact that Spain and the Catholic faith had already established themselves in the New World, the very act of English colonization indeed demonstrated that America had now become another stage upon which the apocalyptic drama between the true and the false church was playing itself out.

Closely associated with the prominent role he assigned to England in sacred history was Hakluyt's sense of England's divine election in providential history. Hakluyt's vision of England as an elect nation was based upon reading "Bale" and "Foxe," who had developed this concept to its highest in Protestant England. Writing shortly after the destruction of the Spanish Armada, Hakluyt boasted in the *Principal Navigations*, 1598:

I thinke that never was any nation blessed of Johavah, with a more glorious and wonderfull victory upon the Seas, then our vanquishing of the dreadfull Spanish Armada, 1588.

By this victory, God had "made fearfull spectacles and examples of his judgements unto all Christendom." Obviously, this sense of national election in providential history was not limited in Hakluyt's mind only to the victory over Spain. Identifying Elizabeth with King Solomon – "the person of our Salomon her gratious Majesty" – Hakluyt believed that England was indeed the New Israel, God's chosen nation.[6] Obviously, as compared with Spain and Portugal, Hakluyt developed a very different apocalyptic interpretation of America, in which the Protestant faith, carried to America by a chosen Protestant nation, would conquer the New World for Protestantism.

Hakluyt's *Discourse on Western Planting* was written in order to precure royal support for the English colonization of America. Yet it was more than two decades before England was able to establish a permanent colony in Virginia in 1607. With this, England's first successful colony in the New World, a major transformation took place in Protestant England concerning the role of America in sacred, providential history. That the Virginia colony

[5] *Ibid.*, pp. 158–9.
[6] Richard Hakluyt, *The Principal Navigations, Voyages & Traffiques & Discoveries of the English Nation* (1589), in *Hakluyt's Voyages*, edited, with introduction, by John Masefield, 8 vols., (London, 1907), vol. I, pp. 7, 37, 35.

was primarily an economic enterprise is well known. What is not so well known, however, is that from its very beginning Virginia inspired apocalyptic visions and eschatological expectations in Protestant England. Having become accustomed to viewing England as an elect nation, now, with the settlement of Virginia, Protestants had to address themselves to the question of the relationship between the elect nation and its overseas enterprise. For this reason, a host of Protestant preachers and laymen took upon themselves the task of defining the appropriate relationship between the center in England and its periphery in Virginia. Yet, while attempting to arouse the spirit of Englishmen toward the young colony in America, they developed, as well, a unique interpretation of English colonization which was based essentially upon the premises of sacred, ecclesiastical history as a mode of historical thought. More specifically, these Protestants' advocacy of the settlement of Virginia defined England's warrant to colonize America upon the *Genesis* type of religious migration, or upon God's divine warrant to a sacred, elect nation, to spread and conquer lands appointed by the Lord to His chosen people. This type of Protestant religious imperialism, the obvious outcome of the *Genesis* type of religious migration, is the most charcteristic feature of the Protestants' justification of the settlement of Virginia.

Before turning to a detailed discussion of the Protestant vision of the settlement of Virginia, it is important to note that the incorporation of America as a sacred space within the confines of providential history is always, according to the *Genesis* type of religious migration, dependent and contingent. This is so because the *Genesis*-type migration necessarily entailed the concept of a sacred center in providential history, such as an elect nation or a Promised Land, which could serve as the nucleus for the realization of prophetic revelations. Therefore, as was also the case with regard to Spain and Portugal's apocalyptic interpretation of the New World, for English Protestants America acquired the title of sacred place in the history of salvation only so far as it was connected with the sacred center of England as the elect nation. America, in other words, had no independent, autonomous, sacred meaning of its own in ecclesiastical history, but only by virtue of its relationship with the sacred center in England. As we will see, in clear contrast to the Protestant incorporation of America as a sacred space which was ultimately dependent upon its relationship to the sacred center of England, the Puritans who emigrated to New England had incorporated America as a sacred space within the confines of ecclesiastical history in a radically different – even revolutionary – way. The Puritan migration, which was based upon the *Exodus* type of religious migration, had rather established America as an independent and autonomous sacred place in providential history, which necessarily and indeed intentionally entailed the severing of ties with England which the Puritans no longer considered a sacred center. The *Genesis* and the *Exodus* types of religious migration, as two different means with which Englishmen interpreted and explained the colonization of the New World, had led, eventually, to two totally different modes of incorporating America as a sacred place within the confines of providential, ecclesiastical history.

THE ESCHATOLOGY OF THE PROTESTANT SETTLEMENT OF VIRGINIA

After the first planting of Virginia in 1607, the fate of the little colony at Jamestown was greatly dependent upon the arrival of new immigrants from England. For this reason, the Virginia Company in London spared no effort to arouse the interest of the public in England. In its vigorous attempt to save the little colony in America, the Virginia Company "chose certain popular ministers to preach before the shareholders and then printed their sermons as quickly as possible so that they might reach a wider audience" in England.[7] In that way, a great body of Protestant works was formed, during a period of several years, in which one can clearly see how Protestants incorporated America within the confines of sacred history, through the *Genesis* type of religious migration. Furthermore, this body of Protestant works constituted, in fact, the ideological context of the settlement of Virginia, which we shall later compare with the Puritan reasons for emigrating to New England.

Robert Johnson and 'Nova Britannia'

The first official sermon on behalf of the Virginia Company was delivered by Robert Johnson, chaplain to the bishop of Lincoln, under the title *Nova Britannia* (1609). Any attempt to justify the English colonization of America ought to begin, according to Johnson, with Pope Alexander VI's donation to Spain of the title to America. Obviously, Johnson ridiculed the

---

[7] Louis B. Wright, *Religion and Empire: The Alliance Between Piety and Commerce in English Expansion 1558–1625* (Chapel Hill, 1943), p. 90. See also Alexander Brown, *The Genesis of the United States*, 2 vols. (Boston and New York, 1890); Nichols P. Canny, "The Ideology of English Colonization: From Ireland to America," *William and Mary Quarterly* 30 (1973), 575–98; Carole Shammas, "English Commercial Development and American Colonization 1560–1620," in *The Westward Enterprise: English Activities in Ireland, the Atlantic, and America 1480–1650*, ed. K. R. Andrews, N. P. Canny, and P. E. H. Hair (Detroit, 1989), pp. 151–74; Hugh Kearney, "The Problem of Perspective in the History of Colonial America," in *The Westward Enterprise*, pp. 290–302; John Parker, "Religion and the Virginia Colony 1609–1610," in *The Westward Enterprise*, pp. 245–70; and Perry Miller, "Religion and Society in the Early Literature of Virginia," in *Errand into the Wilderness* (Cambridge, Mass., 1956), pp. 99–140.

Alexandrian bull of 1493 as a false one, exactly as Protestants generally rejected the Donation of Constantine which gave Rome its predominance in western Christianity. The Alexandrian bull, argued Johnson, "is much like that great Donation of Constantine where by the pope himself doth hold and claime, the citie of Rome and all the Westerne Empire, a thing that so crosseth all Histories of truth, and sound Antiquitie." Consequently, the "two Donations," the one in which "the whole West Empire" was given "from a temporall Prince to the Pope," and the other in which America was given "from the pope to a temporal Prince," were both false, according to Johnson, "the one an olde tale" and the other "ridicolous." In sum, both claims are just "legendari fables."[8]

Having freed the New World from any Catholic claim and having opened it to English colonization efforts, Johnson developed two ultimate justifications for the settlement of Virginia. The first was "to advance and spread the kingdom of God, and the knowledge of his truth, among so many millions of men and women, savage and blinde," and the second was "for the honour of our King, and enlarging his Kingdomes." Religion and empire went hand in hand; therefore, the title Johnson gave to his sermon – *Nova Britannia* – was, indeed, a most appropriate one, because for him, as for many Protestants after him, America was an extension of England and the Church of England. Yet, in this context, America had, of course, a prominent role in providential history. In order to explain the English colonization of America, Johnson used the story of the two spies sent out by Moses to search out the land of Canaan (Numbers 13, 14). In this context, evidently, America the "earthly Paradice," as Johnson called it, lay wide open to capture by England, the elect nation, exactly as Canaan was conquered by the Israelites under God's divine warrant. Furthermore, according to Johnson, the English conquest of America would be a "just conquest," because as "Divine testimonies shew," the "honour of a King consisteth in the multitude of subjects, and certainly the state of the Jewes was farre more glorious by the conquests of David, and under the ample raigne of Solomon, then ever before or after." England's "just Conquest by sword" of America, according to Johnson, would be "honourable" not only "in the sight of men and ages to come, but much more glorious in the sight of God."[9]

The analogy between England and the ancient imperialistic kingdom of Israel under Kings David and Solomon would enable English Protestants to justify the settlement of Virginia. Its importance, however, lay in the fact that it illuminated clearly the *Genesis* type of religious migration in which

---

[8] Robert Johnson, *Nova Britannia, Offering Most Excellent Fruites by Planting in Virginia* (1609), pp. 2–3.
[9] *Ibid.*, pp. 15, 5, 13, 14.

an elect nation possessed a divine warrant to conquer foreign territories. So, as was the case with ancient Israel, "the Prince and people of God" had a "good warrant" to take over and settle the "earthly Paradice" of America, according to Johnson. Eschatological expectations also gave strength to England's divine mission to settle America: "We may verily beleeve, that God hath reserved in this last age of the world, an infinite number of those lost and scattered sheepe, to be wonne and recovered by our meanes" to the saving grace of the Gospel.[10]

Evidently, in order to lure settlers to Virginia, America had to be formulated in a meaningful and appealing context. Here was, indeed, a land devoid, in the English mind, of any history and tradition. Protestants could therefore easily project into it whatever meaning and significance they wished, in order to facilitate the ultimate goal of English expansion to the New World. Robert Johnson's first official sermon on behalf of the Virginia Company claimed a singular religious aim in settling America, thereby setting the tone for later Protestant writings concerning Virginia. For what Protestants were doing, in fact, was to reconstruct a religious context for the English settlement of America, based upon the premises of ecclesiastical history as a mode of historical thought. And since ecclesiastical history was the dominant philosophy of history at the time, it should come as no surprise that Protestants used sacred, providential history to transform America from *Terra Incognita* into *Terra Cognita* in the English mind.

The religious warrant to colonize America is further seen in Richard Crakanthorpe's important sermon of March 24, 1609, at Paul's Cross, in celebration of King James I's coronation. Crakanthorpe, chaplain to the bishop of London and a violent opponent of the Roman Church, called upon the godly prince in England "not only to see a New Britain in another world, but also to have those as yet heathen barbarians and brutish people, together with our English, to learn the speech and language of Canaan."[11] Crakanthorpe's appeal was not for money and worldly gain, but was a purely religious one. For him the ultimate goal of English colonization of America was a spiritual mission, a kind of spiritual imperialism, indeed, to teach the Indians the mystery of Christ's Gospel of salvation.

Robert Gray and the theocratic rule of colonization

If Crakanthorpe stressed the spiritual, educational, aspect of English colonization of America, there were of course other Protestant preachers who

---

[10] *Ibid.*, pp. 14, 5, 13.
[11] Richard Crakanthorpe, *A Sermon Solmnizing the Happie inauguration of Our Most Gracious and Religious Soveraigne King James* (1609), in Alexander Brown (ed.), *The Genesis of the United States*, vol. I, p. 256.

boldly proclaimed England's right as the elect nation to conquer the New World. Prominent among them was Robert Gray, rector of St. Bennet Sherehog in Cheapward, who developed in his sermon, *A Good Speed to Virginia*, 1609, one of the most explicitly militant views concerning England's right to conquer America. Dedicating his sermon to the "Aduenturers for the plantation of Virginia," Gray had no doubt that God made them "instruments for the inlarging of his Church militant upon earth," and argued that "the same God [shall] make you members of his Church triumphant in Heaven." More specifically Gray's militant colonial policy is based upon a theocratic view: "The heavens saith *David*, even the heavens are the Lords, and so is the earth." Therefore, "the Lord hath given the earth to the children of men." Yet, this earth which was given to men "by deede of gift from God, is the greater part of it possessed and usurped by wild beasts, and unreasonable creatures, or by brutish savages." Christians, therefore, according to Gray, had a full right to conquer this land and take it "out of the hands of beasts, and brutish savages, which have no interest in it, because they participate rather of the nature of beasts then men."[12]

Having set the theocratic rule of colonization, by claiming the right of God's people to take over lands inhabited by "beasts" and barbarian people, Gray chose as the biblical text for this sermon the passage from Joshua, the most militant book in the Bible, which describes the capture of the land of the Perizzites and of the Giants by the children of Joseph (Josh. 17: 14–18). In the same vein, declared Gray, "we may justly say, as the children of *Israel* say here to Joshua, we are a great people, and the land is too narrow for us." Accordingly, upon the same divine warrant which directed Joshua to capture Canaan for the Israelites, "our Joshua, and mighty Monarch, that most religious and renowned King James" gives now his "charter for the plantation of *Virginia*." For "we gather from the text," continues Gray, "that the cause why the children of Joseph desired to inlarge their borders, was the multitude and greatness whereunto they are growne." This population growth was a sure sign of God's favor. Likewise, "this should teach us of this kingdome and country, prudence and providence, the Lord hath blessed us, and we are growne to be a great people, so that one lot is not sufficient for us." According to such reasoning, the English colonial expansion to America constituted clear evidence of this realm's election in providential history. So, like the children of Joseph, "the duty of the people" of England "is to enlarge their territories and dilate their [geographical] borders." Consequently, Gray had no doubt that "all Polititians doe with one consent, holde and maintaine, that a Christian King may lawfullie make warre uppon barbarous and Sauage people, and such as

[12] Robert Gray, *A Good Speed to Virginia* (1609), "The Epistle Dedicatorie," pp. 5–6.

live under no lawfull or warrantable gouernment, and may make a conquest of them."[13]

Robert Gray's *A Good Speed to Virginia* presents one of the most militant, imperialist Protestant views of the colonization of America. In the context of providential history, he asserted, a godly Christian king has a divine warrant, exactly as was the case with Israel's conquest of the land of Canaan, to take hold of America as a land of barbarian people and transform it into the dominion of God's people. Gray transformed the notion of the "Militant Church" (i.e. the concept of the church engaged in an ongoing earthly struggle against Satan), into the gospel of colonization: "to bring the barbarous and savage people" of America "to a civill and Christian kinde of government," so that these people "may learn" to live "holily, and soberly in this world."[14] Gray presented a militant way, indeed, of incorporating America into the confines of sacred, ecclesiastical history. If the English settlement of Virginia was analogous to Joshua's conquest of the land of Canaan, then America could become a sacred place in providential history only through the dimension of English colonization, or through the transfer of England's superior religious and cultural institutions to the New World. In the context of providential history, English colonization of America signifies the expansion of God's elect nation in the world. Hence, in a world created by God for the glory of His chosen people, England was possessed of a full divine warrant to conquer foreign territories and to spread there the Gospel of Salvation. Later, other Protestant preachers, in their attempts to justify the settlement of Virginia, would further articulate this expansionist vision by citing the conquests of Kings David and Solomon. Yet, it was Gray who provided the most explicitly militant dimension to the English settlement of America by identifying it with Joshua's conquest of the land of Israel.

William Symonds and the 'Genesis' type of religious migration

During the year 1609, many tracts and sermons were published in England in order to aid further the new colony in Virginia. Among them, one is especially important for our purposes because it offered an important model from sacred, ecclesiastical history, as the justification for the settlement of America. This was William Symonds' *Virginia*, a sermon preached before the Virginia Company in London on April 25, 1609. Symonds' sermon clearly defined the colonization of America in the context of a powerful model of religious migration in sacred, ecclesiastical history, which was

---

[13] *Ibid.*, pp. 8–9, 11–13, 18–19.   [14] *Ibid.*, p. 15.

indeed to become the most characteristic feature of the Protestant justification for the settlement of Virginia – the *Genesis* type of religious migration.

Symonds, a preacher at Saint Savior's, Southwark, had acquired an early reputation with the publication of his book *Pisgah Evangelica* (1605), a commentary upon the Book of Revelation, in which he attempted to present to "the publike view those Canaanites," or the Papists, "over whom our Lord Jesus Christ and his holie Church shall triumph after severall Battailes." A true heir of the apocalyptic tradition in England, Symonds saw the "propheticall spirit" in Revelation, a book which foretells "the steps" of God's "providence, by which he would rule the *Christian* world, from the time of the Apostles to the last days." Most important, Symonds regarded the Apocalypse as "a perfect Ecclesiastical historie," because it shows "to the servants of God" the history of the church "from the time of the being of St. John in Patmos, to the end of the world." He argued, therefore, that "nothing of importance can be found in the Christian world, which may not be referred to some part" of the Revelation. He strove "to reduce all stories of importance," or main historical events of the church, "to their certain heads of the Revelation." Symonds, then, was well qualified among English Protestants to provide the fullest incorporation of America into the confines of sacred, prophetic, ecclesiastical history. It was Symonds who introduced so powerfully the concept of the *Genesis* type of religious migration in regard to the English settlement of America.[15]

Symonds chose for his sermon *Virginia* the text from Genesis 12:1–3, in which God promised Abraham that if he would emigrate from his native country, God would make out of him and his seed a great nation. Naturally, and according to his exegesis on the Apocalypse, Symonds transformed this magnificent divine promise from Abraham to the English people, as God's chosen people, who possessed a divine warrant to settle America. Yet, writing during the reign of James I, Symonds evidently had to accord a glorious and prophetic role to the first Stuart king as a godly prince who would lead the great revelatory migration to America. So, if in the apocalyptic tradition in England in the past Foxe identified Elizabeth with Constantine the Great, because the queen's triumph signified the victory of the Protestant faith in England, which according to Foxe was equivalent to the triumph of Christianity in the Roman empire during the reign of Constantine, Symonds now identified James I with Constantine the Great in relation to the glorious task of spreading the Gospel to America. Therefore, he emphasized the profound similarities between "our most sacred

[15] William Symonds, *Pisgah Evangelica, By the Method of the Revelation, presenting to the publike view those Cananites over whom our Lord Jesus Christ and his holie Church shall triumph . . .* (1605), "The Epistle Dedicatorie," and "To the Reader."

Soveraigne," James I, "in whom is the spirit of his great Ancestor, *Constantine the pacifier of the world, and planter of the Gospell in places most remote.*" Likewise, as Constantine planted Christianity in the whole Roman empire, so now, according to Symonds, James "desireth to present this land a pure Virgine to Christ." And knowing that the little colony in Virginia was in much need of help and resources from the English crown, Symonds appealed to the king:

Lord finish this good work thou hath begun; and marry this land, a pure Virgine, to thy kingly soone Christ Jesus; so shall thy name bee magnified: and we shall have a Virgin or Maiden Britaine, a comfortable addition to our Great Britaine.[16]

Symonds' eschatological expectations, which he presented in his earlier book *Pisgah Evangelica* of 1605, had a profound impact on his apocalyptic vision of the settlement of America. From its very beginning to its very end, the history of the church is characterized by an apocalyptic struggle between the church and the Devil. This long and continuous war "hath beautified the world with admirable and pleasant varieties," such as, for example,

the Flood, the burning of Sodom; the drowning of *Pharoh*: the subduing of the Cananites by *David* and his sonnes; the breaking of Monarchies into chaffe: the surprising & conquering of great nations, by Fisher-men, *with the sword of the spirit*; the stamping of the Dragon (the Heathen Empire) into peeces by *Constantine*; the desolation, and nakedness of Anti-Christ now readie to cast into fire.

All these events are "manifested demonstrations of the Serpent bruished head." But they all related to time past, and they were small "in comparison of that which is at hand, and remaineth to be accomplished at the last judgement." English colonization of America, thus, was placed by Symonds in the final stage of sacred, providential history. "Now the Lord hath made bare his holy arm, in the sight of all the Gentiles; and all the ends of the earth shall see the salvation of our God." Now, in this last act in the drama of salvation, when "many Mighty Kings have set their Crownes up on the head of Christ," and the "true Nobilitie, have upon their horse bridles, *Holinesse to the Lord*," was the time, declared Symonds, "to carry the Gospell abroad" and conquer America for Christ and his Gospel. No wonder, then, that in this apocalyptic context, Symonds warned the Virginia Company to be very "carefull to carry" to America "no Traitors, nor Papists that depend on the Great Whore" of Babylon.[17] The Apocalypse of the Age of Discovery was thus transformed into the apocalypse of colonization.

The justification for such an eschatological mission of conquering America for Christ is to be found, according to Symonds, in God's promise

---

[16] William Symonds, *Virginia, A Sermon Preached at White-Chappel* . . . (1609), "The Epistle Dedicatorie."

[17] *Ibid.*, "The Epistle Dedicatorie."

to Abraham (Gen. 12:1–3). Abraham's migration was based upon a "heavenly calling" which commanded him "to take a journey" out of his native land. But this calling, Symonds stressed, "is not described Cosmographically," in terms of specific territory, but rather "Morally." Abraham did not emigrate because of the granting of any particular land, but only because of "the promise of God." Yet, even if this migration is a moral one, still it was "subject to the general law of replenishing the earth." This general law of inhabiting all lands is derived from the belief that "the Lord would have his workes to be knowne" upon the whole earth, and not only in special, limited places. Consequently, "the implication is manifest, that his Saints must be witnesses of all his works, in all Climates; for else they cannot blesse him in all his workes." Another reason for Abraham's migration is, of course, derived from ecclesiastical history; namely, the spread of the Gospel upon earth. "One that hath the knowledge of the feare of God," argued Symonds, "should communicate it to others," for otherwise God may withhold "some mercy from us, til all nations haue the meanes of salvation." Accordingly, given the belief that "Christ our Saviour . . . revived the olde law, of filling the earth" by his call to his disciples to preach the Gospel in all the world, then clearly God's call to Abraham "doth binde all his sonnes, according to the faith, to go likewise abroad." Symonds concluded by asking – "can there be any doubt, but that the Lord that called Abraham into another Country, doeth also by the same holy hand, call you," the Adventurers of the Virginia Company, "to goe and carry the Gospell to a Nation that never heard of Christ"?[18]

Like other Protestants, Symonds was very sensitive to the problem of lawful "Conquest," or the right "to enter other Princes Territories." Yet, the solution was clear enough: because "the most worthies of the Scriptures," such as "the true type of Christ, King Salomon," made "holy conquerers," no one has the right of "telling them that they must not make offensive warres, if it were to gain the whole world to Christ." Furthermore, not only the Old Testament bears witness to this rule, but the whole history of Christianity is based upon the divine right to spread the Gospel in the world:

What wrong I pray you did the Apostles in going about to alter the lawes of nations, even against the expresse commandement of the princes, and to set up the throne of Christ.

Yet Symonds was careful to draw a distinction between Spain's "bloudy invasion" of America and England's "planting of a peaceable Colony, in a waste country, where the people doe live but like Deere in hearde." A peaceful colonization of America was much needed "in this stouping age, of

[18] Ibid., pp. 3–9.

the gray headed world, ful of yeres and experience," because the Indians "have not as yet attained unto the first modestie that was *Adam*, that knew he was naked, where they know no God but the divell, nor sacrifice, but to offer their men and children unto *Moloch*."[19] By making a distinction between Spain's bloody invasion and England's peaceful colonization of America, and by defending the urgent need to convert the Indians in the last age of the world, Symonds justified the lawful conquest of the New World.

Having established the ecclesiastical context for the just conquest of America, Symonds argued that Englishmen being "the sonnes of Abraham" had an obligation to settle Virginia. The colonization of America was not only a matter of human choice, but of divine duty, for "where God giveth a due vocation to spread abroad and inhabit the earth, neither the love of the country," nor "the love of kindred," nor "the love of a mans fathers house . . . nor the largenes of possession ought to be any impediment to keep us from obedience." Symonds, indeed, was fully aware that many in England "are not willing to goe abroad and spread the gospell, in this most honorable and Christian voyage of the Plantation of Virginia." To persuade them, he used again and again the symbol of Abraham's migration from Mesopotamia which was "the sweetest, and most fruitful soyle that was in the world." Yet Abraham had to leave this earthly paradise only because he had to follow God's divine promise. The same divine call is awaiting England now. For "how sweete soever" England might be, "I am sure," continues Symonds, "it cannot compare with Mesopotamia, where Abraham dwelt." Ultimately, in the providential scheme of history, "where God doth commaund, he is to be obeyed, without asking of any questions; *Abraham* must goe to a land hee knoweth whither, because God will haue it so." And "how much more, when" America was discovered "to bee as much better than the place in which we live, as the land of Canaan, was better than the roaring wilderness, ought we to be willing to goe, whither God calleth?" It was, then, England's divine duty to settle America:

Let us bee cheerefull to goe to the place, that God will shew us to possesse in peace and plentie, a land more like the garden of Eden: which the Lord planted, then any part else of all the earth.[20]

Through the comparison with Abraham's migration, Symonds had established a meaningful sacred, ecclesiastical context for the English settlement of Virginia. And based upon the *Genesis* type of religious migration, the English colonization of America was set within a providential context. This type of religious migration was particularly appealing to Protestant England. Since Abraham was considered "a type of Christ," therefore "what the Lord promised to Abraham, was also promised to all those that

[19] *Ibid.*, pp. 10–15.   [20] *Ibid.*, pp. 16–24.

are of the same faith and obedience with him."[21] So, as Abraham signified in ecclesiastical history a sacred locus for the fulfillment of prophetic revelations, now England, as God's elect nation, was the sacred center for the realization of divine prophecies.

With the settlement of Virginia the apocalyptic struggle taking place in Europe between the forces of Reformation and Counter-Reformation was transferred to the New World. England, or more generally "every true hearted Protestant" according to Symonds, should not hesitate to settle Virginia because of "the perill" of the "Papists" and the "popish Church." Evidence of God's favor upon England was provided by the fate of the Armada "that came into the Narrow seas in the yeere 1588." In the same vein, argued Symonds, "feare not" from the Spanish fleet in the New World, because "Babilon, saith the Angell" in Revelation "is fallen; never to rise again: sing *Hallelu-iah*, and you shall see her smoake ascend for evermore." "The only perill," concerning the settlement of Virginia, therefore, "is in offending God, and taking of Papists in to your company," or to the Protestant colony in America. For "if once they come creeping into your houses, then looke for mischiefe: if treason or poyson bee of any force: know them all to be very Assasines, of all men to be abhorred."[22]

The apocalyptic dimensions of the colonization of America are intrinsically associated with eschatology. Like other Protestant preachers, Symonds stressed the divine errand of spreading the Gospel in all the world in the context of God's promise to Abraham and his seed, "seeing the seed is Christ." Therefore, "*Abraham* must get him out of his Countrie: that he may begin that, which God, by him and his seed, will accomplish in due time: namely that all nations embrace the gospel of Christ unto their salvation." This "so great an errand," however, calls immediately upon the issue of millennialism, or the transformation of the kingdoms of the world into the Kingdom of God and his son Christ. "But stay, saith one" to Symonds, "you run too fast without good ground: you seeme to encline to the Millenaries, or such as looke for the gospell to be spread over all the world." Such a millennial quest is not attainable; it is "safer to tremble at the last judgement, whose trumpet is ever sounding in our eares: *Arise from the dead and come to judgement*." These words of caution, intended to soften the radical plea of the pursuit of the millennium, Symonds flatly rejected. For "no doctrine," according to him, "can makes a wise man depart from the doctrine of the *Canonicall Scriptures*," or from the Apocalypse. Even the Catholics, he claimed, affirmed that "the gospell must be preached universally through the world before the last judgement."[23]

The issue of the relationship between millenarianism and the Last Judg-

---

[21] *Ibid.*, pp. 33–4.   [22] *Ibid.*, pp. 43, 45–6.   [23] *Ibid.*, pp. 47–8.

ment is a critical one in the Christian philosophy of history. Those who denied that millennialism was an earthly phenomenon and argued for a patient waiting until the Last Judgment, evidently upheld the view that the meaning of history is to be found beyond the confines of history itself. Those, on the other hand, who believed in the millennium as taking place within time, argued that the meaning of history lies within history, not beyond it. Seen in this context, Symonds is truly representative of the English apocalyptic tradition, for he claimed that the millennium would precede the Last Judgment. The millennial quest, then, serves him well in the incorporation of America as a sacred place within the confines of ecclesiastical history. Taking the example of "the Jewes" who argued that "all the world must bee subdued by force and violence unto *Messiah*," Symonds argued that this option "prevailed much in the time of Christ" and was professed "by the Apostles." Later, with the Ascension of Christ, this belief found its expression in the millennialism of the Book of Revelation. For him, therefore, millennialism signifies an earthly, terrestrial phenomenon, before the last act in providential history, or the Last Judgment. "But what shal [Christ] abolish kings, and bring all to Popularity?" No, this is not the case with Symonds' understanding of the millennial rule of Christ. For according to him, "*God is the author of order, and not of confusion.*" Therefore, "*the kingdomes of this world shall bee our Lords, and his Christs, and he shall raigne for evermore.*" Symonds recited Revelation 11:15 in the Geneva Bible, rather "by Kings converted to the Gospel. For godly Kings *doe fit on the throne of the Lord, and by them the Lord reigneth.*"[24]

The pursuit of the millennium, therefore, signified order and stability, a quest for a utopian godly society, which ought not to be confused with the Antinomianism of the lunatic fringe during the Puritan Revolution. Ultimately, according to Symonds, millennialism denoted the spread of the Gospel in the world and conquering the earth for Christ:

The summe is, what blessing any nation had by Christ, must be communicated to all Nations: the office of his Prophecie to teach the ignorant; the office of his Priesthood, to give remission of sinnes to the sinnefull: the office of his kingdome, by word, and Sacraments, and spirit, to rule the inordinate.

An elect nation, such as England, had a divine duty to spread the Gospel in the world, because God "made the world" so "that his Sonne might rule over all."[25] Millennialism and colonialism, in Symonds' Protestant vision of the settlement of Virginia, went hand in hand.

For Symonds, the *Genesis* type of religious migration turned into a revolutionary model for justifying the colonization of America. Viewing religious migration as a prophetic, revelatory event, Symonds infused the

English settlement of Virginia with eschatological visions and millennial expectations: through the spreading of the Gospel to America the prophecy of the millennial rule of Christ would be accomplished within time and history. In this way, the millennial dimension became an integral part in the Protestant justification of the settlement of Virginia. With Symonds, Protestant colonialism and imperialism had reached its highest level of sophistication, because he radically transformed the *Genesis* model of Abraham's peaceful migration into an ultimate apocalyptic event in providential history – Christ's millennial rule upon the earth. Hence, according to Symonds, the English settlement of America ought to be considered in the larger context of the pursuit of the millennium.

The settlement of Virginia and Protestant apocalyptic consciousness

The settlement of Virginia aroused a deep apocalyptic consciousness among many Protestants in England, even those who had no clear interest in the young colony in America except in that it revealed England's divine election. Apart from sermons patronized by the Virginia Company, there is ample evidence that Protestant preachers used the English settlement of Virginia as a sign of the realization of prophetic revelation. For example, Robert Tynley, Doctor of Divinity and Archdeacon of Ely, preaching in April 1609, claimed that the colonization of Virginia was an evidence "of the true miracles" of the Church of England as against "those false & fabulous sorts" of miracles of the Church of Rome. Inasmuch as "the faith of the Church of Rome . . . is new and strangely degenerating from the ancient Catholic faith, so it is no marvell," according to Tynley, that it is based upon a "false" ground. On the other hand, with the Protestant Reformation, and through the great work of "our reverend Pastors, *Luther*, *Calvin*, *Beza*," and "with the extraordinary and powerful working of almighty God," there occurred "the restoring of the purity of religion, in these late times, from the drosse and corruptions of *Antichrist*."[26]

As against the Antichristian "Romish Synagogue," the Protestant religion in England had miraculously prevailed against "all the conspiracies and forces of our enemies," who waged a war "against our Princes and our people." This itself, claimed Tynley, "*is the Lords, and it is wonderfull in our eies*." As evidence for such a great divine favor toward England, "witness abroad the planting intended, or rather already happily begun of our English Colonie in *Virginia*," whose ultimate goal is

the gaining and winning to Christ his fold, and the reducing unto civill societies . . .

---

[26] Robert Tynley, *Two Learned Sermons. The One, of the Mischievous Subtiltie and Barbarous Crueltie, the Other of the False Doctrines, and Refined Heresies of the Romish Synagogue* . . . (1608, 1609), pp. 66–9.

of so many thousands of those sillie, brutish, and ignorant soules, now fast bound with the chaines of error and ignorance, under the bondage and slavery of the Divell.

Obviously, in such a glorious Protestant imperial vision, the English crown acquired a most singular role in providential history:

with all thankfulnesse we acknowledge, and with most hearty praiers we commend to almighty God the happy preservation and continuance amongst us, of the noble instrument of his glory, our most gratious Sovereigne Lord *King James*, by whom he effected so powerfully his miraculous workes now daies in our Church, to the wonder and astonishment of the world, not wilfully malignant.[27]

Like Tynley, George Benson, a Fellow of Queen's College, Oxford, had no visible interest in Virginia. Yet the praise of the little colony which he expressed in his sermon of May 1609 shows clearly how Virginia became an integral part of Protestant eschatology, or how it served as a symbol for the realization of prophetic revelations. "The publication of the Gospel over the world" is, according to Benson, a sure sign that "the ends of the world are drawing neere unto us." In this eschatological moment, "one most pregnant, most fresh [prophetic event] is that of Virginia which now (by God grace) through our English shal heare news of Christ." And he was thoroughly confident that "the gospel of Christ shall be published" in America by Englishmen who "are of that metall, that having in their hands *the key of the kingdome of god*, they will not keepe those weak ones out," namely, the Indians, from knowing the mystery of God's salvation. Accordingly, among the many "forerunners of the end," the settlement of Virginia, as Benson told his audience, was a clear sign "before the ends of the world come upon you."[28]

Incorporating the colonization of America into the sacred annals of ecclesiastical history, Protestants thus depicted the settlement of Virginia in eschatological and apocalyptic terms. Ultimately, they provided a much needed ideological context for interpreting Virginia's significance in providential history, and hence, for luring new settlers to the new colony in Virginia. Divine prophecy and colonization of the New World went hand in hand in the Protestant vision of America. "The Angel of Virginia crieth to this Land," preached Daniel Price, Chaplaine in ordinaire to the Prince in 1609, "as the Angele of Macedonia did to Paul, *O! Come and help us*," and "watered the Gospel in so great, fair, fruitful a Country."[29] And R. Rice, who emigrated to Virginia and later wrote the poem *News From Virginia* (1610), proclaimed:

---

[27] *Ibid.*, "To the Reader," and pp. 66–8.
[28] George Benson, *A Sermon Preached at Paulles Crosse* . . . (1609), pp. 90–2.
[29] Daniel Price, *Saules Prohibition Staide: Or the Apprehension and Examination of Saule* . . . (1609), in Alexander Brown (ed.), *The Genesis of the United States*, vol. I, pp. 314–15.

Let England knowe our willingnesse,
For that our worke is good,
Wee hope to plant a nation,
Where none before hath stood.
To glorifie the Lord 'tis done,
And to no other end;
He that would crosse so good a work,
To God can be no friend.[30]

William Crashaw and the civilized mission to the Indians

In William Crashaw's sermon before the Virginia Company in London, 1609, the Protestant mission to America was placed in the larger context of England's mission to civilize the Indians. Crashaw, a preacher at the Inner Temple, who is known also as the father of the Catholic poet Richard Crashaw, came to preach his sermon when Lord de la Ware, the governor of the Virginia Company, was ready to sail to America with new immigrants and a great amount of supplies for the little colony. In this crucial moment for the Virginia enterprise, Crashaw aimed to show "the lawfulnesse of that Action," and "the necessity therefore," and this "not so much out of the grounds of Policie, as of Humanity, Equity, and Christianity."[31]

Any discussion of Virginia ought to begin, according to Crashaw, with the larger apocalyptic context in which Satan fights against the godly who aim at the establishment of the Kingdom of God upon earth, both in England and in America. So, "though satan seeke to make us desist" and his goal is to hurt the godly "by all his power," yet "we have Christ Jesus on our side, whose kingdome we goe to inlarge" in America. It was Satan's work to raise all the objections in England against the colonization of Virginia, but Crashaw pleaded with his audience to remember that "the end of this voiage is the destruction of the divel kingdome, and propagation of the Gospel." Crashaw then proceeded to expound on England's divine obligation to convert the Indians in America. His lesson was from Luke 22:32, "But I have praied for thee, that thy faith faile not: therefore when thou are converted strengthen thy brethren." Yet, "this commandment" of Christ to Peter "is not voluntary or left indifferent to a mans choice, but (plainly) a necessarie dutie, for every Christian to labour the conversion and confirmation of others that are not." This argument, obviously, serves to prove "not only the lawfulnesse" of the settlement of Virginia,

---

[30] R. Rich, *News from Virginia. The Lost Flocke Triumphant* . . . (1610), p. 8.
[31] William Crashaw, *A Sermon Preached in London before the Right Honorable the Lord Lawarre, Lord Governour and Captaine General of Virginia* . . . (1610). The quotation is taken from the title page of Crashaw's sermon.

but even the excellencie and goodnesse, and indeed the plaine necessity . . . of this present action: the principal ends thereof being the plantation of a Church of English christians there, and consequently the conversion of the heathen from the divel to God.[32]

Defining the settlement of Virginia as a divine necessity, Crashaw described James I as a godly prince obeying God's decree to convert the heathen in America. "Our *most gratious and christian king* hath shewed himselfe conscionable obedient to this commandment, setting forward this blessed businesse by his princely priviledges and gratious grants under his great seale," which can be found in the Charter of Virginia. So, James I, "out of his duty to God, love of his religion, and care of [the Indians'] soules . . . thus put to his roiall hand for the furtherance of this blessed and worthy work," to wit – the settlement of Virginia. And if the king willingly obeyed God's commandment, "who art thou that wilt be free from the bonds of this duty?"[33] According to Crashaw, under a godly prince, England had to take upon herself this most glorious task of converting the Indians in America.

It would be a great mistake, however, to see in Crashaw's words only a missionary zeal. For to him civilization and culture were crucially associated with religion. Indeed, once Englishmen themselves "were savage and uncivill, and worshipped the divell, as now" the Indians do, but "then God sent some to make us civill, others to make us christian." And now it had become England's duty to Christianize and civilize the savages in America. Failing to do so would signify that "we are not truly and effectually converted: for if wee be, then assurredly as by vertue of Gods commandment *Wee must* . . . procure" the Indians' "salvation." Any opposition to such "a most excellent and holie action," according to Crashaw, was "a sure sign of a profane man." No wonder that – in Crashaw's view – anyone who inclined not to assist the English plantation in America "discovers himselfe to be an unsanctified, unmortified, and unconverted man, negligent of his own and other mens salvation."[34]

Crashaw, like so many Protestants before him, defined the colonization of Virginia according to the *Genesis* type of religious migration. The justification for the "*plantation of an English colonie in Virginia*" was to be found in the sacred biblical model of Abraham who bought his burial place in Canaan, and "so must all the children of *Abraham* doe." It was upon this biblical model that all the actions of Englishmen in America ought to be grounded: they ought to "exchange" with the Indians for everything the native "*may spare*," such as, for example, "*land and roome* for us to plant in." Englishmen, in their turn, would provide the savages "such things as they greatly desire," such as "1. *Civilitie* for their bodies," and "2.

---

[32] *Ibid.*, pp. 9, 17, 22–3.   [33] *Ibid.*, pp. 25–6.   [34] *Ibid.*, pp. 26–9.

Christianitie for their soules." The first would "make them *men*, the second *happy men*; the first to cover their *bodies* from the shame of the world; the second, to cover their *soules* from the wrath of God." Colonization, then, was justified as a "lawfull bargaine," based upon a mutually advantageous exchange between two partners. Yet, it was also a cultural trade because Englishmen would make the Indians "much richer, even for matter of this life," by making them "*civilized*." But if Englishmen would offer the gift of civilization in exchange for land, the most important thing, "namely, *religion*," they would "have from us for nothing: and surely so it is, they shall have it freely for Gods sake, and for their soules sake."[35]

With all the importance he attached to the exchange with the Indians, however, Crashaw never abandoned the ecclesiastical context, or the *Genesis* model of migration, as the ultimate justification for the settlement of Virginia. Even as "the Israelites had *a commandment* from God to dwell in *Canaan*, we have *leave* to dwell in *Virginia*." There was a crucial difference, however, according to Crashaw, between biblical times and the present enterprise to Virginia: for while the people of Israel, "were *commanded to kill* the heathen, we are *forbidden to kill them*, but are commanded to *convert* them." Consequently, Crashaw appealed to the members of the Virginia Company, "looke not at the gain, the wealth," or other worldly ends, "but looke at those high and better ends that concerne the kingdom of God. Remember thou art a Generall of English men, nay a Generall of Christian men: therefore principally looke to religion" in the settlement of America. Crashaw then turned to Virginia, saying:

Thou hast thy name from the worthiest Queene that ever the world had: thou hast thy matter from the greatest King on earth: and thou shalt now have the forme from one of the most glorious Nations under the Sunne.[36]

No other tract during this time captured more beautifully and brilliantly than Crashaw's sermon the glorious Protestant vision of the settlement of Virginia. Indeed, "there is no nobler sermon than this of the period."[37]

Continuity and change in the glorious Protestant vision of the settlement of Virginia

In the next decade the great Protestant crusade for Virginia of 1609–10 "bogged down in problems of management and mere survival."[38] This transformation had a great effect on Protestant writings advocating the

---

[35] *Ibid.*, pp. 30–4.
[36] *Ibid.*, pp. 46–8, 82, 85.
[37] A. B. Grosart, cited by Alexander Brown (ed.), *The Genesis of the United States*, vol. I, p. 373.
[38] Parker, "Religion and the Virginia Colony," p. 270.

settlement of America. The prophetic, militant, and apocalyptic vision of the colonization of the New World was replaced by more practical language depicting the struggle for survival in Virginia. For example, Robert Johnson's *The New Life of Virginea* (1612) had lost much of the militant vision which so characterized his earlier tract *Nova Britannia* of 1609. And William Symonds' *The Proceeding of the English Colonie in Virginia* (1612) had almost nothing of the great eschatological expectations and apocalyptic visions which were the ultimate mark of his previous work *Virginia* of 1609.[39] Seen in this context, the Protestant crusade of 1609–10 constituted a unique phenomenon in terms of the incorporation of America into the confines of sacred, ecclesiastical history. Indeed, "never again would there be anything like this brief, enthusiastic hour in English and American history, when religion spoke more loudly for empire than either the state or the merchant community."[40]

Yet the Protestant vision of the settlement of Virginia as a prophetic, apocalyptic event in sacred history, continued to be heard in England. Such was the case with William Crashaw's introduction to Alexander Whitaker's *Good News from Virginia*, 1613, in which he continuously claimed "*Virginia*" to be a "world without end" for the fulfillment of divine, prophetic revelations.[41] The Protestant vision of Virginia was fully intact, with all its previous militant and apocalyptic zeal, in the Reverend Samuel Purchas' *Purchas His Pilgrimes*, 1613, which aroused the enthusiasm of James I and his contemporaries, and later in Purchas' *Hakluytus Posthumus or Purchas His Pilgrimes* of 1625. In the second work Purchas claimed that Christians possessed a "natural" and "Evangelical Charter" from God "to replenish the whole earth," and this "Divine Ordinance" constituted the justification for settling Virginia: "Loe here the scope of Christian Plantations, to plan Christianity, to produce and multiply Christians, by our words and works to further the knowledge of God in his Word and Works." Consequently, Purchas provided a highly apocalyptic vision of Virginia:

And let men know that hee which converteth a sinner from the errour of his way, shall save a soule from death, and shall hide a multitude of sinnes. And Saviours shall thus come on Mount Zion to judge the Mount of Esau, and the Kingdome (of Virginia) shall be Lord. Thus shall wee at once overcome both Men and Devilles, and espouse Virginia to one husband, presenting her as a chast Virgin to Christ.[42]

---

[39] Robert Johnson, *The New Life of Virginea: Declaring the Former Successe and Present Estate of that Plantation* . . . (1612); William Symonds, *The Proceedings of the English Colonie in Virginia* (1612).

[40] Parker, "Religion and the Virginia Colony," p. 270.

[41] William Crashaw, "The Epistle Dedicatorie," to Alexander Whitaker, *Good News from Virginia* (1613), p. 22.

[42] Samuel Purchas, *Hakluyt Posthumus or Purchas His Pilgrimes* (1625), vol. XIX, pp. 218, 220, 222, 223, 230–1. See also, Loren E. Pennington, *Hakluyt Posthumus: Samuel Purchas*

The glorious Protestant vision of Virginia in providential history can be further seen in Patrick Copland's *Virginia's God be Thanked* (1622). Copland, a preacher of the East India Company, became an enthusiastic advocate of Virginia and raised funds for the free school there. Preaching before the Virginia Company, he called on his audience to praise God for transforming Virginia from a "Heathen" into a "Christian Kingdome." His was a most optimistic sermon about the prospects of the colony in America. Yet, he argued, religion and profit are closely connected: for "as when you advance religion, you advance together with it your own profit." He was sure that the English plantation in Virginia "shall continue there till the second comming of our blessed Saviour." And he therefore beseeched his audience to continue in their efforts for "this noble Plantation, tending so highly to the advancement of the Gospel; and to the honouring of our drad Soveraigne, by inlarging of his Kingdomes."[43]

Yet it was left perhaps to Dr. John Donne, the famous poet and dean of St. Paul's, to summarize so beautifully and powerfully the premises of the Protestant ideology of the settlement of Virginia. Preaching before the Virginia Company in 1622, Donne told all those who aided the Virginia enterprise to consider their colonization efforts in the context of "the *Acts* of the *Apostles*" who were to spread "that name of Christ Jesus" over all the world: "beloved you are *Actors* upon the same Stage too: the uttermost part of the Earth are your *Scene*." Therefore he urged them to "act over the *acts* of the *Apostles*; bee you a light to the *Gentiles*." Placing the settlement of Virginia in the context of the sacred, providential drama of salvation, Donne invoked the eschatological dimension, as well:

Before the end of the world come . . . before al things shal be subdued to *Christ*, his kingdome persisted, & the last Enemy Death destroied, the Gospell must be preached to those men to whom ye send.

And he concluded his marvelous sermon with a unique prophetic imagination of Virginia's role in sacred, providential history:

You shall have made this Iland, which is but as the *Suburbs* of the old world, a Bridge, a Gallery to the new; to joine all to that world that shall never grow old, the Kingdome of heaven. You shall add persons to this Kingdome, and to the Kingdome of heaven, and adde names to the Bookes of our Chronicles, and to the booke of Life.

In the hands of the great poet, the incorporation of America into the confines of sacred, ecclesiastical history, reached, perhaps, its highest degree.

and the Promotion of English Overseas Expansion, in *The Emporia State Research Studies*, vol. XIV (Emporia, 1966).
[43] Patrick Copland, *Virginia's God be Thanked, or A Sermon of Thanksgiving for the Happie Successe of the Affayres in Virginia this Last Yeare* (1622), pp. 2, 28, 33, 35.

America became a necessary means for the transformation of the world into the Kingdom of God. Donne, therefore, told his audience how crucial the settlement of Virginia was in providential history:

Christ Jesus himselfe *is yesterday, and to day, and the same for ever.* In the advancing of his glory, be you so too, yesterday, and to day, and the same fore ever; and hereafter, when time shall be no more, no more yesterday, no more to day, yet for ever and ever, you shall enjoy that joy, and that glorie, which no ill accident can attaine to diminish, or Eclipse it.[44]

THE PROTESTANT SACRALIZATION OF VIRGINIA

The Protestant vision of the settlement of Virginia as a glorious, prophetic and apocalyptic event, had thus become inseparable from the premises of the Protestant apocalyptic tradition in which England conceived itself as God's elect nation, guided by divine providence and ruled by a godly prince. Accordingly, the colonization of America, grounded upon the *Genesis* type of religious migration, constituted a singular revelatory event in the unfolding history of salvation, drawing now to its eschatological moment. That Protestants chose the *Genesis* type in order to justify the colonization of America is not hard to understand, since according to this model of religious migration God's chosen people – "the seed of Abraham" – are obligated to fulfill the divine prophecy of transforming the world into the Kingdom of God through the preaching of Christ's Gospel of salvation all over the world. The Protestant incorporation of America as a sacred space within the confines of ecclesiastical history, was intrinsically interwoven with the Protestant apocalyptic tradition in England. Consequently, America's role as a sacred space in providential history was essentialy determined by the migration of God's chosen people to the New World, which spread the Gospel to America and, in that way, transformed it from *Terra Incognita* into *Terra Cognita* in the course of the history of salvation.

When we turn now to the Puritan "errand into the wilderness" in New England, it will become clear that the Puritan apocalypse of the New World defined itself in a radically different way. For, based upon the Puritans' failure to reform the Church of England under Elizabeth and the early Stuart kings – a failure which eventually led to the desacralization of England's role in sacred history and to its desacralization as a sacred space in providential history – the Puritan migration to America was, in their thought, a flight from a corrupted nation, a sinful land, and an ungodly prince. Where Protestants emphasized the association between England the elect nation and its divine mission in settling America, the Puritans, on the

---

[44] John Donne, *A Sermon Upon the VIII Verse of the I. Chapter of the Acts of the Apostles* (1622), pp. 1–2, 41–2, 44, 46, 51.

other hand, stressed rather the saints' divine duty to cut their ties with sinful England, or Laodicea, and to fly out of doomed England, or Babylon, upon which God would pour his divine wrath. Accordingly, as we are about to see, in sharp contrast to the *Genesis* type of religious migration used by Protestants to justify the settlement of Virginia, the Puritans rather chose to justify their flight into the wilderness in New England upon the *Exodus* model of religious migration. The Puritan incorporation of America as a sacred space within the confines of sacred, ecclesiastical history, differed radically from that of the Protestants, and was based upon a divine call to cut all ties and relationships with England, the corrupted nation. Now, then, for the first time since the "discovery" of the New World, America finally was construed as a sacred space of its own, independent and autonomous, in providential history, through the conscious Puritan attempt to create an apocalyptic gulf separating the New World from the Old, corrupted World, in sacred, providential history. In this context, indeed, one can clearly see in the Puritan migration to New England the beginnings of American ideology.

4

The creation of sacred space III

Time, history, and eschatology in the Puritan migration into the wilderness

ERRAND INTO THE WILDERNESS

Ever since Perry Miller wrote his brilliant and most influential essay, "Errand into the Wilderness" (1952), historians of early Puritan New England have debated continuously and persistently the question of the ultimate goal and mission of the Puritan migration to America. Indeed, in the historiography of Puritan New England, no other issue seems to generate more heat and controversy than that of the Puritan "Errand into the Wilderness." The reasons for this debate are not hard to find. For what Miller did in his wonderful essay was in fact to call attention to the ideological origins, or goals, of the Puritan migration, without which it would be difficult, indeed impossible, to interpret the Puritan experience in early New England as a whole. So, according to Miller, "the large unspoken assumption in the errand" of the Puritan migration to New England, was that if the Puritan emigrants could realize the true religious reformation in America, Jehova "would bring back these temporary colonials to govern England." Consequently, whereas the first phase of the Puritan Errand entailed the fulfillment of the goals of reformation in America, the second involved influencing the Puritan reformation back in England. According to Miller, the Puritan migration to New England

was an organized task force of Christians, executing a flank attack on the corruption of Christiandom. These Puritans did not flee to America; they went in order to work out that complete reformation which was not yet accomplished in England and Europe, but which would quickly be accomplished if only the saints back there had a working model to guide them.

Following Miller, the majority of scholars have indeed accepted some sort of Puritan Errand, or ideology, as underlying the settlement of New England, though they have continuously and consistently tended to modify

120

Miller's arguments regarding its meaning. There are even some who have totally denied the existence of a founding Errand in the Puritan migration to America.[1]

In the historiography of American Puritanism, Perry Miller's essay inaugurated a lively and fruitful debate over the ideology of the settlement of New England. However, in focusing on the nature and meaning of the Puritan "Errand into the Wilderness," the most important concept appears to have been neglected; namely the very concept of the "wilderness." Yet, it would seem evident that any discussion of the Puritan errand in New England ought to begin first with some definition of the meaning of the term "wilderness" in Puritan thought. Furthermore, it is clear that before there could be any adequate analysis of the Puritan mission in America, the very concept of the "wilderness" must be fully explored and defined.[2] For as we are about to see, in the Puritan mind the very terms "errand" and "wilderness" were intrinsically interwoven. Above all, the concept of the "wilderness" is one of the most crucial and critical concepts in sacred, ecclesiastical history. No wonder, then, that New England Puritans of the first and second generation had intentionally chosen the term "wilderness" to describe their migration to, and their holy experiment in, New England. In other words, the Puritan errand has no meaning separate from the significance Puritans attached to the term "wilderness" in providential history. Only within the context of sacred, ecclesiastical history can the Puritan "Errand into the Wilderness" be fully understood.

For the Puritans who emigrated to New England, as for Protestants and Catholics during this period, sacred, ecclesiastical history constituted the very ideology, or philosophy, of history. Therefore, the Puritans defined and explained their actions in time in accordance with the sacred patterns of ecclesiastical history, deeming themselves actors playing out their role on the stage of providential history whereon the drama – indeed the tragedy – of the mystery of salvation and redemption from the very beginning to the

---

[1] Perry Miller, "Errand into the Wilderness," in *Errand into the Wilderness* (Cambridge, Mass., 1976), p. 11. A good summary and analysis of the debate over the Puritan "errand" can be found in Theodore D. Bozeman's important study, *To Live Ancient Lives: The Primitivist Dimension in Puritanism* (Chapel Hill, 1988), ch. 3. See also my essay, "Epiphany at Matadi: Perry Miller's *Orthodoxy in Massachusetts* and the Meaning of American History," *Reviews in American History* 8 (1985), 627–41.

[2] Only a few studies have dealt with the term "wilderness" and its relationship to the Puritan migration to New England. Most important is, of course, George H. Williams' excellent general study, *Wilderness and Paradise in Christian Thought: The Biblical Experience of the Desert in the History of Christianity* (New York, 1962). See also Peter N. Carroll, *Puritanism and the Wilderness: The Intellectual Significance of the New England Frontier, 1629–1700* (New York, 1969), and Alan Heimert, "Puritanism, the Wilderness, and the Frontier," *New England Quarterly* 26 (1953), 361–82.

very end of time and history can be seen to unfold. Thus for example, according to John Cotton:

The principal cause of all passages in the world: which is not mans weaknesse, or goodness, but chiefly the wise and strong and good providence of God: who presenteth every age with a new stage of acts and actors.[3]

The ultimate role of divine providence signified, according to Samuel Willard, teacher of the Third, or South Church, in Boston, that "the whole world is a sucking infant depending on the breasts of divine providence." Accordingly, the Puritan world-view, it should be emphasized, was that of a theocratic universe, ruled directly and immediately by God's divine providence. For

[God] never intended to make a world, and then put the government of it out of his own hands, nor yet to lose the liberty of governing of it as he sees meet.

Hence, God "is not the idle spectator, but an agent in all" the actions taking place upon the stage of history as a mystery of salvation.[4]

In the context of a theocratic universe, then, the Puritan migration to America transformed the New England wilderness into the "new stage of acts," with the Puritan emigrants as the new "actors," in sacred, providential history. Based upon the desacralization of England in ecclesiastical history, and led directly by God's divine providence, the Puritan migration was indeed a great revelatory and prophetic event. But unlike John Donne who compared the settlement of Virginia to the glorious Acts of the Apostles in spreading the Gospel in the world, Puritans rather tended to justify their migration upon "the rule of Christ to his Apostles and Saints, and the practise of Gods Saints in all ages . . . to fly into the Wilderness from the face of the Dragon." This was the "new stage of acts and actors" which God's divine providence assigned to the Puritan settlement of New England in the unfolding drama of providential history. Separation from – and not identification with – England constituted, then, the very theme of the Puritan migration to America, and this was what made it so radically different from the Protestant ideology of the settlement of Virginia. For according to the Puritans only alienation from sinful England could bring them to a true reformation, and hence to reconciliation with God. Therefore, "God gave liberty" to his saints "to escape with their lives" from the Dragon's rage in England and led them to a place of "liberty," where they would be able "to serve the Lord according to his Word."[5]

---

[3] John Cotton, *A Brief Exposition with Practicall Observations upon the whole Book of Ecclesiastes* (1654), p. 131.
[4] Samuel Willard, *A Complete Body of Divinity* (1726), cited by Ernest B. Lowrie, *The Shape of the Puritan Mind: The Thought of Samuel Willard* (New Haven, 1974), pp. 71, 64.
[5] Thomas Shepard and John Allin, *A Defence of the Answer made unto the Nine Questions or*

Perry Miller's arguments in "Errand into the Wilderness" may not be acceptable today. Yet in many other places in his work he captured quite marvelously the essence of the Puritan migration to New England as a revelatory, prophetic event in the course of providential history, as for example when he wrote that for the Puritans

New England was the culmination of the Reformation, the climax of world history, the ultimate revelation through events of the objective toward which the whole of human activity had been tending from the beginning of time.[6]

Any analysis of the Puritan migration to New England, and hence of the Puritan Errand, obviously should take into consideration how the Puritans viewed their holy mission within the context of sacred, providential history, and what significance they attached to it within the unfolding drama of the history of salvation. By the very definition of their migration as based upon the *Exodus* type of religious migration, the Puritans provided us with a crucial clue in regard to their "Errand into the Wilderness." For in accordance with the *Exodus* type of religious migration, theirs was a migration based upon a flight from the impending divine judgments which would soon come upon England and the old corrupt European world; theirs was the flight of God's chosen remnant whom the Lord chose to save from the general conflagration.

Seen in this context, the Puritan apocalypse and eschatology of the New World was indeed radically different from that of the Protestants of Virginia. Hence, the Puritan incorporation of America as a sacred place within the confines of ecclesiastical history presented a revolutionary shift from that of Catholic Spain and Portugal, and from that of Protestant England. For whereas previously Spain, Portugal, and England, construed America as a sacred space by justifying the colonization of the New World upon God's divine warrant to his chosen nation to go out and spread the Gospel in the New World, now with the Puritan migration it was evident that the sacralization of America was essentially dependent upon the desacralization of England and the Old World in providential history, and the Puritans, therefore, saved no efforts to prove that an apocalyptic gulf was separating the New World from the Old in the all-time drama of the history of salvation. In sum, the Puritan migration signified a flight from a corrupted world and history. The truth of this assertion can be clearly seen from the very beginning of the Puritan migration to New England.

Positions Sent from New England against the Reply thereto by Mr. John Ball (1648), "The Preface," in *The Puritans*, ed. Perry Miller and Thomas H. Johnson (New York, 1963), vol. I, pp. 119–20.
[6] Miller, *The Puritans*, vol. I, p. 86.

THE PILGRIMS' IDEOLOGY OF THE SETTLEMENT OF NEW PLYMOUTH

In 1622, in the same year in which John Donne preached his marvelous sermon comparing – in the context of providential history – the Protestant settlement of Virginia with the glorious Acts of the Apostles in spreading the Gospel in the world, a small tract was published in London which provided the earliest expression of the Puritan ideology of the settlement of New England for the public in England. This was Robert Cushman's *A Sermon Preached at Plimmoth in New England* (1622), which he delivered to the poor and tiny band of Separatists at Plymouth in 1621, a year after the Pilgrim Fathers had landed in New England. Cushman (1579–1625), a deacon of the Leyden congregation and at that time a business agent of the Pilgrim colony, was in Plymouth during the months of November and December 1621, and during this time preached his lay sermon on the subject of "The Sin and Danger of Self-Love,"[7] admonishing his Separatist brethren against an excessive individualism which might threaten their entire holy experiment in the wilderness of America, including the young colony's economic survival. (Cushman's lay sermon, together with John Winthrop's lay sermon, "A Model of Christian Charity" (1630), supplies a unique picture of the Puritan fears of excessive individualism which would undermine the ultimate religious mission to be accomplished in America. Both, therefore, spared no efforts to show that the Puritan religious goal in settling New England would be realized only through the collective endeavors and means of a Christian society as a whole.) Yet, Cushman's sermon is important to study, because it provides the first instance of a written rendering of the Puritan justifications for emigration to America which were so radically different from those of the Protestants of Virginia.

Cushman made it very clear in the preface to his sermon, which also was written during his stay at Plymouth during the winter of 1621, that New England was designed by God to be a shelter and a place of refuge for God's chosen remnants whom the Lord aimed to save in the face of the imminent divine judgments soon to befall the sinful Old World:

And if it should please God to punish his people in the Christian countries of *Europe* (for their coldnesse, carnality, wanton abuse of the Gospel, contention, &c.) either by Turkish slavery, or by Popish tyrannie, which God forbid, yet if the time be come, or shall come (as who knoweth) when Satan shall be let loose, to cast out his flouds against them, here is a way opened for such as have wings to flie into this Wilderness.[8]

---

[7] Robert Cushman, *A Sermon Preached at Plimmoth in New England, December 9, 1621 . . . Wherein is Shewed the Danger of Selfe-Love, and the Sweetnesse of True Friendship* (1622).
[8] Cushman, *A Sermon Preached at Plimmoth*, "The Epistle Dedicatory," p. 2.

These eschatological expectations and apocalyptic visions, which were in time to become the predominant reasons and justifications for the Puritan migration to New England, clearly reveal the Puritans' revolutionary way of incorporating America as a sacred space within the confines of ecclesiastical history. For in clear contrast to the Protestant eschatology of the New World, based on the glorious role of England as the elect nation in spreading the Gospel in America, the Puritan eschatology of America rather stressed that an essential apocalyptic gulf separated the New World from the Old in the course of providential history. New England's singular role in the history of salvation, therefore, was based upon its total disassociation from the sins and corruptions of the Old World. Therefore, continued Cushman,

as by the dispersion of the Jewish Church thorow persecution, the Lord brought in the fulnesse of the Gentiles, so who knoweth, whether now by tyrannia and afflication, which he suffereth to come upon them, he will not by little and little chase them, even amongst the Heathens, that so a light may rise up in the darke and the kingdome of heaven be taken from them which now have it, and given to a people that shall bring forth the fruit of it.

Consequently, looking back on the annals of sacred history, and "considering Gods dealing of olde" time, "and seeing the name of Christian to be very great, but the true nature thereof almost quite lost in all degrees & sects" in Europe, Cushman was deeply convinced that God's divine wrath would very soon fall upon doomed Europe:

I cannot think but that there is some judgement not farre off, and that God will shortly, even of stones, rayse up children unto *Abraham*.[9]

Here Cushman was making use of the famous eschatological vision in Matthew: "for I tell you, God is able from these stones to raise up children to Abraham. Even now the axe is laid to the root of the trees; every tree thereof that does not bear good fruit is cut down and thrown into the fire" (Matt. 3: 9–10).

When Robert Cushman returned to England, he "helped to compile and wrote the dedication to a collection of narrative and description concerning the Atlantic voyage" to New England, and the Pilgrim "colony's first tentative months."[10] At the end of this volume Cushman published an important tract, entitled, *Reasons and Considerations Touching the Lawfulness of Removing out of England into the Parts of America* (1622).[11] This tract, in

[9] *Ibid.*, p. 3.
[10] Alan Heimert and Andrew Delbanco (eds.), *The Puritans in America: A Narrative Anthology* (Cambridge, Mass., 1985), p. 41.
[11] Robert Cushman, *Reasons and Considerations Touching the Lawfulness of Removing out of England into the Parts of America* (1622), in *The Story of the Pilgrim Fathers, 1606–1623, A.D. as Told by Themselves, their Friends, and their Enemies*, ed. Edward Arber (New York, 1969), pp. 495–505.

Cushman's own words, was "the first attempt that hath been made, that I know of, to defend those enterprises" of the Separatists in the wilderness of America. Yet, apart from its great value as the first conscious attempt in England to vindicate the Pilgrim colony, the importance of Cushman's *Reasons and Considerations* is that it provides us again with one of the earliest expressions of the Puritan ideology of the settlement of New England which was so radically different from the Protestant ideology of settling Virginia. Apparently, Cushman's tract was an appeal to the Nonconformist Puritans in England. Therefore, as compared to the Protestant justification of the settlement of Virginia, Cushman formulated a very different set of premises for the Puritan migration to New England. His problem, evidently, was to persuade the Nonconformists in England to flee to America, and convince them that even in the wilderness of the New World they would be able to serve God and His Christ by establishing the true church there. His ultimate problem, however, was to convince his brethren in England that they could not wait for sudden divine revelations to lead them out of England, as had been the case with the Jewish Exodus from Egypt. Rather, Cushman argued, nothing bound the Nonconformists to live in England, because the essence of Christian life in this world was a constant wandering and pilgrimage upon earth. Instead of claiming that the settlement of America revealed England's glorious role in providential history, as the Protestants argued, Cushman rather developed the notion, along with many other Puritan emigrants, of "that poor persecuted Flock of Christ" flying into the wilderness in face of Satan's malice and rage in England.[12]

Cushman's ultimate goal in writing the *Reasons and Considerations* was to convince Nonconformist Puritans in England that their migration to New England had a full divine warrant. These Nonconformists, who "out of doubt, in tenderness and conscience and fear to offend God, by running" to New England "before they were called" by God's explicit command, declined to remove themselves to the New World and hindered "others from going" to New England. They, obviously, had waited for a definitive divine revelation, as was the case with Israel's Exodus from Egypt, before they would dare to emigrate from England into New England. Cushman, therefore, had to prove for them the great difference between the time of the "ancient Patriarchs," in which God used "extraordinary revelations," and the present time in which such revelations could no longer "be expected":

we must first consider, That whereas God, of old, did call and summon our fathers by predictions, dreams, visions, and certain illuminations, to go from their countries, places, and habitations, to reside and dwell here, or there; and to wander up and

---

[12] Edward Winslow, "The Reasons that Moved most of the Pilgrim Church to Migrate to America," in *The Story of the Pilgrim Fathers*, ed. Edward Arber, p. 262.

down from city to city, and land to land, according to his will and pleasure: now there is no such calling to be expected, for any matter whatsoever; neither must any so much as imagine that there will now be any such thing.

In biblical times the migration of God's chosen people was guided directly by certain prophetic and revelatory divine signs. In the past, indeed, "God did once so train his people: but now he doth not; but speaks in another manner. And so we must apply ourselves," declared Cushman, "to God's present dealing; and not to his wonted dealing."[13]

Within the confines of a theocratic universe, evidently, God's divine providence did not leave the saints without prophetic directions and signs to guide them in the mystery of the history of salvation. Thus what had changed during time and history was not that God had gradually removed His saving grace from His created world, for the Lord continued as strongly and as persistently as ever to take care of His people, but only that the manner and mode with which He communicated himself to His chosen ones was transformed from "extraordinary revelations" in past times into men's ability in modern times to discern God's "Voice and Word." So, according to Cushman,

as the miracle of giving manna cease, when the fruits of the land became plenty: so God, having such a plentiful storehouse of directions in his holy Word; there must not now any extraordinary revelations be expected. But now the ordinary examples and precepts of the Scriptures, reasonably and rightly understood and applied, must be the Voice and Word that must call us, press us, and direct us in every action.[14]

The realm of history, again, became an essential dimension for the true understanding of divine, prophetic revelation, because in the historical examples in the Scriptures the sacred history of the church was exhibited. At the same time, in an age in which "extraordinary revelation" could no longer be expected, human reason became a crucial agent in the application of the sacred examples of ecclesiastical history to present times and present situations.

Having directed Nonconformist Puritans not to expect in their age some sudden "extraordinary revelations," but rather to search diligently in the Scriptures for "the Voice and Word" of God, Cushman's next step was to prove that "neither is there any land or possession now, like unto the possession which the Jews had in Canaan; being legally holy, and appropriated unto a holy people, the Seed of Abraham: in which they dwelt securely, and had their days prolonged." This land, the Promised Land, which "the Lord gave" to his chosen nation "as a land of rest after their weary travels" in the wilderness, signified indeed "a type of eternal rest in heaven." Yet, according to Cushman, this Holy Land existed no more in the world, and

---

[13] Cushman, *Reasons and Considerations*, p. 496.   [14] *Ibid.*, p. 496.

therefore no nation could appropriate to itself the title of the Promised Land in the sacred history of salvation. Most significant in this passage is, of course, Cushman's refusal to identify England with the Promised Land, the very identification which had become the ultimate mark of the Protestant vision of England during this time. Instead, Cushman argued that the existential condition of Christian life in this world was that of constant wandering and pilgrimage: "But now we are all, in all places, strangers and pilgrims" upon earth. "Our dwelling is but a wandering; and our abiding, but as a fleeting; and in a word, our home is nowhere but in heavens."[15] The vision of pilgrimage supported Cushman's endeavors to prove to the Nonconformist Puritans that nothing should bind them to continue to dwell in England, and that they, in fact, were fully at liberty to emigrate to New England.

In the Puritan mind, therefore, nothing remained of the Protestant glorious vision of England as God's elect nation, or of England as the Promised Land. And it was this desacralization of England in sacred, providential history which provided the ultimate justification for the Puritan migration to New England. Thus, continued Cushman, although "there may be reasons to persuade a man to live in this or that land; yet there cannot be the same reasons which the Jews had" in regard of Canaan as God's Promised Land. England, however, was not the Promised Land, nor its people God's chosen people, and therefore, according to Cushman, Nonconformist Puritans who were "living as outcasts, nobodies, eyesores"[16] in England were under no divine obligation to stay there.

Yet, Cushman himself was fully aware of the Puritans' deep hesitations and strong fears concerning their removal to America. "I know many who sit here still," he wrote,

with their talent in a napkin, having notable endowments, both of body and mind; and might do great good if they were in some places; which here do none: and yet, through fleshly fear, niceness, straitness of heart, &c., sit still and look on; and will not hazard a dram of health, no a day of pleasure, nor an hour of rest, to further the knowledge and salvation of the sons of Adam in that New World; where a drop of the knowledge of Christ is most precious, which is here not set by.

Furthermore, he urged his fellow Nonconformists in England to consider the advantage of establishing a colony "chiefly to display the efficacy and power of the Gospel, both in zealous preaching, professing, and wise walking under it, before the faces of these poor blind infidels" in America. Ultimately, however, Cushman pleaded with Puritans to consider the migration to New England in the context of the impending apocalyptic judgments which would soon come upon the Old World:

---

[15] *Ibid.*, p. 497.   [16] *Ibid.*, pp. 497–8.

And who can tell but God, what danger may lie at our doors, even in our native country? or what plots may be abroad? or when God will cause our sun to go down at noonday? and in the midst of our peace and security, lay upon us some lasting scourge for our so long neglect and contempt of his most glorious Gospel?[17]

An important source for these apocalyptic visions concerning England's gloomy fate in providential history was indeed "the bitter contention" in this realm "about Religion, by writing disputing and inveighing earnestly one against another." "The heat" and "zeal" of these religious controversies in Jacobean England, claimed Cushman, "might easily drive the zealous" Nonconformists "to the heathens" in America. Likewise, the very fact, according to Cushman, that England "groaneth under so many close-fisted and unmerciful men . . . may quickly persuade any man to a liking of this course, and to prectice a removal" to New England. He made it very clear that only "honest godly and industrious men" would be "right heartily welcome" in the Pilgrim colony in America, "but for others of dissolute and profane life, their rooms [or absence] are better than their companies."[18]

The earliest formulation of the Puritan ideology of the settlement of New England had thus differed in a revolutionary way from the Protestant ideology of the colonization of Virginia. The Puritan eschatology and apocalypse of the New World was radically different from that of Protestant Virginia. Gone were visions of England as God's elect nation, and of the Church of England's glorious and singular role in providential history. Gone, too, was the concept of the English people as God's chosen people. Instead, the Puritan call to emigrate to New England was also a call to leave behind them in England a corrupted nation, a sinful church and profane people, upon whom the Lord would pour his divine wrath. Thus, in accordance with the transformation in English apocalyptic tradition from John Bale and John Foxe's glorious vision of England as God's chosen nation into William Perkins and Thomas Brightman's identification of England with the sinful church of Laodicea in the Book of Revelation, the Puritan migration to America was essentially based upon the desacralization of England in sacred, ecclesiastical history. Consequently, this Puritan desacralization of England led eventually to the sacralization of the wilderness in America as a shelter and a place of refuge for Nonconformist Puritans. Evidently, then, with the Puritan migration to New England a new and revolutionary way of incorporating America into the confines of sacred, ecclesiastical history was established for the first time: the role of the New World in providential history was no longer dependent upon its connection with the Old World; rather, it had become totally and absolutely dissociated from the degeneration of the Old World and its corrupted history.

---

[17] *Ibid.*, pp. 498–9, 501–2.   [18] *Ibid.*, pp. 503–5.

In the past Protestants had viewed the meaning of America in sacred history as essentially connected with, and hence totally dependent upon, England's singular role in providential history. But now, with the beginnings of the Puritan migration to America the eschatology of the New World was radically transformed. For Puritans emphasized rather that an essential apocalyptic gulf was separating the New World from the Old in the sacred history of salvation, and that the creation of New England as a sacred place within the confines of providential history was grounded upon its total separation from the corruptions and sins of old England. Within sacred history as the theatre of God's judgment, and within the confines of a theocratic universe, then, the Old and the New World were totally antagonistic and mutually exclusive entities. So, according to the Puritan ideology of the migration to New England, the "discovery" of America was a great revelatory and prophetic event in the course of the progress of the church upon earth in which God's divine providence transformed the locus of the history of redemption and salvation from the corrupted Old World to the New World. In the context of sacred, ecclesiastical history, therefore, the Puritan incorporation of America as a sacred space in providential history signified indeed a revolutionary shift: they no longer required the New World to rely upon the Old in order to acquire its significance in sacred history. On the contrary, it acquired its singular role in the providential history of salvation by severing all ties with the corruption of the Old World. According America a uniquely independent role within the confines of providential history, Puritans construed the first original American ideology which stressed, for the first time since the "discovery" of America, that the New World had a unique destiny of its own within the boundaries of sacred, ecclesiastical history.

Cushman, indeed, was the first Puritan, but by no means the last one, to fashion a new vision of America as an indepenet and autonomous sacred space within the confines of providential history – as the place divine providence had assigned for God's chosen remnants to flee to, out of the general conflagration which would soon come upon the Old World. Evidently, eschatological expectations and apocalyptic visions constituted the very theme of the Pilgrims' migration to Plymouth, and later they constituted the very motive of the great Puritan migration to New England. So, for example, according to William Bradford, one of the ultimate reasons for the Pilgrims' removal from Holland to America in 1620 was in accordance with "the divine proverb, that a wise man seeth the plague when it cometh, and hideth himself, Proverbs xxii, 3." He therefore envisioned the Separatists as those "skillful and beaten soldiers" who "were fearful either to be entrapped or surrounded by their enemies so as they should neither be able to fight nor fly." Bradford too, like Cushman, raised the theme of pilgrimage as the existential mode of Christian life in this world, yet in his highly eschatological conscience the fears of divine judgment also played an important role. The Separatists lived in Holland, he wrote, "but as men in exile and in a poor condition," and could anticipate only that "great miseries might possibly befall them in this place." Furthermore, with the beginning of the Thirty Years' War (1618–48), the Pilgrims could expect from Europe "nothing but beating of drums and preparing for war." Twice, then, the Pilgrim Fathers were driven into exile because corruption and degeneration in England and Europe threatened to bring God to pour his divine wrath upon the sinful world. But now, finally, the migration to America put an end to all their suffering and miseries in the Old World, because "In this wilderness" of America, as Bradford wrote, the Lord "Us shelter still in th' shadow of" His "wings," and

> His great and marvellous works they here saw,
> And he them taught in his most holy law.[19]

JOHN WINTHROP AND THE APOCALYPSE OF THE PURITAN MIGRATION TO AMERICA

Eschatological expectations and apocalyptic visions constituted the core and the heart of the great Puritan migration of the 1630s to New England as well. This contention is clearly substantiated by John Winthrop's crucial decision to emigrate to New England in 1630 as the governor of the newly formed Massachusetts Bay Company. As early as 1616, he acutely described the gloomy situation of the Puritan in Jacobean England in these words: "all experience tells me," he wrote, that those who adhered to the Puritan way of godly life "shalbe despised, pointed at, hated of the world, made a byword, reviled, slandered, rebuked, made a gazing stocke, called Puritans, nice fools, hipocrites, hair-brainde fellows, rashe, indiscreet, vain-glorious," and so forth. He was, then, fully sensitive to the fact that his and his fellow Puritans' attempt to establish a "society of saints" and to lead a godly life had nothing but the contempt of the majority of English society. This depressing situation had led to the rise of his eschatological conscience, and eventually, to his desacralization of England as a sacred place in providential history. In 1622 he was still sure that "the Lo: looke mercifully upon his sinful lande, and turne us to him by some repentance, otherwise we may feare" that England "hath seene the best dayes." This he wrote in January 1622, but in August of that very year there occurred a radical change in his eschatological conscience. Writing to his son, John Winthrop, Jr., he told

---

[19] William Bradford, *Of Plymouth Plantation*, pp. 24, 27; "Verses by Governor Bradford," Massachusetts Historical Society, *Proceedings* 11 (Boston, 1869–70), 471–3.

him: "but remember still that the tyme is at hande when they shall call to the [mountains to] hide them from the face of him whom now they slight and neglect etc." (Luke 21:20–2). A year later, in 1623, Winthrop's gloomy eschatological expectations concerning England's ability to retain its singular role in providential history became even more desperate. "We have cause to feare the worst," he wrote to his wife in August 1623, "in regarde that all thinges are so farre out of order, and that the sinnes bothe our owne and the whole lande doe call for judgementes rather than blessinges."[20]

In 1629, however, when Winthrop became deeply involved with the plans to establish a Puritan colony in Massachusetts Bay, his eschatological conscience reached its climax. As was the case with Cushman before, Winthrop abandoned any hope concerning England's fate in providential history. In his mind the sacralization of New England in sacred history had been intrinsically associated with his total desacralization of England. In a letter to his wife, Margaret, in May 1629, Winthrop wrote:

the increasinge of our sines gives us so great cause to looke for some heauye Scquorge and Judgment to be cominge upon us: the Lorde hath admonished, threatened, corrected, and astonished us, yet we growe worse and worse, so as his spirit will not allwayes strive with us, he must needs give waye to his furye at last.

Furthermore, considering the historical events taking place in Europe during the Thirty Years' War exclusively in the context of sacred, ecclesiastical history, or as evidence of divine fury against the churches and nations of the continent, Winthrop could not but foresee that the divine wrath would soon come upon England too. He therefore took the apocalyptic vision from Revelation concerning Babylon ("and God remembered great Babylon, to make her drain the cup of the fury of his wrath" [Rev. 16:19]), in order to describe the desperate fate of England in the course of providential history. The Lord, he wrote,

hath smitten all other Churches before our eyes, and hath made them to drinke of the bitter cuppe of tribulation, even unto death; we sawe this, and humbled not overselves, to turn from our evill wayes, but have provoked him more than all the nations rounde about us: therefore he is turning the cuppe toward us also, and because we are the last, our portion must be, to drinke the verye dreggs which remaine.[21]

It was within this general context of God's imminent apocalyptic judgments that Winthrop wrote to Margaret, "my dear wife, I am veryly perswade, God will bringe some heavye Afflicacion upon this lande, and

---

[20] "John Winthrop's Experiencia," *Winthrop Papers*, vol. I, pp. 196–7; "John Winthrop to Thomas Fones," *Winthrop Papers*, vol. I, p. 268; "John Winthrop to John Winthrop Jr.," *Winthrop Papers*, vol. I, p. 271; "John Winthrop to his Wife," *Winthrop Papers*, vol. I, p. 286.
[21] "John Winthrop to his Wife," *Winthrop Papers*, vol. II, p. 91.

that speedylye." Yet since Winthrop was already, in 1629, contemplating a move to Massachusetts – and this not the least because God pleased "to frame" his and fellow Puritans' "mindes" to pursue this direction – he therefore could conclude this letter to his wife with these consolatory words:

If the Lord seeth it wilbe good for us, he will provide a shelter and a hiding place for us and ours as a Zoar for Lott, Sarephtah for his prophet etc.[22]

This passage is the most famous and most oft-quoted in the correspondence between Margaret and John Winthrop. Yet, the most important aspect of this passage is indeed the biblical references (Gen. 19:17–22, 1 Kings 17:8–24, and Luke 5:26), which Winthrop used here, because they sharply illuminate the dimension of sacred, ecclesiastical history, as a mode of historical thought, within which Winthrop consciously sought to place the future Puritan migration to New England of the 1630s. Furthermore, reading these biblical references, it becomes immediately clear that Winthrop, in fact, intentionally chose these sacred passages from the annals of ecclesiastical history in order to construe an indispensable eschatological and apocalyptic dimension for the Puritan migration to Massachusetts which was already under serious consideration. For, taken as a whole, Winthrop's biblical references depicted indeed a prophetic journey in providential history in which God's divine providence was leading His saints to escape out of doomed Sodom into a place of safety where they would glorify the Lord for their deliverance. Or more specifically, these passages present in fact three crucial *acts* in the drama of human salvation and redemption – deliverance, pilgrimage, and glorification.

The first biblical passage which Winthrop used in this letter, is taken from Genesis 19. This chapter tells the story of Lot's miraculous escape from Sodom. The first *act*, then, in the drama to which Winthrop referred in his letter, was that of deliverance. So, before the Lord "rained on Sodom and Gomor'rah brimstones and fire" from heaven, He sent two angels to warn Lot to depart immediately from that city of sin and corruption. Lot eventually escaped to Zoar, and there he found a shelter and a hiding place while God brought about the destruction and total devastation of Sodom and Gomorrah (Gen. 19:17–25). The second *act* in the drama Winthrop set in his letter was that of a pilgrimage. Here he used the passage from 1 Kings 17, which describes how the Lord sent his chosen prophet, Elijah the Tishbite on a pilgrimage to Zarephath, near the city of Sidon, in order to save him from the rage of Ahab, the most sinful king of Israel who married the notorious Jesebel and worshiped the Baal. All during his journey and escape, God furnished his beloved prophet and maintained all his needs.

---

[22] *Ibid.*, pp. 91–2.

This was especially true in regard to Elijah's stay in the village of Zarephath where, as the Lord promised him, "The jar of meal shall not be spent, and the cruse of oil shall not fail" (1 Kings 17:8–24). After the *act* of deliverance, then, came the *act* of pilgrimage revealing God's endless care and support of his saints in all their ways in the world. Finally, the last *act* in Winthrop's dramatic vision of the Puritan migration, was that of glorification. For this Winthrop chose the passage from Luke 5, which described how after Jesus cured a paralyzed man, "they were all amazed" who had been present when this miracle took place, "and they glorified God and were filled with fear, saying, 'We have seen strange things today'" (Luke 5:26).

Evidently, then, with the growing prospects of settling a Puritan colony in Massachusetts, Winthrop's eschatological conscience reached its zenith, and he now envisioned the Puritan migration to America in striking apocalyptic terms; as a daring providential flight from doomed Sodom and a fearless pilgrimage under the wings of divine providence, which eventually would lead the Puritan saints to a place of safety and refuge in the wilderness of America where they would praise the Lord and glorify His name. In Winthrop's mind, therefore, the sacralization of America went hand in hand with the desacralization of England within the confines of the sacred history of the church. Consequently, once he defined in these words the apocalyptic dimension of the Puritan migration within providential history, nothing could keep him from dedicating all his efforts to furthering this crucial and glorious event in the course of the history of salvation. No wonder, then, that since May 1629, when he described this apocalyptic dramatic vision of the Puritan removal to America in the letter to his wife, Winthrop was wholly preoccupied with the great task of defining the ideological, apocalyptic, premises of the Puritan migration which he eventually led to Massachusetts in 1630. His eschatological zeal, therefore, was responsible more than anything else for his existential decision to lead the Puritan exodus out of the sins of the Old World and its corrupted history.

We find, then, that Winthrop had already, in the spring of 1629, defined the migration to New England as a prophetic flight from the much-feared impending judgments God's divine wrath would pour upon England and the Old World. The same view of course, as we saw earlier, constituted the theme of Cushman's justification of the Pilgrim colony in Plymouth. However, when compared with the Protestant ideology of the settlement of Virginia, based, as it was, upon the *Genesis* type of religious migration, it becomes clear that the Puritans had developed a radical new ideology for their settlement of New England, and that this new ideology was based upon a new sacred model taken from the annals of ecclesiastical history; namely, the *Exodus*, or judgmental, type of religious migration, which stressed the Saints' divine duty and obligation to separate from, and not to take part in, the sin and corruption of the Old World. This ideology not only stood behind the Pilgrims' decision to emigrate to Plymouth, but it was also fundamental to the origins of the great Puritan migration to Massachusetts. So, for example, when Francis Higginson preached his farewell sermon to his congregation in Leicester, in old England, shortly before he left for Salem in America on behalf of the Massachusetts Bay Company in April 1629, he told his godly brethren:

When you see Jerusalem compassed with armies, then flee to the mountains.[23]

The members of Higginson's godly congregation, who were, as were all Puritans, well acquainted with the various passages in the Bible through constant reading and exercise, recognized immediately that their much-beloved departing minister used here an important sacred prophecy in order to describe for them the role of the Puritan migration in providential history. For what Higginson did was to combine in one short yet powerful sentence two long sentences from Luke, the very same ones which Winthrop in fact used in his letter to his son in 1622, and thus to draw a forceful prophetic image of the Puritan migration to Massachusetts: "But *when you see Jerusalem surrounded by armies, then* know that its desolation has come near. Then let those who are in Judea *flee to the mountains*" (Luke 21:20–2; my italics).

THE ESCHATOLOGY OF THE PURITANS' "GENERAL OBSERVATIONS FOR THE PLANTATION OF NEW ENGLAND"

It seems evident, then, that before there could be any Puritan migration to New England, there would first have to be formulated a certain well-defined and coherent ideology with which Puritans would be able to interpret the meaning of their mission into the wilderness in America. So, before engaging themselves in the actual arrangements and preparations for the long and perilous sea voyage to New England, Puritans first drew a long series of "Reasons" and "Considerations" in which they debated among themselves the justification for their holy experiment in New England.[24] These import-

---

[23] Francis Higginson, cited in *Magnalia Christi Americana*, by Cotton Mather, vol. I, p. 327.
[24] "General Observations for the Plantation of New England" (1629), *Winthrop Papers*, vol. II, pp. 111–49. In the following discussion I use "General Observations" as an inclusive name for a whole series of papers, arguments, objections, letters, etc., which characterized the debate among Puritans in England in 1629 concerning the plan to settle Massachusetts Bay. In so doing I follow the editors of volume II of the *Winthrop Papers*. On the relationship between the leaders of the great Puritan migration and Parliamentary leaders during that time, men like Sir John Eliot and John Hampden, who also took an active part in the debate on the "Observations," see A. P. Newton, *The Colohnial Activities of the English*

ant tracts, most of them written by John Winthrop but some also by other leaders of the great Puritan migration of the 1630s, had been widely circulated among Puritans who had already expressed their inclination to go to America, or among those Puritans who seemed greatly in favor of the holy enterprise in the wilderness. The ultimate significance of these writings, however, lies in the fact that they provide us with first-hand evidence as to the Puritan mind at work in regard to fashioning the ideological premises of the migration to America. Furthermore, because this body of writings illuminates the shape of the Puritan ideology of the settlement of New England, it may serve as a basis for comparison with the Protestant ideology of the settlement of Virginia, as well. For these Puritan tracts, above all, reveal definitively that the desacralization of England in providential history was an essential precondition for the Puritan migration to New England, and that it was the *Exodus* type, and not the *Genesis* type, of religious migration upon which the Puritans based their settlement of Massachusetts.

In the spring of 1629, the leaders of the Puritan migration circulated in England among themselves and their friends an important pamphlet entitled "General Observations for the Plantation of New England." This important tract was the outcome of several meetings which the future Puritan leaders of the great migration held in Lincolnshire and at Bury, Suffolk, during July and August of 1629.[25] Both in the grievances it listed as justification for the pending migration and in the general picture it presents of one group of Puritans critically reviewing the state of England in the early seventeenth century, this revealing document offers an excellent summary of the arguments and justifications – economic, social, political, and religious – employed by the Puritans themselves to explain why they were exploring the prospects of settling in the wilderness of America.

One searches these "Observations," and other related tracts pertaining to the Puritans' plan to settle Massachusetts, in vain for any reference to the recent "crisis" in England of the late 1620s and early 1630s so frequently associated with the Puritan migration in modern historiography.[26] The 1629 "crisis of the Parliament," or its dissolution by Charles I on March 10,

---

Puritans (New Haven, 1914), and J. H. Hexter, *The Reign of King Pym* (Cambridge, 1948). For the Puritans' involvement in colonization, see T. K. Rabb, *Enterprise and Empire: Merchant and Gentry Investment in the Expansion of England, 1575–1630* (Cambridge, 1967).

[25] Editors' "Introduction" to the "Arguments for the Plantation of New England," *Winthrop Papers*, vol. II, p. 110.

[26] For modern interpretations which seek to explain the origins of the Puritan migration to New England by a sudden economic, social, political, or ecclesiastical "crisis" within English society, see, for example, James Truslow Adams, *The Founding of New England* (Boston, 1921 [1949]), pp. 122–4; Perry Miller, *Orthodoxy in Massachusetts* (Gloucester, 1964 [1933]), p. 99.

1629, issues of Puritan conformity and nonconformity with the rites and ceremonies of the Church of England, ecclesiastical questions of separation and non-separation from the established church, even the specter of William Laud, bishop of London and his anti-Puritan policy – none of these explanatory staples of modern scholarship appear. From a reading of the "General Observations," it would seem that these particular events and issues did not determine the Puritans' decision to emigrate to the New World. More than an isolated series of recent political, social, and economic crises, we must then conclude, motivated the Puritan migrants of 1629–30.

This is not to deny that the Puritans of the "Observations" viewed England as reeling in the mist of an ominous crisis; they did. But the crisis they feared was neither political in nature nor of recent vintage; it was, instead, a general historical crisis which they traced back to the second half of the sixteenth century, or to the Puritan failure during the reign of Elizabeth to bring a more perfect religious reformation in England. Ultimately, it was a crisis of enormous proportions in the course of sacred, ecclesiastical history which Puritans discussed in terms of the meaning of England's place in the progress of the history of salvation, and the future significance of Massachusetts Bay colony in providential history. These, indeed, were the prominent concerns of the "General Observations," and here lies their ultimate importance for any analysis of the Puritan ideology of the settlement of New England.

Puritans, like Protestants as a whole, thought of history exclusively in terms of ecclesiastical history. Therefore, in their vision, the church constituted the ultimate agent in the progress of history. History was the story of the church, the true church, its successes and failures, from the very act of Creation to the very final Day of Judgment. "Dothe not the history of the Churche give us many examples," so runs the common rhetorical refrain of the "General Observations."[27] Accordingly, the ultimate goal of the Puritans of the "Observations" was to locate the sacred meaning of the future Puritan migration to New England within the context of providential history, and to prove the ultimate significance thereof in the drama of the history of salvation. It is, indeed, within this context – of the meaning Puritans rendered to their migration – or within the ideological context, that the crucial differences between the Protestant settlement of Virginia and the Puritan settlement of New England can be most fully revealed.

The "General Observations for the Plantation of New England," along with the various tracts connected with it, consisted in fact of eight arguments for the settlement of New England and objections attached to each argument. The beginning, or the first argument, read thus:

[27] "General Observations for the Plantation of New England," p. 122.

It wilbe a service to the church of great consequens by carryinge the gospell into those parts to raise a bullworke against the kingdom of antichrist which the Jesuits labour to rere in all parts of the world.

The resemblance here to the Protestants' arguments should not mislead us concerning the revolutionary character of this tract. For immediately in the second argument the Puritans fully exposed the apocalyptic role they assigned to their migration in providential history:

All other Churches of Europe are brought to desolation, and it cannot be, but the like Judgement is comminge upon us: and who knows, but that God hathe provided this place [New England], to be a refuge for manye, whome he meanes to save out of the general destruction.[28]

This eschatological scenario was radically different from that of the Protestant ideology of the settlement of Virginia, because it stressed that an apocalyptic gulf was separating the Old World from the New World, and consequently that it was the saints' duty to flee into the wilderness in face of God's impending divine judgments which would soon fall upon the Old World.

Having set the eschatological and apocalyptic context for their future migration to New England, Puritans in the following arguments strove to prove that the desacralization of England in providential history was a sufficient, if not a necessary, condition for the saints' migration to America. Their attitude was clearly opposite to that of the Protestants who settled Virginia, to whom England's glorious role in providential history provided the ultimate sanction for its colonial enterprises in the New World. So, for example, the Puritans of the "Observations," argued that, economically, "noe mans estate" in England "will suffice him to keep sayle with his equall and he that doeth not must live in contempt," and that "it is almost impossible for a good upright man to maynteyne his charge and to live comfortably in his profession." Not only is social and economic life in England unbearable, but also "the fountaynes of learning and religion are soe corrupted" in England that "most children, (even the best wittiest and of fayerest hopes) are perverted, corrupted, and utterly over powered by the multitude of evill examples and licentious governors of those seminaries."[29] Nothing indeed could be further away from the Protestants' glorious vision of England as God's chosen nation than this gloomy and despairing Puritan image of England. The Puritans' total desacralization of England retained nothing from the proud and magnificent vision of the elect nation in providential history.

After successfully establishing the eschatological and apocalyptic dimensions of the Puritan migration through the desacralization of England,

---

[28] *Ibid.*, p. 111.   [29] *Ibid.*, pp. 111–12, 118.

Puritans evidently had to prove the right of colonizing New England, and, most importantly, to define the divine warrant for their flight out of England into the wilderness in America. So, in the first place, Puritans, like the Protestants of Virginia, claimed that "the earth is the lords garden and he hath given it to the sonns of men to be tylled and improved." Again, the fact that Puritans used a similar argument as that of the Protestants concerning the right to colonize America should not prevent us from seeing the revolutionary thrust of the Puritans' "General Observations." For the crucial difference between the Protestants of Virginia and the Puritans of New England had to do with the Church of England's role in the colonial enterprise in America.

Believing their church to be the true reformed church, Protestants evidently assigned an important role to the Church of England in the settlement of Virginia by transferring the Protestant faith to the New World against the Catholics there. Puritans, on the other hand, presented a radical, yet different picture; having identified the Church of England with Laodicea, the most sinful church in Revelation, they sought rather to cut any association with this corrupted church, and to erect in the wilderness of America what they considered to be the true apostolic church. "What can be better or more honorable worke" declared the Puritans "then to help rayse and support a particular church," and they beseeched other Puritans "to joyne our forces" and their "company of faithfull people" in laying the ground for the holy experiment in the wilderness.[30]

Yet, by defining the migration to New England as the flight of the godly from corrupted England, and by declaring explicitly that the purpose of their removal to America is to establish "a particular church," or congregational church, Puritans showed that they regarded the Church of England as nothing but an apostasy in the drama of the history of salvation. Hence, the Puritans maintained in their final argument for the plantation of New England, that only migration to America could save the saints from living scandalous lives in England, or in sum, that migration was indeed itself an act of religious reformation:

If such as are knowen to be godly and live in welth heare shall forsake all this to joyne themselves with this church and to runne their hazard it wilbe an example of great use boeth for the removinge of the scandall of wor[l]dly and sinister respects to give more lyfe to the faith of godly people in their prayers for the plantation and alsoe to encourage others to joyne the more willingly in it.[31]

The Puritans' reasons for, and considerations regarding, the settlement of New England, thus presented a radical shift from those of the Protestants of Virginia. For both groups the vision of England and the Church of England

---

[30] *Ibid.*, p. 112. [31] *Ibid.*, p. 112.

had essentially affected the ideology of the settlement of America. Accordingly, while Protestants exalted England's singular role in providential history, they naturally tended to justify the ground for their colonial activities in America upon the *Genesis* type of religious migration, stressing to the utmost England's duty as God's chosen nation to spread the Gospel of the true Protestant faith in the world. Puritans, on the other hand, while grounding their arguments for emigration to America upon the desacralization of England and its church, obviously inclined rather to justify their settlement of New England upon the *Exodus* type of religious migration, emphasizing the saints' ultimate duty to sever their ties with corrupted England and the Church of England. Conflicting visions, therefore, concerning England's role in sacred, ecclesiastical history, had thus led to contrasting ideological premises among Protestants and Puritans concerning the meaning of the settlement of the New World.

Based, as it was, upon the *Exodus*, judgmental, sacred type of religious migration, the Puritan ideology of the settlement of New England emphasized, time and again, the immediate threatening presence of God's divine judgments which would soon come upon the English nation. So, according to the Nonconformist Puritan Francis Higginson, who left for Salem in the summer of 1629 to serve as a minister of the church there,

New England might be designed by heaven, as a *refuge* and *shelter* for the *nonconformists* against the storms that were coming upon the nation.[32]

And the Puritans of the "Observations" saved no efforts to reveal the extent to which eschatological expectations and apocalyptic visions played a crucial role in their quest to establish a Puritan colony in Massachusetts Bay: "We have feared" they declared "a judgement a long tyme yet we are safe." Therefore they asked themselves if "it were better to stay till it come and either we may fly then or if we be overtaken we may content our selves to suffer with such a church as this," namely the wicked Church of England.[33]

This was indeed the greatest and the gravest choice Puritans had to contend with: namely, whether to wait patiently until God would pour his unavoidable and long-expected divine wrath upon the corrupted Old World, or instead to flee beforehand out of doomed England into the wilderness of America. As for the answer to this most crucial, not to say existential, problem, Puritans found it easily in their own contemporary history by looking at the terrible fate of the Protestant Churches in France and Germany during the course of what was to become known as the Thirty Years' War. So, as against those who opposed emigration to New England and rather preferred to stay in England until it would have to confront its

---

[32] Francis Higginson, cited in *Magnalia Christi Americana*, by Cotton Mather, vol. I, p. 328.
[33] "General Observations," pp. 112–13.

own unavoidable destruction for its sins and corruptions, the Puritans of the "Observations" called attention to the fact that this was the very same stand taken by the Protestant churches on the continent which had eventually led to their fateful destruction:

It is likly that this consideration made the church beyounde the seas viz: the Palatinate [and] Rochell to sit still and not labour for shelter whyle they might: but the wofull spectackle of their ruine may teach us wysdome to avoyd the plague whyle it is forsenne [Proverbs 22:3] and not to tary as they did till it overtake us.[34]

During the Thirty Years' War, it will be recalled, the army of the Catholic League under Johannes Tilly defeated the Protestants in the Palatinate in 1623, and in France Richelieu had captured the Protestant, Huguenot, stronghold in the port city of La Rochelle in 1628. In both cases Protestants and Puritans in England vehemently demanded that James I and Charles I aid the Protestant cause on the continent against the forces of the Counter-Reformation, but to no avail. Hence, the fateful destruction of the Protestant churches on the continent had played a prominent role in the Puritan eschatology and apocalypse of the settlement of New England.

In clear contrast to the Protestant ideology and the settlement of Virginia, the ultimate goal of the Puritans was to prove in most explicit terms the saints' divine necessity to relinquish all their ties with doomed England before God would pour his judgments upon that sinful land. So, for example, when some Puritans rejected the idea of emigration to New England, claiming that "we have here" in England "a plentyfull land of all thinges with peace," John Winthrop took upon himself to demolish this contention at once. As applied to individuals, he wrote, "it may best receive answere from such as it concerns." Yet, in regard of "the estate of our Churche and Com[mon]w[ealth] let the grones and fears of Gods people give a silent answer." More specifically, continued Winthrop,

If our condition be good, why doe his Embassadours turne their messages into complaintes and threateninges? why doe they so constantly denounce wrathe and judgment against us? why do they pray so muche for healing if we be not sicke? why doe their soules wepe in secret? and will not be comforted, if there be yet hope that our hurt may be healed? One Calfe set up in Israel removed the tabernacle out of the host, and for 2 God forsooke them for ever.[35]

Such uncompromising zeal concerning the desacralization of England in providential history constituted the foundation of the Puritan migration to New England, and any understanding of the ideological origins of the Puritan settlement of America ought to begin first with this deep-seated Puritan eschatological consciousness. Furthermore, continued Winthrop,

---

[34] *Ibid.*, p. 113.
[35] *Ibid.*, p. 113; "John Winthrop to . . ." (1629), *Winthrop Papers*, vol. II, p. 121.

even the presence of godly men in England could not save this sinful land from God's imminent divine wrath:

Israel had such priviledges when her destruction was at hand, Elias and Elisha and above 400: good prophettes and 7000 good protestants in Ahabs time . . . yet she came downe wonderfully.

This was now England's fate in providential history as well, even though some godly people still lived there to bear witness to Christ and his Word. It was in this all-embracing eschatological context that Winthrop raised the powerful apocalyptic image concerning the saints' duty to flee out of Sodom and Laodicea:

if we imytayte Sodom in her Pride and intemperance, if Laodicea in her lukewarmnesse, if Eph[esus] Sardis etc. in the sins for which their candlesticke was removed, if the turks and other heathen in their abominations, yea if the Sinagogue of Antichrist in her superstition, where is yet the good should content us?[36]

This gloomy apocalyptic vision had been ascribed to the state of the Church of England. Yet, could the Puritan saints find the civil sphere in England more cogent and compatible with their holy, godly aspiration? According to Winthrop, the answer was totally negative because in the church and state of England God's saints could not expect any more peace and rest:

what means then the bleating of so may oppressed with wronge, that drink wormwood [Jer. 9:15; Rev. 8:11], for righteousness? why doe so many seely sheep that seeke shelter at the judgment seates returne without their fleeces? why meet we so many wandering ghostes in shape of men, so many spectacles of misery in all our streetes, our houses full of victuals, and our entryes of hunger-starved Christians? our shoppes full of riche wares, and under our stalles lye our own fleshe in nakednesse.[37]

In this desperate situation of the saints in England, Winthrop attempted to raise the historical conscience of his brethren, by asking, "dothe not the history of the Church," or sacred, ecclesiastical history, "give us many examples" concerning those saints who chose to stay in their place, despite many divine warnings, until their very destruction. Winthrop used the example of the Albigenses, a sect in southern France, against whom Pope Innocent III led a Crusade (1208–18), and whom Pope Gregory IX handed to the Dominican Inquisition in 1233, bringing about their final extirpation. These people "were in the Covenant, and a holy seed," continued Winthrop, and therefore "it had been better suche had fled." Apparently, the Albigenses attached so much sacred significance to their land that they, therefore, were unwilling to flee to a place of safety; "yet we ascribe no such

---

[36] "John Winthrop to . . . ," pp. 121–2.   [37] *Ibid.*, p. 122.

vertue to the soile" of England, declared Winthrop, and therefore Puritans should remove themselves to New England.[38]

Point after point, then, the Puritans of the "General Observations" demolished the image of England's singular role in providential history, until at the end nothing was left of the Protestants' glorious and magnificent vision of England as God's chosen nation. And so, out of the desacralization of England in sacred history, the sacralization of New England and its glorification within the confines of ecclesiastical history began slowly to evolve:

How woonderfull is the lorde in mercye, that hathe reysed this newe plantation, for so comfortable a refuge, for all suche whom he hathe exempted owte of that generall divastation, which our Synnes have so muche deserved.

Accordingly, the Puritans argued that

seeinge the Church hath noe place lefte to flie into but the wilderness, what better worke can there be, than to goe and provide tabernacles and foode for here against she comes thether [Rev. 12:6, 14].[39]

Viewing history exclusively in terms of sacred, ecclesiastical history, or in light of the course of the Church upon the earth, it was no wonder that the Puritans chose to describe their migration to New England in accordance with the powerful apocalyptic and prophetic vision of the flight of the Woman, or the church, into the wilderness in face of the Dragon's rage (Rev. 12:6, 14). So, according to the Puritans of the "Observations," just as "when the woman" in Revelation "was persecuted by the dragon," and was "forced to flye into the wilderness,"[40] so now they themselves must follow this divine prophetic revelation, leave England at once and escape into the American wilderness. By identifying their migration to New England with the sacred, prophetic revelations of the Apocalypse, Puritans revealed that they conceived of their exodus as a crucial stage in the course of providential history, and that sacred, ecclesiastical history, as a mode of historical thought, had been their ultimate guide in interpreting the redemptive significance of their errand into the wilderness. This apocalyptic and prophetic context, as we shall see, is of crucial importance for any possible understanding of the Puritan "errand" into New England.

In sum, any attempt to analyze the meaning of the Puritan "errand into the wilderness" obligates us first to explore seriously the apocalyptic and prophetic vision of the Woman's flight into the wilderness, or of the church's escape to the desert, upon which Puritans construed their ideology of the migration of New England, and the redemptive significance they

---

[38] *Ibid.*, p. 122.
[39] "Robert Ryece to John Winthrop," (1629), *Winthrop Papers*, vol. II, p. 129; "Reasons to be Considered, and Objections with Answers," *Winthrop Papers*, vol. II, p. 139.
[40] "General Conclusions and Particular Considerations," *Winthrop Papers*, vol. II, p. 125.

rendered to their migration within the confines of ecclesiastical history. For in the history of salvation, as we are about to see, the wilderness constituted in fact a special dimension of sacred "time-space" in the drama of human salvation: here existed the Church of the Wilderness, or the congregation of the saints in the wilderness, wandering in its prophetic, revelatory pilgrimage from the bondage in Egypt on her road to the Land of Promise (Acts 7:38); and here was forged the wilderness experience, or the wilderness state and wilderness condition, of the church as an essential stage in the drama of human redemption after the saints' flight from doomed Babylon and before God's divine providence led them on the road to the New Jerusalem (Rev. 12:6, 14).

Historically speaking, this powerful prophetic image of the Church of the Wilderness, along with the important concepts closely associated with it, such as the eschatology and the apocalypse of the wilderness, had been widely used by radical religious groups and movements throughout the Middle Ages and during the Protestant Reformation to describe their flight from the corruptions and degenerations of the established Church. Yet, this powerful imaginative vision of the Church of the Wilderness is also of the utmost importance for understanding how the Puritans themselves perceived of their "errand" into the wilderness. Any discussion, therefore, of the Puritan "errand into the wilderness" ought to begin first with the redemptive significance, or indeed the sacralization, of the wilderness in Puritan thought. For the Puritans' view of the wilderness, as a place of refuge for God's chosen remnants and as a shelter for the Church of the Wilderness, constituted the conceptual basis of the Puritan "errand into the wilderness," and consequently, of the ultimate redemptive significance Puritans assigned to their migration to New England.

THE CHURCH OF THE WILDERNESS: THE PROPHETIC REDEMPTIVE SIGNIFICANCE OF THE PURITAN MIGRATION INTO THE WILDERNESS OF AMERICA

In defining their migration to New England along the lines of the prophetic and apocalyptic vision of the Woman's flight into the wilderness, Puritans provided, in vivid terms, a crucial dimension of the ideology of the settlement of the New World; namely, within the confines of sacred, providential history, they envisioned themselves as God's saints in the midst of an apocalyptic scenario described by the prophetic visions and symbols of the Book of Revelation. And as saints in the midst of cosmic occurrences, so to speak, they sought out the best place to ride out the storm; a place, that is, which according to divine prophecy, ought to be in the wilderness, away from corrupted history and degenerated human traditions, and out of the reach of

Satan's fury. After many deliberations and discussion, Puritans found this secured place for the Church of the Wilderness away from the shores of the unscrupulous Old World, in the wilderness of America. This was why the Puritans of the "Observations" were so deeply convinced "that God hath provided" the New England wilderness "to be a refuge for many whom he meanes to save out of the generall callamity."[41]

Here lay, therefore, the ultimate significance of the Puritan migration in sacred ecclesiastical history, and therefore its greatest importance concerning the rise of a unique American ideology. For in contrast to the many radical religious groups and movements during the Middle Ages and the proponents of the Radical Reformation during the era of the Protestant Reformation, who according to their geographical lore could find the wilderness only in Europe, Puritans were, in fact, the first radical religious group which attempted to apply to America the redemptive significance of the wilderness in providential history. In contrast to Catholic Spain and Portugal, and Protestant England, which based their ideology of settling the New World upon the *Genesis* type of religious migration, or upon each nation's claim to be God's chosen people, Puritans rather based their ideology of the migration to New England upon the *Exodus* type of religious migration, or upon the vision of the Church of the Wilderness in its prophetic flight from the doomed Old World. Furthermore, in the light of the impending general conflagration which would soon come upon the Old World, no other place had been left for the true church in her attempt to live in purity and in accordance with God's Word, but to hasten to escape into the American wilderness. For the wilderness is the place which the Lord had assigned for the true church to flee into in times of peril and danger, there to exist in shelter until God would restore it to its most prominent role at the center of the sacred history of salvation. Or, according to the Puritans, the true church "should returne" to the center stage of providential history "after the storm,"[42] or the general devastation which God would bring upon the wicked Old World.

The Puritan ideology of the settlement of New England is, thus, radically different from any previous European colonial enterprises in the New World. For, having now imbued America with the redemptive significance of the wilderness, which derived essentially from the very premises of ecclesiastical history as a mode of historical thought, Puritans were the first to formulate a unique American ideology according to which the sacred concept of the "wilderness" was totally removed from the stage of European history and became inextricably associated with Puritan life and

[41] "Reasons to be Considered and Objections with Answers," *Winthrop Papers*, vol. II, p. 139.
[42] "General Conclusions and Particular Considerations," *Winthrop Papers*, vol. II, p. 125.

experience in America as such. Furthermore, with the removal of the "wilderness" from the geographical scene of Europe, the very center of providential history was shifted from Europe into the New World. Seen in this apocalyptic context of the church's flight into the wilderness, the Puritan ideology of the settlement of New England was indeed the first original American ideology, in the sense that here for the first time Puritans accorded to America, or more specifically to the American wilderness, a prominent and singular role of its own in the drama of the history of salvation. This contention may become clearer after we illuminate more fully the redemptive significance of the "Church of the Wilderness" concept in sacred, ecclesiastical history, a concept which had a crucial influence on the Puritan "Errand into the Wilderness."

The wilderness held a most prominent place in the history of salvation because it constituted a special dimension of sacred "time-space" in the course of providential history, being the intermediate zone between Egypt and the Promised Land, or between Babylon and the New Jerusalem. For, looking on sacred history as a drama, or indeed as a tragedy played out in three acts according to the Puritans, the wilderness connects the two most antagonistic poles of Egypt and the Promised Land, or Babylon and the New Jerusalem, and it thus signifies the pilgrimage from alienation to reconciliation with God. Here lay the crucial redemptive significance of the wilderness condition in ecclesiastical history, and the apocalyptic and eschatological dimension assigned to the Church of the Wilderness in the drama of salvation.

The term the "Church of the Wilderness" referred to the wilderness state of God's chosen remnants after their flight from Egypt, or to the wilderness condition of the church in its escape from the Dragon's rage. In both cases the wilderness acquired its redemptive significance in providential history because it was into this space that divine providence led the church to find a place of refuge and a shelter. So, in the first instance, during their wandering in the wilderness as the intermediate zone between Egypt and the Promised Land, the Israelites were called "the congregation of the wilderness" (Acts 7:38). In the second instance, the wilderness was assigned a crucial role in the framework of the prophetic apocalyptic visions of the Book of Revelation. In the revelation, while living in heaven and being "with child cried, travailing in birth, and pained to be delivered," the Woman must escape from her heavenly place because a seven-headed "red dragon" in heaven "stood before the woman . . . for to devour her child as soon as it was born." The Woman "brought forth a man-child who was to rule all nations with a rod of iron," and with him she "fled into the wilderness, where she hath a place prepared of God" (Rev. 12:1–6). Later on, "there was war in heaven" wherein Satan "the great dragon was cast out" from the heavenly realm. "And when the dragon saw that he was cast unto earth, he persecuted the woman which brought forth the man *child*." Again, with Satan on earth, the woman was given wings "that she might fly into the wilderness . . . from the face of the serpent." Yet, Satan continues upon earth "to make war with the remnant of her seed, which keep the commandments of God, and have the testimony of Jesus Christ" (Rev. 12:13–17).

The eschatological and apocalyptic vision of the Church of the Wilderness thus signified a crucial "event-horizon" in providential history; it was an event of great portent which reconstituted the boundary of the region of sacred "time-space" in the history of salvation with the migrations from Egypt and Babylon into the wilderness. For the saints' flight was the outcome of the desacralization of Egypt and Babylon in ecclesiastical history, which would eventually yet inevitably lead to the total destruction of these wicked countries. The removal of God's grace from these sinful states had thus shifted the boundary of sacred "time-space" into the wilderness. Accordingly, with the church's flight into the wilderness, the central stage of providential history had itself been transferred to the wilderness. Consequently, in accordance with the prophetic revelatory migration of the church in the world, in which the desacralization of one place leads necessarily to the sacralization of another in providential history, it was now the wilderness which had become the ultimate stage in the drama of the history of salvation. In sum, the wilderness acquired its most prominent role in providential history through the power of prophetic, apocalyptic imaginative conceptions.

Before turning to the issue of the role of the wilderness in Christian thought, which will provide us with the necessary historical and ideological context with which to interpret the meaning of the Puritan "errand into the wilderness," we still have to deal with the notion of the wilderness state, or the wilderness condition, which refers to the essence of the wilderness experience. For the wilderness acquired its singular role in sacred history not only because it was the place into which the saints fled in times of danger, but also because it possessed an important formative and redemptive role as the place in which the Lord forged the congregation of the wilderness before leading it to the Promised Land. Accordingly, the wilderness was a place of temptation and danger, or the realm of demons and death. And yet, it was also the place of the covenant, as well as the place of refuge, shelter, purgation, and consecration. It was into the wilderness that the Lord called his saints to gather during the times of danger and persecution in order to save them from Satan's furious rage, and yet only divine providence could save them from their constant and endless wandering in the wilderness and lead them on the glorious road to the New Jerusalem.

The wilderness, then, was an essential condition in providential history, a crucial stage in the prophetic and revelatory pilgrimage from the house of bondage and death in Egypt, or Babylon, into the house of life and grace in the Promised Land, or the New Jerusalem. Eric Voegelin brilliantly summarized the redemptive significance of the wilderness, or the desert, as the symbol of the sacred historical impasse:

The Events of Exodus, the sojourn at Kadesh, and the conquest of Canaan became symbols because they were animated by a new spirit. Through the illumination by the spirit the house of institutional bondage became a house of spiritual death. Egypt was the realm of the dead, the Sheol, in more than one sense. From death and its cult man had to wrest the life of the spirit. And this adventure was hazardous, for the Exodus from Sheol at first led nowhere but into the desert of indecision, between equally unpalatable forms of nomad existence and life in high civilization. Hence, to Sheol and Exodus must be added the Desert as the symbol of the historical impasse. It was not a specific but the eternal impasse of historical existence in the "world," that is, in the cosmos in which empires rise and fall with no more meaning than a tree growing and dying, as waves in the stream of eternal occurrence. By attunement with cosmic order the fugitives from the house of bondage could not find the life that they sought. When the spirit bloweth, society in cosmological form becomes Sheol, the realm of death; but when we undertake the Exodus and wander into the world, in order to found a new society elsewhere, we discover the world as the Desert. The flight leads nowhere, until we stop in order to find our bearings beyond the world. When the world has become Desert, man is at last in the solitude in which he can hear thunderingly the voice of the spirit that with its urgent whispering has already driven and rescued him from Sheol. In the Desert God spoke to the leader and his tribes; in the Desert, by listening to the voice, by accepting its offer, and by submitting to its command, they at last reached life and became the chosen people of God.[43]

The wilderness condition of the church, then, had a crucial formative and redemptive significance in the course of providential history. For this was the intermediate stage which sharply divided the most antagonistic poles in sacred history: Egypt from the Promised Land, or Babylon from the New Jerusalem. Most important, in spiritual terms, the wilderness state was the space of time in which God forged his chosen people by having them forget the corruption of past times and by preparing them for their future glorious role at the culmination of the history of salvation. Hence the wilderness condition is indeed inextricably associated, on the one hand, with the eschatology of the wilderness, or the prophetic vision of the church's flight into the wilderness in face of God's divine judgments, and, on the other hand, with the apocalypse of the wilderness, or the prophetic redemptive significance of the pilgrimage through the wilderness as a necessary condition in order to reach the New Jerusalem.

Analyzing the redemptive significance of the wilderness in sacred,

---

[43] Eric Voegelin, *Order and History*, vol. I, *Israel and Revelation* (Baton Rouge, 1956), pp. 113–14.

ecclesiastical history, it is no wonder that in the history of Christianity the quest for the wilderness had become the common trait of many radical religious groups and movements whose uncompromising zeal for a thorough religious reformation according to the premises of the primitive, apostolic church, had led them to separate themselves from the sins and corruption of the established church. These radical religious groups, such as the Paulicians of the seventh century, the Waldenses of the twelfth century, the Albigenses of the twelfth to thirteenth centuries, the Spiritual Franciscans of the fourteenth century, the Taborites of the fifteenth century, to name only a few, tended to define their situation in sacred, providential history according to the divine prophecy concerning the persecuted Church of the Wilderness. Deeming themselves as God's chosen remnant who momentarily had to fly into the wilderness, they would, in due time, return as God's chosen people to conquer the world and history. The quest for the wilderness, or that firm determination to leave behind them corrupted history and sinful human traditions, was the common characteristic feature of these various religious movements, which, in accordance with their unbroken zeal for a total religious reformation, denounced the world around them and looked for the wilderness as the only place available for them to live according to the purity of God's word and his ordinances. In that way, evidently, they sought to inaugurate a new age in sacred, providential history, which was indeed the ultimate mark of the wilderness condition of the Church as the intermediate "time-space" dimension which separated Egypt from the Promised Land, or Babylon from the New Jerusalem.

The sacred, prophetic dimension of the wilderness in Christian thought is of the utmost importance for any examination of the Puritan "errand," because it was within this redemptive context of the Church of the Wilderness that the Puritan migration to New England should be placed, in order to appreciate fully the significance of the Puritan "errand into the wilderness." Not only did Puritans define their migration in terms of the prophetic vision of the Church of the Wilderness; but also, and most significantly, they identified themselves with those radical religious movements, such as the Waldenses and Albigenses, or those Churches of the Wilderness whose history exemplified to the utmost the quest for the wilderness. Nothing more clearly illuminates the sacred, ecclesiastical context of the Puritan migration, and hence the essence of the Puritan "errand."[44]

According to George H. Williams in his important study, *Wilderness and Paradise in Christian Thought*, the concept of the Church of the Wilderness arose in Western Christianity, on the one hand, because of the rise of

[44] For the Puritans' identification with the Waldensian and Albigensian Churches of the Wilderness, see "General Observations," pp. 122, 134–5, 143.

eschatological expectations during the twelfth and thirteenth centuries, and, on the other hand, because of the deep despair resulting from the worldly and corrupted monarchy of the papacy:

Schematically one can say that a renewed eschatological intensity, coupled with dissatisfaction or even despair with the apostolic see [of Rome] – finally transformed into a papal monarchy under Innocent III (1198–1216) – tended to convert the monastic impulse into fully separatist sectarianism and to encourage the replacement of the cloistered paradise with the conventicle of the wilderness.[45]

At this crucial juncture in the history of Christianity, in which dissatisfaction with the worldly role of the papacy had led to separation from the Church of Rome, the concept of the Church of the Wilderness, as prophesied in Revelation 12, became an important weapon in the hands of those who sought to return to the premises of the primitive, apostolic church. So, for example, the followers of Peter Waldo, the Waldenses, had fled into the wilderness of the Piedmontese Alps for protection from the papal ban (1179), Inquisition, and Crusade (1209). At this moment, wrote Williams, "it was inevitable that the aptness of the description of the Church of the Wilderness of Revelation 12:6 would come to be recognized as the scriptural sanction of their flight and their meaningful suffering as a remnant."[46]

The ultimate mark of the Church of the Wilderness is the urgent call to cut all ties with the established, corrupted church, and to fly into the wilderness. Hence, based upon the same prophetic writing such as Revelation 12, it comes as no surprise that the Waldensian writings are so similar to those of the Puritan migrants to New England in their urgent call to "flee out of Babylon," or in their unshaken belief that the Lord would take care of His Church in the Wilderness:

God, who blessed the five barley loaves and two fishes for His disciples in the wilderness (Matt. 14:17], bless this table, whatever is upon it, and whatever may be brought to it.

Later, when Samuel Moreland, Oliver Cromwell's representative, visited the Waldensian Piedmont, he was thoroughly convinced that this place "is the Desert whither the Woman fled when she was persecuted by the Dragon with seven heads and ten horns. And where she had a place prepared of God, that they should feed her one thousand two hundred and sixty daies," as prophesied in Revelation 12. Moreland captured in vivid terms the Waldensians' interpretation of their church as the Church of the Wilderness:

That here it was that the Church fled, and where she made her Flocks to rest at noon . . . it was in the clefts of these Rocks, and in the secret places of the stairs of these

---

[45] Williams, *Wilderness and Paradise*, p. 57.   [46] *Ibid.*, p. 62.

Valleys of Piedmont, that the dove of Christ then remained, where also the Italian Foxes then began to spoil the Vines with their tender Grapes although they were never able utterly to destroy or pluck them up by the roots.[47]

The same can be said about the Albigenses of southern France, another Church of the Wilderness which Puritans used, along with the Waldensian church, in their reasons and considerations for the migration to New England. In their radical and uncompromising quest for a thorough religious reformation, along with their unbroken zeal to teach the true (i.e. Albigensian) doctrine, the Albigenses denounced the Catholic Church as the one which was doing the work of the devil. Consequently, they were condemned by several councils of the Church of Rome during the late twelfth and early thirteenth centuries. Pope Innocent III sought to convert them by several missions, but in the face of Albigensian insistence not to come to terms with the devilish papacy, he launched a Crusade against them (1208). The actual Crusade, which was conducted with great cruelty, ended in 1218. Later in 1233, Pope Gregory IX charged the Dominican Inquisition with the final extirpation of this heresy, of which no trace was left at the end of the fourteenth century.

With the rise of Protestant historiography during the sixteenth century, historians strongly emphasized the historical connections between Protestantism and the persecuted Churches of the Wilderness, such as the Waldenses and the Albigenses, in order to provide the ecclesiastical historical context of the Protestant Reformation. The identification of the Waldensian and Albigensian churches as the Churches of the Wilderness goes back to John Bale's *Image of both Churches* of 1550. Bale adopted this identification after reading the work of the Anabaptist Melchior Hoffmann.[48] Later, John Foxe followed the lead of his friend John Bale and provided a detailed historical description of these churches of the wilderness in his most influential book *Acts and Monuments*.[49] The theme of the Church of the Wilderness, of course, had played an important role not only in the Puritan migration to New England, but also in the Puritan Revolution in England. Its use, however, among English Puritans was much different from that among the American Puritans. So, for example, according to John Milton, the wilderness denotes rather a negative meaning in providential history. Speaking bitterly against those who justified the course of the Church of England since the Reformation in England, Milton declared that until the Puritan Revolution England had lived "in this our wilderness since Reform-

---

[47] *Ibid.*, pp. 62–3. On the Waldenses, see, Norman Cohn, *The Pursuit of the Millennium* (London, 1972 [1957]), pp. 157–8, 210–11.

[48] Williams, *Wilderness and Paradise*, p. 75.

[49] John Foxe, *Acts and Monuments*, edn. of 1610, vol. I, p. 211; vol. II, pp. 859–70.

ation began" and with "these rotten principles" of religion which the Puritan Revolution came to totally extirpate.[50]

In the great debate among Puritans in the summer of 1629 concerning the justifications for the migration to New England, the Waldensian and Albigensian Churches of the Wilderness served as a great exemplary model from the annals of sacred, ecclesiastical history, by which Puritans came to define the context of their removal to the New World in providential history. Indeed, Puritans of the "General Observations" justified their migration to America upon the fateful destruction of the Protestant churches in La Rochelle and the Palatinate as well. Yet, these were negative examples upon which it was hardly possible to conduct a full scale religious errand into the wilderness in America. On the other hand, by utilizing the important vision of the Church of the Wilderness, Puritans of the "Observations" could portray their migration to America as a great redemptive errand in the course of sacred, providential history. Here, then, lay the crucial role the Puritans assigned to the Waldensian and Albigensian Churches of the Wilderness in their "General Observations for the Plantation of New England."

If the Puritans of the "Observations" were united in their common denunciation of the sins and corruption within the state and Church of England, still they were much divided among themselves in the summer of 1629 as to whether emigration to New England was the most appropriate course available for the godly at this moment. In order to convince those who were reluctant to emigrate, John Winthrop invoked before them the example of the Albigenses. "For the Albiennes," or the Albigenses, he wrote to his Puritan brethren, "you will grant that it had better suche had fled" in face of the Crusade against them which eventually brought to their total extirpation. "They were in the Covenant, and a holy seed, and so suche as the Churches might have a good hope of," and therefore instead of insisting on staying in their place and facing annihilation, the Albigenses according to Winthrop should have fled out of the storm of persecution against them.[51] Such was the lesson the Puritans drew from the fateful destruction of the Albigensian Church of the Wilderness. Facing now only gloomy prospects in England, the Puritan migration to New England had become a matter of necessity.

In another place in the "Observations," the Albigenses were used again as a sacred, historical model for the Puritans. Debating fervently the fearful contention that their future migration "will certainly overthrowe our lives and estates," the Puritans in order to calm this frightening thought boldly

---

[50] John Milton, *Animadversions upon the Remonstrants against Smectymnuus,* 1641, cited in Williams, *Wilderness and Paradise,* p. 76.
[51] "John Winthrop to . . . ," *Winthrop Papers,* vol. II, p. 122.

declared that "there is no apparent reason to feare this, for" in New England "there is no suche danger either of sworde, famine, or pestilence, as is supposed." Yet, living within a theocratic universe, ruled directly and immediately by divine providence, Puritans of course could not deny that the fate of their future migration to New England was totally dependent upon God's will and pleasure, as for example was the case with the Albigensian Church of the Wilderness:

If the Action be good, then is it of Godes worke, and he who gave us our lives and estates must have libertye to dispose of them at his pleasure, as he hathe doone with others of his faithfull servantes: thus he disposed of the lives and estates of 80: of his priestes, whom Doeg slue [1 Samuel 22:18], thus he disposed of the life and estate of [the] Earl of Bezier in France, and of his subjects [the Albigenses] who mantained a just Cause of Religion and right against the unjust violence of the Earl of Montfort and the Popes Legatt.[52]

The prophetic vision of the Church of the Wilderness served, as well, the Puritans of the "Observations" in their attempt to refute the contention that the small and tiny Puritan churches in the wilderness of New England would have almost no impact upon the course of sacred, ecclesiastical history. Against this argument, Puritans claimed that "the wellfare of a bodye consistes not so muche in the quantitye, as in the proportion of disposition of the partes," and that "it is no wonder for great things to arise from smale and contemptible beginnins." More particularly, Puritans used the example of the Waldenses in order to prove how the small number of godly congregations could gain a glorious role in providential history:

The Waldenses weare scattered into the Alps, and mountaines of Peidmont by small companies but they became famous Churches whereof some remaine to this day.[53]

Finally, in "A Model of Christian Charity" (1630), John Winthrop – seeking to explain the meaning of true love among Christians – invoked the sacred model of the Waldenses who "use to love any of theire own religion even before they were acquainted with them."[54]

The great affinity between the Puritans of the "Observations" and the Waldensian and Albigensian movements stemmed from the fact that all these churches defined their situation in providential history along the prophetic and revelatory vision of the Church of the Wilderness. The medieval saints and the Puritan saints tended to describe their actions in time and history as based upon the premises of the eschatology and apocalypse of the Church of the Wilderness as described in Revelation 12; they deemed themselves the persecuted Church of the Wilderness which had to fly out of a

[52] "Objections Answered," *Winthrop Papers*, vol. II, pp. 134–5.
[53] *Ibid.*, p. 135; "Reasons to be Considered, and Objections with Answers," *Winthrop Papers*, vol. II, p. 143.
[54] John Winthrop, "A Model of Christian Charity," *Winthrop Papers*, vol. II, p. 202.

corrupted world and history to the wilderness in order to maintain God's ordinances in their purity. The underlying theme of these radical religious movements was indeed the quest for the wilderness, a radical and uncompromising quest to separate themselves from the corruption and degeneration of the established church, be it the Church of Rome or the Church of England, and in a place devoid of any corrupted human traditions and history to inaugurate a new age in the history of salvation. This was the ultimate redemptive meaning of the Church of the Wilderness concept in sacred, ecclesiastical history.

Yet, the close affinity between the Waldenses and Albigenses, on the one hand, and the Puritans, on the other, should not hinder us from seeing the great revolutionary character of the Puritan migration to New England in the context of the prophetic vision of the Church of the Wilderness. So far in the history of Christianity in the West, radical religious groups sought after the wilderness within the geographical boundaries of Europe. So, for example, according to their geographical lore, the Waldenses had found the wilderness in the Piedmontese Alps, while the Albigenses had found it in southern France. The Puritans' historical uniqueness, in the context of the quest for the wilderness, lies in the fact that they were the first religious group, or movement, to seek out the redemptive meaning of the wilderness outside the geographical boundaries of Europe. For the Puritans, who had already incorporated the New World into their geographical lore, found the wilderness in New England. In that way, evidently, Puritans had in a radical and revolutionary way shifted the redemptive significance of the wilderness from Europe to America. The Puritans, consequently, transferred the center of sacred, providential history from the Old World to the New World, claiming for the first time in the history of Christianity that America was the site of the sacred wilderness, and thus established for the first time the notion of an apocalyptic gulf separating the New World from the Old, a notion which later, more secular, generations were to use so widely in terms of the struggle between freedom and slavery, liberty and bondage.

The roots of the first authentic American ideology lies, therefore in the prophetic, redemptive vision of the wilderness with which Puritans were the first to invest America. Here, then, for the first time the New World acquired its prominent role in providential history. America attained its singular role in sacred, ecclesiastical history through a total separation from the corruptions and sins of the Old World. In the fashioning of the first unique American ideology, that is the first ideology which invested America with an independent sacred historical role of its own in providential history, lies the crucial significance of Puritanism in American history. In this context, then, Perry Miller, though for apparently different reasons, was not so far from the truth when he claimed that "without some understanding of

Puritanism, it may safely be said, there is no understanding of America."[55] Yet, it is equally safe to say, as we shall see in the next chapter, that without some understanding of the term "the Church of the Wilderness," there could hardly be any understanding of the Puritan "Errand into the Wilderness."

[55] Miller, *The Puritans*, vol. I, p. 1.

5

The creation of sacred errand

Exile and Kingdom: The redemptive significance of the Puritan Errand into the Wilderness

ESCHATOLOGY AND APOCALYPSE OF THE PURITAN ERRAND INTO THE WILDERNESS OF AMERICA

Any discussion of the Puritan mission in the settlement of America, clearly must take into account not only Perry Miller's famous essay "Errand into the Wilderness," but the revisions of his arguments as well. Such discussion ought to deal, for example, with the important contention that "the fathers may have founded the colonies, but the sons invented New England."[1] This powerful argument, along with other attempts to revise Miller's thesis about the presence of a well-defined and highly coherent founding Puritan errand in the settlement of New England, has led some critics to accuse later generations of Puritans as having created the "myth of New England,"[2] or even to the bold assertion that

had the founders of Massachusetts actually intended an overarching Errand, surely it would have been a persistent theme in their many explicit statements of purpose, and especially in the tabulation of "arguments" by Winthrop, Cotton, Thomas Shepard and Richard Mather, and others. But it was not.[3]

This important contention of modern Puritan historiography, that a conscious "invention" of New England and a deliberate fashioning of its "myth" was perpetrated by the Puritans of the second generation, inevitably raises serious suspicions about the very existence of any founding Errand on the part of the first generation of American Puritans who emigrated from England to New England during the 1620s and 1630s. Recognizing,

[1] Robert Middlekauff, *The Mathers: Three Generations of Puritan Intellectuals* (New York, 1968), p. 98.
[2] Harry S. Stout, *The New England Soul: Preaching and Religious Culture in Colonial New England* (New York, 1986), p. 70.
[3] Theodore D. Bozeman, *To Live Ancient Lives: The Primitivist Dimension in Puritanism* (Chapel Hill, 1988), p. 114.

however, that a serious evaluation of an original Puritan Errand is essential to any understanding of the Puritan migration as an ideological movement, and hence crucially important to any understanding of Puritan life and experience in seventeenth century New England, and in order to disperse the cloud of suspicion over the very presence of such a founding Puritan Errand at the beginning of the Puritan migration, our task is to show that indeed the sacred, prophetic, and redemptive vision of the Church of the Wilderness constituted the very essence of the Puritan Errand into the Wilderness in America. Not only was this unique sense of the Errand of the Church of the Wilderness genuinely formulated by the Puritans of the "General Observations" in 1629 in order to construe the sacred, historical–ecclesiastical context for their removal to New England, but most importantly, it was this very sense of the Errand of the Church of the Wilderness to which the second and third generations of Puritans in New England heartily and steadfastly adhered during the seventeenth century.

The Errand of the Church of the Wilderness, in the sense of opening a new age in the unfolding history of salvation, was the underlying theme both of the Puritan migration to New England, from its very inception by the Puritans of the "Observations" in 1629, and of Puritan life and experience in seventeenth-century New England. For it was according to this divine prophetic vision that Puritans in America tended constantly and continuously to define their holy experiment in the wilderness both in terms of sacred time and sacred space. Accordingly, from the Puritans of the "Observations" to the lamentations of the second generation Jeremiads, and even later as far as the utterances of the third generation, the prophetic vision of the Errand of the Church of the Wilderness incorporated the entirety of Puritan existence and experience in New England within a single coherent and well-defined redemptive, providential framework.

Originating in the debates among Puritans in England in 1629 concerning the settlement of New England, where it was first invoked in order to construe the sacred ecclesiastical ideological origins for the future Puritan migration, the prophetic vision of the Church of the Wilderness provided New England Puritans with an enduring and powerful divine image according to which they consistently tended to define and examine their holy experiment in the wilderness throughout the seventeenth century. Furthermore, since the redemptive flight of the Church of the Wilderness constituted, in fact, the very essence of the Puritan Errand into the Wilderness in America, it is not surprising that, throughout the seventeenth century, New England Puritans persistently identified the significance of their abode in the wilderness with this sacred, revelatory vision. In 1629, the Puritans of the "Observations" were deeply convinced that "seeinge the Church hath noe place lefte to flie into but the wildernesse, what better worked can there be, than to goe" to New England "and provide tabernacles and foode for her against she comes thethere."⁴ Later, for example, it was utilized by John Allin and Thomas Shepard in 1645 in defending the Puritan migration to America upon "the rule of Christ to his Apostles and Saints . . . to fly into the Wilderness from the face of the Dragon."⁵ And later on, with the Restoration of the House of Stuart in England in 1660, when English authorities accused the Puritan colonies in America of being "sectaries," "schismatics," and "fanatics," John Norton, in his election sermon in 1661, identified the Puritan Errand in America with that of the Church of the Wilderness in order to refute these charges coming from England: "the woman in the wilderness may have the vomit of the dragon cast in her face [Rev. 12:15]," yet, he assured his audience, "God will look after his outcasts, and care fore us being outcasts for the truth."⁶

This very identification of the Puritan Errand in America with the redemptive, prophetic flight of the Church of the Wilderness passed without change from the first to the second and third generations of Puritans in New England. So, for example, in the light of the growing "mist of error and heresy" in New England, Thomas Shepard, Jr., in 1672 warned that "this poor woman in the wilderness" might be utterly destroyed by "that very vomit of the dragon" from which she had fled from England.⁷ And according to Cotton Mather in 1693, the American wilderness before the Puritan migration had been the empire of Antichrist. Hence, with the first Puritan colony,

the Devile thus Irritated, immediately try'd all sorts of Methods to overturn this poor Plantation and so much of the Church, as was fled into this Wilderness, [Revelation 12], immediately found, the Serpent cast out of his Mouth a flood for the carrying of it away.⁸

The remarkable affinity New England Puritans found between their enterprise in the wilderness and the sacred symbol of the Woman in the wilderness clearly indicates that the prophetic vision of the Errand of the Church

⁴ "Reasons to be Considered, and Objections with Answers," *Winthrop Papers*, vol. II, p. 139.

⁵ Thomas Shepard and John Allin, *A Defence of the Answer* (London, 1648), "The Preface," in *A Library of American Puritan Writings: The Seventeenth Century*, ed. Sacvan Bercovitch, vol. IX, *Histories and Narratives* (New York, 1985), p. 33.

⁶ John Norton, *Sion the Outcast Healed of Her Wounds* (1661), in Alan Heimert and Andrew Delbanco (eds.), *The Puritans in America: A Narrative Anthology* (Cambridge, 1985), pp. 227–8.

⁷ Thomas Shepard, Jr., *Eye-Salve, or a Watch-Word from Our Lord Jesus Christ unto His Churches in New England* (1672), in Heimert and Delbanco (eds.), *The Puritans in America*, pp. 254–5.

⁸ Cotton Mather, *The Wonders of the Invisible World*, 1693, cited in G. H. Williams, *Wilderness and Paradise in Christian Thought: The Biblical Experience of the Desert in the History of Christianity* (New York, 1962), p. 108.

of the Wilderness cast the whole of Puritan experience in New England throughout the seventeenth century within a single intelligible redemptive context. Accordingly, Puritans of the first, as well as the second and third generations, never ceased seeing the significance of their holy experiment in terms of sacred, ecclesiastical history.

The contention that the redemptive vision of the Church of the Wilderness constituted the very essence of the Puritan Errand into the Wilderness in America should not come as a surprise to anyone familiar with the role of sacred, prophetic visions in Christianity. Many religious movements, in various ages and periods, have used divine and revelatory symbols to explain the significance of their role and location within the confines of the history of salvation. Therefore, having rejected entirely the glorious Protestant vision of England as God's elect nation, and deeming themselves God's persecuted chosen remnant surrounded by an environment fiercely hostile to their premises of religious reformation, the Puritans borrowed a potent vision from ecclesiastical history by which to define their providential Errand to America, namely the redemptive flight of the Church of the Wilderness.

Like many other religious movements in the history of Christianity which tended to describe their role in the history of salvation along the lines of the prophetic vision of the flight of the Woman into the wilderness, such as the Waldenses and Albigenses, Puritans indeed were drawn to define the Errand of their migration to America as that of the Church of the Wilderness because of their total denunciation of the prevailing corrupted religious life and culture in England. Here, then, a most powerful prophetic image was available, by which the Puritans could easily explain their separation from corrupt England, serving at one and the same time as a potent sacred vision according to which they could immediately locate the role of the Puritan settlement of New England within the confines of the history of salvation. Hence, with the desacralization of England in providential history, the prophetic vision of the Church of the Wilderness not only enabled Puritans to endow their migration to New England with singular prophetic meaning in the history of salvation, but it also helped them to imbue the American wilderness with sacred, redemptive significance. The vision of the Church of the Wilderness, therefore, provided Puritans with what they needed most: on the one hand, an image of themselves as the true persecuted church, which could explain their flight from corrupted England, and on the other hand, a redemptive significance for their existence in the wilderness of America.

Considering, therefore, the Puritan Errand in terms of the prophetic, redemptive, and revelatory vision of the flight of the Church of the Wilderness, it will become clear not only why this sacred notion comprised an integral part of first-generation Puritan ideology of the settlement of New England, but why this prophetic vision continued to constitute for later Puritans as well the essential ideological context for examining the significance of Puritan New England in providential history. This is why the sermons of the second and third Puritan generations concerning the Errand are so nearly identical to those of the first generation despite the obviously different historical circumstances which lay behind them. For, ultimately, it was through sacred divine prophecies and symbols that Puritans defined the meaning of their existence and experience in the wilderness of America and not the other way around. Furthermore, the presence of the founding Puritan Errand from the very beginning of the migration to New England may explain the fact that, once that Errand was construed in terms of the sacred Errand of the Church of the Wilderness, later Puritan generations in America adhered to it steadfastly rather than fashioning and inventing a unique Errand of their own concerning Puritan New England's singular role in the mystery of the history of redemption and salvation.

Indeed, the last thing that the Puritans of the second and third generations wanted to do was consciously "invent" or create a "myth" of their own liking of the Errand of the Church of the Wilderness. For the sacred revelatory vision of the Church of the Wilderness is rooted within Christian apocalyptical thought and has a history and tradition of its own in Christianity. It portrays the existential wilderness condition of the church situated in the middle of apocalyptic and eschatological occurrences and describes, in vivid terms, the redemptive flight of the Church of the Wilderness from the rage of Satan and his minions. No wonder, then, that radical religious movements, such as the Waldenses, the Albigenses, and the Puritan emigrants to America, who attempted to separate themselves from corrupted established religious life and traditions, tended to identify themselves with the prophetic vision of the Church of the Wilderness. Hence, it is clear that the Errand of the Church of the Wilderness could not be merely "invented" and fashioned into a "myth" by certain religious movements, according to their liking. For this prophetic vision deals with the church's revelatory separation from sin and corruption and with the redemptive flight into the wilderness when the world around it no longer seemed a safe place in which the true church could dwell. Thus, instead of trying to evaluate the lamentations of the Puritans of the second and third generations, or the Jeremiads, as a conscious attempt to "invent" or create a "myth" of their own of the Puritan errand, it is more useful to examine the redemptive significance of the Puritan Errand in the context of the prophetic vision of the Church of the Wilderness as it was formulated by the Puritans on the eve of their migration to New England. The prophetic vision of the Church of the Wilderness not only constituted the very essence of the

Puritan Errand into the Wilderness. Thanks to it, later Puritan generations in New England as well were able to incorporate their whole Puritan enterprise in America within a well-defined providential historical context.

It is evident from our discussion so far that this providential sense of the Puritan Errand has its origins neither with John Winthrop's famous lay sermon "A Model of Christian Charity" of 1630, as some historians have argued, nor with Samuel Danforth's "A brief Recognition of New England's Errand into the Wilderness" of 1670, from which Perry Miller took the title for his famous essay "Errand into the Wilderness." Although Winthrop's lay sermon and Danforth's address to the General Court present important dimensions of the Puritan errand of the Church of the Wilderness, neither should be considered as the original source for the Puritan Errand into the Wilderness. Rather, the Puritan sense of the Errand of the Church of the Wilderness had its origins in the great and painful debates among the Puritans of the "General Observations" when Puritans searched fiercely and diligently into the annals of sacred, ecclesiastical history for the most appropriate divine model by which to define, in the context of providential history, their reasons for emigrating to New England. In these debates lay the origins of the Puritan ideology of the settlement of America, and it was there that for the first time Puritans identified the Errand of their future migration to New England with the prophetic, redemptive vision of the Errand of the Church of the Wilderness.

For the Puritans of the "Observations," then, the prophetic flight of the Church of the Wilderness constituted a crucial stage in the course of the history of salvation. For their understanding of the redemptive significance of the term "wilderness," they drew, as in many other places, upon Thomas Brightman's apocalyptic interpretation. They not only inherited from Brightman the identification between England and Laodicea, the most sinful church in the Apocalypse, but they were also influenced by his exegesis upon Revelation concerning the prophetic and redemptive Errand of the Church of the Wilderness. In English apocalyptic tradition before Brightman, the church's flight into the Wilderness was not associated with any English historical context. So, for example, according to the commentaries appended to the Geneva Bible, the Woman's flight into the wilderness signifies that "the Church was remoued from among the Jewes to the Gentiles, which were as bare wilderness" (Rev. 12:6). In his exegesis, however, Brightman transformed the prophetic passages from Revelation concerning the Woman and wilderness by relating them to a concrete historical context in England. "The Woman which is seen," he argued,

"doth very fittly carry the image of the Church." Her son, of course, is
Christ, yet the wilderness is no longer the gentiles' wilderness in general to
which, according to the Geneva Bible, the church fled after the Jews' refusal
to accept Christ's teaching but rather a real geographical space endowed
with sacred, redemptive significance. Concerning the wilderness, *"the place
is the wilderness* that is *the* Temple." Thus, the wilderness is the place in
which "the poor handsome of the Elect lurke," and where "there was a
meere solitary wilderness in respect of that place, where the Innumerable
company lived, that possessed *the holy city*." The Woman fled to the wilderness in Brightman's explanation, because "God care[d] for her, [and there]
he provide[d] her an hiding place." In the wilderness the Woman, or the
church, "was fed by the help of certain men," who maintained her there.
Because "this *wilderness* is that *Temple*," according to Brightman, "the
continuance of banishment in the wilderness is that abode that was made in
the Temple."[9]

It is important to note that the biblical concept of the wilderness, as
transformed by Brightman, no longer signified the place of trial or the
intermediate zone between the corrupted past and the Promised Land, but
rather the place in which church and temple, the house of God, would
become one, that is, a solitary place far away from corruption and sin. The
flight of the Woman into the wilderness occurred in the time of the seventh
trumpet, Brightman noted, when the whole mystery of time and history
would be revealed, and in the time of the "sealing of the Elect" when the
Lord would elect the saints. Why did the Woman flee, asked Brightman, just
when her son and his father came to conquer the world? "Certainly it could
not be the feare of the enemy but the intollerable irkesomenes" stemming
from the lack of "true piety" and the "yoke of tyranny." For once in the
wilderness, "she had the leasure to seek out the Reliques of Saints, to
consecrate Temples to the Martyrs, and to make supplication for every
shrine." In the wilderness, argued Brightman, "there were no outward
troubles that did molest men" such as those that caused men "to corrupt
Religion" and "the simple purity which Christ ordained."[10] Likewise for the
Puritans of the "General Observations," this redemptive Errand of the
Church of the Wilderness held a prominent role in their reasons for emigrating to America. So they argued that when the church was "eclipsed in parte,
darkened, or persecuted," it is "juste to seeke refuge for saftye, especially
were safest hope maye be founde." For them, then, emigration was imperative because "nowe the doore is opened, and were a great forgetfull

[9] Thomas Brightman, *Apocalypsis Apocalypseos, or a Revelation of the Revelation* (Leyden,
   1616), pp. 503, 512, 514–15.
[10] *Ibid.*, pp. 512–16.

unthankefullnes to the lorde, to refuse imployment in so hie an ordinance."[11]

An essential feature of Brightman's interpretation, as we have previously seen, was to abolish the Augustinian dualism between heaven and earth. In so doing, he projected Augustine's heavenly city into the wilderness. That is to say that, for Brightman, the wilderness became a "heavenly place" on earth, a place remote from human corruption and sin. Consequently, when the Woman, or the church, fled to the wilderness, she did so because she "could not endure" the corruption of religion in a nation "where no publike assemplies [were] to be found, wherein the Ordinances of God did not flourish in their integrity." This Woman also represented, for Brightman, the congregation of the faithful, or the company of the saints: she "doth not bear the person of the faithful one by one, but of the whole assemblies of the faithfull."[12]

By this point in his exegesis, Brightman had clearly drawn out the seventeenth-century applications of Revelation. He presented the Dragon's persecution of the Woman in a way most suggestive for early seventeenth-century Puritan readers, who could not miss the contemporary relevance of the Woman's flight into the wilderness. For, according to Brightman's interpretation, the Woman was the "whole Church generally" and at the same time the "particular congregation," and the flight into the wilderness signified the migration of the saints from a corrupted nation:

The Womans flight then is either the *dissolution* or the depraving of the *particular assemblies*, so as God should not be porely worshipped in of them according to his will alone, the which thing when once it commeth to passe, *the Church fleet away* . . .

But if the Woman were the "Holy assemblies of the faithfull," Brightman continued, then "her *seed* are *the faithfull in particular*," or those who "hold the true Religion," and those "who can not come together to worship God in publike assemblies, because [of] the iniquity of the times."[13]

The double meaning of the term "wilderness" in Revelation, as interpreted by Brightman, constituted an essential dimension of the prophetic and redemptive Errand into the Wilderness as understood by those of the Puritan migration. The wilderness was, first, a place of escape, or a shelter from the corrupted state and Church of England, or Laodicea as Puritans defined it. Second, it was the only place in which the true church could flourish in the face of impending divine judgments. Hence, the wilderness, on the one hand, was a shelter, a place of refuge or a hiding place, and, on

---

[11] "Robert Ryce to John Winthrop" (1629), *Winthrop Papers*, vol. II, pp. 128–9.
[12] Brightman, *Apocalypsis Apocalypseos*, pp. 517, 526.
[13] *Ibid.*, pp. 517, 526, 533.

the other hand, a Temple of the Lord, or indeed a Garden of the Lord according to Puritans' commentary on Canticles 6:2. This complexity is clearly revealed in the debates among Puritans in England concerning the future Errand of the Puritan migration to New England.

An ultimate dimension of the redemptive flight of the Church of the Wilderness was, indeed, the urgency of separating from an established corrupted religion, and the necessity of fleeing to the wilderness wherein lay the only hope of living according to God's word and ordinances. This was, of course, exactly what Puritans felt in 1629 about England,

> where every place mourneth for want of justice, where the cryenge synnes goe unponished, or unreproved, crueltye and bloodde is in our streetes, the lande abowndeth with murthers, slawghters Incestes Adulteryes, whoredome dronkennes, oppression and pride where well doinge is not maytayned, or the godly cherished, but Idollatrye popery and what so ever is evyll is cowntenanced, even the least of these, is enowghe, and enowghe to make haste owte of Babylon, and to seeke to dye rather in the wylderness then styll to dwelle in Sodome Mesheck and in the tentes of Keder.[14]

Thus, out of the fear of God's impending judgment, the saints' exodus from England became an essential dimension of the Puritan Errand into the Wilderness sanctuary of New England.

Yet, apart from the vision of the wilderness as a shelter and a hiding place, and particularly following Brightman's exegesis, Puritans of the "Observations" were fully aware of the redemptive significance of the wilderness. They knew that it was in the wilderness that God would redeem his chosen ones from the sin and corruption of Egypt, as in past times the Lord "carried the Isralites into the Wildernesse and made them forgette the fleshpotts of Egipt."[15] Indeed, it was this ultimate redemptive significance of the wilderness, as a Temple or a Garden of the Lord, to which John Winthrop referred in one of his most moving farewell letters to his friends in England before sailing to America. Few passages indeed depict so deeply the great redemptive expectations the future Puritan emigrants attached to the American wilderness:

> Nowe thou the hope of Israell, and the sure helpe of all that come thee, knitt the heartes of thy servantes to thy selfe, in faith and puritye: Drawe us with the sweetnesse of thine odours, that we may runne after thee, allure us, and speak kindly to thy servantes, that thou maist possesse us as thine owne, in the kindnesse of youthe and the loue of marriage: sealle us up by that holy spirit of promise, that we may not feare to trust in thee: Carrye us into thy Garden, that we may eate and be filled with those pleasures, which the world knows not: let us heare that sweet voyce of thine, my love my doue, my undefiled: spread thy skirt over us and cover our

---

[14] "Robert Ryce to John Winthrop" (1629), *Winthrop Papers*, vol. II, pp. 129–30.
[15] "Reasons to be Considered, and Objections with Answers" (1629), *Winthrop Papers*, vol. II, p. 144; "Objections Answered: First Draft," 1629, *Winthrop Papers*, vol. II, p. 136.

deformitye, make us sicke with thy love: let us sleep in thine armes, and awake in thy kingdome: the soules of thy servantes, thus united to thee, make as one in the bond of brotherly affection.[16]

It should be noted, however, that in the English apocalyptic interpretation, along with the eschatological, redemptive concept of the wilderness in Revelation, there existed, as well, the notion of the biblical wilderness, or that geographical space which Israel had crossed after the exodus from Egypt on the road to the Promised Land. "The Wilderness," noted Joseph Mede, the famous early seventeenth century commentator on Revelation, is that place where "God is encamping with Israel," or where "God [is] marching before his people" after their miraculous deliverance out of corrupted Egypt.[17] Yet, as G. H. Williams has argued convincingly, "in the colonial period, it was not the wilderness of Sinai that New England forefathers had mostly in mind, but rather much more commonly the eschatologically oriented conception of the wilderness in Revelation 12:6 and the mystically saturated imagery of the wilderness in Canticles and the allied texts of the pre-exilic prophets."[18]

This important contention about the eschatological significance Puritans rendered to the American wilderness should be seen again in the wider context of the double character assigned to the redemptive Errand of the Church of the Wilderness which the Puritans inherited from Thomas Brightman's exegesis on the Apocalypse. As we have already seen, according to Brightman, the wilderness acquired its eschatological meaning through the flight of the church in its quest for a shelter and a hiding place from the rage of the Dragon. At the same time, the wilderness attained its revelatory significance through the existence of the church in a wilderness-state which constituted a necessary precondition for a thorough religious reformation. For only in the wilderness-condition could the church live according to God's word and the purity of His ordinances. Originating, thus, in Brightman's exegesis on Revelation, Puritans stressed the double meaning of the Errand of the Church of the Wilderness, consisting, on the one hand, of the apocalyptic flight of the church into the wilderness for a shelter and a refuge, and, on the other hand, of executing a clear-cut reformation in a wilderness devoid of any corrupted religious life and experience.

The eschatology and apocalypse of the American wilderness in Puritan thought, then, was inextricably linked to the twofold prophetic and redemptive Errand of the Church of the Wilderness in sacred, ecclesiastical history. Thus, for example, the Puritan redemptive Errand into the Wilderness in

---

[16] "John Winthrop to Sir William Spring" (1620), *Winthrop Papers*, vol. II, p. 206.
[17] Joseph Mede, *The Brief Meaning or Summary Exposition of the Apocalypse*, in *The Works of ... Joseph Mede*, ed. John Worthington (London, 1672), pp. 917–18.
[18] G. H. Williams, *Wilderness and Paradise in Christian Thought*, pp. 98–9.

America is beautifully described by Michael Wigglesworth, on the one hand, in the negative sense of an apocalyptic flight into a sanctuary:

> Here was the Hiding place, which thou,
>   Jehova, didst provide
> For thy redeemed ones, and where
>   Thou didst thy jewels hide
> In per'lous times, and saddest dayes
>   Of sack-cloth and of blood,
> When th' overflowing scourge did pass
>   Through Europe, like a flood.[19]

On the other hand, the eschatological revelatory significance of the Puritan holy enterprise in the wilderness, in the positive sense of holding the ultimate key to the all-time mystery of human salvation and redemption, is clearly described, for example, by Edward Johnson:

I am now prest for the service of our Lord Christ, to re-build the most glorious Edifice of Mount Sion in a Wilderness, and as John Baptist, I must cry, Prepare yee the way of the Lord, make his paths strait, for behold hee is comming again, hee is comming to destroy Antichrist, and give the whore double to drinke the very dregs of his wrath. (Rev. 18:6)[20]

So far we have seen that the rise of a coherent, well-defined Puritan Errand into the Wilderness in America took place in the many and long debates among Puritans in 1629 concerning their future migration to New England. Most importantly, we have found that the Puritans who discussed the "General Observations for the Plantation of New England," had already in 1629 identified their Errand to America with the prophetic, redemptive vision of the Errand of the Church of the Wilderness described in the Apocalypse. Furthermore, we have noted as well that it was Brightman's exegesis upon the Revelation that ultimately influenced the Puritans in their understanding of the double character of the Errand of the Church of the Wilderness, conceiving it both as an apocalyptic flight into shelter in the wilderness and as an eschatological act inaugurating a new age in the history of salvation and redemption. The prophetic, redemptive Errand of the Church of the Wilderness, therefore, may be considered as the ideological origin of the Puritan migration to New England, for it was according to this divine revelatory vision that Puritans persistently examined the meaning of their removal to New England within the confines of sacred, ecclesiastical history. Having found, thus, the presence of an original Puritan Errand at

---

[19] Michael Wigglesworth, *God's Controversy with New England* (1662), in *Seventeenth-Century American Poetry*, ed. Harrison T. Meserole (New York, 1968), p. 45.
[20] Edward Johnson, *Wonder-Working Providence of Sions Saviour in New England* (1654), ed. J. Franklin Jameson (New York, 1952), p. 52.

the very inception of the Puritan migration, it will be our task now to illuminate the continuous presence of this Errand in the settlement of New England, and to show that the vision of the Errand of the Church of the Wilderness constantly supplied New England Puritans with the sacred, ideological context according to which they were able to evaluate the significance of their holy experiment in the wilderness of America within the confines of providential history.

JOHN COTTON AND THE ESCHATOLOGY OF THE PURITAN MIGRATION

In March 1630 the Winthrop fleet was gathering at the port of Southampton ready to sail to New England. An almost year-long preparation had come to an end, both in terms of ideological debates and actual material arrangements. Now the eyes of the Puritans aboard the ships were directed toward the holy mission they had dedicated themselves to accomplish in the wilderness of America. They had already made their choice to join in body and spirit this Errand into the Wilderness. But aboard the ships at Southampton, the Puritan emigrants could only have had a dim vision of New England, and obviously many fears lurked in their hearts concerning their wilderness-exile in America. It was at this grave and solemn moment that John Cotton, a famous Puritan divine and a long-time friend of the Puritan holy enterprise to America, came down to Southampton on March 21 to preach a farewell sermon, "Gods Promise to His Plantations."

At this moment in his life John Cotton was not contemplating a removal to New England. Yet, because he was so familiar with the Puritan mission to America, it was no mere accident that the Puritans who were ready to sail to the New World chose Cotton to preach the farewell sermon. And in his sermon Cotton did not waste the great solemnity of that occasion, wonderfully depicting the Puritan Errand as based upon God's prophetic promise to his chosen people that he would lead them to the Land of Promise. Accordingly, Cotton's farewell sermon is an essential source regarding the formation of a founding Puritan Errand in the settlement of New England, and hence provides persuasive evidence concerning the decisive process taking place in the Puritan mind in which the desacralization of England had led inevitably to the sacralization of Puritan New England in providential history.

Taking the text for his sermon from 2 Samuel 7:10, Cotton told his Puritan audience at Southampton to consider their migration to New England along the lines of God's divine promise to Israel: "Moreover, I will appoint a place for my people Israell, and I will plant them, that they may dwell in a place of their owne, and move no more." Viewing the Puritan migration in this providential context, Cotton argued that "the placing of a people in this or that Country is from the appointment of the Lord." Within a theocratic universe, then, first "God espies or discovers a land" for his chosen people, and second, "God [is] leading them from one Country to another." Like the Protestants of Virginia, Cotton emphasized the view that colonization is based upon God's "grand Charter given to Adam and his posterity in Paradise, Gen. 1.28." Therefore he concluded that the "placing of people in this or that Country, is from Gods soveraignty over all earth, and the inhabitants thereof." Evidently, in this divine process of colonization, a special role is ascribed to God's chosen people. Thus, while "others take the land by his providence . . . Gods people take the land by promise:"

And therefore the land of Canaan is called a land of promise. Which they discerne, first, by discerning themselves to be in Christ, in whom all the promises are yea, and amen.[21]

Discovery and prophecy, promise and election, are therefore closely connected in this theocratic universe; sacred space is appointed only for God's chosen people whose election in God's providence is revealed through their settlement of a holy, sacred land.

The close association between geographical discovery and divine prophecy served Cotton well in his attempt to illuminate for his Puritan brethren the providential context of their migration to America. God's people know his "holy presence with them" when God "giveth them the liberty and purity of his Ordinances." Accordingly, Cotton argued, the Promised Land is "a land of promise where they have provision for soule as well as for body." It is obvious, then, that a certain space acquires the prominent title of the Promised Land not through history or tradition, but rather through divine prophecy and the presence of God in that place. Indeed, no historical claims, nor historical traditions, could bestow upon a certain geographical space the title of the Land of Promise. Only God could do this. Through divine prophecy, God reveals this land to his chosen people so that they could worship him in that place according to the purity of his ordinances. Consequently, Cotton argued: "When God wrappes us in his Ordinances, and warmes us with the life and power of them as with wings, there is a land of promise."[22]

All this discussion, of course, was not merely academic for Cotton. On the contrary, he had a far more important goal in mind. For many years Englishmen were conditioned by the premises of English apocalyptic tradition to regard their land and people as God's elect nation. And as we saw earlier, this glorious vision of England in providential history provided an

    [21] John Cotton, *Gods Promise to His Plantation* (1634 [1630]), pp. 3, 5, 6.
    [22] *Ibid.*, pp. 6–7.

important dimension to the Protestant ideology of the settlement of Virginia. Cotton's Puritan audience at Southampton, of course, did not adhere to this glorious Protestant vision of England, but rather denounced it. Evidently, then, in clear contrast to the Protestant ideology of the settlement of Virginia which was based upon the vision of England as God's elect nation, Cotton had to construct a very different ideology for the Puritan settlement of New England. Thus, instead of grounding the justification for the colonization of America upon a historical model of England as the embodiment of God's chosen nation, as the Protestants believed, Cotton vindicated the Puritan exodus on the basis of God's promise to his chosen people, Israel, that he would settle them in the Land of Promise. That is why Cotton told the Puritans at Southampton that wherever they would plant the true religion and worship God according to the purity of his ordinances, there is the Promised Land. This was, then, the divine warrant by which Cotton justified the Puritan migration to America. In that way indeed Cotton was successful in vindicating the Puritan migration, not upon the historical model of England, but upon God's prophetic promise to his chosen people.

Having established the divine warrant for the Puritan migration by arguing that the Promised Land may lie wherever God provides for "the liberty and Purity of His Ordinances," Cotton next turned to deal with the actual issue of "what may warrant" the Puritans "removall" to New England. Among the various reasons for people emigrating, such as the gaining of knowledge and commercial advantages, Cotton noted that they included as well "the liberty of the Ordinances" of God. In this context he begged his audience to compare their migration with that of the Marian exiles, or the flight of many Protestants to the continent during the reign of Bloody Mary (1553–8). "This case was of seasonable use to our fathers in the dayes of Queene Mary; who removed to France and Germany in the beginning of the her Reign, upon Proclamation of alteration of religion, before any persecution began." Furthermore, continued Cotton, "there be evills to be avoyded that may warrant removall." So, for example, "when some grievous sinnes overspread a Country that threaten desolation," then a man has a mandate to fly out of the approaching calamity. For according to Cotton, "as in a threatning a wise man foreseeth the plague, so in the threatning he seeth a commandement, to hide himself from it."[23]

Point after point Cotton delineated for the Puritans who gathered at Southampton the apocalyptic and eschatological context of their Errand into the Wilderness in America. And he was always cautious to show that the Puritan exodus had ample warrant in God's providence. Led by divine

[23] *Ibid.*, pp. 6, 9, 10.

providence to flee from the impending judgments about to befall England, the Puritan migration, according to Cotton, was directed by God's promise to his people that he would settle them safely in a place appointed by him. So he concluded by saying:

Here is then the eye of God that opens a doore there [New England], and set him loose here [England], inclines his heart that way, and outlookes all difficulties. When God makes a roome for us, no binding here [England], and an open way there [New England], in such a case God tells them, he will appoint a place for them.[24]

It is within this overall providential context of God's promise to his people that Cotton pleaded with the Puritans who were ready to go to America to consider their Errand:

When you have found God making way and roome for you, and carrying you by his providence unto any place, learne to walke thankfully before him, defraud him not of his rent, but offer your selves unto his service.

They were, he continued, "a choice generation," namely a chosen people embarking on a mission to plant "the Ordinances of God amongst them in a more glorious manner," and therefore he exhorted them to "have a speciall care that you ever have the Ordinances planted amongst you, or else never look for security." Defining, therefore, the Puritan Errand in terms of God's promise to his chosen people that he would settle them in the Land of Promise, a land in which God's holy presence is evident in the purity of his Ordinances, Cotton closed his sermon by saying that the whole fate of the Puritan enterprise in the wilderness would be determined by the establishment of God's ordinances in the Puritan plantation in New England:

Looke into all the stories whether divine or humane, and you shall never finde that God ever rooted out a people that had the Ordinances planted amongst them, and themselves planted into the Ordinances: Never did God suffer such plants to be plucked up; on all their glory shall be a defence.[25]

In 1630, Cotton still preferred to stay in England in order to aid the forces of reformation. Therefore, in his sermon he admonished his Puritan friends who were about to sail to America: "be not unmindfull of our *Jerusalem* at home, whether you leave us, or stay at home with us."[26] Yet, a radical transformation was about to take place in Cotton's thought with his own migration to New England in 1633. Once in America, Cotton heartily adhered to the identification of the Puritan Errand with that of the prophetic, redemptive Errand of the Church of the Wilderness, which was laid down in the Puritan debates of 1629. And as we will see later, Cotton became the most prominent, indeed the most radical, spokesman of the Puritan Errand as the embodiment of the prophetic Errand of the Church of

---

[24] *Ibid.*, p. 12.   [25] *Ibid.*, pp. 13, 15, 17–18.   [26] *Ibid.*, p. 18.

the Wilderness. These changes of thought, however, should not hinder us from seeing the importance of his unique contribution to the issue of the Puritan Errand which he had made in his sermon of 1630. As constructed by Cotton, the Puritan Errand was based upon God's promise to his chosen people Israel that he would plant them in the Land of Promise. Likewise, argued Cotton, this sacred prophecy constituted the divine warrant for the Puritan migration to New England. For where God's people worship Him in liberty and according to the purity of His holy ordinances, there lies the land of Promise. Consequently, for Cotton, the Puritan Errand signified the purest establishment of God's ordinances in the wilderness of America.

This explicit institutional dimension of the Puritan Errand into the Wilderness was indeed widespread in the thought of the Puritans of the first generation of New England. Yet it should not, by any means, be regarded as opposing the vision of the Puritan Errand in terms of the Errand of the Church of the Wilderness. These different visions of the Puritan Errand were not mutually exclusive, but rather complementary. For both were based upon divine prophecy assigned to God's chosen people, and served to reveal the sacred meaning of the Puritan migration in the providential history. The differences between them, however, can be ascribed to the variety of views among Puritans concerning the mission of the great Puritan migration to America, which were ultimately derived from a different reading among Puritans concerning the prospects of reforming the Church of England. Accordingly, those Puritans, like John Cotton and the many friends of the Puritan emigrants, who yet preferred to stay in England in order to fight with the forces of reformation, still thought about "Jerusalem at Home"[27] though they had been full and ardent supporters of the migration to New England. Therefore, as Cotton's sermon shows, they tended to define the Puritan Errand to New England in less apocalyptic and eschatological terms, unwilling as yet to consider it, as indeed the Puritan emigrants did, as holding the ultimate clue to the mystery of salvation and redemption.

On the other hand, those Puritans already in America, like the Pilgrims, or those who had already resolved to emigrate, like the Puritans aboard the ships at Southampton, had already relinquished all hope for reforming the Church of England. For them nothing was left from the vision of Jerusalem at home. They therefore identified their Errand with that of the Errand of the Church of the Wilderness, considering, as it was, their Errand as an apocalyptic and eschatological separation from the sin and corruption of England. For these Puritans indeed the desacralization of England lends itself inevitably to the sacralization of New England in providential history. This essential process, which lay at the roots of the Puritan ideology of the

27 *Ibid.*, p. 18.

settlement of New England, can be clearly seen in one of the boldest and most radical identifications of the Puritan Errand with the prophetic and redemptive Errand of the Church of the Wilderness – Thomas Hooker's sermon, *The Danger of Desertion* (1631).

THOMAS HOOKER AND THE APOCALYPSE OF GOD'S DEPARTURE FROM ENGLAND

Thomas Hooker's *The Danger of Desertion*, 1631, which is commonly subtitled "A Farewell Sermon," is important to the discussion of the Puritan Errand because it further establishes the apocalyptic and eschatological context for the Puritan migration. In this regard, indeed, it should be understood along with the writings of the Pilgrim Fathers and the Puritans of the "General Observations," which identified the Puritan Errand to New England with the prophetic, redemptive visions of the Errand of the Church of the Wilderness. These writings sharply reveal how the Puritan failure to execute the true reformation in England greatly stimulated the rise of Puritan apocalyptic and eschatological consciousness concerning New England's unique role in providential history. Consequently, these writings provide not only clear evidence of the growing tendency among Puritans to relinquish any hope for reforming England, except of apostasy, but they illuminate as well the essential process taking place in the Puritan mind concerning the sacralization of New England. In this context, indeed, the uniqueness of Hooker's "extraordinarily moving sermon" can be seen not only in the fact that it "admirably sets forth the Puritan mood of desperation"[28] concerning England, but also in the wonderful description of the gradual removal of God's grace from England and of its placement upon Puritan New England.

It is of the utmost significance that Hooker preached his sermon in 1631 while he was preparing to leave for Holland, yet it was not Europe but rather New England that constituted the ultimate solution for the sins and corruptions of England and the Old World in general. For Hooker, therefore, as was the case in relation to the Pilgrims and the Puritans of the "General Observations," England and New England represented the ultimate boundaries within which the drama of salvation took place. Hence, the desacralization of the former led inevitably to the sacralization of the latter. Indeed, like many other Puritans, Hooker was not satisfied with the course of the Reformation in England. Yet, as of 1626, he was truly convinced that "the Lord hath had an eye" upon England and had chosen it to

---

[28] George H. Williams, "Introduction" to Thomas Hooker's *The Danger of Desertion*, in *Thomas Hooker: Writings in England and Holland, 1626–1633*, ed. George H. Williams, Norman Pettit, Winfried Herget, and Sargent Bush, Jr. (Cambridge, 1975), p. 221.

be his chosen nation "above all the rest" in the world. For "when the fire of God's fury hath flamed and consumed all the countries round about us; Bohemia, the Palatinate, and Denmark" during the Thirty Years' War, "this little cottage, this little England" lay in rest and peace. So, continued Hooker, it was the mark of God's favor and grace toward England that

when the sward hath ruinated and overcome all the other parts of Christiandom where the name of the Lord Jesus is professed, we sit under our vines and fig trees, there is no complaining in our streets, our wives are not husbandless, our children are not fatherless. Mark the reason and ground of all is nothing else but God's mercy toward us.[29]

In 1631, however, nothing remained from this admirable vision concerning England's singular place in providential history as is clear in his sermon, *The Danger of Desertion.*

The text which Hooker chose for his sermon is taken from one of the most gloomy and desperate chapters in Jeremiah in which the prophet warned sinful Israel of the approach of God's impending divine wrath and judgments (Jer. 14). And placing his words in this eschatological context of Israel's destruction, Hooker warned his congregation that, as it had been the case in the past in regard to Israel, now in regard of England, "God might cast off a people, and unchurch a nation." In a time in which "a domination of a judgment" leads God to "take his providence" from England, Hooker turned to the dreadful vision in Revelation in order to arouse fear and trembling in the hearts of his brethren concerning the fate which would fall upon England because of God's wrath:

My brethren, cast your thoughts afar off, and see what is become of those famous Churches of Pergamum and Theatira and the rest mentioned, Rev. 1:11. And who would have thought that Jerusalem should have been made a heap of stones and a wagabond people? And yet we see God hath forsaken them, showing us thereby that, although God will never forsake his own elect ones, yet he may forsake such as are in outward covenant with him.[30]

These are the lessons Hooker drew from the historical model of Israel and from the prophetic revelations in the Apocalypse, showing clearly what both history and prophecy teach about a people deserting God and his word. Furthermore, these awful lessons from the annals of providential history were awaiting England now, according to Hooker, for God was now saying to England:

Plead, plead with England, all ye that are my ministers in the way of my truth, and say unto her, let her cast away her rebellions, lest I leave her as I found her in the day of captivity and bondage under the blindness of popery and superstitions.[31]

---

[29] Thomas Hooker, *The Church's Deliverance* (1626), in G. H. Williams, Pettit, Herget, and Bush (eds.), *Thomas Hooker*, p. 67.
[30] Thomas Hooker, *The Danger of Desertion*, pp. 230, 228, 230.   [31] *Ibid.*, p. 231.

For many years, Englishmen had been conditioned by English apocalyptic tradition to look upon England as God's chosen nation. Throughout his sermon, therefore, Hooker time and again tried to persuade them that, as the historical model of Israel indicated, God indeed may "un-church or discarge a people, and cast a nation off." Admittedly, continued Hooker, Englishmen "cannot entertain a thought of England's desolation." Yet, when "there are so many prophecies in it of its destruction," who, declared Hooker, may dare to overlook them. God's people in particular should take his divine warnings seriously. For "God may leave a nation, and his elect may suffer, and why may not England?" After all, as Puritans well knew about their native land,

England's sins are very great, and the greater, because the means are great, and our warnings are and have been great; but yet our mercies are far greater. England hath been a mirror of mercies. Yet now God may leave it, and make it the mirror of his justice.[32]

Hooker found evidence for his views, like so many other Puritans at that time, in the Thirty Years' War. These fierce battles between the forces of the Reformation and the Counter-Reformation seized the eyes of many Puritans, and played an important role in the Puritan reasons and justifications for the migration to New England. Yet, it was Hooker who drew the most dreadful vision for England from the Catholic victories in Europe:

Go to Bohemia, and from thence to the Palatinate (and so to Denmark) and from thence to other parts of Germany. Do but imagine that you were there, or do but mark what travellers say. God's churches are made heaps of stone, and those Bethels wherein God's name was called upon, are now defiled Temples for Satan and superstition to reign in.

"You cannot go three steps" in those areas of Europe in which the fury of the Thirty Years' War raged, continued Hooker, "but you shall see the head of a dead man. And go a little further, and you shall see the heart picked out by the fowls of the air, or some other sad spectacle." And now, with the devastation of the Protestant churches throughout the continent, argued Hooker, "may not this be the condition of England, and who knows but it may?"[33]

Indeed, in all the Puritan apocalyptic and eschatological writings relating to the migration to New England, one can hardly find a more awful vision than Hooker's description of the horrible fate awaiting England in providential history because of its failure to execute the true reformation. To the Puritans, in general, the Thirty Years' War served as a great prophetical and

---

[32] *Ibid.*, pp. 231–2.   [33] *Ibid.*, pp. 232–3.

historical symbol for the degenerate course of the Reformation in England. For them, this war was a frightful revelatory sign of God's wrath against the sins of the Old World. So far England had been saved from the terrible calamities that God's fury had brought upon Europe through this war. Yet, as Hooker told his congregation, England should not be over-confident that God would not turn his rage upon her. "Who would have thought that Jerusalem, the Lady City of all Nations . . . should become a heap of stones and a vagabond people?" And if God brought destruction upon his beloved city, "why may it not be England's case?" "For assuredly," continued Hooker, "God can be God without England's prosperity." England's ultimate problem in providential history, argued Hooker, lay in the fact that it as "yet hath to be reformed" according to God's will and his word. Otherwise, Hooker proclaimed boldly, God "will rather go into Turkey and say unto them, 'Thou are my people, and I will be your God'." God, for his own part, had no problem leaving England, yet England, according to Hooker, cannot afford to "let Christ go and God go," because this will be the surest sign of its doom and ruin.[34]

Hooker's apocalyptic and eschatological visions concerning England's gloomy fate in sacred, ecclesiastical history, are based upon his belief that England could no longer boast of being God's elect nation. For a nation which forsakes God's word and his ordinance faces the terrible danger of God's imminent desertion and the removal of God's presence from her. "But what is the presence of God?", asked Hooker. "In a word, it is the particular favor of God which he expresseth in his ordinances, . . . it is all the good and sweetness that flows from the purity of God's worship, whereby God reveals himself unto us." Most important, argued Hooker, "it is God's ordinances purely administrated that brings God's presence to a people," and therefore "the saints are so urgent for God's ordinances in the purity of them." Consequently, continued Hooker, "the saints of God are marvelous importunate to keep God in his ordinances, . . . the want of which is under the penalty of death and demnation." Now, it is precisely because the people in England were seeking "to be freed from the ordinances of God" that they "be the everlasting object of his never dying wrath." And in these horrible words he admonished his brethren: "A hundred hells thou hast deserved, and in those hells to lie a hundred years, nay forever, Hold theyself contented with thy condition."[35]

This terrible exhortation, however, was directed to the English nation as a whole, and not to Hooker's Puritan congregation in particular. For Hooker made it perfectly clear what he had in mind concerning the English people's

---

[34] *Ibid.*, p. 234.   [35] *Ibid.*, pp. 236–7, 241.

fortune in the ensuing apocalyptic and eschatological occurrences which would soon take place in England:

when thou shal hear the trumpets sound, and when thine ears shal tingle with the sound of wars; then depart forever. Fulfill your base lusts.

These profane and ungodly people, according to Hooker, had prevented the Reformation in England from being fulfilled, and hence, caused God's grace to desert England. Yet, those who deserted God cannot but expect that God would forsake them. Consequently, Hooker declared in unmistakable words, "Christ is departing" out of England, because he is going "to seek better entertainment" for him and his Gospel.[36]

At this point in his sermon, Hooker's apocalyptic and eschatological consciousness reached its height. "As sure as God is God," he proclaimed, "God is going from England." At this tremendous moment, God had invested Hooker with a sacred prophetic mission from heaven to promulgate to his brethren what would be the outcome for England if God and Christ should leave that sinful nation. "I am a poor ambassador sent from God to do his message unto you," Hooker said, "and, although I be low, my message is from above, and he that sent me is great, and from above." Now, invested with God's divine, prophetic mission, Hooker relentlessly and passionately admonished his brethren about the near-destruction and desolation of England:

Will you have your young women widows, and your virgins defiled? Will you have your dear and tender little ones tossed upon the pikes and dashed against the stones? Or will you have them brought up in Popery, in idolatry, under a necessity of perishing their souls forever, which is worst of all? Will you have these temples wherein we seem to worship God, will you have them and your houses burnt with fire? And will you see England laid waste without inhabitants?

Indeed, at such an alarming eschatological moment, in which God's sword is already lifted up ready to strike against England, Hooker even told his audience that because of England's grave sins, the saints in fact should welcome God's wrath. "But if desolation do come, thank yourselves for it, it is your own fault if you be destroyed, and not God's; for he delights not in the death of any."[37]

Armed thus with God's divine mission, Hooker announced the prophetic message of destruction which God would soon inflict upon England. Evidently for Hooker, the desacralization of England led inevitably to the sacralization of New England in providential history:

So glory is departed from England; for England hath seen her best days, and the reward of sin is coming on apace; for God is packing up of his gospel, because none will buy his wares (not come to his price). God begins to ship away his Noahs, which

---

[36] *Ibid.*, pp. 242–3.   [37] *Ibid.*, pp. 244–5.

prophesied and foretold that destruction was near; and God makes account that New England shall be a refuge for his Noahs and his Lots, a rock and shelter for his righteous ones to run unto; and those that were vexed to see the ungodly lives of the people in this wicked land, shall there be safe.[38]

As this passage shows, in 1631 Thomas Hooker had reached the same conclusions the Pilgrim Fathers and the Puritans of the "General Observations" had already arrived at concerning the redemptive significance of the Puritan migration to America within the confines of providential history. For Hooker now, like the Puritans who had already settled in New England, believed that the clue for the history of salvation and redemption lay in the immediate utmost separation from sinful England whose foreordained doom was at hand. In this eschatological and apocalyptic moment, Hooker recognized, like the Puritans before him, that nothing was left for the true church but to assume upon herself the prophetic, revelatory Errand of the Church of the Wilderness; to cut all ties with corrupt England and fly into the wilderness in America.

Hooker's sermon is indeed the ultimate expression of the desacralization process which lay behind the Puritan migration to New England. He emphasized time and again that God's wrath was soon to fall upon corrupt England

The same sins that were found in the old world, are found in us. Sodom's and Gomorah's sins were but straws in respect of ours! And yet God rained down fire and brimstone upon them. Tell me, are there not as great sins amongst us as were in Jerusalem, who were carried captives, and their city destroyed, and they a vagabond people unto this day? Are we better than other brethren and neighbor nations, that have drunk so deeply of God's wrath? I tell you truely, we are a burden to God; he cannot long bear us, and he will think his burden well over when he hath destroyed us.[39]

In 1631 Hooker was ready to escape to the continent. Therefore his sermon carries nothing but a prophetic message of destruction and desolation for England. A year before, in his farewell sermon of 1630, John Cotton admonished the Puritan emigrants to remember "Jerusalem at home." Yet with Hooker, nothing indeed remained from the vision of establishing Jerusalem in England. Therefore he concluded his sermon with the horrible vision Christ had at Capernaum:

And thou, Capernaum, which are exalted to heaven, shall be brought down to hell . . . (and) I say unto you, That it shall be more tolerable for the land of Sodom in the day of judgment, than for thee (Matt. 11:23).

And at that moment in his life, Hooker unhesitatingly identified England's fate in providential history with that of Capernaum: "Capernaum's place is England's place, which is the most scalding tormenting place of all."[40]

[38] *Ibid.*, pp. 245–6.   [39] *Ibid.*, p. 250.   [40] *Ibid.*, p. 252.

No other sermon of that time captured so brilliantly the Puritan's desperate eschatological and apocalyptic consciousness concerning England than Hooker's *The Danger of Desertion*. Indeed, no other sermon in this period described so vividly what terrible consequences England would face because of the imminent removal of God's grace from this land. Consequently, with Hooker's sermon, the Puritan desacralization of England had reached its culmination. As for Hooker himself, immediately after admonishing England so mercilessly, he had fled to Holland. Yet his prophetic message was not uttered in vain. For in 1632, as John Winthrop recorded in his *Journal*, "Mr. Hooker's company" came to the Bay colony.[41] His prophetic words, then, had their effect upon the consciousness of his godly congregation who fled doomed England into the shelter of the wilderness in America. This, in general terms, was exactly the case with so many other Puritan congregations who came to New England. Thus, the Puritan migration as a prophetic revelatory event in providential history was based essentially and inevitably upon the desacralization of England. For according to the Puritan apocalyptic interpretation of history as a mode of historical thought, their migration to America was taking place between two antagonistic poles in sacred history, Egypt and the Promised Land, or Babylon and the New Jerusalem. Hence, the Puritan eschatology and apocalypse of New England was fundamentally constructed upon the prophetic and redemptive vision of the Errand of the Church of the Wilderness, or upon the revelatory event of God's people migrating to the Land of Promise and thereby inaugurating a new era in the history of salvation and redemption. It was indeed in this eschatological and apocalyptic context that Thomas Hooker raised his magnificent vision of the Puritan migration, in which, according to the divine scheme of providential history, "God begins to ship away his Noahs" out of doomed England, "which prophesied and foretold that destruction was near; and God makes account that New England shall be a refuge for his Noahs and his Lots, a rock and a shelter for his righteous ones to run unto."[42]

JOHN COTTON AND THE AMERICANIZATION OF THE ERRAND OF
THE CHURCH OF THE WILDERNESS

So far we have seen how the prophetic, redemptive vision of the Errand of the Church of the Wilderness powerfully informed the Puritan ideology of the settlement of New England, and how, through this sacred vision, Puritans had been able to construe the meaning and significance of their

---

[41] John Winthrop, *The History of New England, from 1630 to 1649*, 2 vols., ed. James Savage (Boston, 1853), vol. I, p. 74.
[42] Hooker, *The Danger of Desertion*, p. 246.

removal to America within the boundaries of providential history. This divine vision, however, did not cease to influence Puritans' modes of conviction and of action after their actual migration to America. On the contrary, the eschatologically oriented conception of the Church of the Wilderness in the Apocalypse was a crucial animating force not only in shaping the ideological premises of the Puritan migration, but also played a most significant role in explaining the meaning of the Puritan life and existence in the wilderness of New England. The vision of the Church of the Wilderness, then, had been transferred to America by the Puritans of the first generation, and later it continuously constituted an essential part of the ideological and theological universe of the second and third Puritan generations in the New World. For it was according to this prophetic vision that later Puritan generations persistently defined the importance of their abode in the wilderness of America. Considering, therefore, the Errand of the Church of the Wilderness in terms of a founding Puritan Errand in the settlement of New England, it will be hard not to recognize how this prophetic Errand incorporated the whole Puritan experience in seventeenth-century New England within a single, coherent sacred, ecclesiastical context.

The most important example of the persistent use of the apocalyptic conception of the wilderness in Revelation made by New England Puritans is perhaps that of John Cotton. After his emigration to New England in 1633, Cotton not only wholeheartedly adopted the eschatologically oriented conception of the wilderness in the Apocalypse, but more important, he wholly adhered to Brightman's apocalyptic exposition of the Errand of the Church of the Wilderness in terms of inaugurating a new era in providential history. This great transformation in one of the most prominent minds among the Puritans in New England can be clearly seen in Cotton's *An Exposition upon the Thirteenth Chapter of the Revelation*, in which the Errand of the Church of the Wilderness was identified in the most radical way with the Congregationalist, or Independent system of church-government as professed by the New England Puritans. Indeed, among New England Puritans, Cotton's exegesis of the Errand of the Church of the Wilderness was the most radical. For according to him, this Errand represented the gradual apocalyptic and historical progress of the rise and establishment of Congregationalism. Furthermore, Cotton's interpretation was deeply historical because, in his discussion of the Errand of the Church of the Wilderness, he took into consideration the whole course of sacred, ecclesiastical history. This wide historical perspective enabled Cotton to claim later that with the Puritan migration and establishment of Congregationalism in New England, the history of salvation and redemption had reached its culmination. Seen in this context, Cotton's interpretation of the Church of the Wilderness may be considered as the first instance of the

Puritan American apocalyptic tradition, or as the first example of an apocalyptic interpretation of history based upon the Puritan experience in
America.

At the end of 1639 and at the beginning of 1640, during his weekly
sermons at his Boston church, Cotton preached extensively about the
thirteenth chapter of the Apocalypse.[43] These lectures were later published
in London in 1655 under the title, *An Exposition upon the Thirteenth
Chapter of the Revelation*. Chapter 13 of Revelation, as may be recalled,
deals with the rise of the Beast to predominance in the world, which occurs
immediately after the vision of the Woman's flight into the wilderness in
chapter 12. Having failed to destroy the Woman, or the church, in her
shelter in the wilderness, the Dragon then "went to make war with the
remnant of her seed, which keep the commandments of God, and have the
testimony of Jesus Christ" (Rev. 12:17). Later, immediately after that
vision, chapter 13 describes the rise of the Beast to whom was given the
power to rule "over all kindreds, and tongues, and nations" (Rev. 13:7).
Now, in accordance with the premises of English apocalyptic interpretation
as a mode of historical thought, Cotton attempted to explain historically
this prophetic revelation of the Beast's rise to predominance in the world by
indicating the period of Christianity to which this sacred prophecy should
be applied. And for his correlation between sacred prophecy and history,
Cotton drew ultimately upon "holy Brightman,"[44] claiming that the
Woman's flight into the wilderness took place during the time of the Beast's
rise to rule over all the world. Thus, by calculating the historical period of
the Beast's rise, Cotton had been able to reckon as well the historical time of
the Woman's flight into the wilderness and to expound in the most radical
way the Errand of the Church of the Wilderness.

Drawing fundamentally upon Brightman's apocalyptic interpretation of
Revelation, Cotton argued that "Mr. Brightman rightly observes" that "the
woman fled into the wilderness at the Constantine coming to the Crown,"
or at that crucial moment in the history of Christianity in which it was
transformed from a persecuted church into the official church and faith of
the Roman empire by Constantine the Great (288?–377). At this decisive
moment in the history of Christianity in which "The Roman Catholick
visible Church" was established, continued Cotton, "there is given two
wings of an Eagle unto the woman, that she might flee into the wildernesse
into her place" of refuge "from the face of the Serpent." So, it was from
the time of "Constantine Reigne" (312–337), that the Beast began to rule

---

[43] John Cotton, *An Exposition upon the Thirteenth Chapter of the Revelation* (London,
1655). On the date on which Cotton preached these sermons, see Thomas Allen's "Preface"
to Cotton's book.
[44] *Ibid.*, pp. 87–88.

the world, and it was this satanic rule which caused the church to fly into the wilderness. Now, "the expiration" of Satan's rule, according to Cotton who followed Brightman's exegesis, "will fall somewhat after the beginning of the reigne of Queene Elizabeth." Furthermore, grounding his apocalyptic interpretation upon Brightman's exegesis of Revelation, Cotton placed the reign of Elizabeth in the time of the seventh trumpet, or during that time in which the whole mystery of the history of salvation would be revealed:

[Elizabeth] renounced the Catholick Church, that is this great beast, and cut off his head to her best understanding, which was about the sounding of the seventh Trumpet, Rev. 11.15. When the Kingdomes of this world became the Kingdomes of our Lord, and of his Christ.[45]

The revolutionary radicalism embodied in Cotton's historical interpretation of the Church of the Wilderness, which was ultimately and essentially derived from Brightman's apocalyptic exegesis, should not be overlooked. In the English apocalyptic tradition before Brightman and Cotton, by contrast, as we saw earlier, John Foxe had seen in Constantine the Great's reign one of the most glorious periods in the history of Christianity. Therefore, when seeking to compare Elizabeth's accession to the throne which brought about the triumph of Protestantism, Foxe had in mind no other historical example but Constantine's glorious establishment of Christianity as the church and the faith of the Roman empire, claiming that as Constantine ceased persecuting Christians and brought them to the citadels of power and authority in Rome, so Elizabeth stopped persecuting Protestants and made Protestantism the faith of the English nation. Hence, like "Constantine the greate and mightie Emperour" in the past, who "pacified and established the churche of Christ" in the Roman empire, so now it was into England that "the Lord sent this mild Constantine," namely, Elizabeth, "to cease bloud, to staye persecution, [and] to refresh his people." No wonder, then, that by favorably comparing Elizabeth's and Constantine's role in sacred history, Foxe chose to identify himself with Eusebius, the "father of church history." Just as Eusebius wrote during the time of Constantine the Great about "the names, sufferinges, and actes, of all such as suffered . . . for the testimonie and faith of Christ Jesus," so did Foxe in his *Acts and Monuments* during Queen Elizabeth's reign.[46]

As against the glorious role Foxe accorded to the godly prince in providential history, such as, for example, to Elizabeth and Constantine, Brightman presented a radically different picture concerning the prince and the pursuit of religious reformation. Writing from the gloomy perspective of the Puritan failure under Elizabeth, and in clear contrast to Foxe's optimistic

---

[45] *Ibid.*, pp. 89, 95, 89, 90–1.
[46] John Foxe, *Acts and Monuments*, "To the Queene's Most Excellent Majestie, Queene Elizabeth," vol. I, pp. vi–vii.

prospects of the triumph of Protestantism in England, Brightman held that the godly prince hindered rather than advanced the true reformation of the church. In Brightman's thought, therefore, nothing was left from Foxe's magnificent vision of Constantine's role in providential history but that of apostasy. For according to Brightman, it was during Constantine's reign that the Beast rose to power in the world with the creation of the Roman Catholic Church. (Writing at the end of Elizabeth's reign, Brightman's explicit denunciation of Constantine's apostasized role in providential history should also be seen as an implicit criticism of Elizabeth's abandonment of the pursuit of the Reformation in Protestant England.) Having thus placed the rise of the Beast during Constantine's times, Brightman, and later Cotton who followed closely his apocalyptic interpretation, consequently argued that the Woman's flight into the wilderness took place during that period in the history of Christianity in which Constantine transformed it from being a persecuted church into the official faith of the Roman empire. Changing historical circumstances and prospects for the Reformation in England had thus led to a radical reevaluation within English apocalyptic tradition of Constantine's role in sacred, ecclesiastical history. This great revolutionary shift of abandoning altogether Foxe's glorious vision of a godly prince in providential history is evident not only in Brightman's thought but also in Cotton's interpretation of the nature and significance of the Errand of the Church of the Wilderness.

Constructing his apocalyptic interpretation upon Brightman's desacralization of Constantine's role in providential history, Cotton emphasized time and again that it was during Constantine's rule that the church fled into the wilderness:

It is true from Constantine time, the Church might fly into the wildernesse; for it is true, the Church is made a wildernesse if you see the doores of the Church so wide and pull down the walls, that whereas before, *it was a Garden inclosed*, Can. 4.12. now you let in vast territories, bring in the whole world, now you make it Catholick.

From this moment in the history of Christianity rose "the whore of Rome," and "this great Beast (the Roman Catholick visible Church) bewitched the world for so many ages." Furthermore, it "had power to make warre against the Saints, yea to overcome them," as was the case, for example, with the Beast's wars "against the Waldenses and Albingeses in the 12. Century after Christ." Following Brightman's reckoning that Elizabeth's accession to the throne inaugurated the time of the seventh trumpet, Cotton calculated that "so far as God helps by Scripture light," or by his divine prophecies, "about the time 1655, there will be then such a blow given to this beast, and to the head of this beast, which is *Pontifex maximus*," or the Pope.[47]

---

[47] Cotton, *An Exposition Upon the Thirteenth Chapter of the Revelation*, pp. 92–3, 111.

In this eschatological context of the papacy drawing to its apocalyptic end, Cotton was able to tell his brethren in New England that "the Beast of Rome still live, his 42. moneths" as foretold in the Apocalypse "is not yet out (though his power he much weakned) but his Agents still live." Consequently, Cotton warned repeatedly that their ultimate enemy had always been and was still the papacy:

And if Wars come against New England, it will be from *Principalities and Powers*, and flesh and blood will not be able to with-stand them; They will be Principalities from Hell, or the great Beast, the Catholick Church, or from the Image of that Beast, otherwise there is no feare of any War.[48]

By placing the Puritan Errand into America within the eschatological and apocalyptic context of the providential flight of the Church of the Wilderness from the Beast of Rome, Cotton revealed the deepest, sacred, ideological origins which lay at the roots of Puritan life and experience in New England. In this sense, indeed, Cotton's interpretation of the Puritan Errand is the most historically conscious among New England Puritans.

The Puritan Errand into the Wilderness in America was inextricably associated with the prophetic, redemptive Errand of the Church of the Wilderness, according to Cotton, because in his thought the essence of both Errands was the pursuit of Congregationalism as a system of church-government. Hence, the ultimate mark of Cotton's apocalyptic interpretation of the Beast's rise to dominance in the world, and consequently of the Woman's flight into the wilderness, should be seen in the context of the Congregationalist opposition to the Roman Catholic Church. Accordingly, following the Apocalypse in which the Beast would rule the world "for 1260. years together," Cotton argued that one should reckon "from Constantine time" that people around the world began to "worship the great Beast," or the Church of Rome. The rise of the Beast, however, stood in a clear contrast to the "Apostolicall Church" and "The Apostles Doctrine" about Congregationalism. For "in the dayes of the new Testament [sic], the Church that Christ instituted reacheth no further then to their own members, and their own members reach no further than to one Congregation." The Church of Rome's usurpation of ecclesiastical and civil power caused the rise of the Beast according to Cotton. Especially in ecclesiastical matters, the "Apostles Doctrine" held that "Church power extends no further then the bounds of one Congregation." Yet, with the rise of the Church of Rome, it usurped into her hand that power which Christ gave to each congregation. Therefore, Cotton declared:

that Church that swelleth and strechet forth her power all the world over, Kindreds, and Tongues, and Nations; what an out-ragious swelling Beast is that, that reacheth such vast dominion beyond the proportion that the Lord gave to his Church?

[48] *Ibid.*, pp. 110–11.

The ultimate mark of such a church is "not of an Apostolicall Church, but it may be a note of an Apostaticall Church that is fallen away from the Apostles Doctrine." This is so, argued Cotton, because during the time of primitive Christianity, "the Lord had limited the power of the Church within it selfe."[49]

Congregationalism was therefore the true apostolic tradition in the Christian world before the Church of Rome had usurped the "Soveraignty" Christ had enjoyed within each of his congregational churches. Consequently, declared Cotton,

as soon as Constantine brought the world to become Christian, the woman she fled into the wildernesse: The true worshipers of Christ were soon troden under the hatches, a mountain of corruption in Church Government overwhelmed them amain.

This beastly reign of the Church of Rome in the world, however, had no warrant at all in "the Kingly, Priestly, and Prophetical Office of Christ." For "never did the Christian world give that Authority to Christ, as they have done unto the Pope, and his Institutions, which are not Ordinances of Christ." With the rise of the Beast of Rome, then, "it hath been a very rare and singular case when any man would acknowledge a particular visible Church, depending on no power, but Independent within it selfe." Furthermore, when the papacy gradually assumed power in the world, the Church of the Wilderness, or the Congregational, Independent church, had almost disappeared from the face of the world. That is why, Cotton told his brethren, "it is very rare to heare" of such a true church "till you come down to the Waldences, and Albedences, and those poor Churches that were scattered in the Wildernesse." Since Constantine's time, therefore, an apocalyptic struggle had taken place between the Roman Beast and the congregational, apostolic churches. And glancing at the course of the history of Christianity since the rise of Rome, Cotton could not but sadly acknowledge the fact that

it is very hard to find the Church of Christs Institution to remain in the world, whereas this Roman Catholic Church reigns in the world: This is a great power, and yet this power the Church of Rome had. The Harlot reigns over Kindreds, Tongues, and Nations, whereas the true Spouse of Christ hath scarce a subsistance in the world.[50]

Cotton's apocalyptic interpretation of the Errand of the Church of the Wilderness rested on a wide historical context within which the Puritan Errand into New England was placed. In contrast, then, to earlier Puritan expressions which identified the Puritan migration to New England with that of the Woman's flight into the wilderness and yet placed its origins and

---

[49] *Ibid.*, pp. 120–1.   [50] *Ibid.*, pp. 122, 110, 123.

causes within the context of English history during Elizabeth's and the early Stuarts' reign, Cotton boldly claimed that the New England Errand into the Wilderness should be seen in the larger sacred, ecclesiastical context of the Beast of Rome's rise to predominance in the world. In this way, he unfolded before the eyes of his Puritan brethren in America the whole course of providential history, claiming that, with the Puritan migration to New England and the establishment of Congregationalism there, the history of salvation and redemption had reached its culmination. Furthermore, viewing Congregationalism as the essence of the Woman's flight into the wilderness, Cotton enabled his audience in Boston to consider their life and existence in America within the widest historical perspective yet offered. And by telling his Puritan brethren that the New England Errand was inseparable from that of the Church of the Wilderness, Cotton beseeched them to evaluate their singular role in providential history:

let it be of much praise and thanksgiving to God, that hath delivered us and ours, from these Contagions and pollutions, in which you see all that dwell on the earth have been intangled and polluted in time past; That he hath delivered us from the power of this Beast (the Roman Catholick Church) that he hath freed us from making an Image to that Beast; we own none of his Ordinances, and that God hath removed us from the mark of this Beast, that we desire not to be accounted Catholicks, nor Hirarchies, nor standing members of a Diocesan, or Provinciall, or Cathedrall, or Nationall Church, but beare witnessed against them all.[51]

Having defined the prophetic, redemptive Errand of the Church of the Wilderness in the context of the apocalyptic struggle between the Beast of Rome and the true Church, which was based upon the Congregationalist way in terms of church-government, it is no wonder that Cotton could declare that Puritan New England signified the climax of providential history. As described in Revelation, the Woman fled into the wilderness from the face of the Dragon's rage, and she was maintained there by God's divine providence for 1,260 years (Rev. 12:6). This span of time, according to Cotton, represents the fate of the true church under the rule of the Beast of Rome who persecuted it and eventually destroyed all attempts to establish the Congregationalist way in the Christian world as was the case, for example, with the Waldenses' and Albigenses' churches. Now, this 1,260-year span began with Constantine and it came to an end, according to Cotton, with the establishment of Congregationalism in New England. The uniqueness of Puritan New England, therefore, lay precisely in the fact that there, for the first time since the Beast's rise, Puritans had succeeded, in the long historical apocalyptic struggle with Rome, to erect Congregationalism on the face of the earth. In this context, evidently, Puritan New England, according to Cotton, signified the climax of sacred, ecclesiastical history for

[51] *Ibid.*, p. 241.

the establishment of Congregationalism there symbolized the ultimate realization of the prophetic, redemptive Errand of the Church of the Wilderness. Accordingly, Cotton declared that the Puritans in America should be most exalted and glorified:

The Lord hath given us to enjoy Churches, and Congregational Assemblies by his Covenant, to whorship him in all his holy Ordinances; that he hath given us to look for no Laws but his Word, no ruler nor forms of worship, but such as he hath set downe in his word; no platforms of Doctrine, but such as are held forth in the word of the Prophets and Apostles: It is such a priviledge, that for 1260. years, the Christian world knew not the meaning of it.[52]

Puritan New England signified, therefore, the utmost embodiment of the Errand of the Church of the Wilderness, which according to Cotton was essentially characterized by the Congregationalist system of church-government. Indeed, continued Cotton, "there is a great deale of these things in sundry other Churches" in Protestant Europe, "but yet there is a tang of the image of the Beast" in all of them, being national, provincial, or diocesan by their very nature as was, for example the Church of England. It was left, therefore to Puritan New England to bring about the fullest realization of the Errand of the Church of the Wilderness by establishing Congregationalism in its purest form according to God's word and his ordinances. Consequently, proclaimed Cotton, the Lord had singled out New England by giving it "such liberty" to erect an ecclesiastical polity totally free from any image of the Beast:

all our Churches are not subordinate one to another, and none arrogate or plead Supremacy, but are preserved and kept from all contagion of the first and second beast [the Church of Rome, on the one hand, and the Pope, on the other], this calls us to abundant thankfulnesse, and we are to desire that the Lord would keep us at such a distance, that we may never return to the image of either of the beasts.[53]

Such a radical apocalyptic interpretation of the Woman's flight into the wilderness, however, had decisive social and political implications for the Puritans in America and Cotton did not hesitate to reveal them fully for his fellow brethren in New England. Preaching at the time of growing prospects for the reformation in England with the convening of the Long Parliament in 1640, Cotton was fully aware that some Puritans in New England had begun to contemplate a return to England in order to assist the Puritans there in the wars of the Lord. It was against these people that Cotton directed his great ire in his lectures upon the Apocalypse. "You shall have many poore creatures that came hither to this Country, and will be ready to go back again" to England, he told his congregation. But he admonished them in unmistakable words that those who were thinking of going back to

---

[52] *Ibid.*, pp. 241–2.   [53] *Ibid.*, p. 242.

England would have "much adoe to escape the paw of the Bear." More specifically, Cotton warned in stern words, that going back to England meant a return to worshipping the Beast in their native land. For according to Cotton's apocalyptic interpretation of the Puritan Errand, a return to England meant *ipso facto* joining forces with the Beast "from which the Lord by his stretched arme hath delivered you." Puritan emigration back to England, in other words, would totally undermine all the foundations upon which the whole Errand of Puritan New England was based. For, according to Cotton,

If you be once incorporated into any of their Parishes, you will finde such beastly work in Church Government . . . you must worship the beast or the Image of the beast; A Diocesan, or Nationall Church, is but an Image of the great beast.[54]

Cotton's severe denunciation of Puritan migration back to England was founded, evidently, upon his apocalyptic, historical interpretation of the struggle between the Beast, or the Church of Rome, and the true church, or Congregationalism. The "kinde of Church the Lord instituted" during the times of golden, primitive Christianity, argued Cotton, was "the Church of a particular Congregation." Hence, Cotton proclaimed boldly, "Leave every church Independent," because the Lord in his divine providence did not intend that "one Church shall have power over the rest." Here lay the ultimate difference between the Protestant movement in Europe and the Puritan migration to New England. "Christian Protestant Churches wrong themselves that leave any footsteps of this [beastly] government in their Churches." These Protestant churches continued to carry the mark of the Beast because they erroneously thought that "they must have Provinciall and Diocesan Churches, and National Churches," and thus wrongfully incorporated "many hundred congregations into one Nationall Church," which is indeed the "image of this beast" of Rome. So, in clear contrast to all Protestant churches in Europe, Puritan New England Congregationalist churches were the only ones to have rid themselves totally and absolutely from the images and the marks of the Beast. Cotton, therefore, earnestly pleaded to his Puritan brethren in America

to raise up our hearts in holy thanksfulnesse to God, that hath delivered us from this Monster, both our Fathers from this great beast, and our selves from the remnants of the Image of this beast, from all Diocesan and National Churches, and from Metropollitan & Catholick visible Churches that are Images of this great beast.[55]

Among New England Puritans, Cotton's apocalyptic interpretation

---

[54] *Ibid.*, p. 20.
[55] *Ibid.*, pp. 14, 30–1, 16–18. On Congregationalism in Puritan New England, see my essay, "The Ministers' View of Church and State in Early Massachusetts," *Scripta Hierosolymitana* 32; *Studies in American Civilization*, E. Miller Budick, Arthur A. Goren and Shlomo Slonim (eds.) (Jerusalem, 1987), pp. 1–25.

enjoyed a great reputation, and was considered one of the most cherished philosophies of history which lay out the uniqueness of the Puritan Errand into the Wilderness in America. Thus, along with other "reverend Ministers of Christ" in New England, who "for many yeers have studied and laboured for the finding" of "the time of the fall of Antichrist," wrote Edward Johnson, "that holy man of God Mr. John Cotton, among many other, hath diligently searched for the Lords mind herein, and hath declared some sudden blow to be given to this blood-thirsty monster."[56] Another contemporary of Cotton, Captain Roger Clap, heard "Mr. Cotton preach out of the Revelation, that Christ's Church did come out of great Tribulation." This apocalyptic interpretation, most probably Cotton's *An Exposition upon the Thirteenth Chapter of the Revelation*, continued Clap, "was no little Support unto me," both in terms of personal conversion and in terms of the general significance of the Puritan existence in America.[57] And according to John Fiske, a pastor to the tiny church in Wenham, who wrote an anagram upon the death of Cotton, it was Cotton

> Hee who the knotts of Truth, of Mysteries
> Sacred, most cleerly did ope 'fore our eyes.[58]

Indeed, during the years of the Puritan Revolution in England, and with the growing debates among Puritans on both sides of the ocean "about the Kingdom and Government of Christ in his Churches; which is the great work of this age, and of this nick of time,"[59] Cotton wrote extensively on the issue of Congregationalism, especially, in *The Keys of the Kingdom of Heaven* (1644), and in *The Way of Congregational Churches Cleared* (1648). Both works, however, were more theoretical in their character than historically apocalyptic.[60] Cotton's earlier work upon Revelation, therefore, provided the most explicit apocalyptic and historical exposition of the Puritan Errand into the Wilderness. His identification of the historical course of Congregationalism with the sacred, apocalyptic vision of the Woman's flight into the wilderness was, then, the most radical interpretation of the Errand of the Church of the Wilderness. It is in this sense that Cotton's revolutionary exposition of the Errand of the Church of the Wilderness, as based upon the course and progress of Congregationalism in

---

[56] Johnson, *Wonder-Working Providence*, p. 228.
[57] Roger Clap, *Memoirs of Captain Roger Clap* (Boston, 1731), p. 11.
[58] John Fiske, "Upon the Much-to-Be Lamented Decease of the Reverend Mr. John Cotton," in *Seventeenth-Century American Poetry*, ed. Meserole, p. 188.
[59] Thomas Shepard and John Allin, *A Defense of the Answer made unto the Nine Questions* (1648), "The Preface," in *Library of American Puritan Writings: The Seventeenth Century*, ed. Sacvan Bercovitch, vol. IX; *Histories and Narratives*, p. 29. Shepard and Allin's "Preface" was written in 1645.
[60] Larzer Ziff (ed.), *John Cotton on the Churches of New England* (Cambridge, Mass., 1968), "Introduction," p. 1.

sacred history, may be regarded as one of the earliest expressions of the Puritan philosophy and ideology of history molded on the Puritan experience in America.

Further analysis of Cotton's radical apocalyptic and historical interpretation of the Errand of the Church of the Wilderness may enable us to illuminate the significance of two of the most dominant themes in Puritan thought, Exile and Kingdom, and to clarify why Puritans in America considered their Exile in the Wilderness a necessary condition for their pursuit of the Kingdom of God. In his revolutionary exposition, Cotton identified the Woman's Errand into the Wilderness with Congregationalism as the true system of church-government prescribed by Christ. Moreover, he claimed that since the reign of Constantine the Great, Congregationalism had to fly into Exile in the Wilderness. Now, according to Cotton, the Congregationalist church was the Kingdom of Christ because it holds "the keys of the kingdom of heaven," or the keys of "the kingdom of grace." These keys were necessary means instituted by Christ in his Church in order to reach salvation and redemption. "The keys of the kingdom" of Heaven or Grace, continued Cotton, "are the ordinances which Christ hath instituted, to be administrated in his church." Hence, being God's true church, only Congregationalism possessed these keys to the Kingdom of Heaven. Consequently, the Puritans went into "voluntary exile" in America, according to Cotton, in order to reach "the kingdom of Christ in the government of each holy congregation of saints." Indeed, "making these [congregational] churches little sanctuary" of Christ explained why Puritans "have suffered this hazardous and voluntary banishment into this remote wilderness" of America.[61]

These important themes of Exile and Kingdom, which featured so prominently in the thought of John Cotton as well as in the New England mind in general, were derived from the existential condition of the Church of the Wilderness. Obviously, the fact that the New England Puritans tended to describe their existence in the wilderness of America in terms of Exile and Kingdom, shows unmistakably that they identified their migration to, and abode in, America with the prophetic, redemptive vision of the Church of the Wilderness. Having situated their migration within the apocalyptic and eschatological context of the Woman's flight into the wilderness, it is clear why New England Puritans interpreted the motives of Exile and Kingdom as inextricably tied to the existential state and condition of the Church in the Wilderness of America. Furthermore, it may explain as well why, for the New England Puritans, the state of Exile in the Wilderness of America had

[61] John Cotton, *The Keys of the Kingdom of Heaven* (1644), in *John Cotton on the Churches of New England*, ed. Ziff, pp. 87–8; John Cotton, *The Way of Congregational Churches Cleared* (1648), in *John Cotton on the Churches of New England*, ed. Ziff, pp. 201, 304–5.

been inseparable from the pursuit of the Kingdom of God. For being unable
to accomplish the true reformation in the Church of England according to
their premises, the Puritans, in order to justify their migration to America
within the context of providential history, envisioned it alongside the sacred
vision of the Woman's flight into the wilderness. And like the Woman in the
Apocalypse which symbolized the true church's flight into the wilderness
from the face of the Dragon's persecutions, Puritans had to fly into exile in
the wilderness in America in order to reach the Kingdom of Christ in the
framework of the Congregational Church. This was the most common
argument used by Puritans in order to justify their migration to New England within the confines of sacred, ecclesiastical history. And that is why, as
we will see in the next section, the themes of Exile and Kingdom were
associated in Puritan thought with the prophetic, redemptive Errand of the
Church of the Wilderness.

EXILE AND KINGDOM: THE EXISTENTIAL CONDITION OF THE CHURCH OF THE WILDERNESS

Evidently, the important themes of Exile and Wilderness appeared in
Puritan thought only after the actual settlement of New England took place.
Yet, these important motives, which permeated Puritan thought and
imagination so powerfully throughout the seventeenth century, were inextricably entangled with the sacred vision of the Church of the Wilderness.
Exile and Kingdom constituted the two ultimate dimensions of the existential state of the Church of the Wilderness; namely, the need to be in an Exile
condition away from corrupted human traditions, in order to execute the
true reformation, and hence, eventually reach the Kingdom of God. Here
lies the crucial importance of the themes of Exile and Kingdom for the
Errand in the Puritan migration to, and existence in, New England.

Earlier it was argued that the Puritan Errand was based upon the prophetic, redemptive vision of the Errand of the Church of the Wilderness as
described in the Apocalypse. And we have already seen how the Pilgrim
Fathers, the Puritans of the "General Observations," Thomas Hooker and
John Cotton, interpreted the significance and meaning of Puritan New
England in sacred, ecclesiastical history according to the eschatological and
apocalyptic vision of the Woman's flight into the wilderness. Now, the rise
of the themes of Exile and Kingdom in Puritan New England, which are
intrinsic to the sacred vision of the Church of the Wilderness, further enable
us to explore the presence of a founding Puritan Errand, based upon the
vision of the Woman's flight into the wilderness, in many other expressions
of first generation Puritans in America. Later we will see that this very sense
of the Puritan Errand reappeared in various expressions of second and third

generations of Puritans in New England. Consequently, the Puritan's continuous and persistent identification of their Errand with that of the Woman's flight into the wilderness clearly reveals that this sense of the Errand of the Church of the Wilderness had indeed incorporated the whole Puritan experience in the wilderness of America throughout the seventeenth century within a single, coherent, sacred, providential context.

The vision of the Puritan migration to, and existence in, New England as based upon the eschatological and apocalyptic Errand of the Church of the Wilderness is clearly seen, for example, in John Allin and Thomas Shepard's justification of the holy experiment in America. New England Puritans, they claimed, "were sent into this Wilderness" by God's providence in order "to bear witness to his Truth." Believing that "the great work of this age" is "about the Kingdom and Government of Christ in his Churches," or about the ultimate "necessity of Reformation of the Church," Puritans went to America in order to execute "a general and holy Reformation." For such a great enterprise, the Lord "inclines their hearts rather to fly" into the wilderness instead of staying in England where "Human Worship and Inventions were grown to such an intolerable height, that the Conscience of Gods Saints and Servants, inlightened in the truth, could no longer bear them." The ultimate goal of their migration to America was to see that "God will have his Church and the Kingdom of Christ" in the wilderness of America:

How many longings and pantings of heart have been in many after the Lord Jesus, to see his goings in his Sanctuary, as the one thing their Souls desired and requested of God, that they might dwell in his house for ever; the fruit of which prayers and desires this liberty of new England hath been taken to be, and thankfully received from God.

Consequently, Puritans went into exile "to a Wilderness, where we could forecast nothing but care and temptations; only in hopes of enjoying Christ in his Ordinances, in the fellowship of his people." And equating their migration to that of the Woman's flight in Revelation, Shepard and Allin declared that it was "the singular Providence of God" which brought "so many Shiploads of his people, through so many dangers, as upon Eagles wings" safely to America, and after their arrival continued to take care of his saints by "feeding and cloathing [them] in a Wilderness."[62]

In the thought of Roger Williams, the wilderness and the Church of the Wilderness occupied a prominent place. This "Prophet in the Wilderness," as Perry Miller rightly observed, with his highly radical mind closely followed Cotton's identification of Congregationalism with the Church of the Wilderness. Therefore he proclaimed that with the rise of Rome "there were

[62] John Allin and Thomas Shepard, *A Defence of the Answer*, "The Preface," pp. 28–32, 35, 37–8.

no churches since those founded by the apostles and evangelists" because, from the papacy's rise to power, the true Congregational Church "continued in the Wilderness."[63] In the same way, Henry Vane argued that the whole drama of salvation and redemption is fought "between the seed of the woman and the seed of the serpent." Therefore, he continued "those that are in this Kingdom" of Christ,

are fitted to fly with the Church of the Wilderness, and continue in such a solitary, dispersed, desolate condition till God call them out of it. They have wells and springs opened to them in the wilderness, whence they draw the waters of salvation, without being in bondage to the life of sense.[64]

The quest after Exile in the Wilderness as a precondition to the establishment of the Kingdom of Christ is further seen in the writings of John Eliot of Roxbury, the "apostle to the Indians" in New England. According to him, the ultimate goal of the Puritan "enterprise" was "to go into a wilderness where nothing appeareth but hard labour, wants, and wilderness-temptations," and this in order that the Puritan exiles could have "the enjoyment of Christ in his pure Ordinances."[65] Likewise, Captain Roger Clap emigrated to New England with his company of saints because "times were so bad in England, that they could not Worship God after the due Manner prescribed in his most holy Word, but they must be Imprisoned, Excommunicated, &c." And having settled safely in the wilderness of New England, he could not but with great admiration acknowledge:

what a wonderous Work of God was it, to stir up such *Worthys* to undertake such a difficult Work, as to remove themselves, and their Wives and Children, from their Native Country, and to leave their gallant Scituations there, to come into this Wilderness, to set up the pure Worship of God here![66]

The presence of a founding Puritan Errand based upon the sacred image of the Church of the Wilderness is evident in many other expressions of first-generation Puritans in New England. For John Norton, teacher of the church at Ipswich, history presents the gradual revelation and fulfillment of divine truths:

Even Fundamental Truths which have been the same in all generations, have been, and shall be transmitted more clear from age to age in the times of the Reformation until that which is perfect is come, and that which is imperfect is done away.

[63] Perry Miller, *Roger Williams: His Contribution to the American Tradition* (Indianapolis, 1953), p. 52; Roger Williams, *The Hireling Ministry* (1652), p. 2, cited by G. H. Williams, *Wilderness and Paradise*, p. 104.

[64] Henry Vane, *An Epistle to the Mystical Body of Christ on Earth: The Church Universal in Babylon* (1662), cited by G. H. Williams, *Wilderness and Paradise*, p. 105.

[65] John Eliot, "The Learned Conjectures Touching the Americans," 1650, cited by G. H. Williams, *Wilderness and Paradise*, p. 102.

[66] Roger Clap, *Memoirs of Captain Roger Clap*, p. 14.

Norton argued that one should view the discovery of America in this providential context of the spread of God's "Fundamental Truths" upon the
earth. For "Columbus did not make a New World, when he made a new
discovery of the old World." The same applied to the Puritan holy experiment in the wilderness of America. Rather, Puritan New England acquired
its singular and prominent place in sacred history because of its testimony
against human innovations in terms of religion. So, according to Norton,
with the migration,

God purposed to uperadd unto what had formerly been, a practical and more
notable Testimony against the intermixing of human inventions with Institutions
Divine.

Accordingly, in order to maintain "the Gospel Church-worship, and politie
in their purity," continued Norton, the Lord

in his All-wise providence transplants many of his Faithful servants into this vast
Wilderness, as a place in respect of it's remoteness so much the fitter for the fuller
inquiry after, and free exercise of all his holy ordinances, and together therewith for
the holding forth a pregnant demonstration of the consistency of Civil-Government
with a Congregational-way God giveth Moses the pattern of the Tabernacle in the
Wilderness.[67]

The church's flight into the wilderness in order to reconstitute the Kingdom of Christ within the framework of the Congregational Church recalls,
then, the existential issue of the Exile state and condition of the Church of
the Wilderness. Thus, as "Moses" received "the pattern of the Tabernacle in
the Wilderness," so, according to Norton, the history of the church proves
many times that Exile is a precondition for Kingdom:

Ezekiel seeth the formes of the House in exile. John received his revelation in
Patmos. Jotham upon mount Gerizim is bold to utter his Apologie: and David can
more safely expostulate with Saul, when he is gotten to the top of the Hill a far off, a
great space between them.

And now, with the Puritan migration, this prophetic, revelatory "Act" in
providential history is assigned to New England. Consequently, Puritans
fled "unto this vast Jeshimon," wrote Norton, in order "to set up the
worship of Christ in this desart" of America.[68]

Distinguishing, as he did, between "Acts and the Agents [in] the Mystery
of God, concerning all the transactions of his eternal purpose upon the
Theatre of this World, throughout the whole time of time," Norton
declared that the Puritans, being the Lord's "Agents" in the drama of
salvation and redemption, were forced to go to America when "Providence

---

[67] John Norton, *The Orthodox Evangelist* (1654), "The Epistle Dedicatory;" John Norton,
Abel Being Dead yet Speaketh, or The Life and Death of . . . Mr. John Cotton (1658), p. 19.
[68] Norton, *Abel Being Dead yet Speaketh*, pp. 19, 5, 19.

Divine" was "shutting up the door of service in England, and on the other hand opening it in New England." In this providential context, he argued, the Puritan "tempestive Flight" to New England was indeed "a kind of Confession" of their "faith; it being an open profession, that our faith is dearer to us than all that we flie from, for the defence therefore." Furthermore, by considering the Puritan migration to America in terms of the sacred vision of the Woman's flight into the wilderness, Norton could claim that the Puritan holy experiment in New England was inaugurating a new era in the drama of salvation:

How would it sweeten the bitter waters of this Wilderness to live and dye in the Mount, in the sight of this *Canaan* unto the comparative speediness of Christ coming at the Resurrection.

Yet, if the establishment of Congregationalism in New England signified the opening of a new era in providential history, then the bitter disputes among Puritans in England during the Puritan Revolution concerning the issue of church-government, argued Norton, keep away the fulfillment of the Kingdom of Christ in England. Therefore, he warned that

The discord of brothers about the polity of the Gospel holds Christ away from his dominion, [and] keeps the woman in the wilderness, and the [Anglican–Papal] harlot on the throne.[69]

Envisioning the gradual progress of fulfillment of God's "Fundamental Truths" within time and history, Norton claimed further that the Puritan Errand, being based upon the prophetic, redemptive Errand of the Church of the Wilderness, would eventually enable the Puritans in America to receive God's divine revelations in a clearer light. Therefore, he asked his congregation at Ipswich to consider their Exile in the Wilderness of America in the context of St. John's exile at Patmos where he received the Apocalypse. There were, he told his brethren, "comparisons" with St. John "in the tribulations of this *Patmos*" in America. And remember, he continued, that you are "exiles" in "this *Patmos*" of New England: "you know the hearts of strangers" because "ye are strangers" indeed in this earthly world, for you belong to another kingdom, the Kingdom of Christ whose attainment necessarily leads through an Exile in the Wilderness.[70] Thus, just as St. John was led into Exile at Patmos in order to receive the Apocalypse which revealed the realization of the whole mystery of time and history, so now Puritans were directed by God's divine providence into an Exile in the

---

[69] *Ibid.*, pp. 19–21, 39; Norton, *The Orthodox Evangelist*, p. 354; Norton, *Answer to the Whole Set of Question of the Celebrated Mr. William Apollonius* (1648), "A Letter from the Author," p. 7. Norton wrote this "Letter" in 1645.

[70] Norton, *The Orthodox Evangelist*, "The Epistle Dedicatory;" Norton, *Abel Being Dead yet Speaketh*, p. 39; *The Orthodox Evangelist*, "The Epistle Dedicatory."

Wilderness of America in order to discover and build the Kingdom of Christ upon the earth.

This magnificent vision of Puritan New England's singular role in sacred history was used as well by John Cotton. Rejoicing at the Wilderness-Exile state of the Church in New England, where Puritans could fashion their congregational way, Cotton was more than confident that here the way was open not only for the realization of the Kingdom of Christ but even for the imminent coming of the New Jerusalem as foretold in the Apocalypse:

Let no one despise this [Congregationalism] as the inelegant production of exiled and abandoned brethren, far removed by land and sea, voices crying in the wilderness, as long as it can be said of them, as Jehoshaphat once said of Elisha, who was living temporarily in the wilderness of Edom: The word of the Lord is with them. John, the beloved disciple of Christ, writes that he himself was carried away into the wilderness that he might see more clearly not only the judgment of the great whore but also the coming down from heaven of the chaste bride of Christ, the new Jerusalem (Revelation 17:1,3; 21:2).[71]

The Restoration of the House of Stuart in England in 1660 brought to an end nearly a century of fierce conflict over the soul of the English people. The failure of the Puritan Revolution put an end to Puritan visions of reforming the state and the Church of England. For Puritans in New England, the failure of the godly in England carried serious consequences for the holy experiment in the Wilderness of America. Hence, they were greatly dismayed with the events taking place in England during the Restoration. As was the case during the 1630s when Puritans fled to America, a Stuart monarch, who was hostile to the Puritans both in England and New England, sat at the citadel of power in England. Restoration policies contrasted sharply with those of Oliver Cromwell, a godly ruler, who looked upon the Puritan experiment in New England favorably. But now, with the accession of Charles II to the throne in England in 1660, the saints in the wilderness could expect nothing but growing hostility toward their religious utopia from English authorities. Furthermore, all over Europe in general, Protestantism seemed under siege. This desperate situation was the subject of John Davenport's sermon, *The Saint's Anchor-Hold*, of 1661, in which he portrayed for the Puritans in America the fateful "narrative of the Protestant churches in Europe." And he sadly concluded his remarks by saying "that the antichristian party had never so great advantage against the churches of Christ since the reformation began, as now." Therefore he admonished his Puritan brethren to cleave more faithfully to God "who will never leave nor forsake his people in their distress."[72]

[71] John Cotton, "The Foreword Written in New England" to John Norton's Book, *The Answer*, p. 14.
[72] John Davenport, *The Saint's Anchor-Hold*, 1661, in *The Puritans in America: A Narrative Anthology*, ed. Alan Heimert and Andrew Delbanco (Cambridge, 1985), pp. 220–1.

In face of such a desperate situation, it is no wonder that the Puritan apocalyptic and eschatological consciousness of Exile and Kingdom in the Wilderness of America reached its height after 1660. For now once again, as was the case with their flight to America during the 1620s and 1630s, Puritans vividly felt that they alone had been left to bear witness to God and His Word in their Exile and sanctuary in the wilderness of New England. The poor prospects for reformation in Europe, and especially the defeat of Puritanism in England, once again brought the Puritans in America up against the situation they faced prior to their migration to New England; namely, that in the face of God's imminent judgments coming upon the Old World, only in Exile in the Wilderness of America could the saints realize their pursuit of the Kingdom of God.

It will come as no surprise, then, that after 1660 and with the reemergence of apocalyptic and eschatological visions concerning the Old World, Puritans in New England continued more strongly than ever to identify their Errand with the prophetic, redemptive Errand of the Church of the Wilderness. Having been left in the Wilderness of America to execute alone the true reformation, New England Puritans steadfastly and consistently adhered to the sacred vision of the Church of the Wilderness in order to explain and interpret their singular role in providential history. And as we shall see now, this sacred vision which lay at the roots of the Puritan migration to New England, and constantly sustained the meaning and significance of the Puritan Exile in America, passed intact from the first to the second generation of Puritans in New England.

In 1661, a year after the Restoration in England, John Norton, who was nominated by John Cotton to be his successor at Boston, was called on to deliver the annual election sermon in Massachusetts. After almost two decades in which New England Puritans had found favor in England during the Puritan Revolution for their holy enterprise in America, now, with the accession of Charles II, Puritans vividly felt again the sense of being isolated from England as "outcasts" in the Wilderness of America. Hence, they had to assess their acts and deeds with care *vis-à-vis* the newly restored Stuart king. It was in this context that Norton exhorted his audience: "It is not a gospel spirit to be against kings; 'tis neither gospel nor English spirit for any of us to be against the government by King, Lords, and Commons" in England. Furthermore, Norton told his brethren in Massachusetts to be very careful not to present themselves as an enemy of the English crown: "God make us more wise and religious then so to carry it, that they should not sooner see a Congregational-man, than to have cause to say they see an enemy to the crown."[73] Now, with the Restoration in England taking place,

---

[73] Norton, *Sion the Outcast Healed of Her Wounds* (1661), pp. 226–7.

as Norton knew too well, the years in which Puritan New England enjoyed almost total independency were gone, and therefore he tried to convince the Puritans in America to comply with the new Stuart regime in England.

Yet, with all his spirit of compromise, Norton could not relinquish the Puritan Errand into the wilderness of America. "Let us show it," he declared, "that we mistook not ourselves, pretending to come into this wilderness to live under the gospel. We are outcasts indeed [from England] and reproached" there, he continued, "but let us be such outcasts as are caring for the truth" of God. Many indeed in England "represent[ed]" the Puritans in America "as disaffected to government, and as sectaries, and schismatics, and as fanatics," but Norton assured his audience that they, as "god's outcasts" in the Wilderness of America, "are not fanatics" but rather "orthodox" in their faith and religion. Nevertheless, Norton identified the fate of the Puritan "outcasts" in America with the sacred vision of the Church of the Wilderness in order to comfort his audience and refute the charges against them coming from England: "The woman in the wilderness may have the vomit of the dragon cast in her face," he argued, but as concerns God, he was more than confident that the Lord "will look after his outcasts, and care for us, being outcasts for the truth." And based upon this prophetic, redemptive vision of the Errand of the Church of the Wilderness, Norton claimed that the Puritan "outcast condition in this wilderness" of America is ultimately directed toward the establishment of the Kingdom of Christ. For "we came into" Exile in America, he continued,

not only with the spirit testifying, according to the scripture, against the inventions of men, but also that we do come up unto the institutions of Christ; that as we have departed from inventions humane, so we may not be found to be, or here continue, opposers against institutions divine; that we are not negligent of, but faithful to, that order of the gospel which we are outcast for.[74]

With the passing away of the founding fathers of Puritan New England, the sons did not abandon the legacy of their fathers concerning the Errand of the Church of the Wilderness. "This was and is our Cause," preached John Higginson in his election sermon, *The Cause of God and His People in New England* (1663),

that Christ alone might be acknowledged by us, as the only head, Lord, and Law-giver, in his Church, that his written word might be acknowledged as the onely Rule, that onely and all his Institutions might be observed and enjoyed by us, and that with puritie and libertie with peace and power.

Preaching three years after the Restoration in England, Higginson told the crowd who gathered to hear him that "the History of the Church in all ages hath informed us of this, that after a time of *peace*, comes a time of *trouble*,

---

[74] Norton, *Sion the Outcast Healed of Her Wounds*, pp. 227–8.

after a time of *liberty* . . . there comes a time of *restraint*." Yet, even in this
gloomy situation, Higginson preached boldly, "*to serve the time in matter
of Religion*," or to conform to the Church of England, "*we must not*," for
Puritan New England "*must obey God rather than men*." And thus, according to Higginson, the very founding Errand of the Puritan fathers was the
one and the same as that of the sons:

Our Fathers fled into this Wilderness from the face of *a Lording Episcopacie, and
humane injunctions in the Worship of God: now if any of us their children should
yeild unto, or be instrumentitall to set up in this Country, any of the wayes of mens
inventions, such as Prelacie, imposed Leiturgie, humane Ceremonies in the Worship
of God . . . this would be a backsliding indeed*: it would be a backsliding to the
things which we and our Fathers have departed from, and have openly testified
against, to be not of God.[75]

Second-generation Puritans did not abandon the sense of their fathers'
Errand into the Wilderness in terms of instituting Congregationalism as the
due system of church-government in order to realize the Kingdom of Christ
upon the earth. Nor did they relinquish the prophetic, redemptive vision of
the Errand of the Church of the Wilderness by which their fathers explained
the significance of Puritan New England in providential history. Consequently, Puritans of the second generation continued to invoke the sense of
Exile and Kingdom in the wilderness, the two essential dimensions of the
existential state of the Church in the Wilderness, in order to expound the
uniqueness of Puritan New England in sacred, ecclesiastical history.

So, for example, Increase Mather, one of the most prominent outspoken
of the second generation, accorded the saints in the wilderness a singular
role in the unfolding drama of salvation and redemption, which according
to him would reach its culmination in the second half of the seventeenth
century. In his work *The Mystery of Israel's Salvation* (1667), he claimed
that "the salvation of all Israel, it is now near to be revealed," and hence
that "the time of fulfilling prophecies is at hand." And believing his time to
be the time of the Seventh Angel in the Apocalypse, in which "the mystery of
God shall be finished," Mather was convinced that Puritan New England
was assigned by God to play a decisive role in the drama of salvation then
reaching its culmination. For being "in an exiled condition in this wilderness," he wrote, the saints in America "are under special advantage to
understand these mysterious truths of God" pertaining to the actual realization of His prophetic revelations which were then taking place within time
and history. For the Puritans went to the wilderness in order that "they
might bear witness not only against the name of the beast, and against his
character, but also against his number . . . [and] against all human inven-

[75] John Higginson, *The Cause of God and His People in New England* (Cambridge, Mass.,
1663), pp. 13, 10, 20–1, 14.

tions in the worship of God." Furthermore, the Puritan migration was initiated by God, according to Mather, in order that the Lord "will discover much of his counsel" to the saints in their Exile in the Wilderness concerning the final acts in sacred, ecclesiastical history exactly as God "hath declared" his prophetic revelations to "his servants the Prophets."

Where was John when he had the Revelation of Jesus Christ? He was . . . banished into the Isle of Patmos, Revelation 1:9. So Daniel and Ezekiel were exiles when they saw vision of God. And I have often thought upon that which is said, Revelation 17:3. Namely, that *John was led into the wilderness* to see the destruction of Rome.[76]

Thus, following the founding Puritan fathers, such as John Cotton and John Norton, Increase Mather identified the Puritan Errand with the prophetic, redemptive Errand of the Church of the Wilderness, claiming that the Puritan Exile in the Wilderness of America was a precondition for the establishment of the Kingdom of God upon earth. Therefore, he comforted his New England brethren concerning the significance of their Exile in America saying:

God hath led us into a wilderness, and surely it was not because the Lord hated us but because he loved us that he brought us hither into this Jeshimon. Who knoweth but that he may send down his spirit upon us here if we continue faithful before him.[77]

Exploring the expressions of both first and second Puritan generations in New England reveals indeed that, thanks to the prophetic, redemptive vision of the Errand of the Church of the Wilderness, Puritans never lost sight of the revelatory meaning of their Exile in the Wilderness of America within the framework of providential history. In this context, we may see as well how inseparable were the themes of Exile and Kingdom in Puritan thought from the sacred vision of the Errand into the Wilderness. Plainly, then the meaning of an Exile in the Wilderness should be seen in the context of the pursuit of the Kingdom of God. In this vein, for example, Jonathan Mitchell, one of the intellectual leaders of New England in the second generation and minister of the church at Cambridge and the tutor and mentor of Increase Mather, preached in his election sermon in 1667 that the Puritans "retired into these Ends of the Earth, for known ends of Religion and Reformation, to serve God in his *Temple* and *Ordinances* according to his appointment." The people of New England, he argued, are "a part of Gods *Israel*," and therefore he told the civil magistrates in Massachusetts:

The Lord Jesus Christ, having ask'd and obtained this piece of the *uttermost ends of*

---

[76] Increase Mather, *The Mystery of Israel's Salvation (1667), in Heimert and Delbanco, The Puritans in America*, pp. 242, 239, 245.
[77] *Ibid.*, pp. 245–6.

the Earth for his possession, doth commit it unto you, as Instruments under him, to keep and maintain his possession in it. The eyes of the whole *Christian world* are upon you; yea which is more, the eyes of *God* and of his holy *Angels* are upon you, to see and observe how you Manage and Discharge this Trust now at such a time.

Evidently, for Mitchell, as well as for Puritans in general, this sense of Exile and Kingdom in America had determined the content and the scope of the Puritan Errand into the Wilderness:

And it is our Errand into the Wilderness to study and practise true Scripture-*Reformation*, and it will be our Crown (in the sight of God and man) if we find it, and hold it without Adulterating *deviations*.[78]

Undoubtedly, second-generation Puritans in New England lived in a much different world compared to their fathers. Yet, what was so remarkable about them was that even in such different historical circumstances, the universe of their thought was so much like that of their fathers. This is nowhere clearer than in the persistent use that Puritan sons made of the founding Puritan Errand into the Wilderness inherited from their fathers. So, for example, according to William Stoughton of Dorchester, who preached the election sermon in Massachusetts in 1668 under the title *New Englands True Interest*,

The solemn work of this day is *Foundation-work*; not to lay a new Foundation, but to continue and strengthen, and beautifie, and build upon that which hath been laid.

This sense of continuity with their fathers' work is everywhere present in this wonderful sermon. From the very beginning of Puritan New England to this very moment, continued Stoughton, the Lord is "so wonderfully preserving of us, displaying his banner over us, holding underneath the Everlasting Arms, and making us to taste so much of his loving kindness and tender mercies every way." And this continuous divine blessing upon New England, according to Stoughton, is clear evidence that the Lord "have singled out New England . . . above any Nation or people in the world."[79]

This glorious vision of Puritan New England as God's elect and chosen people, which is so prominent in the expressions of second generation Puritans, cannot be understood without taking into consideration the Errand of the church into Exile in the Wilderness of America in order to pursue the Kingdom of Christ. For it was ultimately because of the establishment of the Kingdom of Christ in the wilderness that the Lord had singled out the Puritans in America to be his chosen people. Accordingly, Stoughton asked, "whom hath the Lord more signally exalted then his

---

[78] Jonathan Mitchell, *Nehemiah on the Wall in Troublesom Times* (Cambridge, Mass., 1671), pp. 18–19, 28.
[79] William Stoughton, *New Englands True Interest; Not to Lie* (1668), in Miller (ed.), *The Puritans*, vol. I, pp. 243–4.

people in this Wilderness?" Nobody else, of course. Hence, "the Name and Interest of God, and Covenant-relation to him, it hath been written upon us in Capital Letters from the beginning" of the Puritan settlement of New England. In the same vein, the Puritans were those whom the Lord took "to be a peculiar portion to himself" because "if any people in the world have been lifted up to the heaven as to Advantages and Priviledges, we are the people." This marvelous blessing which God's divine providence continued to bestow upon New England had its origins with the Puritan migration. From the founding "fathers" to Stoughton's time, American Puritans did "entertain the Gospel, and all the pure Institutions thereof, and those Liberties . . . in the Administration of the Kingdom of Christ." Conse-quently, it was in light of this Errand that "God sifted a whole Nation that he might send choice Grain over into this Wilderness."[80] Over and over again, the Puritans of the second generation expounded the meaning and significance of their Exile in America according to the prophetic, redemptive Errand of the Church of the Wilderness as it had been previously defined by the founding Puritan fathers.

The fashioning of New England's glorious vision in providential history, however, did not prevent second-generation Puritans from seeing that even in their "present wilderness state," as Thomas Shepard, Jr., acknowledged, there were frightening things in New England concerning "the loss of first love, first to Christ and so to the subjects and order of his kingdom." Furthermore, he said, this "radical disease [is] too tremendously growing upon so great a part of the body of professors in this land unto a Laodicean lukewarmness in the matters of God." Shepard, consequently, admonished his brethren that in face of such "declension," the Puritans should "review and consider in earnest their errand into this wilderness." Furthermore, he exhorted them not to be "strangers to the first intention of the people of God in their planting in this wilderness," and not to forget the Errand "of the poor woman" who fled "into this wilderness" of America."[81]

Thomas Shepard, Jr., wrote these words in his preface to Samuel Dan-forth's *A Brief Recognition of New Englands Errand into the Wilderness* (1670). In his preface, Shepard told his readers that Danforth's election sermon was a "testimony of his solicitude for the poor woman" in her flight "into this wilderness" of America, and that its message ought to be taken into serious "consideration of all such as are wise-hearted in Israel."[82] That

---

[80] *Ibid.*, pp. 245–6.
[81] Thomas Shepard, Jr., "The Preface" to Samuel Danforth's *A Brief Recognition of New Englands Errand into the Wilderness* (1670), in *The Wall and the Garden: Selected Mas-sachusetts Election Sermons, 1670–1775*, ed. W. Plumstead (Minneapolis, 1984), pp. 54–5, 57.
[82] *Ibid.*, p. 57.

was indeed the ultimate goal of Danforth's election sermon. For the whole thrust of his sermon lay in its urgent call to Puritan New England:

Attend we our errand upon which Christ sent us into the wilderness and he will provide bread for us. "Seek ye first the kingdom of God, and his righteousness; and all these things shall be added unto you" (Matt. 6:33).[83]

Danforth's sermon was in fact one of the most serious expositions of the prophetic, redemptive Errand of the Church of the Wilderness made by Puritans of the second generation. From the very beginning of his sermon to its end, Danforth attempted to elaborate the revelatory significance of the Church of the Wilderness in America. For this aim, he chose the text of Matthew 11:7–9: "What went ye out into the wilderness to see? . . . A prophet? Yea, I say unto you, and more than a prophet." These passages in Matthew are of the utmost importance as they concern the revelatory and prophetic service of John the Baptist in the Judean wilderness as the herald of Christ and the Kingdom of God. For these words in Matthew refer to Jesus' words to the crowd who went to see John in the wilderness: that John is not only a "prophet," but "more than a prophet." Now, it is within this revelatory and prophetic context of "seeing" and "hearing" John in the wilderness that Danforth set the direction and content of his sermon. He immediately drew an important distinction. The Lord, he claimed, "saith not 'Whom went ye out to hear,' but 'what went ye out to see?'" This important distinction between the "culture of seeing" and the "culture of hearing," Danforth told his audience, is crucial in terms of understanding the Lord's words.[84] For, according to him,

The phrase agrees to shows and stage plays, plainly arguing that many of those who seemed well affected to John and flock'd after him were theatrical hearers, spectators rather than auditors; they went not to "hear," but to "see"; they went to gaze upon a new and strange spectacle.[85]

This crucial distinction between the "culture of hearing" and the "culture of seeing," according to Danforth, lay behind the Lord's words in Matthew concerning John the Baptist. For "John preached in the wilderness which was no fit place" for theatrical plays and spectacle shows. On the contrary, argued Danforth, "John preached in the wilderness" in order to convince his audience and listeners about the coming of the Kingdom of God:

His work was to prepare a people for the Lord, by calling them off from worldly pomp vanities, unto repentance and mourning for sin.

---

[83] Danforth, *A Brief Recognition*, p. 77.

[84] *Ibid.*, p. 58. For a brilliant exposition of the differences between the "culture of hearing" and the "culture of seeing" in Renaissance England, see D. R. Woolf, "Speech, Text, and Time: The Sense of Hearing and the Sense of the Past in Renaissance England," *Albion* 18 (1986), 253–70.

[85] Danforth, *A Brief Recognition*, pp. 57–8.

Therefore for Danforth, as Christ's words in Matthew signified, John was "a prophet," or the "one who by the extraordinary inspiration of the Holy Ghost, made known the mystries of salvation (Luke 1:76,77)." Yet, as implied by Christ's words, John the Baptist was "more than a prophet." And the reason for this, preached Danforth, lay in the fact that

John was Christ's herald sent immediately before his face to proclaime his coming and kingdom and prepare the people for the reception of him by the baptism of repentance.

Indeed, Danforth continued, "all the prophets foretold Christ's coming, his suffering and glory," yet "the Baptist was his harbinger and forerunner that bare the sword before him, proclaimed his presence, and made room for him in the hearts of the people." Consequently, the ultimate significance of John's ministry in the wilderness should be seen "in respect of the degree of the revelation of Christ, which is far more clear and full in him than in the other prophets."[86]

Now, evidently, it was within the glorious prophetic and revelatory context of John the Baptist's Errand into the Wilderness, as the harbinger and forerunner of Christ, that Danforth sought to root the Errand of the Puritan migration to New England. As we saw earlier, this prophetic and revelatory vision of the Puritan Errand had already been formulated by Edward Johnson, when he boldly proclaimed:

I am now prest for the service of our Lord Christ, to re-build the most glorious Edifice of Mount Sion in a Wilderness, and as John Baptist, I must cry, Prepare yee the way of the lord, make his paths strait, for behold hee is comming again, hee is comming to destroy Antichrist, and give the whore double to drinke the very dregs of his wrath.[87]

So, like Johnson before him, Danforth identified the Puritan Errand with the "prophetical office and function" of John in providential history. Like John the Baptist, the Puritans were led into the wilderness in order "to proclaime" Christ's "coming and kingdom," and like the Baptist, their Errand in the Wilderness was "to prepare the people for the Lord, by calling them off from worldly pomp and vanities, unto repentance and mourning for sin."[88] In both cases, therefore, prophecy and revelation, Exile and Kingdom, constituted the essential dimensions of the Errand into the Wilderness.

It is obvious, therefore, that Danforth, like other spokesmen of the second generation in New England, did not intend, nor consciously sought, to construct an original Errand of his own. On the contrary, he directed all his zeal to arousing his generation to continue steadfastly the realization of the

[86] *Ibid.*, pp. 59–60.
[87] Johnson, *Wonder-Working Providence*, p. 52.
[88] Danforth, *A Brief Recognition*, p. 59.

prophetic and revelatory Puritan Errand of the Church of the Wilderness which he and the other sons in America inherited from their Puritan fathers. Hence, the lamentations about sickness and decay in religious life in New England made by second- and third-generation Puritans should not hinder us from seeing that they inherited a clear and coherent vision of a founding Puritan Errand in terms of the prophetic, redemptive, and revelatory Errand of the Church of the Wilderness in sacred, ecclesiastical history. Indeed, what makes the repeated use of the Errand of the Church of the Wilderness by second- and third-generation Puritans so interesting is that they were thereby able to explain their own special experience in New England by justifying it along lines akin to their fathers' Errand into the Wilderness. Seen in this context, his sermon was indeed, as Danforth declared, an "exhortation" aiming "to excite and stir us all to attend and prosecute our errand into the wilderness."[89]

But, as Danforth and his generation knew too well, there was a crucial difference between the founding fathers' zeal and enthusiasm toward the accomplishment of the Errand of the Church of the Wilderness and the "decays and languishing" in the sons' "affection to, and estimation of, that which we came into the wilderness to enjoy." Danforth, therefore, turned to the great exemplary model of John's Errand into the Wilderness in Judea in order to explain to his audience what the Lord expected of them. Accordingly, he claimed, "one of John's excellencies" which characterized his Errand in the Wilderness was "his eminent constancy in asserting the truth:"

The winds of various temptations both on the right hand and the left blew upon him, yet he wavered not in his testimony concerning Christ; "he confessed, and denied not; but confessed" the truth (John 1:20).[90]

This magnificent testimony of Christ and his truth signified what Danforth and other spokesmen of the second generation now demanded from New England. They knew of course the dangers and temptations awaiting God's people in the wilderness. So, according to Danforth,

Such as have sometime left their pleasant cities and habitations to enjoy the pure worship of God in a wilderness are apt in time to abate and cool in their affection thereunto.

New England itself now faced such risks of decline and decay in terms of religion. Danforth therefore told his audience that in face of the present declension in Puritan New England,

the Lord calls upon them seriously and thoroughly to examine themselves, what it was that drew them into the wilderness, and to consider that it was not the expec-

---

[89] *Ibid.*, p. 71.   [90] *Ibid.*, pp. 69, 59.

tation of ludicrous levity nor of courtly pomp and delicacy, but of the free and clear dispensation of the Gospel and kingdom of God.[91]

Moreover, Danforth called upon his brethren to reconsider, and in fact to restore, the founding Errand of the Church into the wilderness of America. For what purpose, he asked, had the Puritans fled to America, and "what expectation drew them into the wilderness?" And according to him, following the Lord's words regarding John the Baptist, "it was to see a great and excellent prophet and that had not they seen rare and admirable things in him they would never have gone out into the wilderness unto him." Or more precisely, the Puritans went into the wilderness in order to have "the free and clear dispensation of the Gospel and kingdom of God." Yet, in view of such a glorious Errand, Danforth sadly proclaimed,

Of solemn and serious enquiry to us all in this general assembly is whether we have not in a great measure forgotten our errand into the wilderness.

And he begged them as well to consider "whether our ancient and primitive affections to the Lord Jesus, his glorious Gospel, his pure and spiritual worship, and the order of his house, remain, abide, and continue firm, constant, entire, and inviolate."[92]

New England's religious decline was a sure sign of God's judgment. "In the whole Evangelical history," Danforth proclaimed, "I find not that ever the Lord Jesus did so sharply rebuke his disciples for anything as for that fit and pang of worldly care and solicitude about bread." Before closing his sermon, therefore, he demanded of New England "to give glory to God by believing his Word and we shall have real and experimental manifestations of his glory for our good and comfort." For only "in this way we have the promise of divine protection and preservation." Finally, Danforth concluded his wonderful sermon with the Lord's words in his epistle to his beloved Church of Philadelphia in the Apocalypse:

Because thou hast kept the word of my patience, I also will keep thee from the hour of temptation, which shall come upon the world, to try them that dwell upon the earth (Rev. 3:10).[93]

When taking into full consideration the Jeremiads' lamentations about the sickness and decay spreading through the religious life of the second and third generations of Puritans in America, it is of the utmost importance to remember that these utterances reflected as well the unbroken adherence to the redemptive and revelatory vision of the Errand of the Church into the Wilderness of America which the sons had inherited from their founding Puritan fathers. In this context, for example, Danforth's sermon is especially important. For like so many other examples during this time, Danforth's

[91] *Ibid.*, p. 61.   [92] *Ibid.*, pp. 64–5.   [93] *Ibid.*, pp. 76–7, 75, 77.

sermon reveals unmistakably how consistently Puritans of the second and third generations cleaved to the original, founding Puritan Errand laid down by their fathers when they fled to the wilderness in America. Earlier we saw that John Cotton and John Norton identified the Puritans' Errand with St. John's prophetic and revelatory Exile in the wilderness of Patmos. And now, as we have seen above, Danforth continued in the same vein by identifying the Puritan Errand with the redemptive role of John the Baptist in the wilderness of Judea. Though fathers and sons lived in different historical circumstances, the sacred vision of their Errand did not change. In both cases, the sacred image of the Errand of the Church into the Wilderness of America constituted indeed the ultimate vision by which they could, and did, interpret the meaning and significance of their Exile in the Wilderness of America within the confines of sacred, ecclesiastical history. For all of them, fathers and sons alike, the Puritan Errand signified Exile in the Wilderness of America where the pursuit of the Kingdom of God could be realized.

6

The creation of a sacred Christian society

The Gospel of reformation: the creation of holy Christian fellowships

The idea of society is a powerful image. It is potent in its own right to control or to stir men to action. This image has form; it has external boundaries, margins, internal structure. Its outlines contain power to reward conformity and repulse attack. There is energy in its margins and unstructured areas.

Mary Douglas, *Purity and Danger*, 1979

ENGLAND: "SPUED OUT OF CHRIST MOUTH"

At the turn of the sixteenth century it was all too evident for some Puritans that God had "A controversy with the inhabitants of this land," because of England's continuous failure to execute the true reformation.[1] William Perkins, one of the most influential Puritan theologians of his age and fellow of Christ's College, Cambridge, powerfully depicted the gloomy state of religion in England. Pointing to the period between Elizabeth's accession to the throne when Protestantism was established in England in 1558 and the middle of the 1590s, he declared

Religion hath been amongst us this thirty-five years, but the more it is published, the more it it is contemned and reproached of many, etc. Thus not profaneness nor wickedness but religion itself is a byword, a mockingstock, and a matter of reproach; so that in England at this day the man and woman that begins to profess religion and to serve God, must resolve with himself to sustain mocks and injuries even as though he lived amongst the enemies of Religion.[2]

Perkins' disappointment with the condition of religion in English society during the last decades of Queen Elizabeth's reign led him, exactly as was the case with Thomas Brightman, to elaborate a very desperate and gloomy vision concerning England's future role in sacred, providential history.

[1] John Downame, *Lectures upon the Four First Chapters of the Prophecy of Hosea* (1608), cited in Michael McGiffert, "God's Controversy with Jacobean England," *American Historical Review* 88 (1983), 1,151.
[2] William Perkins, *Exposition of Christ's Sermon Upon the Mount* (1618), p. 421.

Thus, in his *Lectures Upon the Three First Chapters of the Revelation* delivered at Cambridge in 1595, Perkins foresaw terrible consequences awaiting England "in this last age" of the world because of the "common neglect of the duties of religion." "We may flatter our selves," he told his audience, "and thinke all is well, as they did in *Noahs* time: but know it, we are in danger of most grievous judgement, namely, to be cut off from Christ, & to be made no people." Within the apocalyptic and eschatological context of sacred, ecclesiastical history, England was "in danger to be *Spued out of Christ mouth*," either "by taking the Gospell from us, or sending in our enemies among us."[3]

Viewed in terms of the Puritan sense of sacred time as described in the previous chapters, Perkins' words reflect the unmistakable process of the desacralization of England in sacred, providential history by which Puritans gradually denied God's divine grace to England. Because they found it increasingly difficult to maintain and realize religious reformation within English society, Puritans stripped England of its elective preeminence. They came to dismiss England's singular role in the history of salvation, or in sacred time, and hence its unique geographical place within the course of ecclesiastical history, as a sacred space. Thus, according to William Bradford, from the very beginning of the Reformation in England, "Satan hath raised maintained, and continued" to wage war "against the Saints." Rather than a nation of God's elect in providential history, England was a place in which godly people were both "scoffed and scorned by the profane multitude," and were forced to conform to "unlawful and antichristian" ecclesiastical practices by the "lordly and tyrannous power of the prelates." Therefore, being unable to accord England any role within sacred, providential history, except that of an obstacle, Bradford, along with the other Pilgrim Fathers, "shook off this yoke of antichristian bondage" in England by first fleeing to the continent and later to Plymouth, New England, in 1620.[4] Likewise, John Winthrop found it increasingly hard, if not impossible, to maintain the premises of reformation in the surrounding ungodly English society. As he wrote in 1616, to be a Puritan in this society meant to be "despised, pointed at, hated of the world, made a byword, reviled, slandered, made a gazing stock," and so forth.[5] He concluded, like Bradford, that England had no place for God's saints.

This process of the desacralization of England, by which Puritans gradu-

[3] William Perkins, *Lectures upon the Three First Chapters of the Revelation* (1604), pp. 308–10. See also, Perkins, *A Godly and Learned Exposition or Commentary upon the Three First Chapters of the Revelation* (1606), pp. 200–17.

[4] William Bradford, *Of Plymouth Plantation*, ed. S. E. Morison (New York, 1967), pp. 3, 8, 9.

[5] John Winthrop, "Religious Experiencia," *The Winthrop Papers*, ed. Allyn Forbes, 5 vols. (Boston, 1929–1947), vol. I, p. 196.

ally withdrew God's divine grace from England, reached its climax with the Puritan migration to New England and with their construal of America, and not England, as the Promised Land for God's people. "God is packing up his gospel," preached Thomas Hooker in England in 1631 before leaving the country, "because none will buy his wares" in England. Furthermore, declared Hooker,

God begin to ship away his Noahs, which prophesied and foretold that destruction was near; and God makes account that New England shall be a refuge for his Noahs and his Lots, a rock and a shelter for his righteous to run into.

And because God had removed his divine grace from old England, its destruction was imminent. "My brethren, cast your thought afar off, and see what is become of those famous Churches of Pergamum and Thyatira and the rest mentioned" in the Book of Revelation. "Glory is departed from England; for England hath seen her best days, and the reward of sin is coming in apace." The time had come, Hooker argued, for the sounding of the trumpets as foretold in the Apocalypse. Therefore, he warned his audience: "When thou shalt hear the trumpets sound, and thine ears tingle with the sound of war; then depart forever" from England.[6] Likewise, Francis Higginson, one of the earliest Puritan ministers in Massachusetts, depicted Puritan migration to America in eschatological terms when he admonished his congregation in his farewell sermon, "When you see Jerusalem compassed with armies, then flee to the mountains."[7]

Thus, because of its sin and corruption and its unwillingness and inability to reform religion and society, England no longer deserved its formerly singular role in sacred, providential history. Instead, according to the Puritans, an eschatological gulf separated it from the course of the history of salvation. Hence, they imparted new meaning and significance to sacred time and sacred space by incorporating America into the confines of ecclesiastical history and by ultimately making New England the very center of the history of salvation. By stripping England of its godly preeminence, then, America became the focus for their eschatological visions and millennial expectations.

It should be remembered, however, that the Puritan revolutionary transformation of English apocalyptic tradition, both in terms of sacred time and in terms of sacred place according to which New England and not old England became the central stage in the drama of salvation, was inextric-

[6] Thomas Hooker, "The Danger of Desertion" (April, 1631), in *Thomas Hooker, Writings in England and Holland, 1626–1633,* ed. George H. Williams, Norman Pettit, Winfried Herget, and Sargent Bush, Jr. (Cambridge, Mass., 1975), pp. 246, 230, 245, 242.

[7] Francis Higginson, "Farewell Sermon" (1629), cited in Cotton Mather, *Magnalia Christi Americana, or the Ecclesiastical History of New England, 1620–1698,* 2 vols. (Hartford, 1820), vol. I, p. 327.

ably connected with the Puritan aspiration to restore God's role and power within a theocratic universe. Only by keeping this quest for a theocratic universe ruled directly and immediately by God's divine providence in mind, is it possible to understand the Puritan attempt to reconstruct all dimensions of human life upon the sacred and to endow significance to human existence upon earth within the unfolding drama (or tragedy as Puritans sometimes preferred to call it) of sacred, providential history. The Puritan failure in Elizabethan and early Stuart England, then, must also be seen in the context of their quest for a theocratic universe in which every sphere of human life would be regulated by the sacred word of God. In that way, as seen previously, Puritans construed new sacred meaning and significance for two of the most important dimensions of human existence – time and space. Accordingly, and in a sharp contrast to the Protestant apocalyptic tradition in England, Puritans came to view New England as holding a unique place within the dimensions of sacred time and sacred space which characterized providential, ecclesiastical history.

In sum, the new meanings and significance which Puritans gave to sacred time and space were prerequisites for their immigration to America. Only by removing God's divine grace from England could New England occupy its singular role in providential history. Hence, the new renderings which they gave to time and space formed the ideological context, or the ideological origins, of their emigration to America. When dealing, however, with the causes and origins of the Puritan migration to New England, we need to look further into the actual world or the social context. In other words, along with the ideological origins of Puritan migration, in terms of the reconstruction of sacred time and space essentially and exclusively associated with the American wilderness, there was the concrete social context of English society which eventually drove thousands of Puritans to America where they could best serve God and live according to his sacred word. This social context can also best be defined by way of the Puritan quest after a theocratic universe, that is, by their endeavor to reconstitute all dimensions of human life upon the sacred. More specifically, the social origins of the Puritan migration to New England can be seen in their attempt, and eventually their failure to reform English society so that visible saints, or those whose lives exemplified their covenant relationship with God, could live and operate in accordance with God's word. In such a godly Christian society, religious values and belief would influence social actions and conduct.

The present chapter, then, examines the causes of the Puritan migration in the light of the Puritan attempt to create a sacred, Christian society. It explores some of the dimensions of the Puritan experience in England in the late sixteenth century and early seventeenth century by focusing on the world of conflict within local communities, parishes, churches, and towns.

Not enough attention has been paid to these conflicts and their relationship to Puritanism in England as a whole and the Puritan migration to America in particular. Hence, this chapter attempts to clarify long-term trends in English society from which Puritanism sprang and revealed itself as an ecclesiastical power and, more important, as a strong social and political force able to disturb and divide communities with its uncompromising plea for full social and religious reformation. The Puritan failure to achieve reformation by creating a godly, Christian society and the increasing strife between the "godly" and the "profane" at the local level caused, in large measure, thousands of English Puritans to emigrate to New England in order to realize in the American wilderness their vision of the holy Christian society.

PIETISTIC PURITANISM

Writing in his diary in 1587, Richard Rogers, a Puritan minister at Wethersfield, Essex, noted time and again his struggle to keep his covenant with God and lead a godly life in the world. Yet he was pleased that

god hath been very merciful to me again when I have been declineinge or growing weak or wearisome in well doeinge to offer me occasions many wayes of continuance by good company, as cul[verwel].

He and his friend, Ezekiel Culverwell, a famous Puritan divine and the author of a *Treatise of Faith*, 1623, consequently made a covenant among themselves to lead a godly life and to watch over each other in that endeavor:

Seinge the lord had graunted to us some sight of the coldness and halfe service of his which is in the world, and our selves also much caryed away with it, and thus we woulde renue our covenaunt more firmely with the lorde, then we had done, to come neerer to the practize of godliness . . . and to indeavour after a more continual watch from thing to thinge that as much as might be we might walk with the lord for the time of our abideinge here below. These and such lik we communed of togither . . . with great inflameing of our hartes farre about that which is common with us.

Later that year, other godly people joined the two covenanters, ministers and laymen alike, and so this godly group came to constitute a "covenant[ed] society" in Wethersfield. "Great hope we have by our private company among our neighbours to woorck as well more consc[ience] in their whole course as knowledge," Rogers wrote in his diary.[8] By mutual scrutiny and admonition, the members of this godly company sought to support each other in their commitment to God.

---

[8] "The Diary of Richard Rogers," in *Two Elizabethan Puritan Diaries*, ed. M. M. Knappen (Chicago, 1933), pp. 61, 63, 64.

Yet, Richard Rogers came to be prominent and famous among Puritans in the early seventeenth century not for his diary, but for his important book of 1603, *Seven Treatises*. By 1630 this book, which in over 600 pages prescribed daily routines of spiritual exercise for its Christian readers, had passed through eight editions. In *Seven Treatises*, Rogers stressed above all else the importance of godly company to a Christian life. He related much of his own hometown experience by way of illustration. There is, he wrote, "rule and dutie, directing us in companie," because men "who are ignorant and carelesse" should be "exhorted, stirred up, called upon and instructed," until they "might be edified and built up in our most holy faith." His aim was not to convert the sinners, but to edify the godly. "Scornefull, prophane and brutish persons" were not to be admitted into godly company. According to Rogers, godly company was but one company among many companies which men entered into in their life, and each of these companies should be made "sutable and correspondent to the other parts of Christian life."⁹ For Rogers, godly company was thus only an extension of other social activities undertaken by men in this world.

Although he made it clear that godly company was not necessarily associated with the making of covenants, Rogers, toward the end of his book, gave "an example of a couenant made by certain godly brethren" that, he hoped, would "help much to such as they are, to make better use of rules to direct them." Here he cited at length from the covenant that his godly company had made in his town in 1588 and pointed out the blessing it had brought. The covenant, he wrote,

did knit them in that love, the bond whereof could not be broken either on their part which now sleepe in the Lord, whiles they heere lived, nor in them which yet remaine, by any adversarie power unto this day.¹⁰

The contribution of Rogers' book was in its call for true "Christian fellowship" and corresponding condemnation of mere religion. In this effort, Rogers ventured forth on a path that Ernest Stoeffler has termed "Pietistic Puritanism": "indifference toward political issues and overriding concern for the religious welfare of individuals."¹¹ For Rogers, this path meant an increasing emphasis on the formation of godly companies "for our reprooving, exhorting, and comforting one another" and a concomitant de-emphasis on the Church of England as the focal religious institution in his

---

⁹ Richard Rogers, *Seven Treatises . . . Called the Practise of Christianitie* (2nd edn., London 1605), pp. 381–2, 385, 389. In the following discussion of "covenant" and its important role in the Puritan experience in the early seventeenth century, I owe much to Patrick Collinson's important article "Toward a Broader Understanding of the Early Dissenting Tradition," in *The Dissenting Tradition*, ed. C. Robert Cole and Michael E. Moody (Athens, 1975), pp. 3–38.

¹⁰ Rogers, *Seven Treatises*, pp. 389, 497–8.

¹¹ F. Ernest Stoeffler, *The Rise of Evangelical Pietism* (Leiden, 1965), p. 28.

life.[12] He inaugurated an important trend with this new emphasis. With many people, longstanding loyalties, both ecclesiastical and national, to the Church of England subsequently gave way to a new personal loyalty, religious and social in nature, to one's own covenanted society.

John Winthrop's "Religious Experiencia," a diary in which he recorded his religious experiences from his early youth until his emigration in 1630, is in many ways quite similar to Rogers' diary, especially in its revelation of a restless striving for the godly life. Although there is evidence that during the late 1620s Winthrop slowly embraced what James C. Spalding has called "the Deuteronomic" interpretation of history by which God acts in and rules through the events of ancient Israel's history, he was mainly guided during his early years by a pietistic yearning.[13] Like Rogers, Winthrop found it hard always to keep his covenant with God, and he vowed many times in his diary "to stand to the Covenant of my baptisme, renued so often since." But once "the Sabbaothe came," noted Winthrop in 1616,

I arose betymes, and read over the covenant of certain Christians sett down in Mr. Rogers booke, and therewith my hearte beganne to breake, and my worldly delights which had heald my heart in such slaverye before, beganne to be distastefull and of meane account with me, I concluded with prayer in teares; and so to my family exercise, and then to Churche, my heart beinge still somewhat humbled under Gods hand, yet could not gett at libertie from my vaine pleasures.

Winthrop's pietistic search, however, led him, as was the case with Rogers, to see the importance of godly company. In 1607, he wrote in his "Experiencia," "I with my companye," met with other godly people in a conference in which everyone promised "to be mindefull one of another in desiring God to grante the petitions that were made to him that day, etc." Again, as with Rogers' experience, mutual surveillance and edification became foundations of covenant society or company. Family exercise also served in the keeping of one's covenant with God.

I found at last that the conscionable and constant teachine of my familye was a speciall businesse, wherein I might please God, and greatly further their and mine own salvation . . . and I perceived that my exercise therein did stirre up in me many considerations and muche life of affection, which otherwise I should not so often meet with.[14]

---

[12] Rogers, *Seven Treatises*, p. 387.

[13] James C. Spalding, "Sermons Before Parliament (1640–1660) As a Public Puritan Diary," *Church History* 36 (1967), 26.

[14] John Winthrop, "Religious Experiencia," in *Winthrop Papers*, vol. I, pp. 194, 199, 169, 213. On the use of family exercise among Puritans during that period see: Christopher Hill, "The Spiritualization of the Household," *Society and Puritanism in Pre-Revolutionary England* (London, 1966), ch. 13. Among the many studies of the life of John Winthrop are Edmund S. Morgan, *The Puritan Dilemma* (Boston, 1958); R. C. Winthrop, *Life and Letters of John Winthrop* (Boston, 1869); and Richard S. Dunn, *Puritans and Yankees, the Winthrop Dynasty of New England 1630–1717* (Princeton, 1962).

William Haller wrote in his *The Rise of Puritanism* that the *Seven Treatises* by Richard Rogers "was the first important exposition of the code of behavior which expressed the English Calvinist, or, more broadly speaking, the Puritan, conception of the spiritual and moral life."[15] The book was widely read by Puritans in old and New England. Thomas Shepard, before he emigrated to the Bay Colony, wrote that "Mr. Rogers' *Seven Treatises* . . . did first work upon my heart."[16] But Rogers' book was more than a book for reading only, it was a guide to the godly life in this world through the instrument of the covenant. The Revd. John Wilson, for example, before he came to Boston in 1630, was influenced by

that famous book of Mr. Rogers, called *The Seven Treatises*; which when he had read, he [was] so affected . . . and pursuant unto the advice which he had from Dr. Ames, he associated himself with a pious company . . . who kept their meeting . . . for prayer, fasting, holy conference and the exercise of true devotion.[17]

Pietistic searching, then, led the way to social action, through which a godly company was formed with the intention of strengthening through mutual effort the resolve of individuals to keep their covenant with God. Understanding the importance of this process of social covenanting is crucial to comprehending the nature of the Puritan emigration. Already, by the early seventeenth century, some Puritans in England were sufficiently dissatisfied with the established church to withdraw into godly covenanted societies formed to aid them in their efforts to lead a godly life.

The covenant that John White drew up in Dorchester, England, in the early seventeenth century shows clearly how pietistic yearning could lead to social reformation. As minister in his town, White wrote the Ten Vows "for lifting up the weak hands and strengthening of the feeble knees" so as "to bind orselves by solemn Vow, and Covenant unto the Ld our God." The vows sought to encourage "true and pure Worship of God according to his owne ordinance, opposing orselves to all wayes of Innovaction or Corruption." They entreated Christians "to labour for a growth in knowledge and understanding by attending to reading, hearing and meditating Gods word," "to instruct O[u]r Children and families in the fear of the Ld," "to watch our owne Wayes dayly," "to submit to brotherly admonicion and to perform that Christian duty towards others," and so on. Here, as employed by White, the covenant formed the basis for a close-knit spiritual society in which religious reformation entailed social reformation as well. Certainly, there were different circumstances surrounding Rogers' covenant and

---

[15] William Haller, *The Rise of Puritanism* (Philadelphia, 1972), pp. 36–7.
[16] Thomas Shepard, "The Autobiography," in *God's Plot, The Paradox of Puritan Piety, being the Autobiography & Journal of Thomas Shepard*, ed. Michael McGiffert (Amherst, 1972), pp. 42–3.
[17] Mather, *Magnalia Christi Americana*, vol. I, pp. 276–7.

White's "Ten Vows," or covenant. The first bound together only a tiny minority of villagers in Wethersfield, while the Dorchester orders, designed for a town under Puritan discipline, were formed in order to embrace all but the ungodly. But, as Frances Rose-Troup shows, the importance of White's covenant in Dorchester was in the fact that it served "as a touchstone to exclude the ungodly from the Sacrament." And others followed White in this effort. In 1633 Hugh Peters, to whom White sent his Ten Vows, closely emulated White's articles in the covenant which he drew up for his own congregation in Rotterdam.[18]

More evidence exists to show that many Puritans who emigrated to Massachusetts Bay during the thirties engaged in forming godly covenanted societies in England prior to their departure. Francis Higginson, who came to Salem on behalf of the New England Company in 1629, lived previously in Leicester, a town divided into two parties. "On one side, a great multitude of Christians, then called *Puritans*," attended the worship of God not only within the framework of the Church of England but also in

their *assemblies* and more secretly in their *families*, but also they frequently had their *private meetings*, for *prayer* (sometimes with *fasting*) and repeating of *sermons*, and maintaining of profitable *conferences*, at all which Mr. Higginson himself was often present.

Against this godly party, "There was a *profane party*, filled with wolvish rage against the flock of the Lord Jesus."[19] Similarly, in John Cotton's Boston, in Lincolnshire,

there were some scores of pious people in the town, who more exactly formed themselves into an *evangelical Church-State* by entering into *covenant* with God, and with one another, *to follow after the Lord, in the purity of his worship*.[20]

The details of the theological developments of the covenant theory need not detain us here. In *The New England Mind: The Seventeenth Century*, Perry Miller has dealt at length with "the covenant theory" and its many varieties, including the covenant of grace, the federal theology, church covenants, and social covenants.[21] Apart from its theological implications, however, covenant theory had important social and political implications for Puritans and non-Puritans in Jacobean and Caroline England. It is evident, as we have seen with Rogers, Winthrop, Cotton, Wilson, and Higginson, that godly people in England during this period entered into

[18] John White, "The Ten Vows" in *John White*, by Frances Rose-Troup (New York, 1930), pp. 418–22, 222.
[19] Mather, *Magnalia Christi Americana*, vol. I, pp. 324, 238–39.
[20] Larzer Ziff, *The Career of John Cotton* (Princeton, 1962), pp. 43, 49.
[21] Perry Miller, *The New England Mind, the Seventeenth Century* (New York, 1939), Book IV, "Sociology," pp. 365–462, and "Appendix B, the Federal School of Theology," pp. 502–5.

covenants among themselves without necessarily forming connections to the established church. "These covenants," wrote Collinson, "were not church covenants but belonged to the Puritan experience of covenant grace, an area quite remote at this time from any overt ecclesiological reference."[22] They were, in this sense, social covenants and, as shown above, they arose partly from the difficulties experienced by individuals in keeping their private covenants with God. "God conveys his salvation by way of covenant," wrote Thomas Cobbet, as minister in Lynn, Massachusetts.

and he doth it to those onely that are in covenant . . . This covenant must every soule enter into, every particular soule must enter into a particular covenant with God; out of this way there is no life.[23]

Godly society, or covenanting company, as Rogers recommended, was a necessary device by which one could keep his covenant through actual involvement with other members of one's company.

Thus, covenants were an essential part of the Puritan experience in early seventeenth-century England and there is evidence that many Puritans, laymen and clergy alike, engaged in the establishment of godly societies in order to shape their lives according to God's word. But covenants were also an essential part of the Puritan migration to New England. The two most famous covenant expressions in relation to the migration are of course the Mayflower Compact and Winthrop's "A Model of Christian Charity." In relation to the first, as Bradford wrote, the pilgrims "solemnly and mutually, in the presence of God and one another, covenant and combine ourselves together into a Civil Body Politic, for our better ordering and preservation."[24] And Winthrop in his lay sermon made it clear towards what end the Puritan emigration was directed:

The end is to improve our lives to do more service to the Lord the comforte and the encrease of the body of christe whereof we are members that our selves and posterity may be the better preserved from the common corrupcions of this evill world to serve the Lord and worke out our Salvacion under the power and purity of his holy Ordinances.

And the means for that aim? "For the meanes whereby this must bee

[22] Collinson, "Toward A Broader Understanding of the Early Dissenting Tradition," p. 21.

[23] Thomas Cobbett, *A Just Vindication of the Covenant*, 1648, cited by Miller, *The New England Mind*, p. 378. For theological developments of the covenant theory, see: Klaus Baltzer, *The Covenant Formulary* (Philadelphia, 1971); Champlin Burrage, *The Church Covenant Idea* (Philadelphia, 1904); S. A. Burrell, "The Covenant Idea as Revolutionary Symbol: Scotland, 1596–1637," *Church History* 27 (1958), 339–50; Jens G. Moller, "The Beginnings of Puritan Covenant Theology," *The Journal of Ecclesiastical History* 14 (1963), 46–67; Everett H. Emerson, "Calvin and Covenant Theology," *Church History* 25 (1956), 234–55; and J. Wayne Baker, *Heinrich Bullinger and the Covenant* (Athens, 1980).

[24] "The Mayflower Compact," in *The Story of the Pilgrim Fathers, 1606–1623, As Told by Themselves, their Friends and their Enemies*, ed. Edward Arber (London, 1897), p. 409.

effected, they are 2fold, A conformity with the worke and end wee aime at."
Conformity and unity were, according to Winthrop, necessary conditions
for the success of the whole emigration, for

thus stand the cause betweene God and us, wee are entered into Covenant with him
for this work, we have taken out a Commission, the Lord hath given us leave to
drawe our owne Articles wee have professed to enterprise these Accion upon these
and these ends, wee have hereupon besought his favour and blessing.[25]

These covenants clearly were not church covenants. Likewise, as Lockridge has shown in *A New England Town*, before Dedham was a town and
before it had a church, its settlers drew up a covenant in 1636, in which it
was stated: "that we shall by all means labor to keep off from us all such as
are contrary minded, and receive only such unto us as may be probably of
one heart with us." Those who were within the company of covenanters had
to work "for the edification of each other in the knowledge and faith of the
Lord Jesus."[26] The earliest covenant in the Bay colony was, of course, that
of Salem in 1629. There, on July 20, according to the deacon of the Salem
church, Charles Gott, "a company of believers . . . joined together in
covenant, to walk together in all the way of God." One month later, with
the establishment of the church there, the members found it necessary to
renew their previous covenant.

We . . . members of the present Church of Christ in Salem, haveing found by sad
experience how dangerous it is to sitt loose to the Covenant we make with our God .
. . Doe therefore . . . renewe that Church covenant we find this Church bound unto . .
. That we covenant with the Lord and one with one another, and doe bynd our selves
in the presence of God, to walk together in all his waies, according as he pleased to
reveal him selfe unto us in his Blessed word of truth.

As a covenanted church, the members of the Salem church consequently
declared that "we willingly doe nothing to the offence of the Church." Yet,
all the other articles of the covenant are similar to the civil covenants cited
previously.[27]

The emigrants who came to Massachusetts Bay were therefore engaged
before and after their migration in an attempt to establish godly societies or
companies based on social covenants. This kind of Puritan activity was
necessarily related to and was indeed a precondition of the Puritan migration. For what these covenants reveal is a special engagement by Puritans to
reconcile here on earth the law of nature and the law of grace. If the law of
nature, or the moral law, was essential to man as a rational being, the law of

---

[25] John Winthrop, "A Model of Christian Charity," *Winthrop Papers*, vol. II, pp. 283–4.
[26] Kenneth A. Lockridge, *A New England Town, the First Hundred Years* (New York, 1970), p. 5.
[27] Richard D. Pierce (ed.), *The Records of the First Church in Salem Massachusetts, 1629–1736* (Salem, 1974), pp. 3–4; and Mather *Magnalia*, vol. I, p. 66.

grace could be realized only by faith and by divine grace. "There is like-wise," preached Winthrop aboard the *Arbella* in 1630, "a double Lawe by which wee are regulated in our conversacion one towardes another . . . the lawe of nature and the lawe of grace, or the morrall lawe and the lawe of the gospell." Thus, while the law of nature came to regulate civil society as such, the law of Gospel, or grace, came to regulate Christian society, a godly society in which one's covenant with God corresponded to the covenant of society at large with God. By maintaining the law of grace or the law of Gospel, which is the essence of the covenants described above, godly people fulfilled the conditions they took upon themselves in entering into covenant with God. At the same time, they could expect that God would fulfill the conditions he had taken upon himself concerning the covenant. "Now, if the Lord shall please to heare us . . . then hath hee ratified this Covenant and sealed our Commission [and] will expect a strickt performance of the Articles contained in it." And if the covenanters should succeed in their attempt, "the Lord will be our God and delight to dwell among us, as his owne people and will commaund blessing upon us in all our wayes."[28]

Above all else, Puritans of the covenant, in England and New England alike, sought to realize the law of grace in this world. In pursuit of this end, Puritans turned their backs, not only on the established church, but on society at large. Not surprisingly, then, it was on this point, the realization of the law of grace in one's life and society, that Puritans clashed with other groups in English society. In parish church, village, town, and city, Puritans faced non-Puritans in what amounted to a battle for social reformation. The question at issue was how man was to live in society. Conflict over this basic social question, and not simply theological disagreement, thus provided the broad social context within which the Puritan migration movement first took root. Ultimately, Puritans would turn to America to attempt what they could not accomplish in England – the shaping of a godly Christian com-monwealth on earth constructed according to God's word.

CONTRASTING COMMUNITIES

The history of early Massachusetts is to a great extent the history of attempts to fulfill the articles of the covenants, to realize on the North American continent the law of grace. Yet, we must ask ourselves, why was it necessary to cross the Atlantic to put into practice the law of grace? What hindered these Puritans from realizing their covenanted society in England? Or what obstructed their vision of a godly society and godly life? Our task here is to explore the broader social situation out of which the Puritan

---

[28] Winthrop, "A Model of Christian Charity," pp. 283, 294.

movement for emigration emerged and the real world from which the Puritan migration came. An examination of the laity's unique and decisive role in the Puritan movement, for example, is important within this context because it clarifies more fully the origins and the causes of the migration.[29]

Apart from studies of Puritan divines, recent studies of English Puritanism have increasingly stressed the decisive role of the laity in the Puritan movement. These studies have thus shifted our attention from ministers' theological writings to the social and political foundations for this movement. In her investigation of English villagers in the sixteenth and seventeenth centuries, Margaret Spufford gives a vivid picture of Puritanism as a popular movement in the diocese of Ely. At one point she quotes from an account of a Jesuit priest who had witnessed Puritan gatherings while a prisoner in Wisbech Castle in the late 1580s and 1590s:

From the very beginning a great number of Puritans gathered here. Some came from the outlying parts of the town, some from the villages round about, eager and vast crowds of them, flocking to perform their practices – sermons, communions and fasts . . . Each of them had his own Bible, and sedulously turned the pages and looked up the texts cited by the preachers, discussing the passages among themselves to see whether they had quoted them to the point, and accurately, and in harmony with their tenets. Also they would start arguing among themselves about the meaning of passages from the Scriptures – men, women, boys, girls, rustics, labourers and idiots . . . over a thousand of them sometimes assembled, their horses and pack animals burdened with a multitude of Bibles.

"There is then, proof, for the first time" in the late sixteenth century, notes Spufford, "that large numbers of the laity in the diocese . . . had been influenced by Puritan teachings, and were actively involved in doctrinal disputes." According to her, the picture of the Puritans described by the Jesuit priest "shows better than any other source the way the common people had been affected by the reformation and the growth of literacy."[30]

Many other studies of Puritanism in England confirm the importance of the laity in the Puritan movement. A. Tindal Hart has pointed out that in many cases, "the laity were much more protestant than their clergy, had little sympathy with the Laudian ideals, and greatly dreaded a re-introduction of popery."[31] In areas in which Puritanism was predominant, as R. C. Richardson shows, laymen "were sometimes even more insistent opponents of the sign of the cross than their ministers."[32] All this points to the fact that popular Puritanism was by no means guided and led by the

---

[29] On the issue of the laity and the church, see two excellent studies by Claire Cross: *Church and People, 1450–1660, The Triumph of the Laity in the English Church* (Wiltshire, 1976), and *Royal Supremacy in the Elizabethan Church* (London, 1969).

[30] Margaret Spufford, *Contrasting Communities, English Villagers in the Sixteenth and Seventeenth Centuries* (Cambridge, 1974), pp. 262–3.

[31] A. Tindal Hart, *The Country Clergy* (London, 1958), p. 27.

[32] R. C. Richardson, *Puritanism in North-West England* (Manchester, 1972), p. 27.

clergy; the voice of the congregation or the laity was important, if not always decisive. Patrick Collinson describes the relationship between the clergy and laity thus:

the popular Protestant element in the Elizabethan society was not subordinate to the preachers, but possessed a mind and will of its own to which the conduct of the Puritan minister, including his own nonconformity, was partly a response.[33]

With regard to the Puritan migration to Massachusetts Bay, the role of the laity can hardly be exaggerated. One need only look at the Adventurers' list of both the New England Company and Massachusetts Bay Company, in which ministers made up only a tiny minority, to see how the laity initiated this migration. More important, the company invariably initiated the movement to send ministers to the colony. "It was fully resolved, by God's assistance," wrote Matthew Cradock, governor of the New England Company and later first governor of the Bay Company, to John Endecott at Salem in February 1628/9, "to send over two ministers." In another letter, dated the following April, Cradock assured Endecott:

We have been careful to make plentiful provision of godly ministers . . . And because their doctrine will hardly be esteemed whose persons are not reverenced, we desire that both by your own example and by commanding all others to do the like, our ministers may receive due honor.[34]

The essential and decisive role of the laity in the Puritan migration can be illustrated through a few examples. When Thomas Hooker departed for Holland in 1631, "Mr. Hooker's company," wrote Winthrop in his *Journal* in 1632, came to the Bay colony.[35] The godly people, the laity, did not follow their minister to Holland but journeyed to Massachusetts and waited for him there. Many parishioners of St. Stephen's in London decided to emigrate to New England with Winthrop's fleet, so that their former vicar, John Davenport, found himself preaching "before pews vacated by the great exodus to Massachusetts Bay."[36] Even before their ministers were ready to emigrate, many laymen had chosen migration.

Captain Roger Clap supplies us with firsthand evidence as to the way godly people had been engaged in preparation for emigration. Upon leaving his parent's house, Clap writes, he went "to live with a worthy Gentlemen, Mr. William Southcot," who lived near the city of Exon (Exeter) in Devonshire. This gentleman "was careful to keep a Godly Family." Proceeding on

---

[33] Patrick Collinson, "The Godly: Aspects of Popular Protestantism in Elizabethan England," cited by Richardson, *Puritanism in North-West England*, p. 74.

[34] Alexander Young (ed.), *Chronicles of the First Planters of the Colony of Massachusetts Bay, from 1623 to 1636* (Boston, 1846), pp. 234, 142, 144.

[35] John Winthrop, *The History of New England from 1630 to 1649*, ed. James Savage, 2 vols. (Boston, 1853), vol. I, p. 74.

[36] Isabel M. Calder, *The New Haven Colony* (New Haven, 1934), p. 16.

in his search for good "preachers of the Word of God," Clap then traveled to Exeter to Puritan gatherings where he met the Puritan minister John Warham. "I did desire to live near him: so I remove[d] . . . into the city." In Exeter, Clap lived with "one Mr. Mossiour, as Famous a Family for Religion as I ever knew." In his house a "conference" of godly people met each week. Clap does not tell us if this godly company was based on a covenant. But he does indicate that he himself "covenanted" with Mr. Mossiour. Later, now in the late 1620s, Clap describes how he came to emigrate to the Bay colony.

I never so much as heard of New England, until I heard of many godly Persons that were going there, and that Mr. Warham was to go also . . . These godly People resolved to live together; and therefore as they had made choice of these two Revd. Servants of God, Mr. John Warham and Mr. John Maverick to be their Ministers, so they kept a solemn Day of Fasting in the New Hospital in Plymouth in England, spending it in Preaching and Praying.[37]

What motivated these "godly people" to emigrate? Surprisingly, no clear answer to this question exists. Historians have dealt almost exclusively with the emigration of clergymen and not with that of the laity. Even in the case of John Winthrop, whose life has been the subject of many books, we still do not know exactly his motivation for emigrating, because (surprisingly again) historians in many cases have tended to overlook his "Religious Experiencia." Yet, if the argument about the decisive role of the laity in the development of Puritanism in England is correct, it seems that this is the place to look for explanations for the migration.

From its beginnings, the Puritan movement in England did not operate in a vacuum. Theological developments accompanied developments in social action and behavior among Puritans; for this reason, Puritanism often drew the critical attention of many sections of English society. Religious reformation, as contemporaries well knew, carried social implications. Illustrating this point are the many satires penned against Puritans in the late sixteenth and early seventeenth centuries. Many in England used this genre to express their dislike of the Puritan concept and practice of the godly life. In 1609, one W.M. satirized the social outcome of the Puritan's ideas:

> My calling is divine
> And I from God am Sent
> I will not chop-church be,
> Nor pay my patron rent.

Satires against the Puritans' way of life were widespread, for to many their religious and social manners and their devotion and pious behaviour

---

[37] Roger Clap, *Memoirs of Roger Clap* (Boston, 1844), pp. 18, 39.

caused irritation and outrage. In Thyne's *Emblemes and Epigrams* (1600) the author wrote of the Puritans that

> They sett upp churches twenties for their one,
> for everie private house spirituallie
> must be their church, for other will they none.

And the Puritans' militancy, along with their pretence to exclusive possession of the requisite knowledge of the true mode of salvation, brought in 1614 one "R.C." in the *Time Whistle* who wrote:

> There is a sort of purest seeming men,
> That aide this monster in her wrongfull cause,
> Those the world nameth – Puritanes I mean –
> Sent to supplant me from the very jawes
> Of hell, I think; by whose apparent shew
> Of sanctity doe greatest evils grow.

Most common were satires against Puritan insistence on the holiness of the Sabbath. Those who preferred recreation and sport often charged the Puritans with hypocrisy: "Upon the Sabbath, they'l no Phisicke take, / Lest it should worke, and so the Sabbath break." Or, in relation to Sunday, "Suppose his Cat on Sunday killed a Rat, / She on Monday must be Hanged for that."[38] Although the term "Puritan" had not been sharply defined in the early seventeenth century, the satires demonstrate that, among contemporaries, Puritanism had come to represent certain manners and modes of behavior.

This contention, was perhaps best understood by Richard Hooker, one of the most eloquent apologists of the Church of England and a staunch defender of the Elizabethan Settlement of 1559. Writing in his most celebrated book, *Of the Laws of Ecclesiastical Polity* (1593), Hooker had no illusions concerning the grave threat that the Puritan movement posed in regard to the social and ecclesiastical life in England during his time. Inspired by the Holy Ghost "to be the author of their persuasion," he wrote, Puritans proceeded to claim "that the same Spirit leading men into his opinion doth thereby seal them to be God's children." Consequently, this contention

hath bred high terms of separation between such and the rest of the world; whereby the one sort are named The Brethren, The Godly, and so forth; the other, worldings, time-servers, pleasers of men not of God, with such like.[39]

---

[38] William Holden, *Anti-Puritan Satire 1572–1642* (New Haven, 1954), pp. 77, 80, 57, 83.
[39] Richard Hooker, *Of the Laws of Ecclesiastical Polity* (1593), ed. Christopher Morris, 2 vols. (London, 1958–60), vol. I, pp. 102–3.

For Hooker, the essential enmity which Puritans drew between themselves and the "profane" posed a grave threat to the well-being of the Church of England in particular and to English society in general. Before him stood the development of the Protestant Reformation on the continent in which many radical and zealous religious groups, with their uncompromising plea to reconstitute all dimensions of human life upon the sacred, greatly disturbed the church and social order by making the struggle between the godly and the profane the central theme of their zeal for religious reformation. It was only appropriate, then, that Hooker warned Puritans in England where their ways might lead by posing the example of the radical religious sects in the continent, who

drew in a sea of matter, by applying all things unto their own company, which are any where spoken concerning divine favours and benefits bestowed upon the old commonwealth of Israel: concluding that as Israel was delivered out of Egypt, so were they spiritually out of Egypt of this world's servile thraldom unto sin and superstition; as Israel was to root out the idolatrous nations, and to plant instead of them a people which feared God; so the same Lord's good will and pleasure was now, that these new Israelites should under the conduct of other Joshuas, Samsons, and Gideons, perform a work no less miraculous in casting out violently the wicked from the earth, and establishing the kingdom of Christ with perfect liberty.[40]

Hooker drew attention to the similarities between the Puritan activities in England and those of the radical sects in Protestant Europe because he was deeply convinced that

when the minds of men are once erroneously persuaded that it is the will of God to have those things done which they fancy, their opinions are as thorns in their sides, never suffering them to take rest till they have brought their speculations into practice.[41]

Ultimately, Hooker's strong opposition of the Puritans was based upon his total rejection of the Puritan quest for a theocratic universe, as exemplified in the Puritan claim that "Scripture ought to be the only rule of all our actions."[42] Thus, he denounced the Puritans who held to the literal following of the Scriptures, or their attempt to reconstitute all dimensions of human life upon the sacred word of God, and instead elaborated a whole theory of law, based on the fundamental of natural law, which governs the whole universe, and to which both ecclesiastical and civil polity are subservient.

The satires of, and attacks upon, Puritans and their ways of life and belief reflected therefore the fears and anxieties they created in English society. Winthrop described this world in his "Religious Experiencia" in 1616, writing from the point of view of being Puritan and addressing God,

---

[40] *Ibid.*, vol. I, p. 139.   [41] *Ibid.*, vol. I, p. 139.   [42] *Ibid.*, vol. I, p. 122.

Thou tellest me that in this way there is least companie, and that those which doe walke openly in this way shalbe despised, pointed at, hated of the world, made a byword, reviled, slandered, rebuked, make a gazing stocke, called puritans, nice fooles, hipocrites, hair brained fellows, rashes, indiscreet, vain glorious, and all that is naught is; all this is nothinge to that which many of thine exellent servants have been tried with, neither shall they lessen the glorie thou hast prepared for them.[43]

Richard Baxter gives a similarly vivid picture as to the making of a Puritan in his youth. He reports that in and near the village where he grew up in the 1620s many ministers lived

scandalous lives and that only three or four constant competent preachers lived near us, and those (though conformable all save one) were the common marks of the people's obloquy and reproach and any that had but gone to hear them, when he had no preaching at home, was made the derision of the vulgar rabble under the odious name of a Puritan.

On Sundays "the reader read the Common Prayer briefly, and the rest of the day . . . was spent in dancing under a maypole and great tree . . . where all the town met together." With all this activity, Baxter continued,

we could not read the Scripture in our family without the great disturbance of the tabor and pipe and noise in the street. Many times my mind was inclined to be among them, and sometimes I broke loose from conscience and joined with them; and the more I did the more I was inclined to do it. But when I heard them call my father Puritan it did much to cure me and alienate me from them; for I considered my father's exercise of reading Scripture was better than theirs . . . and I considered what it was for that he and others were thus derided.[44]

The picture presented by Winthrop and Baxter shows how the Puritan's way of life stood in contrast to that of other people and the extent to which their neighbors detested the Puritan way. This world of contrasting communities is the world of the great migration.

COVENANT AND HOLY CHRISTIAN FELLOWSHIP

By entering into covenants to form godly societies and companies, Puritans not only took a step in determining their own way of life; they also commented adversely upon the way of life followed by those who continued to adhere to the old order. When Puritan ministers refused to wear the surplice, or use the sign of the cross in baptism; when some of them opposed the practice of having godparents, or kneeling during the celebration of the sacrament; or when they opposed and preached against standing at the reading of the Gospel or bowing in the name of Jesus – in all these renunciations Puritan ministers were not involving themselves in matters of narrow

[43] Winthrop, "Religious Experiencia," *Winthrop Papers*, vol. I, p. 196.
[44] Richard Baxter, *The Autobiography of Richard Baxter*, eds. J. M. Lloyd Thomas and M. H. Keeble (London, 1974), pp. 4, 6.

theological import. They were, in fact, challenging the appropriateness of ancient customs and thereby creating the potential for grave social conflict in parish, church, village, and town. For example, when in 1604 Peter White, vicar of Poulton in the Field, did not baptize with the sign of the cross, his manner "cause[d] many to be baptized out of the parish." And when the minister in the Cheshire parish of Tarporley refused "to execute the holy orders of the church" by baptizing with the cross, his action resulted in a child "be[ing] carried to another church" where he could be "baptized according to the lawful rites and ceremonies of the church of England."[45]

In these and other ways, Puritan ministers exercised their ministry to forward social reformation. They excluded "ungodly" parishioners from communion and church, insisted on godly discipline, and attempted to identify the visible saints with the church. By such actions, they offended many of their parishioners and undermined the working framework of the established church, under which the parish church was designed to encompass all people in its jurisdiction. Thus in 1626 did John Swan of Bunbry cause "sundry men that came prepare[d] to the communion to depart thence without any at all."[46] The Puritan quest for reformation, social and ecclesiastical alike, carried with it severe penalties for those who were, as the Puritans defined them, "profane." What seemed to the Puritans as "reformation according to God's word" was to others obviously an attack on the ancient practices, "the lawful rites and ceremonies" of the Church of England.

These conflicts directly raised the issue of separation. The experience of John Cotton shows one of the many ways Puritans could seek after true reformation within the Church of England, and how the parishioners reacted to it. As early as 1615, Cotton "with cautious firmness rather than enthusiastic zeal," as his biographer says, "set about distinguishing the lily from the thorns." The issue he confronted was how to maintain the ideal of the church as a community of visible saints together with the notion of the established church as inclusive of all the inhabitants of a given area. He did so "not by withdrawing from the parish church . . . but by identifying the elect and withdrawing into a tighter inner group with them." This chosen group consequently "entered into covenant with the Lord and with one another." Thus, Cotton formed a godly company within his Lincolnshire parish church. Such an arrangement amounted to what contemporaries referred to as semi-separation, which stopped short of total separation from the parish church and thereby from the Church of England as a whole. What Cotton formed was not a church but a godly company based on

[45] Richardson, *Puritanism in North-West England*, pp. 27–8.
[46] *Ibid.*, p. 48.

covenant, a company that – without leaving the church – could avoid "the offensive ceremonies" and "was truely qualified to receive the sacrament." The social implications of this act were immediately apparent. Those in the parish excluded from Cotton's godly group "were outraged at the action of the covenanters." They ran to the bishop's court in Lincoln, and the bishop suspended Cotton.[47]

But many Congregationalists in England did not stop where Cotton had stopped. In many cases during the 1640s and the 1650s, as Geoffrey Nuttall shows, the godly group of the covenanters took over the parish church and remade it in their own image.[48] Clearly, what could be done in the 1640s and 1650s, with the fall of the ecclesiastical order during the revolution in England, could not have been so easily accomplished in the 1630s, namely the identification of God's covenanted company with the church and the exclusion from the church of all those not belonging to the godly. It is true that most Puritans who demanded separation from the profane, including almost all of those who emigrated to Massachusetts, strongly denounced the stand of rigid separation which would unchurch the Church of England. Emigration as a legal and loyal withdrawal may therefore be seen as an acceptable alternative to separation as, for example, John White wrote in his defense of the Puritan migration to Massachusetts, *The Planters Plea* (1630).[49] Evidence of the actual practices in the Massachusetts Bay churches indicates, however, explicit separation as well as many instances in which the Bay Puritans accused the Church of England of being a false church. Emigration and the unlimited ecclesiastical freedom in Massachusetts thus radically transformed the Bay Puritans' attitudes toward separation from the Church of England. Full discussion of this important historical phenomenon would, however, lead us well beyond the limits of the present study.[50] In short, the option open to Puritans in the 1630s was the moderate course taken by Cotton in Lincolnshire whereby a congregation of godly people assembled within the established church.

From the point of view of the established church, however, Cotton's moderate course carried the revolutionary threat of Congregationalism. The nature of this threat was made explicit by William Ames, the most prominent theologian of this form of church government. "A congregation or particular Church," proclaimed Ames, "is a society of believers joyned

---

[47] Ziff, *The Career of John Cotton*, p. 49.
[48] Geoffrey F. Nuttall, *Visible Saints, The Congregational Way, 1640–1660* (Oxford, 1957), pp. 134–5.
[49] John White, *The Planters Plea* (London, 1630), pp. 59–61.
[50] For a further analysis of the separatist impulses in Massachusetts Bay, see my "Exile and Kingdom: Reformation, Separation, and the Millennial Quest in the Formation of Massachusetts and Its Relationship with England, 1628–1660," Ph.D. dissertation, Johns Hopkins University, 1982.

together by a special bond among themselves, for the constant exercise of the communion of Saints among themselves." In this proclamation, Ames made it clear both that the essential foundation of a particular church was the social covenant made among the godly people and that a necessary connection existed between the two.

> Believers doe not make a particular church, although peradventure many meete and live together in the same place, unlesse they be joyned by a special bond among themselves . . . This bond is a covenant, either expresse or implicite, whereby believers doe particularly bind themselves to performe all those duties, both toward God and one toward another, which pertaine to the respect and edification of the Church.[51]

Ames thus enlarged the covenant's meaning, making it an indispensable feature of a true church. Ames had transformed Rogers' restricted notion of covenant – as a social covenant with an emphasis on mutual edification among godly people – into nothing less than the essential core of the church. Indeed, the godly company only became a church by virtue of the covenant its members drew among themselves.

The transformation defined by Ames was, in broad outline, the history of the early Massachusetts Bay colony. If godly people could not fulfill their religious goals in England, they had no other choice than to emigrate to America and seek those goals there. Already in 1630, the godly company to which Roger Clap belonged drew a covenant and formed a church in Old Plymouth on the very eve of their migration. But such conduct was exceptional in the great Puritan migration. More common was the Dedham pattern in which emigration preceded the drawing of a covenant and forming a church. Cotton's attempt in old Boston was doomed to failure not only because the bishop objected to it, but because many parishioners objected to it as well. Yet, despite their uncomfortable predicament, Cotton and others of like mind were free to contemplate an enticing prospect. What if the godly simply left the parish churches and gathered in the Bay colony? There the way would be open to the proper execution of the premises of the true church. Central to these was the belief that the church should exclude all but visible saints. Precisely on this point Cotton and his associates in England had no hope. But in New England prospects were entirely different. And so contemplation gave way to action. Emigration was far preferable to the forced inclusion of sinners in the church covenant. As Ames wrote, this was indeed the whole reason for the Puritan emigration to Massachusetts. Well informed in Holland concerning the migration, Ames justified the migration on these grounds:

Yet if believers contending for their liberty cannot procure this right in that part, nor

[51] William Ames, *The Marrow of Sacred Divinity* (London, 1642), pp. 140–1.

without most grievous discommodities depart to a more pure Church, and doe keep themselves from the approbation of sinne . . . they sine not.[52]

Only by leaving sinners in England could the true reformation be fulfilled in New England.

The failure to achieve reform in their local societies, the impossibility of reconciling the principle of a church based on visible saints with the established one, the continuing attacks on the Puritan way of godliness – all these stood in the background of the Puritan migration. For the emigrants demanded nothing less than the whole – the transformation of society and state according to God's word. This radical plea could not be fulfilled in England. It only raised the ire of other sections of society, so that the attempt to distinguish and separate godly from ungodly people was accompanied by social struggles within the community and within the parish church. Emigration therefore represented the possibility, not only to establish a true church, but also to achieve social reformation through social covenants. In New England, wrote Captain Edward Johnson, who sailed with Winthrop's fleet, "the Lord will create a new Heaven and New Earth new Churches, and new Common-Wealth together."[53] For without a Christian commonwealth, godly people and their true churches could not be sustained.

Johnson, like Ames before him, revealed how much the social context in England caused and generated the migration:

When England began to decline in Religion, like lukewarme Laodicea, and instead of purging out Popery, a farther compliance was sought not only in vain Idolatrous Ceremonies, but also in prophaning the Sabbath, and by Proclamation through their Parish churches, exasperating lewd and prophane persons to celebrate a Sabbath like the Heathen to Venus, Baccus and Ceres; in so much that the multitude of irreligious lascivious and popish affected persons spred the whole land like Grashoppers.

These "prophane persons" and that "multitude of irreligious lascivious . . . persons" had obstructed Puritans in England; they were a stumbling block to the Puritans' search for further reformation in social life and in the church. The proclamation Johnson mentioned was the Declaration concerning Sports first issued by James I in 1617 and repeated by his son Charles I in 1633. To the Puritans' chagrin, this declaration allowed the populace to play games on Sunday after church service. Yet one needs to go beyond the royal proclamation, as in the case of Baxter above, to see in the interactions

---

[52] William Ames, *Conscience with the Power and Cases Thereof* (London, 1641), p. 63. On the close relationship between Ames and the great Puritan migration from its beginnings, see: K. L. Sprunger, "William Ames and the Settlement of Massachusetts Bay," *New England Quarterly* 39 (1966), 66–79.

[53] Edward Johnson, *Wonder-Working Providence of Sion's Saviour in New England, 1628–1651*, ed. J. Franklin Jameson (New York, 1910), p. 25.

between the Puritans and the "prophane," how the highest interest of the Puritans – keeping the purity of the holy day – clashed with the multitude's interest in having recreation on the same day. Concerning the latter, wrote Johnson, "every corner of England was filled with the fury of malignant adversaries" of God and godly people. So, when the Puritans emigrated to Massachusetts, they intentionally separated themselves not only from ceremonies, popery, and bishops, but also from this multitude of "malignant and prophane" people; for these people, in Puritan eyes, were the reason that further reformation was not attainable in England. It was, they believed, as a result of this struggle between godly and "malignant" people that "in this very time Christ the glorious King of his Churches" had raised "an Army out of our English Nation" and created "a New England to muster up the first of his Forces in."[54]

THE DESACRALIZATION OF ENGLAND AS HOLY SOCIETY – HOLY-LAND NEW ENGLAND

The Puritan migration arose out of the Puritan experience in England in the early seventeenth century. The appropriate context for examining the Puritans' reasons for emigrating is the small world of their individual communities. For it was in their everyday lives that the Puritans faced opposition to their visions of godly life and the dilemma of whether they should or should not continue to live among "prophane" people. This view partly contradicts the traditional assumption that the great Puritan migration was caused by a certain "crisis" in England in the late 1620s or early 1630s.[55] The differences between these two points of departure are clear enough. The former calls our attention to the long-term trends in English society in which Puritanism increasingly revealed itself, not only as an ecclesiastical power but as a strong social and political force able to disturb and divide communities by its uncompromising plea for full social and religious reformation. The latter explanation, or theory of "crisis," in attributing the origins

---

[54] *Ibid.*, pp. 23–5.

[55] The representatives of each view or interpretation which seeks to explain the origins of the Puritan migration to New England by a "crisis" within English society need only to be mentioned. James Truslow Adams in his famous book, *The Founding of New England* (Boston, 1949 [1921]), pp. 122–4, stressed the view that both a political "crisis" and an economic "crisis" in the late 1620s were responsible for the Puritan migration. A decade later, Perry Miller in his *Orthodoxy in Massachusetts* (Gloucester, 1965 [1933]), p. 99, distancing himself from the economic emphasis typified by Adams, stressed the essentially religious motivation behind the Puritan migration. Yet his account tended rather to reinforce Adams' emphasis on the importance of the political "crisis" in the late 1620s. Thus, for Miller, a crisis occasioned by Charles I's dissolution of the Parliament of 1629 had enormous consequences for the Puritan migration. The political "crisis" then, according to Miller, was essentially associated with the ecclesiastical "crisis."

of the Puritan migration to events occurring at the actual time of the migration, ignores some profound developments in English society that took place well before, and continued well after, the Puritans had sailed to the New World. The actual world out of which the great Puritan migration came was a world of conflict in local communities, parishes, churches, villages, and towns, in which Puritans struggled for religious and social reformation against fellow members of their own local societies, who worked to defeat their social and ecclesiastical program. These divided communities and churches provided one of the primary sources of the migration, for godly people alienated not only ecclesiastical authorities, but, more importantly, their own local communities.

The lessening of the prospects for reform on the local level and the interactions there between godly and "prophane" people determined the Puritan migration. Emigration emerged as a possible solution for many, for whom the only alternative was life among the "prophane." After all, Puritans carried with them not only theological tenets, but also new visions of a godly society. And when the attempt to build a godly society in England failed, some of the Puritans turned their eyes to New England, deeming it the ideal place to make their vision a reality. Thomas Tillan, for example, describes this Puritan expectation upon his first sighting of New England in the summer of 1638:

> Hayle holy-land wherein our holy lord
> hath planted his most true and holy word
> hayle happy people who have dispossest
> yourselves of friends, and means to find some rest
> for Jesus-sake . . .
> Posses this Country, free from all anoye
> heare I'le be with yow, heare you shall Injoye
> my sabbaths, sacraments, my minstrye
> and ordinances in their purity.[56]

But the urgency of the need for emigration is perhaps best revealed by the Revd. Thomas Weld in a message he wrote in 1633 in Massachusetts to his friends in England:

Here are none of the men of Gibea the sonnes of Belial knocking at our doors disturbing our sweet peace or threatening violence. Here blessed be the Lord God for ever Our eares are not beaten nor the aire filled with Oaths. Swearers nor Railers, Nor our eyes and eares vexed with the unclea[n] Conversation of the wicked.[57]

[56] Thomas Tillan, "Uppon the First Sight of New England, June 29 1638," in *Seventeenth-Century American Poetry*, ed. Harrison T. Meserole (New York, 1968), pp. 397–8.
[57] Thomas Weld, "A Letter of Master Wells from New England to Old England . . . 1633," Massachusetts Colonial Society, *Transactions* 13 (1910–11), 130–1.

7

The creation of a holy Christian commonwealth

Theocracy in New England: the nature and meaning of the holy experiment in the wilderness

> By the side of every religion is to be found a political opinion, which is connected with it by affinity. If the human mind be left to follow its own bent, it will regulate the temporal and spiritual institutions of society in a uniform manner, and man will endeavor, if I may so speak, to harmonize earth with heaven.
>
> Alexis de Tocqueville, *Democracy in America*, 1835

MIGRATION AS AN ACT OF RELIGIOUS REFORMATION

Throughout the 1630s thousands of Puritans crossed the Atlantic to reach New England where they intended to dedicate their lives to God and His word. They came with the belief that the millennium, or the time in which Christ would reign on earth with his saints, as described in the Book of Revelation, was at hand. "If the servants of Christ be not mistaken," wrote Edward Johnson of his fellow Puritan emigrants' millennial expectations, "the downfall of Antichrist is at hand, and then the Kingdome[s] of the Earth shall become the Kingdome of our Lord Christ." The realization of their millennial expectations and the transformation of the world into the Kingdom of God, the Puritans believed, depended on the saints assuming an active and decisive role in the apocalyptical events preceding the millennium, as vividly portrayed in Revelation. Thus the saints were to gather themselves into fellowships, or congregations, consisting only of "visible saints." "The great design of Jesus Christ in this age," wrote John Higginson from Guilford, Connecticut, to Thomas Thacher of Weymouth, Massachusetts, "is to set up his Kingdom in Particular churches." Therefore, continues Higginson, "the great duty of such as are in church fellowship is to conform themselves to those primitive patterns."[1] Accordingly, the

---

[1] Edward Johnson, *Wonder-Working Providence of Sion's Saviour in New England, 1628–1651*, ed. J. Franklin Jameson (New York, 1910), p. 146. John Higginson, "Part of John Higginson's Letter, of Guilford, dated 25 of the 8th month, 1654, to his Brother the Rev'd

Puritans set out to establish congregational churches as specified in the prophecies of Revelation immediately upon their arrival in New England.

One must not assume, however, that the great Puritan migration to New England was directed solely toward the establishment of Congregationalism. And indeed, perceiving themselves and their migration as crucial in the great providential drama, the Puritans assigned themselves a larger role than constituting the true church in the wildernesse. They were "to rayse a bullwarke against the kingdome of Antichrist" that would help to insure that Christ and not Antichrist would reign in the world. New England was to be the site for the true Christian commonwealth in which Christ would rule over his saints. "We chose not the place for the land," declared Johnson on the cause and origin of the Puritan migration to America,

but for the government, that our Lord Christ might raigne over us, both in Churches and Common-wealth.

In the eyes of the Puritans, then, church and state were but two complementary instruments through which they hoped to defeat Antichristian institutions and governments and realize their pursuit of the millennium. Thus,

Thomas Thacher of Weymouth," in Connecticut Historical Society, *Collections*, vol. III (1895), p. 319.

Millennial expectations and apocalyptical visions played a crucial role in the rise of the Puritan movement in England during the sixteenth and seventeenth centuries. See Bryan W. Ball, *A Great Expectation: Eschatological Thought in English Protestantism to 1660* (Leiden, 1975); Peter Toon (ed.), *Puritans, the Millennium, and the Future of Israel: Puritan Eschatology* (Cambridge, 1970); Katharine R. Firth, *The Apocalyptic Tradition in Reformation Britain 1530–1646* (Oxford, 1979); Charles Webster, *The Great Instauration: Science, Medicine and Reform 1626–1660* (London, 1975); Paul Christianson, *Reformers and Babylon: English Apocalyptic Visions from the Reformation to the Eve of the Civil War* (Toronto, 1978); William Lamont, *Godly Rule: Politics and Religion, 1603–1600* (London, 1969); and the important study by J. G. A. Pocock, "Modes of Action and Their Pasts in Tudor and Stuart England," in *National Consciousness, History and Political Culture in Early Modern Europe*, ed. Orest Ranum (Baltimore, 1975), pp. 98–117.

For the association between millennial and utopian thought, see Ernest L. Tuveson, *Millennium and Utopia: A Study in the Background of the Idea of Progress* (Berkeley and Los Angeles, 1949), and J. C. Davis, *Utopia and the Ideal Society: A Study of English Utopian Writing 1516–1700* (Cambridge, 1981).

There are many studies on millennial thought in America in general and New England in particular. See Joy B. Gilsdorf, "The Puritan Apocalypse: New England Eschatology in the Seventeenth Century," Ph.D. dissertation, Yale University, 1964; James W. Davidson, *The Logic of Millennial Thought: Eighteenth Century New England* (New Haven, 1977); Clark Gilpin, *The Millenarian Piety of Roger Williams* (Chicago, 1979); Cecelia Tichi, *New World, New Earth: Environmental Reform in American Literature from the Puritans through Whitman* (New Haven, 1979); John Seelye, *Prophetic Waters: The River in Early American Life and Literature* (New York, 1977); and Helmut R. Neibuhr, *The Kingdom of God in America* (Hampden, 1955). I have attempted to show the important role of millennial expectations in the shaping of social and political life in early Massachusetts in my "Exile and Kingdom: Reformation, Separation, and the Millennial Quest in the Formation of Massachusetts and Its Relationship with England, 1628–1660" (Ph.D. dissertation, Johns Hopkins University, 1982).

argued Johnson, "Godly civil government shall have a great share in the worke" of the upcoming of the millennium, and in Massachusetts he happily noted,

our Magistrates being conscious of ruling for Christ, dare not admit of any bastardly brood to nurst upon their tender knees, neither any Christian of sound judgment vote for any, but such as earnestly contend for the Faith.[2]

Clearly, the type of political system the Puritans succeeded in creating in the American wilderness would largely determine both their degree of success in effecting the religious and social reformation they had been unable to achieve in England, as well as the fulfillment of their providential mission to defeat Antichristian institutions and usher in the Kingdom of God. Precisely what was the nature of the Puritan commonwealth in New England, however, remains one of the most persistent questions in the historiography of American Puritanism. In the many works dealing with the Puritan colonies in America, whether or not the Puritans actually intended to and succeeded in creating a theocracy in New England, remains one of the essential questions not yet conclusively resolved.[3]

In an attempt to clarify this troublesome issue concerning the basic character of the Puritan commonwealth in America, the premises of the New England Puritans, or more particularly, those of Massachusetts, Connecticut, and New Haven, will first be examined. Second, it will be shown how, out of these premises concerning state, church, and the special dimension of time they believed themselves to live in, the Puritans shaped their

---

[2] "General Observations for the Plantation of New England" (1629), in *Winthrop Papers*, ed. Allyn b. Forber, 5 vols. (Boston, 1929–1947), vol. II, p. 114; Johnson, *Wonder-Working Providence*, p. 146.

[3] Among the many works dealing with the political nature and foundation of the Puritan commonwealths in New England and the special relationship between church and state there, see Paul E. Lauer, *Church and State in New England* (Baltimore, 1892); Aaron B. Seidman, "Church and Society in the Early Years of the Massachusetts Bay Colony," *New England Quarterly* 18 (1945), 211–33; Perry Miller, "The Puritan State and Puritan Society," in *Errand Into the Wilderness* (Cambridge, 1976), pp. 141–52, and "The Theory of State and Society," in *The Puritans*, ed. Perry Miller and Thomas H. Johnson (New York, 1963), vol. I, pp. 181–93; Edmund S. Morgan (ed.), *Puritan Political Ideas* (Indianapolis, 1965); T. H. Breen, *The Character of the Good Ruler: A Study of Puritan Political Ideas in New England, 1630–1730* (New Haven, 1970); T. J. Wertenbaker, *The Puritan Oligarchy* (New York, 1947); Paul R. Lucas, *Valley of Discord: Church and Society Along the Connecticut River* (Hanover, 1976); Mary Jeanne Anderson Jones, *Congregational Commonwealth, Connecticut, 1636–1662* (Middletown, 1968); Isabel M. Calder, *The New Haven Colony* (New Haven, 1934). George L. Mosse put American Puritan political ideas in the context of English Puritanism in a series of studies: *The Holy Pretence: A Study in Christianity and Reason of State from William Perkins to John Winthrop* (Oxford, 1957), "Puritanism and Reason of State in Old and New England," *William and Mary Quarterly* 9 (1952), 67–80. For the Protestants' general view of church and state, see the important article by Winthrop S. Hudson, "Protestant Concept of Church and State," *Church History* 35 (1966), 229.

Christian commonwealth. Finally, the holy experiment in the wilderness will be explored in the context of the transatlantic Puritan movement, in order to verify whether theocracy was a phenomenon peculiar to American Puritanism, or rather an essential feature of English Puritanism, especially during the so-called Puritan Revolution – when Puritans had the opportunity to establish a Christian commonwealth in England. Above all, this study underscores the requirement of the historian to examine closely the ideological context in order to understand men's actions.

In England during the 1620s and 1630s, the Puritans found themselves thwarted from achieving their goal of separating themselves from ungodly people admitted to membership in parish churches. The wilderness offered them a unique opportunity to reconstruct the church as a spiritual society based on the covenant, and thus realize their longstanding aim. As Edmund Morgan has shown, "the English emigrants to New England were the first Puritans to restrict membership in the church to visible saints, to persons, that is, who felt the stirrings of grace in their souls, and who could demonstrate this fact to the satisfaction of other saints." At the same time, the wilderness also provided the possibility of forming a true Christian commonwealth in which the proper relationship between church and state might be achieved. In the late sixteenth and early seventeenth centuries, long before the Puritan migration began, efforts had been made as part of the pursuit of reformation to form civil and social covenants among Puritans, in order to strengthen through mutual edification each individual's resolve to keep his covenant with God. "These covenants," wrote Patrick Collinson in this regard, "were not church covenants but belonged to the Puritan experience of covenant grace, an area quite remote at this time from any overt ecclesiological reference." Accordingly, as Lockridge shows in his study on Dedham, when the godly reached New England they immediately covenanted among themselves before settling a town or establishing a church.[4]

A social or civil covenant, then, was different from a church covenant; the

---

[4] Edmund S. Morgan, *Visible Saints: The History of a Puritan Idea* (Ithaca, 1975), p. 113; Patrick Collinson, "Toward a Broader Understanding of the Early Dissenting Tradition," in *The Dissenting Tradition*, ed. C. Robert Cole and Michael E. Moody (Athens, 1975), pp. 3–38; Kenneth A. Lockridge, *A New England Town: The First Hundred Years* (New York, 1970). For the theological developments of the covenant theory, see Champlin Burrage, *The Church Covenant Idea* (Philadelphia, 1904); Klaus Baltzer, *The Covenant Formulary* (Philadelphia, 1971); J. Wayne Baker, *Heinrich Bullinger and the Covenant* (Athens, 1980); Perry Miller, *The New England Mind: The Seventeenth Century* (New York, 1939), Book IV, "Sociology," and "Appendix B, The Federal School of Theology;" Jens G. Moller, "The Beginnings of Puritan Covenant Theology," *The Journal of Ecclesiastical History* 14 (1963), 46–67; Everett H. Emerson, "Calvin and Covenant Theology," *Church History* 25 (1956), 136–44; Brooks E. Holifield, *The Covenant Sealed: The Development of Puritan Sacramental Theology in Old and New England, 1570–1720* (New Haven, 1974); and William K. B. Stoever, *A Faire and Easie Way to Heaven: Covenant Theology and Antinomianism in Early Massachusetts* (Middletown, 1978).

first related to civil and social affairs, the second to a spiritual fellowship. Both, however, were religious covenants intended to further the premises of reformation in church and state alike. Yet while the one regulated the saints in the commonwealth, the other governed them in the church. This distinction is a crucial one, since the question of the relationship between the social or civil covenant and the church covenant constitutes the very crux of the issue of the right foundations of a Christian commonwealth. When the Puritans sought to follow God's word in both church and the state, their intention was to construct both realms on the basis of covenants. Thus, out of the Puritan premises of reformation, in the state, as in the church, the covenant became a device to keep the ungodly from fellowship with the saints. "Here the churches and commonwealth are complanted together in holy covenant and fellowship with God," wrote John Davenport of New Haven, and therefore "the people that choose civil rules are God's people in covenant with him, that is members of churches."[5] This radical linkage between the civil covenant and the church covenant served to exclude those who were not saints, not only from the church but also from political power in the Puritan commonwealth.

THEOCRACY IN THE WILDERNESS

Two of the most prominent New England ministers, John Cotton and John Davenport, asserted that the best form of government for a Christian commonwealth was a theocracy, a form that assumed a special relationship between church and state, clergy and magistracy, and above all, the social and church covenant. "Theocracy," wrote John Cotton to Lord Say and Sele, an old friend of the Puritan settlement in New England, is "the best forme of government in the common-wealth, as well as in the church." To the same effect, John Davenport had argued that "*theocratic*, or to make the Lord God our Governour, is the best form of Government in a Christian Common-wealth, and which men that are free to chuse (as in new Plantations they are) ought to establish."[6]

Few concepts have changed more radically over time than the concept of

---

[5] John Davenport, in *Collection of Papers Relative to the History of the Colony of Massachusetts Bay*, comp. Thomas Hutchinson, 2 vols. (Boston, 1865), vol. I, p. 184.

[6] John Cotton, "Copy of a Letter from Mr. Cotton to Lord Say and Seal in the Year 1636," in Thomas Hutchinson, *The History of the Colony and Province of Massachusetts Bay*, ed. Lawrence S. Mayo, 3 vols. (Cambridge, Mass., 1936), vol. I, p. 415; John Norton, *Abel Being Dead Yet Speaketh, or, the Life & Death of the Most Deservedly Famous Man of God, John Cotton, Late Teacher of the Church of Christ, at Boston, in New England* (London, 1658), pp. 35–41; John Davenport, *A Discourse About Civil Government in a New Plantation Whose Design is Religion* (Cambridge, Mass., 1663), p. 14. On Davenport's life, see also Isabel M. Calder (ed.), *Letters of John Davenport: Puritan Divine* (New Haven, 1937).

theocracy. According to the *Encyclopedia of Religion and Ethics*, "the term was coined by Josephus . . . to denote a certain kind of national polity. Any tribe or state that claims to be governed by God or Gods may be called a 'theocracy'." Here the implication is that ministers assume no political power at all. According to its more modern definition in the *Shorter Oxford English Dictionary*, however, theocracy is "a system of government by a sacerdotal order, claiming a divine commission," a state in which priests do exercise political power, or, more precisely, it is a state ruled by ministers. When the Puritans in America stated as their aims the establishment of a theocracy, they were using the former and older meaning of the term.

The truth of this assertion can be seen in John Davenport's *Discourse about Civil Government in a New Plantation Whose Design is Religion* (1639). In the past, this work was ascribed to John Cotton, and as Larzer Ziff has argued, it was certainly "representative of Cotton's opinion on that subject." Recently, however, Bruce E. Steiner demonstrated authoritatively that it was indeed Davenport who wrote this tract. The importance of Davenport's *Discourse* lies in its unusually full exposition of the precise meaning of theocracy during the early years of the Puritan settlement in New England, and in its serving as first-hand evidence concerning the Puritans' attempts to shape a Christian commonwealth in America.[7]

In the summer of 1638, after leaving the Massachusetts Bay colony, Davenport and his company reached their destination of New Haven, where they set about establishing a new settlement. Upon their arrival, according to the *Records of the Colony and Plantation of New Haven*, "all the planters assembled together in a ge[nerall] meeting to consult about the settling of civill Government according to God," and also to nominate the people who would lay the foundation of the church there. Concerning civil government, their aim was to establish "such civill order as might be most p[leas]ing unto God." Before taking this step, all the "freeplanters" assembled to make a solemn covenant, "called a plantation covenant to distinguish it from [a] church covenant." In New Haven, as in Massachusetts, a civil or social covenant thus preceded a church covenant. During that meeting, "Mr. Davenport propunded a divers quaeres" concerning the nature and the right foundation of a Christian commonwealth and exhorted the gathering to "consider seriously in the presence and fear of God the weight of the business they met about." What Davenport argued in these queries was that "the civil power" in the new settlement should be "confined to church members." Another minister, the Revd. Peter Prudden,

---

[7] Larzer Ziff, *The Career of John Cotton* (Princeton, 1962), p. 97 n. 35; Bruce E. Steiner, "Dissension at Quinnipiac: the Authorship and Setting of a Discourse about Civil Government in a New Plantation Whose Design is Religion," *William and Mary Quarterly* 38 (1981), 14–32.

objected to Davenport's motion. In order to answer Prudden, Davenport composed his *Discourse*, aiming to show the necessity of confining the civil power to church members.[8]

Davenport's aim, in his words, was

to prove the Expediency and Necessity . . . of entrusting free Burgesses which are the members of Churches gathered amongst them according to Christ, with the power of Chusing from among themselves Magistrates, and men to whom the managing of all Public Civil Affairs of Importance is to be committed. And to vindicate the Same from an imputation of under-power upon the Churches of Christ.

As this passage suggests, Davenport argued that limiting the choice of magistrates to church members would not lead to theocracy in the sense of a state ruled by the church. Rather he contended, "the Church so considered" was "a spiritual Political Body" and would not interfere in any civil affairs. Yet not every church member, he argued, had the right to choose magistrates, but only those who were "free burgesses" or freemen.[9]

Davenport premised his work upon a basic distinction between civil and ecclesiastical affairs. "Ecclesiastical Administration," he contended, was "a Divine Order appointed to believers for holy communion of holy things," while "Civil Administration" was "an Human Order appointed by God to men for Civil Fellowship of Human things." Any attempt to unite both orders – church and state – could place "the Spiritual Power, which is proper to the Church, into the hand of the Civil Magistrate." Or the equally dire possibility existed, as had materialized with the Romish tyranny, that the church might usurp the civil authority of the state. Davenport was concerned to prevent both these dangers. But he was also fearful of yet another, more important threat, that of separating church and state so completely as to set "these two different Orders, Ecclesiastical and Civil . . . in opposition as contraries, that one should destroy the other." What he wanted was that church and state should be in a "co-ordinate state, in the same place reaching forth help mutually each to other for the welfare of both, according to God."[10] In shaping their Christian commonwealth, Puritans thus aimed neither at unification nor at complete separation of church and state. Rather, they thought of church and state as two different means to the same end.

In New Haven in 1638, as in Massachusetts in 1630, the wilderness provided an opportunity for Puritans to create a commonwealth according to their own premises of religious reformation. Two sorts of people existed

---

[8] Charles J. Hoadly (ed.), *Records of the Colony and Plantation of New Haven, from 1638 to 1649* (Hartford, 1857), pp. 11–12 (hereafter cited as *New Haven Records*); Steiner, "Dissension at Quinnipiac," p. 26.

[9] Davenport, *A Discourse About Civil Government*, pp. 3–5.

[10] *Ibid.*, pp. 6–8.

in the colony, "free burgesses" or freemen, and "inhabitants." To exclude the latter from political power was natural because they were "not Citizens" and were "never likely to be numbered among . . . Rulers." Confining civil power to church members did not, therefore, deprive these particular people of any civil right they would otherwise have had. "When we urge, the magistrates be Chosen out of free Burgesses, and by them, and that those free Burgesses be Chosen out of such as are members of these Churches," said Davenport, "we do not thereby go about to exclude those that are not in Church-Order, from any Civil right or liberty that is due unto them as Inhabitants and planters."[11] The only group which lost any civil rights, Davenport made clear, were those freemen who were not church members and could not, therefore, in a godly commonwealth be permitted either to choose magistrates or to exercise political power.

Davenport thus advocated disenfranchisement of all freemen who were not church members, for the reason that only godly magistrates could be entrusted with preserving civil and church covenants. It was his belief, and that of other Puritans also, that the covenant was the foundation of state as well as church, and that by its very nature it belonged only to the "saints," who "by virtue of their Covenant [were] bound" to serve "god and his ends." To invest those who were not saints with civil power would therefore necessarily mean breaking the covenant with God. In this manner, Davenport transformed the religious obligations of the covenant into political obligations in the Christian commonwealth. Because the ungodly were not "consecrated to God and his ends," they could not be given civil power.[12]

It was precisely for this reason that Davenport and other Puritans argued that "Theocratic, or to make the Lord God our Governour" was "the best form of Government in a Christian Commonwealth." Only in this unique political system, according to the Puritans, could there be absolute assurance that the civil covenant in society and the church covenant in the church would be adhered to.

Davenport spelled out precisely what he meant by theocracy. A theocracy, he wrote, was that

Form of Government where 1. The people that have the power of chusing their Governors are in Covenant with God: 2. Wherein the men chosen by them are godly men, and fitted with a spirit of Government: 3. In which the Laws they rule by are the Laws of God: 4. Wherein Laws are executed, Inheritances alloted, and civil differences are composed, according to Gods appointment: 5. In which men of God are consulted with in all hard cases, and in matters of Religion.

This, said Davenport, was "the Form which was received and established

[11] *Ibid.*, pp. 9–11, 14.   [12] *Ibid.*, pp. 15–16, 19–20.

among the people of Israel whil'st the Lord God was their Governour . . . and is the very same that which we plead for."[13]

Davenport gave here the true and comprehensive meaning of Puritan theocracy, which was clearly not to invest ministers with political power, but rather to "make the Lord God our Governour"; that is, to appoint civil magistrates who would govern according to God's word and will. Although Puritans did not believe ministers should assume civil power, they strongly stressed the obligation of magistrates to seek to make civil society conform to God's purpose. Religious reformation was necessary not only in the church but in society as a whole. Because civil magistrates were charged with such weighty responsibilities, it was essential that they be saints.

A theocratic government, then, was one which gave "Christ his due preheminence," and godly people were obliged to make sure that "all things and all Government in the world, should serve . . . Christ ends . . . for the welfare of the Church whereof he is the Head." To meet this obligation civil authorities had to be "wise and learned in matter of Religion" – and therefore church members, or *"Saints by calling."*[14] With the presence of ungodly magistrates in England having been a crucial factor in the emigration of so many Puritans to New England, it was imperative to take whatever steps were necessary to prevent the church from again being persecuted by ungodly magistrates.

Since political society, no less than the church or holy fellowship, was confined to those capable of preserving the covenant, the exclusiveness of church fellowship led directly to the exclusiveness of the political system. Davenport warned that if political authority were delegated to the ungodly, the entire holy experiment in the wilderness would be jeopardized and the saints' capacity to assist Christ in the apocalyptical battle against Antichrist would be undermined. Those who would commit power into the hands of those "worldly spirits" who "hate[d] the Saints and their communion" would provide Satan with an instrument for "resisting and fighting against Christ and his Kingdom and Government in the Church."[15]

It was Davenport who addressed these arguments concerning the establishment of theocracy to the new colony of New Haven, and there, according to Bruce E. Steiner, "the practice championed in Davenport's *Discourse* had [also] triumphed." A "generall meeting of all the free planters" in New Haven in 1639 agreed that "church members only shall be free burgesses, and they only shall chuse among them selves magistrates and officers to ha[ve] the power of transacting all publique civill affayres of this plantation."[16]

---

[13] *Ibid.*, pp. 14–15.   [14] *Ibid.*, pp. 15–16.   [15] *Ibid.*, pp. 20–3.
[16] Steiner, "Dissension at Quinnipiac," p. 32: *New Haven Records*, pp. 14, 17.

These arguments however, were peculiar neither to Davenport nor to New Haven. In Massachusetts, in fact, they had been embodied in the colony's policy from its very beginnings. In 1631, "to the end that the body of commons may be preserved of honest and god men," the Massachusetts General Court ordered "that for the time to come no man shall be admitted to the freedom of this body politic, but such as are members of some of the churches."[17]

A similar belief was implicit in the Fundamental Orders of Connecticut that were drawn up in 1638/39. As Mary J. A. Jones found: "The purpose of the Fundamental Orders was to provide a legal guide for the government of the holy and regenerate." In Connecticut, no less than in Massachusetts and New Haven, a social covenant preceded the establishment of the commonwealth. The Fundamental Orders were indeed a civil covenant in which the godly declared that "the word of god requires" that "an orderly and decent Government be established according to God" and pledged themselves to "associate and conjoyne our selves to be as one Publike State or Commonwealth . . . to mayntain and preserve the liberty and purity of the gospel of our Lord Jesus wch we now professe, as also the disciplyne of the Churches, wch according to the truth of the said gospel is now practised amongst us." As Jones remarks, this was "a covenant between the godly property owners of Hartford, Windsor, and Wethersfield, not between all the residents on the Connecticut River, just as the church covenants were the agreement between the saints only. Civil rights were indeed the privilege of the few."[18] If, then, the essence of theocratic government was maintaining the political realm as the sole and exclusive domain of the saints, the system of government in all these Puritan colonies, Massachusetts, Connecticut, and New Haven may justifiably be defined as theocracy.

The Puritans' rigid insistence upon excluding the ungodly from political power was thus a crucial element in shaping the foundation of their Christian commonwealth in the early years of Puritan New England. With religious reformation going hand in hand with social and political reform, the same drive for reformation that led to the admission into the church of only the "visible saints," led, in the political realm, to the establishment of theocratic government, a political system which entrusted authority only to those in the Puritan colonies who belonged to the "gathered churches" or

[17] *The Records of the Governor and Company of the Massachusetts Bay in New England*, ed. Nathaniel B. Shurtleff, 5 vols. (Boston, 1853–4), vol. I, p. 87 (hereafter cited as *Mass. Records.*)

[18] Paul R. Lucas, *Valley of Discord*, p. 33; Frank Shuffleton, *Thomas Hooker, 1586–1647* (Princeton, 1977), p. 231; Mary Jeanne Anderson Jones, *Congregational Commonwealth*, p. 77; J. Hammond Trumbull and Charles J. Hoadly (eds.), *The Public Records of the Colony of Connecticut*, 15 vols. (Hartford, 1850–1890), vol. I, p. 21; Jones, *Congregational Commonwealth*, p. 79.

the saints. The revolutionary nature of this theocracy in New England government is well illustrated by a few examples.

IN DEFENSE OF THEOCRATIC GOVERNMENT

An important consequence of the Antinomian controversy in Massachusetts was an order, enacted by the General Court in 1637, "that no town or person shall receive any stranger resorting hither," nor "shall allow any lot of habitant to any . . . except such person shall have allowance under the hand of some one of the councile, or two other of the magistrates." In opposing the menace of the Antinomian heresy, civil authorities intended in this manner to restrict entrance into the Bay colony of those "profane persons" who held Antinomian views. This was the very policy over which "Young Henry Vane" and John Winthrop clashed sharply in 1637. "A family is a common wealth," Winthrop wrote in defense of the order of 1637, "and a common wealth is a great family. Now as a family is not bound to entertaine all comers . . . no more is [a] commonwealth." But to Henry Vane the Court's order revealed an alarming tendency in the Puritan concept of the refuge and shelter in the wilderness, "because here is a liberty given by this law to expell and reject those which are most eminent christian, if they suit not with the disposition of the magistrates." The outcome of this policy, argued Vane, would be "that Christ and his members will find worse entertainment amongst us than the Israelites did among the Egyptians and Babilonians." Christ, argued Vane, "is the head of the Church, and the prince of the kings of earth," but the colony's law, by giving the magistrates power to expel whomever they wanted, contradicted "many lawes of Christ." Vane declared further that

Christ commands us to do good unto all, but especially to them of the household of faith. Many other lawes there are of Christ, which this law dasheth against, and therefore is most wicked and sinnefull.[19]

Winthrop's answer to Vane's charges clearly reveals the character of the Puritan theocracy, and how tightly interwoven the social and church covenants were in the early years of the colony. Winthrop's response was that the magistrates were "members of the churches here, and by that

---

[19] *Mass. Records*, vol. I, p. 196; John Winthrop, "A Defence of an Order of Court Made in the Year 1637," in *Collection*, comp. Hutchinson, vol. I, pp. 79, 81; Henry Vane, "A Brief Answer to a Certain Declaration . . ." (1637), in *Collection*, comp. Hutchinson, vol. I, pp. 81, 85, 95, 88, 96.

Antinomianism played a significant role in the sweep of Puritan history in England. See, for example, Gertrude Huehns, *Antinomianism in English History* (London, 1951); Christopher Hill, *The World Turned Upside Down: Radical Ideas During the English Revolution* (London, 1972); R. A. Knox, *Enthusiasm: A Chapter in the History of Religion* (Oxford, 1962).

covenant" could not act in opposition to but were required and "regulated to direct all their wayes by the rule of the gospell." And he continued by stating that this law was not a new policy, but was "an established order" in Massachusetts from the very beginnings of the colony.[20]

Winthrop's aim in his reply to Vane was more than an attempt to justify the court's order. His primary concern was to vindicate the establishment of theocratic government in Massachusetts by confirming the Puritans' adherence to their millennial expectations and to their belief that they were living in a special dimension of time. Winthrop maintained that the providential process which was to culminate in the reign of Christ and his church or saints on earth had already begun. "Whereas the way of God hath always beene to gather his churches out of the world; now," argued Winthrop, "the world, or the civill state, must be raised out of the churches."[21]

In other words, Winthrop declared that the body politic as such was the outcome of the gathering of churches, or more precisely, that the holy society of the churches in Massachusetts constituted the political body of the colony. With this radical approach, he clearly implied that the boundaries of the church covenant were exactly congruent with those of the civil covenant. This stand did not signify that church and state were one, but only reaffirmed the principle that church membership, participation in the church covenant, was a prerequisite to participation in the civil covenant and membership in the colony's holy body politic.

It was, undoubtedly, because of the very radicalism of this outlook on the proper relationship between church and state covenants that many in England were confused by the Puritan theocracy in America. Even staunch Puritans like William Fiennes, Viscount Say and Sele, and Robert Greville, Baron Brooke, all long-time friends of the Puritan migration to America and the Puritan settlements there, found themselves puzzled by the holy experiment in the wilderness. Like Henry Vane, who left the Bay colony in the summer of 1637 because of his failure to come to terms with some of the more radical premises, not to mention the political and social consequences, of theocracy in Massachusetts, the Puritan lords too found themselves at great odds with their brethren in America when they discovered the true nature of theocracy in New England.

In 1636 Viscount Say and Sele and Baron Brooke along with other nobles considered emigration to New England, as did so many other Puritans

---

[20] John Winthrop, "A Reply to an Answer Made to a Declaration . . ." (1637), in *Collection*, comp. Hutchinson, vol. I, pp. 111–12, 100–1. Henry Vane's life and role in Puritan Massachusetts and England are best described in J. H. Adamson and H. F. Holland, *Sir Harry Vane: His Life and Times 1613–1662* (Boston, 1973). For Vane's political ideas, see: Margaret Judson, *The Political Thought of Sir Henry Vane the Younger* (Philadelphia, 1969).

[21] Winthrop, "A Reply to an Answer," pp. 100–1, 111–12.

during the 1630s. Being noble men, however, they sent "Certain Proposals .
. . as conditions of their moving to New England."[22] In their answer, the Bay
Puritans revealed that they could meet almost all of the legal and constitu-
tional demands of the lords, with the notable exception of the issue of the
relationship between church and state, an exception that finally determined
that the lords abandon their plan to join the Puritan commonwealth in
America. The controversy and debates among the Puritans on both sides of
the Atlantic concerning the lords' proposals were based on the nature and
foundation of the Puritan theocracy in America.

What the Puritan lords had demanded was that they be permitted to
continue in New England to exercise the privileges of their noble rank.
Thus, their first "demand" before emigrating to New England was that "the
common wealth should consist of two distinct ranks of men," the one
"gentlemen of the country" and the other "freeholders." In their answer,
the Bay Puritans declared that they "willingly acknowledge" the lords'
proposal about "two distinct ranks." The second condition was that "the
chief power of the common-wealth shall be placed" in the hands of the
"gentlemen and freeholders," which the colonists acknowledged already
characterized the situation in the colony. When, however, the lords demanded that they be admitted as freemen without being church members, Bay
Puritans would not assent, for this would destroy the very foundation of
their theocracy. Thus they answered the lords that though they would
"receive them with honor and allow them pre-eminence and accommoda-
tions according to their condition, yet none are admitted freemen of this
commonwealth, but such as are first admitted members of some church or
other in this country," and only out of those were their "magistrates . . .
Chosen."[23]

A Christian commonwealth, as Winthrop had made clear in "A Model of
Christian Charity," was based upon the law of grace as well as upon the law
of nature. "There is likewise," he preached aboard the *Arabella* in 1630, "a
double lawe by which we are regulated in our conversacion one toward
another . . . the lawe of nature and the lawe of grace, or the morall lawe or
the lawe of the gospel." The law of nature came to regulate civil society as
such, while the law of the Gospel, or that of grace, came to regulate
Christian society. Thus, when the lords demanded admission to freemenship
in the colony according to their noble status, the Bay Puritans replied that
"hereditary authority and power standeth only by the civil law" and not

---

[22] "Certain Proposals Made by Lord Say, Lord Brooke, and Other Persons of Quality, as
   Conditions of Their Removing to New England, with the Answers Thereto," in Hutchinson,
   History, vol. I, pp. 410–13. Although we have only the Massachusetts Bay Puritans'
   answers to the lords' proposals, New Haven and Connecticut Puritans no doubt shared with
   the Bay Puritans their views concerning theocracy.
[23] "Certain Proposals," pp. 410–12.

upon the law of grace. Not material property and hereditary privilege, but spiritual saving grace was the prerequisite for admission to freemenship in the Puritan theocracy. The justification for such a custom, explained the Puritans in their response to the lords, was "a divine ordinance (and moral) that none should be appointed and chosen by the people of God, magistrates over them, but men fearing God . . . chosen out of their brethren . . . saints." The assumption of authority by such men would result in the "joy of a commonwealth;" whereas "calamity" would ensue "when the wicked bear rule."[24]

The most striking element in the Puritans' answer to Viscount Say and Sele and Baron Brooke is the assertion that the exclusion of the ungodly from power was "a divine ordinance." This approach is well reflected in Winthrop's earlier quoted statement that "now, the world, or civill state, must be arised out of the churches."[25] Davenport in his *Discourse* never went so far as to call the premise of theocracy a divine ordinance. It was through reasoning such as Winthrop's that the Christian commonwealth took on the dimensions of the earthly domain in which the saints would exercise their holiness. Although complete identification of the church and civil covenants would occur only in the millennium, when the earthly kingdoms would become the Kingdom of God, Puritan New England would meanwhile seek to link the purity of the church with the holiness of the Christian commonwealth as two means of achieving the New Jerusalem. Only a theocratic political system could give saints exclusive political authority, to the exclusion of the ungodly from all political and ecclesiastical participation in the holy experiment in the wilderness.

Surely, the assertion that neither wealth nor property nor heredity, but faith and godliness were the conditions of citizenship in the Puritan colonies in New England sounded very strange indeed to Lord Say and Sele, Lord Brooke, and those other persons of "quality" who considered emigrating to New England in 1636. The Puritans clarified their position in their answer to the lords and warned that if magisterial power were given "to men not according to their godliness, which maketh them fit for church fellowship, but according to their wealth," they would themselves be "no better than worldly men." Such an alternative was unthinkable, since "worldly men" might become "the major part" of the magistrates, and could possibly "turn the edge of all authority and laws against the church and the members thereof, the maintenance of whose peace is the chief end which God aimed at in the institution of Magistracy."[26]

---

[24] John Winthrop, "A Model of Christian Charity," *Winthrop Papers*, vol. II, p. 294; "Certain Proposals," pp. 412–13.
[25] John Winthrop, "A Reply to an Answer," p. 101; "Certain Proposals," pp. 412–13.
[26] "Certain Proposals," p. 413.

Thus the Massachusetts Puritans finally and definitely rejected the noble lords' proposals to join the holy experiment. Yet the controversy between New England Puritans and the Puritan lords was far from over. Apparently surprised by the reaction to his proposals, Lord Say and Sele wrote directly to the Revd. John Cotton. Although this letter no longer exists, Cotton's answer makes it clear that Lord Say and Sele had accused American Puritans of having created a "theocracy" in the sense of a state ruled by the church. Cotton flatly denied that in Massachusetts "all things [were] under the determination of the church." The colony's magistrates, Cotton pointed out, were neither "chosen to office in the church, nor doe governe by direction from the church, but by civill lawes, and those enacted in generall courts, and executed in courts of justice, by the governors and assistants." Moreover, Cotton insisted, the church had no formal role in the civil realm other than to prepare "fitt instruments both to rule, and to choose rulers, which is no ambition in the church, nor dishonor to the commonwealth." Cotton did not, however, deny that the state was subject to religious influence. On the contrary, because "the word, and scripture of God do conteyne a short . . . platforme, not onely of theocracy, but also of other sacred sciences," including "ethicks, economicks, politicks, church-government, prophecy, academy," Cotton firmly believed that men should follow God's word in the state as well as in the church.[27]

What Cotton argued, in fact, was that God had actually prescribed the proper relationship between church and state:

It is very suitable to Gods all sufficient wisdom . . . not only to prescribe perfect rules for the right ordering of a private mans soule to over-lasting blessedness with himselfe, but also for the right ordering of a mans family, yea, of the commonwealth too so farre as both of them are subordinate to spiritual ends, and yet avolde both the churches usurpation upon civill jurisdictions, *in ordine ad spiritualia*, and the commonwealth invasion upon ecclesiastical administrations, *in ordine* to civill peace, and conformity to the civill state.

Because all human experience ought to be subordinate to spiritual ends, Cotton contended against Lord Say and Sele, the spiritual and temporal realms could hardly be completely separated. Moreover, a certain degree of overlapping (as opposed to usurping) of authority was inevitable: "Gods institutions (such as the government of church and of commonwealth be)" should "be close and compact, and coordinate one to another, and yet not confounded."[28]

God's word, then, according to Cotton, gave full warrant to the constitution of the Puritan commonwealth in Massachusetts, and theocracy was the

---

[27] John Cotton, "Copy of a Letter from Mr. Cotton to Lord Say and Seal, in the Year 1636," in Hutchinson, *History*, vol. I, pp. 414–17.
[28] *Ibid.*, vol. I, pp. 414–17.

proper form of the colony's government, for "it is better that the commonwealth be fashioned to the setting forth of Gods house, which is his Church, than to accommodate the church frame to the civill state."[29] Not only Massachusetts Puritans, but, as was seen earlier, those of Connecticut and New Haven as well, had fashioned the state in such a way that it might preserve the church and to ensure that the commonwealth be subordinated to spiritual ends, without attempting to unite church and state. Theocracy facilitated their purpose by providing an arrangement by which God, the true sovereign in both church and state, would reign over both.

It is worthwhile examining here the famous passage in Cotton's letter to Lord Say and Sele concerning democracy, monarchy, and aristocracy:

Democracy, I do not conceyve that ever God did ordeyne as a fitt government eyther for church or commonwealth. If the people be governors, who shall be governed? As for monarchy, and aristocracy, they are both of them clearly approved, and directed in scripture, yet so as referreth the soveraigntie to himselfe, and setteth up Theocracy in both, as the best forme of government in the commonwealth, as well in the church.

This passage is especially significant, not for Cotton's consideration of the relative merits of democracy, aristocracy, and monarchy, but rather for his treatment of the term "soveraigntie." Cotton's prime concern here is clearly the issue of whom to invest with sovereignty, or who should reign and rule over church and commonwealth. He rejects democracy, not only because it had no warrant in Scripture, but mainly for its failure to provide God with immediate and direct sovereignty over his saints. Likewise, despite their full warrant in Scripture, Cotton rejects aristocracy and monarchy for not providing God with sovereignty over his people. Consequently, Cotton declares "theocracy," the system in which God is the immediate sovereign of both church and state, to be the "best forme of government in the commonwealth, as well as in the church."[30]

State and church in the theocracy in Massachusetts, Connecticut, and New Haven, were thus under the common headship of the Lord. Although separation between church and state was unthinkable to the Puritans, they constantly reiterated that these were two different instruments in the sweep of providential history. Cotton's letter was largely a refutation of Lord Say and Sele's accusation to the contrary, that church and state were united in the Puritan theocracy.

At this point it is necessary to examine the momentous social and political consequences of the ideological premises laid down by the Puritan theocracy in America. Those who advocated a theocratic government which explicitly acknowledged Christ as sole ruler over them, were presenting the revolu-

---

[29] *Ibid.*, vol. I, pp. 414–17.   [30] *Ibid.*, vol. I, pp. 414–17.

tionary view that no one, neither bishop nor king, could stand between God and his people. Furthermore, with the political realm considered the exclusive domain of the saints by virtue of their covenanted relationship with God both in church and state, theocratic government entailed a denial that any rights based on the privilege of property, heredity, and wealth could determine eligibility to participate in the political life.

The revolutionary character of theocracy is best seen in the barring of unbelievers from any participation in the system of civil government. Since the covenant, the foundation of both church and state, belonged strictly to the godly, religious obligations were transformed into political obligations in the Christian commonwealth in New England, and the exclusiveness of the holy fellowship of the church led directly to the exclusiveness of the political system.

THE THEOCRATIC IMPULSE IN PURITAN ENGLAND

As long as England had bishops and kings, the establishment of a theocracy similar to that of New England remained an impossibility. But conditions changed radically in England during the 1640s: the office of bishops was totally abolished and King Charles I was beheaded. When confronted with this new reality, English Puritans also began to consider the idea of erecting a godly civil government in England based on the premises of theocracy. In 1649, for example, shortly after the king's execution, "Certain Queries" were presented to Thomas Lord Fairfax, Lord General of the Army, and to the General Council of War, "by many Christian people" from the county of Norfolk and the city of Norwich who wondered if indeed the time had come to establish a theocratic government. These people asked the leaders of the Army to ponder the question of "the present interest of the Saints and people of God." If indeed "the time (or near upon it) of putting down that worldly government, and erecting this new kingdom" of God on earth had arrived, as the authors of "Certain Queries" believed, the saints would have to assume their important role in the providential drama. Millennial expectations thus led to the demand for social and political action. According to this particular group, the saints' duty was to begin "to associate [themselves] together into several church-societies" in accordance with "the congregational way." The convening of all these gathered churches "in general assemblies, or church-parliaments, choosing and delegating such officers of Christ, and representatives of the churches, as may rule nations and kingdoms," would in turn result in God giving them "authority and rule over the nations and kingdoms of the world" and "the kingdoms of the world" becoming "the churches." Fearing that their aims would be thwarted by the election of the ungodly to positions of authority, this group questioned the "right or claim mere natural and worldly men have to rule and government" in a holy Christian commonwealth and advocated a form of government strikingly similar to the theocracy which had already been founded by the Puritans in the wilderness.[31]

Even before the king's death, millennial expectations and apocalyptical visions had led Puritans in England to propose barring the ungodly from political life and to argue for the exclusive right of the saints to rule in a Christian commonwealth. Thomas Collier, for example, in his sermon, *A Discovery of the New Creation* (1647), contended that "as formerly God hath many times set up wicked men to rule and govern," so now "he will give it into the hands of the Saints." Using similar arguments during the Whitehall debates in 1649, Colonel Thomas Harrison expressed the belief that the day had come, "God's own day," in which "the powers of this world shall be given into the hands of the Lord and his Saints." Harrison tried to calm his opponents who believed that "our business is . . . only to get power into our own hands, that we may reign over them," with the claim that putting the reins of government into the hands of the saints was not usurpation, but rather the necessary consequence of God's "coming forth in glory in the world."[32]

Only after the king was executed, however, did the Puritans in England seriously undertake putting into action the theocratic ideas. This was especially true of the Fifth Monarchists, who "sought to clear the way for the approaching millennium by political measures." Thus the author of *A Cry for the Right Improvement of all our Mercies* (1651) "called for the restriction of membership of Parliament to those who were 'in church fellowship with some one or other congregation'." In the same year, the author of another tract, *A Model of a New Representative*, argued that "borough M.P.s should be replaced by 'two or more members' of the Congregational churches in their respective towns and that county M.P.s should be elected by the gathered churches of their shire."[33]

---

[31] "Certain Queries Presented by Many Christian People" (1649), in A. S. P. Woodhouse (ed.), *Puritanism and Liberty* (Chicago, 1951), pp. 241–7. The similarity of the political proposals of this group to theocracy in America is readily apparent. As Austin Woolrych wrote: the people of this group tried to establish in England "a government based not on the people as a whole but on the 'gathered churches,' that is to say those congregations which had been voluntarily formed by a company of 'visible saints.'" See: Austin Woolrych, "Oliver Cromwell and the Rule of the Saints," in R. H. Parry (ed.), *The English Civil War and After, 1642–1658* (Berkeley and Los Angeles, 1970), p. 63.

[32] Thomas Collier, "A Discovery of the New Creation" (1647), in Woodhouse (ed.), *Puritanism and Liberty*, pp. 290–396; Thomas Harrison's words appeared in "The Whitehall Debates," in Woodhouse (ed.), *Puritanism and Liberty*, p. 178.

[33] Michael R. Watts, *The Dissenters* (Oxford, 1978), pp. 135–6, 143; B. S. Capp, *The Fifth Monarchy Men: A Study in Seventeenth-Century English Millenarianism* (London, 1972), pp. 51, 230–1. On the relationship between the Fifth Monarchists and the American Puritans, see J. F. Maclear, "New England and the Fifth Monarchy: the Quest for the

Nor was the conviction that theocratic government should be established in England limited to radicals such as the Fifth Monarchists. Many other Puritans shared their beliefs and their desire for action. "A hundred and fifty-three members of Morgan Llwyd's Independent church at Wrexham," for example "urged" that "the new representative should be elected by the gathered churches."[34] Those who strove, then, to establish theocratic government in England, like the Puritans in America, assumed the ultimate association between the church covenant and the civil covenant, and therefore claimed the political realm as the exclusive domain of the saints.

Puritan theocratic impulses reached their peak in England during Barebone's Parliament in 1653. Never before had England been so close to the ideal of theocratic government as with this parliament with its revolutionary social and religious reforms. Many of its nominees had been elected upon the recommendations of the gathered churches, and the combination within it of Fifth Monarchists, radical Independents and Baptists, clearly revealed how serious the saints were in their intentions to play their role in providential history. As Woolrych writes, many members of Barebone's Parliament "were not looking for a mere caretaker government to educate the people in the benefits and responsibility of self-governing republic. They wanted a sanhedrin of the saints, a dictatorship of the godly that would prepare for the millennium by overturning every vestige of the old 'carnal' government." The radical goals of these saints were probably no better understood than by the anonymous author of *A True State of the Case of the Commonwealth* (1654); he warned that in "this last Assembly [Barebone's Parliament] there was a party of men . . . who assumed to themselves only the name of Saints, from which Title they excluded all others," and by "pretense to an extraordinary Call from Christ himself [did] take upon them to rule the Nation by virtue of a supposed Right of Saintship in themselves." Their "dangerous attempts," he continued, "extended not only to the abolition of Law, but to the utter subversion of civil Right and Property." Finally, this commentator on the radicals of the Barebone's Parliament admonished against the dangers which would ensue should their policy succeed: "it would have utterly confounded the whole course of Natural and Civil Right, which is the only Basis of foundation of Government in this world."[35]

Millennium in Early American Puritanism," *William and Mary Quarterly* 32 (1975), 223–60.

[34] Watts, *The Dissenters*, pp. 137, 142.

[35] Woolrych, "Oliver Cromwell and the Rule of the Saints," p. 68; "The True State of the Case of the Commonwealth" (1654), in Stuart E. Prall (ed.), *The Puritan Revolution: A Documentary History* (New York, 1968), pp. 264–5. Thus far the best study of Barebone's Parliament is Tai Liu, "Saints in Power: A Study of the Barebones Parliament" (Ph.D. Thesis, University of Indiana, 1969).

Gradually but inevitably, in their attempts to constitute all human life on the basis of a covenant relationship with God, the Puritans reached the conclusion that only one's covenant relationship as manifested in his membership in the church could provide him with political rights. Those who emigrated to New England in the 1620s and 1630s made this premise the basis of their theocracy in the wilderness. When political conditions were ripe in England during the 1640s and 1650s, when English Puritans could seize the opportunity to create a theocratic system of government, they embarked on the very same policy.

The notion of a common ground shared by English and American Puritans concerning theocracy is supported by the case of Richard Baxter. A moderate Puritan, the Presbyterian Baxter clearly did not belong to the lunatic fringe of Puritanism; yet it was he who proposed the establishment of theocracy in England with arguments strikingly similar to those of the Puritans in America. In his book *A Holy Commonwealth, or Political Aphorisms Opening the True Principles of Government* (1659), Baxter demonstrates "how a Commonwealth may be reduced to this theocratical temper" by instituting the rule, among others, that "*no persons . . .* none as Cives (or free subjects, commonly called burgesses or enfranchised persons)" but only "those who have publicly owned the Baptismal Covenant, personally, deliberately and seriously" should have the right to vote in a holy Christian commonwealth. He continues by emphasizing the need to exclude "ordinary despisers of god's public worship, or neglecters of it, and of the guidance of God's ministers," from the body of electors. Above all, Baxter reiterates the principle that the foundation of theocratic government demands that the proper relationship between church and social covenants be maintained:

But that which I mean is, that the same qualification [that] maketh a man capable of being a member both of a Christian Church and Commonwealth . . . is, his Covenant with God in Christ, or his Membership of the Universal Church.[36]

Clearly, then, Puritans of widely differing persuasions were equally concerned with establishing theocracy, and they all agreed that, to reach their goal, a revolutionary approach to defining the political body was absolutely essential. It was partly in response to this extreme Puritan design to reshape the political system that Thomas Hobbes wrote his refutation in the *Leviathan* (1651).[37]

[36] Richard Baxter, *A Holy Commonwealth, or Political Aphorisms Opening the True Principles of Government* (1659), pp. 241, 219, 247, 249, 218. For an excellent study of Baxter's life and his millennial expectations, see William M. Lamont, *Richard Baxter and the Millennium: Protestant Imperialism and the English Revolution* (London, 1979).

[37] Thomas Hobbes, *Leviathan, or the Matter, Forme and Power of a Commonwealth Ecclesiastical and Civil* (1651), ed. Michael Oakeshott (Oxford, n.d.). On Hobbes' thought,

Hobbes began by attacking what he perceived as pretentiousness in the Puritan claim to hold sole spiritual authority to exercise and impose the will of God:

For if every man, should be obliged, to take for God's law, what particular men, on pretence of private inspiration, or revelation, should obtrude upon him, in such a number of men, that out of pride and ignorance, take their own dreams, and extravagant fancies, and madness, for testimonies of God's spirit; or out of ambition, pretend to such divine testimonies, falsely, and contrary to their own consciences, it were impossible that any divine law should be acknowledged.

Hobbes goes on to deny "*that the present church now militant, is the kingdom of God*," and therefore that "the Church and commonwealth are the same persons." Such identification of the Kingdom of God with the church, argued Hobbes, is unwarranted because "by the kingdom of God, is properly meant a commonwealth, instituted by the consent of those which were to be subject thereto, for their civil government." Contrary to Puritan belief that this was the time in which the kingdoms of the earth would become the Kingdom of God, Hobbes asserted that "the kingdom of God is a civil kingdom," and as such should be ruled only by "civil sovereigns" and not by the church or its saints. Comparing advocates of Puritan theocracy to the "Roman clergy," Hobbes denounces them as "a confederacy of deceivers" who seek power on the basis of "dark and erroneous doctrines."[38]

While Puritans on both sides of the Atlantic strove equally to achieve theocratic government, the Puritan experience on each side differed significantly. In New England, Puritans could, and did in fact, try to implement fully the premises immediately upon their arrival. In England, on the other hand, Puritans were given a similar opportunity only during the 1640s and 1650s, and even then faced such strong opposition that their holy scheme was never implemented. Only in light of the experience in England can one sufficiently appreciate the achievement of the New England Puritans in creating a theocracy in the wilderness.[39]

Considering New England within the framework of the larger Puritan

see the brilliant study by J. G. A. Pocock, "Time, History and Eschatology in the Thought of Thomas Hobbes," in his book *Politics, Language and Time* (New York, 1973), pp. 148–201. For the general ideological context of Hobbes' writings, see the series of articles by Quentin Skinner: "Hobbes' Leviathan," *The Historical Journal* 7 (1964), 321–32; "The Ideological Context of Hobbes's Political Thought," *The Historical Journal* 9 (1966), 286–317; "Conquest and Consent: Thomas Hobbes and the Engagement Controversy," in *The Interregnum*, ed. G. E. Aylmer (Hamden, 1972), pp. 79–98, and "History and Ideology in the English Revolution," *The Historical Journal* 8 (1965), 151–78.

[38] Hobbes, *Leviathan*, pp. 254–5, 451, 268, 295, 399, 233, 298, 306, 459, 452, 397.

[39] For evidence of this theocratic quest among Dutch Calvinists in Holland during the first half of the seventeenth century, see: Douglas Nobbs, *Theocracy and Toleration: A Study of the Dispute in Dutch Calvinism from 1600 to 1650* (Cambridge, 1938).

movement, the American Puritans did in fact succeed in their holy experiment to constitute theocracy. In another context, however, this holy experiment was far from successful. As with many millennial and utopian movements in the past, New England Puritans came to learn that human nature can be a tremendous obstacle in the quest to transform the world into a divine domain. Thus, at the moment when it seemed that, while the Puritan movement in England had failed, the holy experiment in the wilderness would survive, sounds arose in New England indicating that there, too, something had gone awry. In his poem *A Word to New England* (1654) William Bradford laments:

> Oh New England, thou canst not boast:
> Thy former glory thou hast lost.

Holiness, Bradford found, did "languish more away," and

> Love, truth, mercy and grace –
> Wealth and the world have took their place.

Likewise, Michael Wigglesworth wrote in *God's Controversy with New England* (1662) that he found in Puritan America

> In stead of holiness Carnality,
> In stead of heavenly frames an Earthly mind.[40]

Thus did the people who succeeded so well in constituting theocracy in the wilderness and in shaping their church and state according to their ideals eventually find that not human institutions but human nature was the real obstacle to the pursuit of the millennium, the quest for transforming the world into the Kingdom of God. However, as the Puritan experiment in New England shows so vividly, human history can hardly be understood without an appreciation of man's search for the ideal society and the fulfillment of utopian visions.

---

[40] William Bradford, *The Collected Verse*, ed. Michael G. Runyan (Minnesota, 1974), pp. 162–3; Michael Wigglesworth, *God's Controversy with New England* (1662), in *Seventeenth-Century American Poetry*, ed. Harrison T. Meserole (New York, 1968), p. 48.

INDEX

Cambridge Studies in Early Modern British History

263